The World of Hedge Funds

Characteristics and Analysis

The World of Hedge Funds

Characteristics and Analysis

editor

H. Gifford Fong

World Scientific

NEW JERSEY • LONDON • SINGAPORE • BEIJING • SHANGHAI • HONG KONG • TAIPEI • CHENNAI

Published by

World Scientific Publishing Co. Pte. Ltd.

5 Toh Tuck Link, Singapore 596224

USA office: 27 Warren Street, Suite 401-402, Hackensack, NJ 07601

UK office: 57 Shelton Street, Covent Garden, London WC2H 9HE

Library of Congress Cataloging-in-Publication Data

The world of hedge funds : characteristics and analysis / edited by H. Gifford Fong.
p. cm.
Includes bibliographical references.
ISBN 9812563776 (alk. paper)
1. Hedge funds. I. Fong, H. Gifford.
HG4530. W67 2005
332.64'5--dc22 2005044180

British Library Cataloguing-in-Publication Data

A catalogue record for this book is available from the British Library.

Typeset by Stallion Press
Email: enquiries@stallionpress.com

Printed in Singapore by Mainland Press

CONTENTS

INTRODUCTION

The World of Hedge Funds is a compendium of distinguished papers formerly published in the *Journal Of Investment Management* (JOIM) focusing on the topic of hedge funds. This area is arguably the fastest growing source of funds in the investment management arena. It represents an exciting opportunity for the investor and manager in terms of the range of return and risk available.

Our goal is to provide a very high quality series of papers which addresses many of the leading issues associated with hedge funds.

The first paper by Das is part of the JOIM "Working Papers" section where literature surveys of typical themes are showcased. This provides an outstanding review of the issues addressed generally in the literature on the topic of hedge funds.

The next two papers address some of the dangers associated with hedge fund strategies. "Sifting Through the Wreckage: Lessons from Recent Hedge-Fund Liquidations" by Getmansky, Lo and Mei provide a pioneering perspective of the characteristics of hedge fund problem cases and the implications for regulatory oversight; "The Dangers of Mechanical Investment Decision-Making: The Case of Hedge Funds" by Kat provides a review of some of the important considerations in making hedge fund investments.

Ben Dor, Jagannathan and Meier provide a basis for hedge fund analysis based on the fund's return series in "Understanding Mutual Fund and Hedge Fund Styles Using Return-Based Style Analysis" followed by Liang's "Alternative Investments: CTAs, Hedge Funds and Funds-of-Funds" where a comparison between these entities is discussed. In "Managed Futures and Hedge Funds: A Match Made in Heaven," Kat describes the benefits of managed futures funds with regard to typical hedge fund investments.

"Fees on Fees in Funds of Funds" by Brown, Goetzmann and Liang and "Extracting Portable Alphas from Equity Long/Short Hedge Funds" by Fung and Hsieh provide analysis on the role hedge funds can play for investors, followed by "AIRAP—Alternative RAPMs for Alternative Investments" by Sharma which describes a framework for evaluating hedge funds.

I would like to thank each of the authors for contributing to this book. They provide the basic input to the production process which includes a rigorous refereeing and editorial process. A well deserved thanks also goes to the Senior Editors, Advisory Board, Editorial Advisors and Associate Editors of the JOIM whose dedication and hard work enable the success we have enjoyed with the JOIM. Last but not least, many thanks to Christine Proctor and the staff of Stallion Press who contribute significantly to the excellence of our product.

Cordially,
H. Gifford Fong
Editor

Journal of Investment Management
3658 Mt. Diablo Blvd., Suite 200
Lafayette, CA 94549
Telephone: 925-299-7800
Facsimile: 925-299-7815
Email: editor@joim.com

Journal of Investment Management
Vol. 1, No. 2 (2003), pp. 76–81

WORKING PAPERS: "HEDGE" FUNDS

*Sanjiv Ranjan Das**

A casual survey of the extant literature on hedge funds suggests that the term itself might be a misnomer. However, a more careful reading lends credence to the nomenclature. In the past few years a vast and insightful literature has built up around the hedge fund business. This literature may be classified into the following major areas of inquiry.[1]

1. What does investing in a hedge fund do for a typical portfolio? What is the evidence on hedge fund diversification and performance?
2. What are the various hedge fund strategies and styles? Is there some sort of classification that appears to be emerging within the literature?
3. What are the unique risks in hedge funds, how is capital adequacy maintained, and risk management carried out?
4. What is special about hedge fund fee structures? How have hedge funds performed? Do fee structures lead to distortions in manager behavior and performance?

We take up each of these in turn.

1 Portfolio Impact

Keynes once stated that diversification is protection against ignorance. Is this true for hedge funds? Long–short positions effect a dramatic change in the return distributions of equity portfolios, resulting in diversification in the mean–variance or "beta" sense.

In an empirical study, Kat and Amin [17] find that introducing hedge funds into a traditional portfolio results in substantial improvements in the mean–variance risk–return trade-off. However, this comes at a cost in terms of negative skewness, and enhanced kurtosis in portfolio returns. Hence, it is not clear whether every investor's portfolio will be well-suited to an addition of the hedge fund asset class. They also find that much more than a small fraction of the additional hedge fund position is required to make a material difference to the portfolio, an aspect that might encounter risk or regulation limits in implementation. Similar results are obtained in a study by Amenc and Martellini [2], who find that return variances are lower out-of-sample as well.

Measurement of the diversification effect is traditionally carried out by regressing hedge fund returns on the market return. A low β in the regression signifies minimal realized systematic risk. Asness *et al.* [3] empirically establish that the illiquid nature of hedge fund assets leads to an understatement of the β. This arises because illiquidity causes the returns of assets to be asynchronous to the benchmark market index, resulting in a lower β, often by a third as much as the true β. Therefore, investors need to

*Santa Clara University, Santa Clara, CA, USA.

be aware that their positions in hedge funds might be less market-neutral than they empirically appear.

A limiting case of diversification through hedge funds comes from the relatively new concept of a fund of funds (FOF). The comprehensive paper by L'Habitant and Learned [21] examines many aspects of FOFs. Diversification across fund style yields greater benefits than diversification by fund selection within style, though it remains hard to find accurate information for the purposes of classifying hedge funds. There are many benefits to the FOF structure. First, less monitoring of individual funds is required. Second, the FOF offers investors better oversight and access to funds they would not otherwise be able to invest in. Third, the authors find that as the number of funds increase, (a) the variance of returns declines, while the mean return does not, and (b) downside measures such as maximum monthly loss and VaR are lower. However, as more funds are added to the FOF, positive skewness is reduced, and negative skewness structures become worse. Kurtosis also increases, hence the tails of the distribution worsen, no doubt on account of the high degree of concurrent idiosyncratic risk in down markets. Moreover, as the number of funds increases, the β of the FOF increases as well, implying that there is an optimal level to the extent of diversification from the addition of hedge funds to the mix. The authors submit that this optimal number ranges from five to 10 funds, which mitigates what they term "diversification overkill" that arises from including too many funds. Another drawback of the FOF model is that fees multiply. Brown *et al.* [9] look at whether the higher fees paid are more than offset by the informational advantage of FOFs—they find that this is not the case.

Another form of portfolio impact arises in the serial correlation of returns. Whereas hedge funds are designed to be market neutral, Getmansky *et al.* [14] show that these market-neutral portfolios may indeed experience greater serial correlation in returns than long-only portfolios. Their research finds empirical support for illiquidity exposure as the source of this serial correlation.

2 Strategies and Styles

Not surprisingly, the literature finds that identifying hedge fund styles is more complicated than in the case of mutual funds. Hedge funds may be affected by factors different from those impacting mutual funds, which may not have been uncovered in extant empirical research. The presence of myriad portfolio techniques and the use of derivatives results in non-linear effects, which may not lend themselves well to deciphering styles using the same techniques as those for mutual funds. Fung and Hsieh [11] provide a useful approach to understanding the empirical characteristics of hedge fund returns. Maillet and Rousset [25] develop a classification approach using Kohonen maps. While it may appear that non-linearities make style analysis difficult, as well as complicate performance measurement, Pfleiderer [26] writes that the non-linearities are in fact only weak, and that linear (factor) models may still be used.

Differing styles amongst hedge funds complicates performance measurement. Fung and Hsieh [12] find five dominant hedge fund styles. Two of these correspond to standard buy and hold equity and high-yield bond classes of funds, while three are typified by dynamic trading strategies over many asset categories. To form a unified set of styles for mutual and hedge funds, they suggest a 12-factor model with nine buy–hold asset classes and three distinct dynamic trading strategies as a basis. It is important to note that the degree to which mutual fund returns are explained by style is still far higher than the extent to which hedge fund returns are (the reported R^2s are approximately double). There are many hedge funds that did not fall within the ambit of the five styles delineated by Fung and Hsieh. Brown and Goetzmann [8] find that the number of styles has grown as the hedge fund industry has grown, and that there are now many more than just the basic few market-neutral styles. Their empirical work determines that about 20% of the difference in performance in the cross-section of hedge funds can be attributed to style differences.

Survivorship bias causes further complexity in fitting styles. Different styles perform differentially during certain economic epochs, and some styles drop out of favor. We do not seem to have much of a framework for handling this kind of econometric problem. Baquero *et al.* [4] study the impact on this issue of "look-ahead" bias, or *ex-post* conditioning that affects estimates of performance persistence. They find that this effect is severe and should be accounted for carefully in persistence studies. Bares *et al.* [6] employ genetic algorithms to determine the impact of survivorship on portfolio choice—they find that portfolio weights are significantly impacted if this effect is accounted for. Survivorship also impacts the higher moments of hedge fund return distributions (see Barry [7] who examines this issue with an interesting look at the data on defunct funds).

3 Risk Measurement and Management

A popular tool for measuring hedge fund portfolio risk is VaR (value-at-risk). A recommended approach is to use a factor technique. In a recent paper, L'Habitant [22] develops a simple factor model which is then subsequently used for determining VaR. Using a sample of close to 3000 funds, he finds that the factor-based VaR approach is a useful way to detect styles and proves to be a good risk approach in- and out-of-sample. For a comparison of different risk measures such as VaR, Drawdown-at-Risk, with mean absolute deviation, maximum loss and market-neutrality approaches see Krokhmal *et al.* [20].

The efficacy of VaR as a risk assessment device obtains further confirmation in the work of Gupta and Liang [16], who examine more than 2000 hedge funds to determine the extent of under-capitalization. Roughly 3% of funds appear to be poorly capitalized, though undercapitalization is a diagnostic for funds that fail, evidenced in 7.5% of dead funds. VaR is computed off the empirical distribution as well as via the use of extreme value theory. The authors conclude that the results are robust to both approaches, which are also found to be consistent with each other.

While some of the literature finds VaR to be a useful measure, there are arguments against its use. Lo [24] reasons thus on several counts. One, the factors for the VaR analysis may be less clear, since there is a poorer understanding of hedge fund styles. VaR does not include features of event risk, liquidity, default, etc., which are more important than merely price risk in the case of hedge funds. Third, since much less is known about the distribution of hedge fund returns, and we are especially certain that drastic non-normality is present, using a purely statistical measure based on standard assumptions may be egregiously erroneous.

Koh *et al.* [19] in a survey of hedge funds, summarize alternate risk measures that may be broadly categorized as "downside" metrics, which are likely more appropriate for hedge funds and which display return distributions with substantial departures from normality. They highlight the use of the Sortino and Price [27] ratio, which modifies the standard Sharpe ratio in both numerator and denominator. The numerator contains a modified excess return, i.e. the return on the portfolio minus a minimum acceptable return (MAR), which may be set to zero, the risk-free rate, or another low barrier chosen by the investor. The denominator is modified by replacing the return standard deviation with the downside standard deviation. Another ratio that has attained much popularity is the "d-ratio" described by Lavinio [23]. This ratio is as follows: $d = |l/w|$, where l is the average value of negative returns, and w is the average value of positive returns. This may be intuitively thought of as a skewness risk measure.

4 Performance and Fee Structures

The recent declining market environment has proven fruitful for market-neutral trading strategies, and hedge funds have performed well in relation to their mutual fund brethren. Can some of this performance also be attributed to manager skill, over and above fund structure? Edwards and Caglayan [10] study the performance of funds over most of the past decade, and assert that while 25% of hedge funds earn significantly positive returns, the persistence of these returns over time suggests that skill is a factor in explaining the differences between funds. Another aspect that supports the presence of skill is that the better performing funds paid their managers richer contracts *ex-ante*, consistent with the idea that these funds attracted better talent.

To measure the persistence of returns, the popular Hurst [18] ratio is often invoked, and is prescribed in Koh *et al.* [19]. This is based on the rescaled range (R/S) statistic, defined over return random variables $x_1, x_2, \ldots, x_n$, with mean μ_x and standard deviation σ_x. The R/S statistic is

$$Q = \frac{1}{\sigma_x}\left[\max_{1\le k\le n}\sum_{i=1}^{k}(x_i - \mu_x) - \min_{1\le k\le n}\sum_{i=1}^{k}(x_i - \mu_x)\right].$$

The Hurst ratio, $H = (\ln Q/\ln n)$, for large n, has the following relationship to return persistence. When $H = 0.5$, returns are non-persistent, i.e. random walks. When $H < 0.5$, there is negative persistence, i.e. mean reversion, and when $H > 0.5$, there is positive return persistence. For an analysis of long- and short-term persistence, see the work of Bares *et al.* [5], who find some evidence of short-term persistence, but none over the long-term.

Traditional linear factor models are unsatisfactory approaches to the measurement of hedge fund performance. Agarwal and Naik [1] develop a model that uses factors formed from excess returns on option-based and buy–hold strategies as benchmarks for performance. They are able to explain a substantial portion of variation in hedge fund returns with a few simple strategies, and also find that hedge fund performance was high in the early 1990s and tapered off in the latter half of that decade. Hedge fund benchmarks are problematic in the performance attribution process. Fung and Hsieh [13] argue that indices built from individual hedge funds contain noise, as measurement errors in the performance of individual funds propagate with aggregation. Instead, they suggest the use of indices based on FOF performance.

Hedge fund strategies, such as long–short portfolios and non-linear returns from the use of derivatives lead to distortions in performance measures. The Sharpe ratio has been the focus of attention of the literature that assesses these distortions. Goetzmann *et al.* [15] develop a strategy to obtain the optimal Sharpe ratio, and suggest that managers with possible upward distortions in their Sharpe ratios should be evaluated against the maximal Sharpe ratio instead. It is posited that Sharpe ratio distortions may in fact lead to portfolios with exaggerated kurtosis, leading to sharp portfolio crashes.

5 Conclusion

The advent of hedge funds has livened up the investing landscape. As covered in this abstract, there are issues relating to diversification and portfolio impact, style and performance evaluation, fee structures and risk management. It has resulted in pushing the envelope on the theory and practice of investing. Hedge funds have lived through an up and down cycle by now. The future promises to be even more illuminating.

Notes

[1] Caveats: this classification is *ad hoc*, and several others may accommodate the extant literature. The classification depends on the working papers reviewed too, and hence is not necessarily representative of all papers in the field.

Many thanks to Robert Hendershott and Meir Statman for their comments on this article.

References

1. Vikas Agarwal and Narayan Naik (London Business School). "Risks and Portfolio Decisions Involving Hedge Funds," Forthcoming, *Review of Financial Studies.*
2. Noel Amenc and Lionel Martellini (Ecole des Hautes Etudes Commerciales du Nord and University of Southern California). "Portfolio Optimization and Hedge Fund Style Allocation Decisions."
3. Clifford S. Asness, Robert Krail and John M. Liew (AQR Capital Management, LLC). "Hedge Funds Hedge?"
4. Guillermo Baquero, Jenke ter Horst and Marno Verbeek (Erasmus University Rotterdam, Tilburg University, and Erasmus) "Look-Ahead Bias and the Performance of Hedge Funds."
5. Pierre-Antoine Bares, Rajna Gibson and Sebastien Gyger (Swiss Federal Institute of Technology Lausanne (EPFL), Universität Zurich—Swiss Banking Institute and Swiss Federal Institute of Technology, Lausanne—Institute of Theoretical Physics). "Performance in the Hedge Funds Industry: An Analysis of Short and Long-Term Persistence."
6. Pierre-Antoine Bares, Rajna Gibson and Sebastien Gyger (Swiss Federal Institute of Technology Lausanne (EPFL), Universität Zurich—Swiss Banking Institute and Swiss Federal Institute of

Technology, Lausanne—Institute of Theoretical Physics). "Hedge Fund Allocation with Survival Uncertainty and Investment Constraints."
7. Ross Barry (Macquarie University). "Hedge Funds: A Walk Through The Graveyard."
8. Stephen J. Brown and William N. Goetzmann (NYU and Yale). "Hedge Funds with Style."
9. Stephen J. Brown, William N. Goetzmann and Bing Liang (NYU, Yale and Case-Western Reserve). "Fees on Fees in Funds of Funds."
10. Franklin R. Edwards and Mustafa Caglayan (Columbia Business School and J. P. Morgan Chase Securities, NY). "Hedge Fund Performance and Manager Skill," Forthcoming, *Journal of Futures Markets.*
11. William Fung and David Hsieh (1997). "Empirical Characteristics of Dynamic Trading Strategies." *Review of Financial Studies*, April, 275–302.
12. William Fung and David Hsieh (Paradigm Financial Products and Duke University). "Performance Attribution and Style Analysis: from Mutual Funds to Hedge Funds."
13. William Fung and David A. Hsieh (PI Asset Management, LLC and Duke University) (2002). "Benchmarks of Hedge Fund Performance: Information Content and Measurement Biases." *Financial Analysts Journal* **58**, 22–34.
14. Mila Getmansky, Andrew W. Lo and Igor Makarov (MIT). "An Econometric Model of Serial Correlation and Illiquidity in Hedge Fund Returns."
15. William N. Goetzmann, Jonathan E. Ingersoll Jr., Matthew I. Spiegel and Ivo Welch (Yale University). "Sharpening Sharpe Ratios."
16. Anurag Gupta and Bing Liang (Case Western Reserve University). "Do Hedge Funds Have Enough Capital? A Value at Risk Approach."
17. Harry M. Kat and Gaurav S. Amin (City University and University of Reading). "Who Should Buy Hedge Funds? The Effects of Including Hedge Funds in Portfolios of Stocks and Bonds."
18. Hurst, H. (1951). "Long Term Storage Capacity of Reservoirs." *Transactions of the American Society of Civil Engineers* **116**, 770–799.
19. Francis Koh, David Lee and Phoon Kok Fai (Singapore Management University, Ferrell Asset Management, FDP Consultants). "Investing in Hedge Funds: Risk, Return and Pitfalls."
20. Pavlo A. Krokhmal, Stanislav P. Uryasev and Grigory M. Zrazhevsky (University of Florida). "Comparative Analysis of Linear Portfolio Rebalancing Strategies: An Application to Hedge Funds."
21. Francois Serge L'Habitant and Michelle Learned (Union Bancaire Privee (Geneva)—General and Thunderbird, American Graduate School of International Management). "Hedge Fund Diversification: How Much is Enough?"
22. Francois Serge L'Habitant (Union Bancaire Privee, Geneva). "Assessing Market Risk for Hedge Funds and Hedge Funds Portfolios."
23. Stefano Lavinio (1999). "The Hedge Fund Handbook." Irwin Library of Investment and Finance, McGraw Hill.
24. Lo, Andrew (2001). "Risk Management for Hedge Funds: Introduction and Overview." *Financial Analysts Journal* **57**(6), 16–33.
25. Bertrand Maillet and Patrick Rousset (Universite Paris I Pantheon-Sorbonne and ESCP-EAP and Centre For Research on Education, Training and Employment). "Classifying Hedge Funds with Kohonen Maps: A First Attempt."
26. Pfleiderer, Paul (2001). "Managing Market-Neutral Long-Short Funds." In *Developments in Quantitative Financial Models*, AIMR Conference Proceedings, pp. 24–39.
27. Frank Sortino and Lee Price (1994). "Performance Measurement in a Downside Risk Framework." *Journal of Investing*, Fall, **3**(3), 59–64.

Journal of Investment Management
Vol. 2, No. 4 (2004), pp. 6–38

SIFTING THROUGH THE WRECKAGE: LESSONS FROM RECENT HEDGE-FUND LIQUIDATIONS*

Mila Getmansky[a], *Andrew W. Lo*[b,†], *and Shauna X. Mei*[c]

We document the empirical properties of a sample of 1,765 funds in the TASS Hedge Fund database from 1977 to 2004 that are no longer active. The TASS sample shows that attrition rates differ significantly across investment styles, from a low of 5.2% per year on average for convertible arbitrage funds to a high of 14.4% per year on average for managed futures funds. We relate a number of factors to these attrition rates, including past performance, volatility, and investment style, and also document differences in illiquidity risk between active and liquidated funds. We conclude with a proposal for the US Securities and Exchange Commission to play a new role in promoting greater transparency and stability in the hedge-fund industry.

1 Introduction

Enticed by the prospect of double-digit returns, seemingly uncorrelated risks, and impressive trading talent, individual and institutional investors have flocked to hedge funds in recent years. In response, many sell-side traders, investment bankers, and portfolio managers have also answered the siren call of hedge funds, making this one of the fastest growing sectors in the financial services industry. Currently estimated at just over $1 trillion in assets and about 8,000 funds, the hedge-fund industry is poised for even more growth as pension funds continue to increase their allocations to alternative investments in the wake of lackluster returns from traditional asset classes. In a December 2003 survey of 137 US defined-benefit pension plan sponsors conducted by State Street Global Advisors and InvestorForce, 67% of the respondents indicated their intention to increase their allocations to hedge funds, and 15% expected their increases to be "substantial."

Although these are exciting times for the hedge-fund industry, there is a growing concern that both investors and managers have been too focused on the success stories

[a] Isenberg School of Management, University of Massachusetts, Amherst, MA 01003 USA.

[b] MIT Sloan School of Management, and AlphaSimplex Group.

[†] Corresponding author. MIT Sloan School of Management, 50 Memorial Drive, E52-432, Cambridge, MA 02142–1347, USA. Tel.: (617) 253–0920; e-mail: alo@mit.edu

[c] MIT Sloan School of Management, Cambridge, MA 02142, USA.

[*] The views and opinions expressed in this article are those of the authors only, and do not necessarily represent the views and opinions of AlphaSimplex Group, MIT, the University of Massachusetts, or any of their affiliates and employees. The authors make no representations or warranty, either expressed or implied, as to the accuracy or completeness of the information contained in this article, nor are they recommending that this article serve as the basis for any investment decision—this article is for information purposes only.

of the day, forgetting about the many hedge funds that liquidate after just one or two years because of poor performance, insufficient capital to support their operations, credit issues, or conflicts between business partners. Of course, as with many other rapidly growing industries, waves of startups are followed by shake-outs, eventually leading to a more mature and stable group of survivors in the aftermath. Accordingly, it has been estimated that a fifth of all hedge funds failed last year,[1] and this year the failure rate for European hedge funds has increased from 7% to 10% per annum.[2]

In this article, we attempt to provide some balance to the optimistic perspective of most hedge-fund industry participants by focusing our attention on hedge funds that have liquidated. By studying funds that are no longer in business, we hope to develop a more complete understanding of the risks of the industry. Although the effects of "survivorship bias" on the statistical properties of investment returns are well known, there are also qualitative perceptual biases that are harder to quantify, and such biases can be reduced by including liquidated funds in our purview.

Throughout this paper, we use the less pejorative term "liquidated fund" in place of the more common "hedge-fund failure" to refer to hedge funds that have shut down. The latter term implies a value judgment that we are in no position to make, and while there are certainly several highly publicized cases of hedge funds failing due to fraud and other criminal acts, there are many other cases of conscientious and talented managers who closed their funds after many successful years for business or personal reasons. We do not wish to confuse the former with the latter, but hope to learn from the experiences of both.

In Section 2 we provide a brief review of the hedge-fund literature, and in Section 3 we summarize the basic properties of the TASS database of live and liquidated hedge funds from 1977 to 2004. We consider the time-series and cross-sectional properties of hedge-fund attrition rates in Section 4, and document the relation between attrition and performance characteristics such as volatility and lagged returns. Across style categories, higher volatility is clearly associated with higher attrition rates, and over time, lagged performance of a particular style category is inversely related to attrition in that category. In Section 5 we compare valuation and illiquidity risk across categories and between live and liquidated funds using serial correlation as a proxy for illiquidity exposure. We find that, on average, live funds seem to be engaged in less liquid investments, and discuss several possible explanations for this unexpected pattern. We conclude in Section 6 with a proposal for the US Securities and Exchange Commission to play a new role in promoting greater transparency and stability in the hedge-fund industry.

2 Literature Review

Hedge-fund data has only recently become publicly available, hence much of the hedge-fund literature is relatively new. Thanks to data vendors such as Altvest, Hedge Fund Research (HFR), Managed Account Reports (MAR/CISDM), and TASS, researchers now have access to historical monthly returns, fund size, investment style, and many other data items for a broad collection of hedge funds. However, inclusion in these databases is purely voluntary and therefore somewhat idiosyncratic; hence, there is a certain degree of selection bias in the funds that agree to be listed, and the most popular databases seem to have relatively few funds in common.[3] Moreover, because hedge funds are not allowed to solicit the general public, the funds' prospectuses are not included in these databases, depriving researchers of more detailed information concerning the funds' investment processes, securities traded, allowable amounts of leverage, and specific contractual terms such as high-water marks, hurdle rates, and clawback agreements.[4] There is even less information about liquidated funds, apart from coarse categorizations such as those provided by TASS (see Section 3 below). In fact, most databases contain only funds that are currently active and open to new investors, and several data vendors like TASS do not provide the identities of the funds in academic versions of their databases,[5] so it is difficult to track the demise of any fund through other sources.

Despite these challenges, the hedge-fund literature has blossomed into several distinct branches: performance analysis, the impact of survivorship bias, hedge-fund attrition rates, and case studies of operational risks and hedge-fund liquidations.

The empirical properties of hedge-fund performance have been documented by Ackermann, McEnally, and Ravenscraft (1999), Agarwal and Naik (2000b,c), Edwards and Caglayan (2001), Fung and Hsieh (1999, 2000, 2001), Kao (2002), and Liang (1999, 2000, 2001, 2003) using several of the databases cited above. More detailed performance attribution and style analysis for hedge funds has been considered by Agarwal and Naik (2000b,c), Brown and Goetzmann (2003), Brown *et al.* (1999, 2000, 2001a,b), Fung and Hsieh (1997a,b, 2002a,b), and Lochoff (2002). Asness, Krail, and Liew (2001) have questioned the neutrality of certain market-neutral hedge funds, arguing that lagged market betas indicate less hedging than expected. Lo (2001) and Getmansky, Lo, and Makarov (2004) provide an explanation for this striking empirical phenomenon—smoothed returns, which is a symptom of illiquidity in a fund's investments—and propose an econometric model to estimate the degree of smoothing and correct for its effects on performance statistics such as return volatilities, market betas, and Sharpe ratios.

The fact that hedge funds are not required to include their returns in any publicly available database induces a potentially significant selection bias in any sample of hedge funds that do choose to publicize their returns. In addition, many hedge-fund databases include data only for funds that are currently in existence, inducing a "survivorship bias" that affects the estimated mean and volatility of returns as Ackermann, McEnally and Ravenscraft (1999) and Brown *et al.* (1992) have documented. For example, the estimated impact of survivorship on average returns varies from a bias of 0.16% (Ackermann, McEnally, and Ravenscraft, 1999) to 2% (Liang, 2000; Amin and Kat, 2003b) to 3% (Brown, Goetzmann, and Ibbotson, 1999).[6]

The survival rates of hedge funds have been estimated by Brown, Goetzmann, and Ibbotson (1999), Fung and Hsieh (2000), Liang (2000, 2001), Brown, Goetzmann, and Park (2001a,b), Gregoriou (2002), Amin and Kat (2003b), and Bares, Gibson, and Gyger (2003). Brown, Goetzmann, and Park (2001b) show that the probability of liquidation increases with increasing risk, and that funds with negative returns for two consecutive years have a higher risk of shutting down. Liang (2000) finds that the annual hedge-fund attrition rate is 8.3% for the 1994–1998 sample period using TASS data, and Baquero, Horst, and Verbeek (2002) find a slightly higher rate of 8.6% for the 1994–2000 sample period. Baquero, Horst, and Verbeek (2002) also find that surviving funds outperform non-surviving funds by approximately 2.1% per year, which is similar to the findings of Fung and Hsieh (2000, 2002b) and Liang (2000), and that investment style, size, and past performance are significant factors in explaining survival rates. Many of these patterns are also documented by Liang (2000) and Boyson (2002). In analyzing the life cycle of hedge funds, Getmansky (2004) finds that the liquidation probabilities of individual hedge funds depend on fund-specific characteristics such as past returns, asset flows, age, and assets under management, as well as category-specific variables such as competition and favorable positioning within the industry.

Brown, Goetzmann, and Park (2001b) find that the half-life of the TASS hedge funds is exactly 30 months, while Brooks and Kat (2002) estimate that approximately 30% of new hedge funds do not make it past 36 months due to poor performance, and in Amin and Kat's (2003b) study, 40% of their hedge funds do not make it to the fifth year. Howell (2001) observes that the probability of hedge funds failing in their first year was 7.4%, only to increase to 20.3% in their second year. Poor-performing younger funds drop out of databases at a faster rate than older funds (see Getmansky, 2004; Jen, Heasman, and Boyatt, 2001), presumably because younger funds are more likely to take additional risks to obtain good performance which they can use to attract new investors, whereas older funds that have survived already have track records with which to attract and retain capital.

A number of case studies of hedge-fund liquidations have been published recently, no doubt spurred by the most well-known liquidation in the hedge-fund industry to date: Long-Term Capital Management (LTCM). The literature on LTCM is vast, spanning a number of books, journal articles, and news stories; a representative sample includes Greenspan (1998), McDonough (1998), Pérold (1999), the President's Working Group on Financial Markets (1999), and MacKenzie (2003). Ineichen (2001) has compiled a list of selected hedge funds and analyzed the reasons for their liquidations. Kramer (2001) focuses on fraud, providing detailed accounts of six of history's most egregious cases. Although it is virtually impossible to obtain hard data on the frequency of fraud among liquidated hedge funds,[7] in a study of over 100 liquidated hedge funds during the past two decades, Feffer and Kundro (2003) conclude that "half of all failures could be attributed to operational risk alone," of which fraud is one example. In fact, they observe that "The most common operational issues related to hedge fund losses have been misrepresentation of fund investments, misappropriation of investor funds, unauthorized trading, and inadequate resources" (Feffer and Kundro, 2003, p. 5). The last of these issues is, of course, not related to fraud, but Feffer and Kundro (2003, Figure 2) report that only 6% of their sample involved inadequate resources, whereas 41% involved misrepresentation of investments, 30% misappropriation of funds, and 14% unauthorized trading. These results suggest that operational issues are indeed an important factor in hedge-fund liquidations, and deserve considerable attention by investors and managers alike.

Finally, Chan *et al.* (2004) investigate the relation between hedge funds and "systemic" risk, usually defined as a series of correlated defaults among financial institutions that occur over a short period of time, often caused by a single major event like the default of Russian government debt in August 1998. Although systemic risk has traditionally been more of a concern for the banking sector, the events surrounding LTCM in 1998 clearly demonstrated the relevance of hedge funds for such risk exposures. Chan *et al.* (2004) attempt to quantify the potential impact of hedge funds on systemic risk by developing a number of new risk measures for hedge funds and applying them to individual and aggregate hedge-fund returns data. Their preliminary findings suggest that the hedge-fund industry may be heading into a challenging period of lower expected returns, and that systemic risk is currently on the rise.

3 The TASS Live and Graveyard Databases

The TASS database of hedge funds consists of both active and defunct hedge funds, with monthly returns, assets under management and other fund-specific information for 4,781 individual funds from February 1977 to August 2004.[8] The database is divided into two parts: "Live" and "Graveyard" funds. Hedge funds that are in the Live database are considered to be active as of the most recent update of the database, in our case August 31, 2004. Once a hedge fund decides not to report its performance, is liquidated, closed to new investment, restructured, or merged with other hedge funds, the fund is transferred into the Graveyard database. A hedge fund can only be listed in the Graveyard database after having been listed first in the Live database. Because TASS includes both live and dead funds, the effects of suvivorship bias are reduced. However, the database is still subject to *backfill bias*—when a fund decides to be included in the database, TASS adds the fund to the Live database, including the fund's entire *prior* performance record. Hedge funds do not need to meet any specific requirements to be included in the TASS database, and reporting is purely voluntary. Due to reporting delays and time lags in contacting hedge funds, some Graveyard funds can be incorrectly listed in the Live database for a short period of time.[9]

As of August 31, 2004, the combined database of both live and dead hedge funds contained 4781 funds with at least one monthly return observation. Out of these 4,781 funds, 2,920 funds are in the Live database and 1,861 funds are in the Graveyard database. The earliest data available for a fund in either database is February 1977. TASS created the Graveyard database in 1994, hence it is only since 1994 that TASS began transferring funds from the Live to the Graveyard database. Funds that were dropped from the Live database prior to 1994 are not included in the Graveyard, which may yield a certain degree of survivorship bias.[10]

The majority of the 4,781 funds reported returns net of management and incentive fees on a monthly basis,[11] and we eliminated 50 funds that reported only gross returns, leaving 2,893 funds in the Live and 1,838 funds in the Graveyard database. We also eliminated funds that reported returns on a quarterly—not monthly—basis, as well as funds that did not report assets under management, or reported only partial assets under management. These filters yielded a final sample of 4,536 hedge funds in the "Combined" database, consisting of 2,771 funds in the Live database and 1,765 funds in the Graveyard database. For the empirical analysis in Section 5, we impose an additional filter in which we require funds to have at least five years of non-missing returns, yielding 1,226 funds in the Live database and 611 in the Graveyard database for a combined total of 1,837 funds. This obviously creates additional survivorship bias in the remaining sample of funds, but since the main objective in Section 5 is to estimate measures of valuation and illiquidity risk and not to make inferences about overall performance, this filter may not be as problematic.[12]

TASS also classifies funds into one of 11 different investment styles, listed in Table 1 and described in the appendix. Table 1 also reports the number of funds in each category for the Live, Graveyard, and Combined databases, and it is apparent from these figures that the representation of investment styles is not evenly distributed, but is concentrated among four categories: Long/Short Equity (1,415), Fund of Funds (952), Managed Futures (511), and Event Driven (384). Together, these four categories account for 71.9% of the funds in the Combined database. Figure 1 shows that the relative proportions of the Live and Graveyard databases are roughly comparable, with the exception of two categories: Funds of Funds (24% in the Live and 15% in the Graveyard database), and Managed Futures (7% in the Live and 18% in the Graveyard database). This reflects the current trend in the industry toward Funds of Funds, and the somewhat slower growth of Managed Futures funds.

Given our interest in hedge-fund liquidations, the Graveyard database will be our main focus. Because of the voluntary nature of inclusion in the TASS database, Graveyard funds do not consist solely of liquidations. TASS gives one of seven distinct reasons for each fund that is assigned to the Graveyard, summarized in Table 2. It may

Table 1 Number of funds in the TASS Live, Graveyard, and Combined hedge-fund databases, grouped by category.

		Number of TASS Funds in		
Category	Definition	Live	Graveyard	Combined
1	Convertible Arbitrage	127	49	176
2	Dedicated Shortseller	14	15	29
3	Emerging Markets	130	133	263
4	Equity Market Neutral	173	87	260
5	Event Driven	250	134	384
6	Fixed-Income Arbitrage	104	71	175
7	Global Macro	118	114	232
8	Long/Short Equity	883	532	1,415
9	Managed Futures	195	316	511
10	Multi-Strategy	98	41	139
11	Fund of Funds	679	273	952
	Total	2,771	1,765	4,536

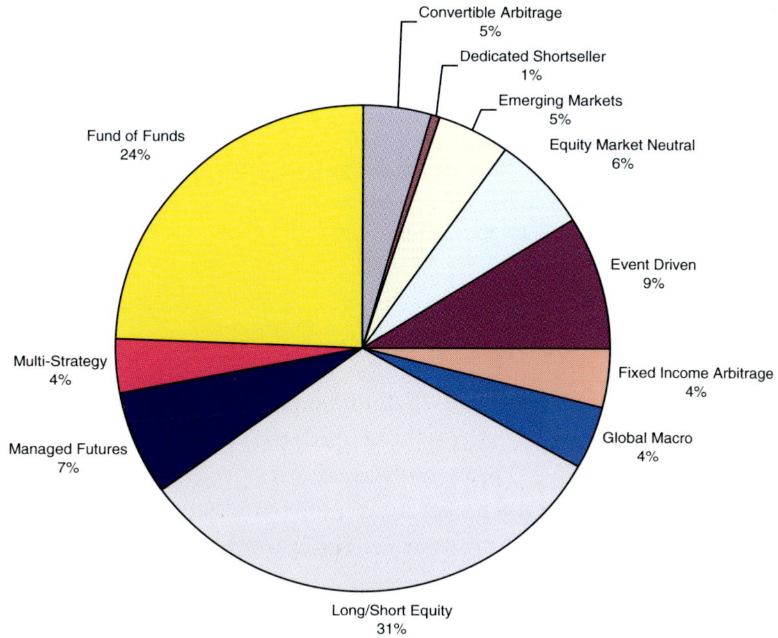

(a) Live funds

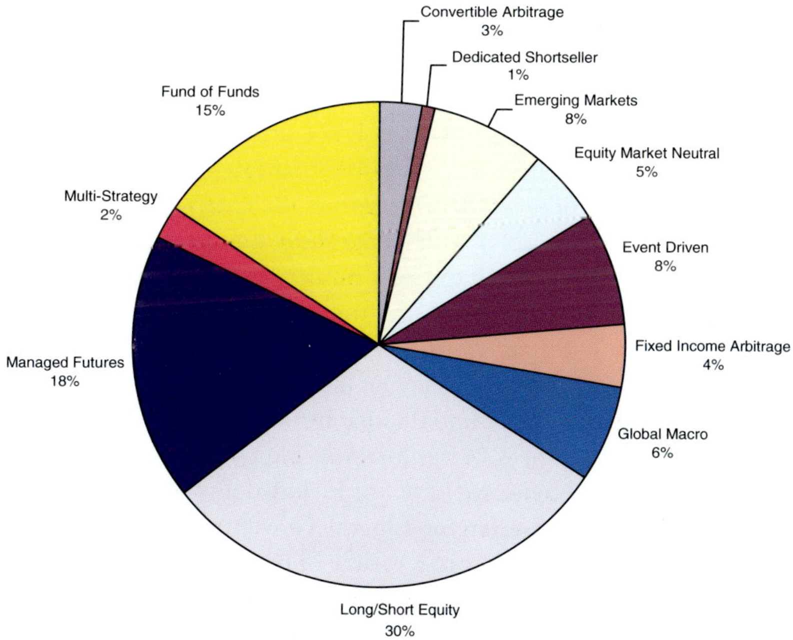

(b) Graveyard funds

Figure 1 Breakdown of TASS Live and Graveyard funds by category.

Table 2 TASS status codes for funds in the Graveyard database.

Status code	Definition
1	Fund liquidated
2	Fund no longer reporting to TASS
3	TASS has been unable to contact the manager for updated information
4	Fund closed to new investment
5	Fund has merged into another entity
7	Fund dormant
9	Unknown

seem reasonable to confine our attention to those Graveyard funds categorized as "liquidated" (status code 1) or perhaps to drop those funds that are closed to new investment (status code 4) from our sample. However, because our purpose is to develop a broader perspective on the dynamics of the hedge-fund industry, we argue that using the entire Graveyard database may be more informative. For example, by eliminating Graveyard funds that are closed to new investors, we create a downward bias in the performance statistics of the remaining funds. Because we do not have detailed information about each of these funds, we cannot easily determine how any particular selection criterion will affect the statistical properties of the remainder. Therefore, we choose to include the entire set of Graveyard funds in our analysis, but caution readers to keep in mind the composition of this sample when interpreting our empirical results.

For concreteness, Table 3 reports frequency counts for Graveyard funds in each status code and style category, as well as assets under management at the time of transfer to the Graveyard.[13] These counts show that 1,571 of the 1,765 Graveyard funds, or 89%, fall into the first three categories, categories that can plausibly be considered liquidations, and within each of these three categories, the relative frequencies across style categories are roughly comparable, with Long/Short Equity being the most numerous and Dedicated Shortseller being the least numerous. Of the remaining 194 funds with status codes 4–9, only status code 4—funds that are closed to new investors—is distinctly different in character from the other status codes. There are only seven funds in this category, and these funds are all likely to be "success stories," providing some counterbalance to the many liquidations in the Graveyard sample. Of course, this is not to say that 7 out of 1,765 is a reasonable estimate of the success rate in the hedge-fund industry, because we have not included any of the Live funds in this calculation. Nevertheless, these seven funds in the Graveyard sample do underscore the fact that hedge-fund data are subject to a variety of biases that do not always point in the same direction, and we prefer to leave them in so as to reflect these biases as they occur naturally rather than to create new biases of our own. For the remainder of this article, we shall refer to all funds in the TASS Graveyard database as "liquidations" for expositional simplicity.

Table 4 contains basic summary statistics for the funds in the TASS Live, Graveyard, and Combined databases, and Figure 2 provides a comparison of average means, standard deviations, Sharpe ratios, and first-order autocorrelation coefficients ρ_1 in the Live

Table 3 Frequency counts and assets under management of funds in the TASS Graveyard database by category and Graveyard inclusion code. Assets under management are at the time of transfer into the Graveyard database.

Code	All Funds	Convert Arb	Ded Short	Emrg Mkts	EqMkt Neutral	Event Driven	Fixed Income Arb	Global Macro	L/S Equity	Mged Futures	Mult-Strat	Fund of Funds
Frequency count												
1	913	19	7	78	65	50	29	53	257	190	30	135
2	511	21	4	34	12	56	26	29	187	43	7	92
3	147	4	1	7	8	17	3	17	54	18	1	17
4	7	0	0	0	0	1	2	0	3	0	0	1
5	56	2	1	5	0	6	3	6	16	9	1	7
7	2	0	0	0	0	1	0	0	1	0	0	0
9	129	3	2	9	2	3	8	9	14	56	2	21
Total	1,765	49	15	133	87	134	71	114	532	316	41	273
Assets under management												
1	18,754	1,168	62	1,677	1,656	2,047	1,712	2,615	4,468	975	641	1,732
2	36,366	6,420	300	848	992	7,132	2,245	678	10,164	537	882	6,167
3	4,127	45	34	729	133	1,398	50	115	931	269	2	423
4	487	0	0	0	0	100	31	0	250	0	0	106
5	3,135	12	31	143	0	222	419	1,775	473	33	3	24
7	8	0	0	0	0	6	0	0	2	0	0	0
9	3,052	42	18	222	9	159	152	32	193	1,671	18	538
Total	65,931	7,686	445	3,620	2,789	11,063	4,610	5,215	16,482	3,484	1,546	8,991

and Graveyard databases.[14] Not surprisingly, there is a great deal of variation in mean returns and volatilities both across and within categories and databases. For example, the 127 Convertible Arbitrage funds in the Live database have an average mean return of 9.92% and an average standard deviation of 5.51%, but in the Graveyard database, the 49 Convertible Arbitrage funds have an average mean return of 10.02% and a much higher average standard deviation of 8.14%. As expected, average volatilities in the Graveyard database are uniformly higher than those in the Live database because the higher-volatility funds are more likely to be eliminated. This effect operates at both ends of the return distribution—funds that are wildly successful are also more likely to leave the database since they have less motivation to advertise their performance. That the Graveyard database also contains successful funds is supported by the fact that in some categories, the average mean return in the Graveyard database is the same as or higher than in the Live database, e.g., Convertible Arbitrage, Equity Market Neutral, and Dedicated Shortseller.

Figure 3 displays the histogram of year-to-date returns at the time of liquidation. The fact that the distribution is skewed to the left is consistent with the conventional wisdom that performance is a major factor in determining the fate of a hedge fund. However, note that there is nontrivial weight in the right half of the distribution, suggesting that recent performance is not the only relevant factor.

Table 4 Means and standard deviations of basic summary statistics for hedge funds in the TASS Hedge Fund Live, Graveyard, and Combined databases from February 1977 to August 2004. The columns "p-Value(Q)" contain means and standard deviations of p-values for the Ljung-Box Q-statistic for each fund using the first 11 autocorrelations of returns.

Category description	Sample size	Annualized mean (%)		Annualized SD (%)		ρ_1 (%)		Annualized Sharpe ratio		Adjusted Sharpe ratio (annualized)		Ljung-Box p-value (%)	
		Mean	SD	Mean	SD	Mean	SD	Mean	SD	Mean	SD	Mean	SD
Live funds													
Convertible Arbitrage	127	9.92	5.89	5.51	4.15	33.6	19.2	2.57	4.20	1.95	2.86	19.5	27.1
Dedicated Shortseller	14	0.33	11.11	25.10	10.92	3.5	10.9	−0.11	0.70	0.12	0.46	48.0	25.7
Emerging Markets	130	17.74	13.77	21.69	14.42	18.8	13.8	1.36	2.01	1.22	1.40	35.5	31.5
Equity Market Neutral	173	6.60	5.89	7.25	5.05	4.4	22.7	1.20	1.18	1.30	1.28	41.6	32.6
Event Driven	250	12.52	8.99	8.00	7.15	19.4	20.9	1.98	1.47	1.68	1.47	31.3	34.1
Fixed Income Arbitrage	104	9.30	5.61	6.27	5.10	16.4	23.6	3.61	11.71	3.12	7.27	36.6	35.2
Global Macro	118	10.51	11.55	13.57	10.41	1.3	17.1	0.86	0.68	0.99	0.79	46.8	30.6
Long/Short Equity	883	13.05	10.56	14.98	9.30	11.3	17.9	1.03	1.01	1.01	0.95	38.1	31.8
Managed Futures	195	8.59	18.55	19.14	12.52	3.4	13.9	0.48	1.10	0.73	0.63	52.3	30.8
Multi-Strategy	98	12.65	17.93	9.31	10.94	18.5	21.3	1.91	2.34	1.46	2.06	31.1	31.7
Fund of Funds	679	6.89	5.45	6.14	4.87	22.9	18.5	1.53	1.33	1.48	1.16	33.7	31.6
Graveyard funds													
Convertible Arbitrage	49	10.02	6.61	8.14	6.08	25.5	19.3	1.89	1.43	1.58	1.46	27.9	34.2
Dedicated Shortseller	15	1.77	9.41	27.54	18.79	8.1	13.2	0.20	0.44	0.25	0.48	55.4	25.2
Emerging Markets	133	2.74	27.74	27.18	18.96	14.3	17.9	0.37	0.91	0.47	1.11	48.5	34.6
Equity Market Neutral	87	7.61	26.37	12.35	13.68	6.4	20.4	0.52	1.23	0.60	1.85	46.6	31.5

Table 4 (*Continued*)

Category description	Sample size	Annualized mean (%)		Annualized SD (%)		ρ_1 (%)		Annualized Sharpe ratio		Adjusted Sharpe ratio (annualized)		Ljung-Box p-value (%)	
		Mean	SD	Mean	SD	Mean	SD	Mean	SD	Mean	SD	Mean	SD
Event Driven	134	9.07	15.04	12.35	12.10	16.6	21.1	1.22	1.38	1.13	1.43	39.3	34.2
Fixed Income Arbitrage	71	5.51	12.93	10.78	9.97	15.9	22.0	1.10	1.77	1.03	1.99	46.0	35.7
Global Macro	114	3.74	28.83	21.02	18.94	3.2	21.5	0.33	1.05	0.37	0.90	46.2	31.0
Long/Short Equity	532	9.69	22.75	23.08	16.82	6.4	19.8	0.48	1.06	0.48	1.17	47.8	31.3
Managed Futures	316	4.78	23.17	20.88	19.35	−2.9	18.7	0.26	0.77	0.37	0.97	48.4	30.9
Multi-Strategy	41	5.32	23.46	17.55	20.90	6.1	17.4	1.10	1.55	1.58	2.06	49.4	32.2
Fund of Funds	273	4.53	10.07	13.56	10.56	11.3	21.2	0.62	1.26	0.57	1.11	40.9	31.9
Combined funds													
Convertible Arbitrage	176	9.94	6.08	6.24	4.89	31.4	19.5	67.47	3.66	1.85	2.55	21.8	29.3
Dedicated Shortseller	29	1.08	10.11	26.36	15.28	5.9	12.2	42.34	0.59	0.19	0.46	52.0	25.2
Emerging Markets	263	10.16	23.18	24.48	17.07	16.5	16.2	55.98	1.63	0.84	1.31	42.2	33.7
Equity Market Neutral	260	6.94	15.94	8.96	9.21	5.1	21.9	75.84	1.24	1.06	1.53	43.3	32.3
Event Driven	384	11.31	11.57	9.52	9.40	18.4	21.0	72.75	1.48	1.49	1.48	34.1	34.3
Fixed Income Arbitrage	175	7.76	9.45	8.10	7.76	16.2	22.9	79.36	9.16	2.29	5.86	40.4	35.6
Global Macro	232	7.18	22.04	17.21	15.61	2.3	19.3	66.88	0.92	0.70	0.90	46.5	30.8
Long/Short Equity	1,415	11.79	16.33	18.02	13.25	9.5	18.8	65.04	1.06	0.81	1.07	41.7	31.9
Managed Futures	511	6.23	21.59	20.22	17.07	−0.6	17.4	60.14	0.91	0.50	0.88	49.8	30.9
Multi-Strategy	139	10.49	19.92	11.74	15.00	14.7	20.9	72.53	2.16	1.49	2.05	36.7	32.9
Fund of Funds	952	6.22	7.17	8.26	7.75	19.6	20.0	69.34	1.37	1.21	1.22	35.8	31.8

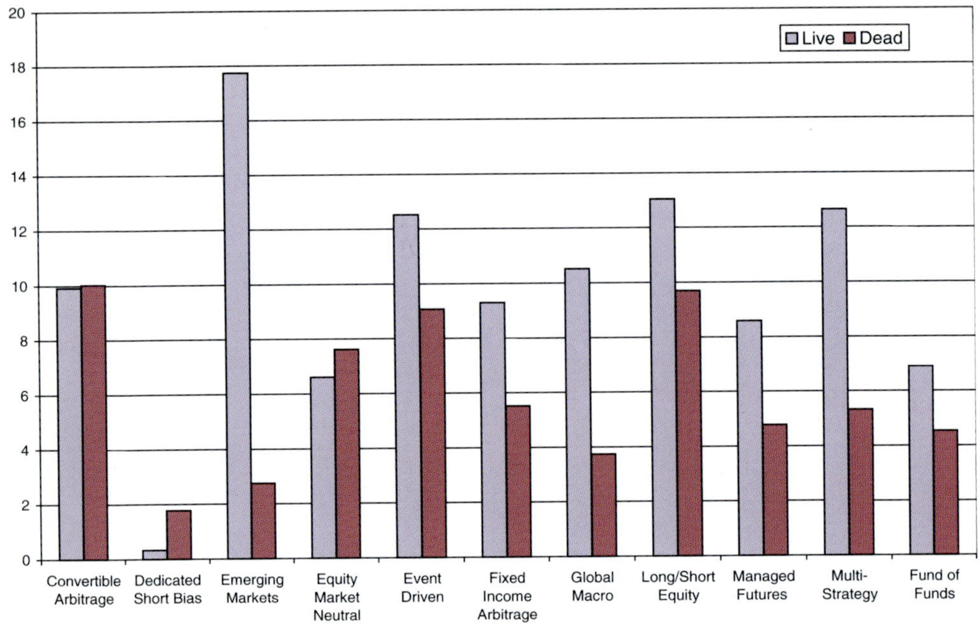

(a) Average mean return

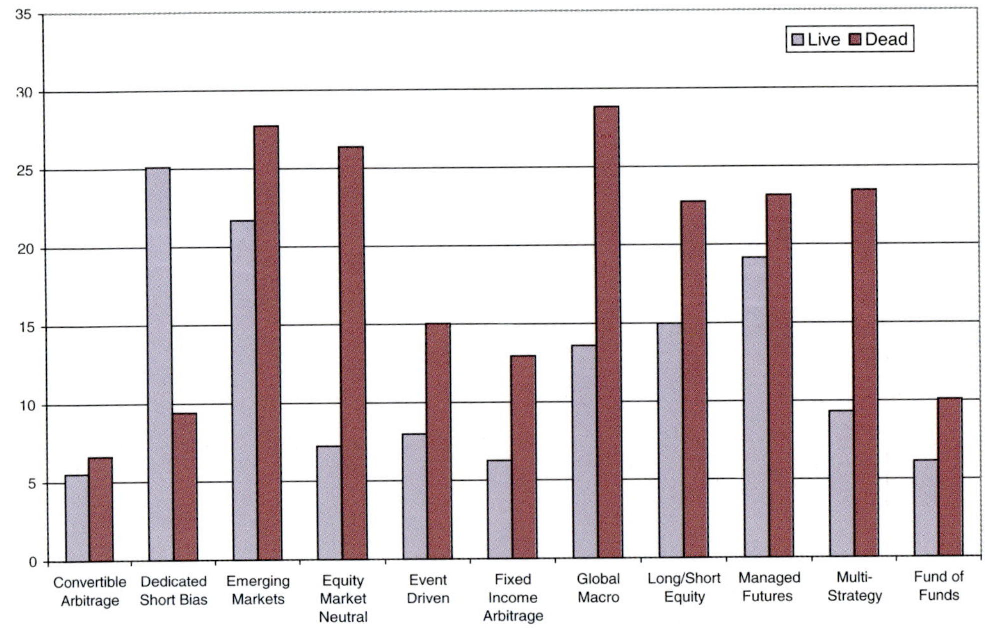

(b) Average standard deviation

Figure 2 Comparison of average means, standard deviations, Sharpe ratios, and first-order autocorrelation coefficients for categories of funds in the TASS Live and Graveyard databases from January 1994 to August 2004.

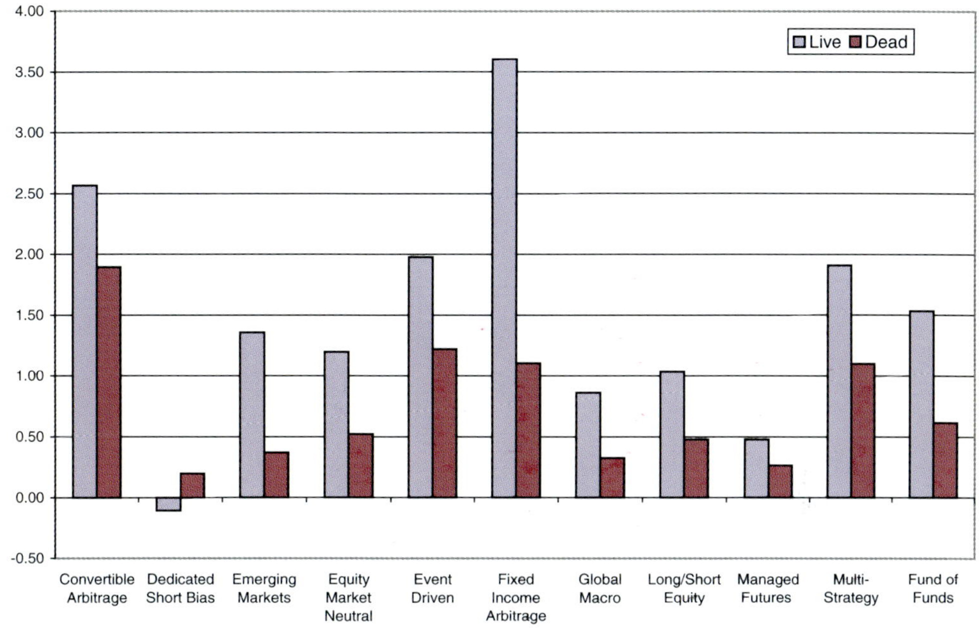

(c) Average Sharpe ratio

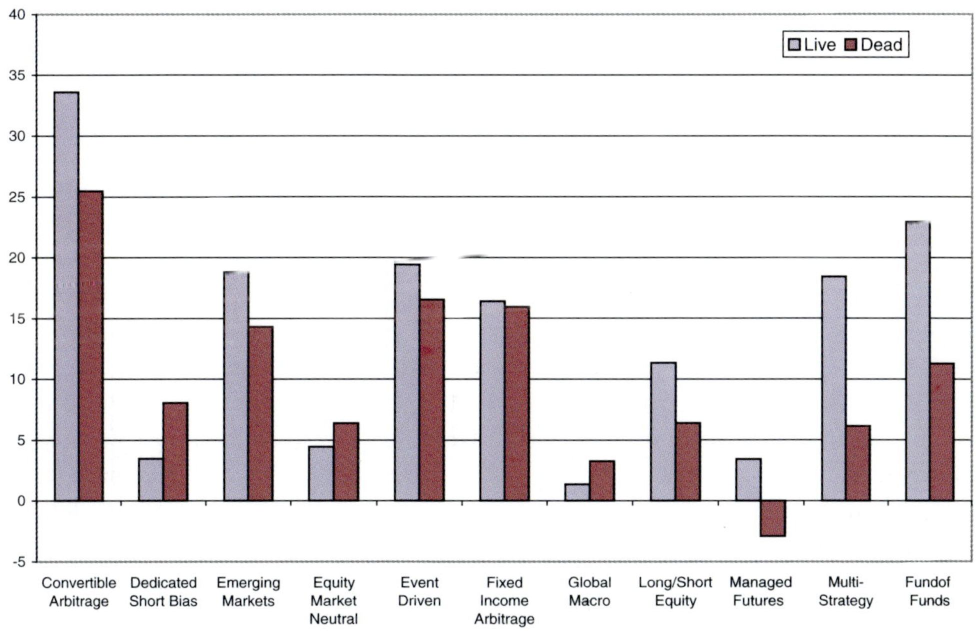

(d) Average autocorrelation

Figure 2 (*Continued*)

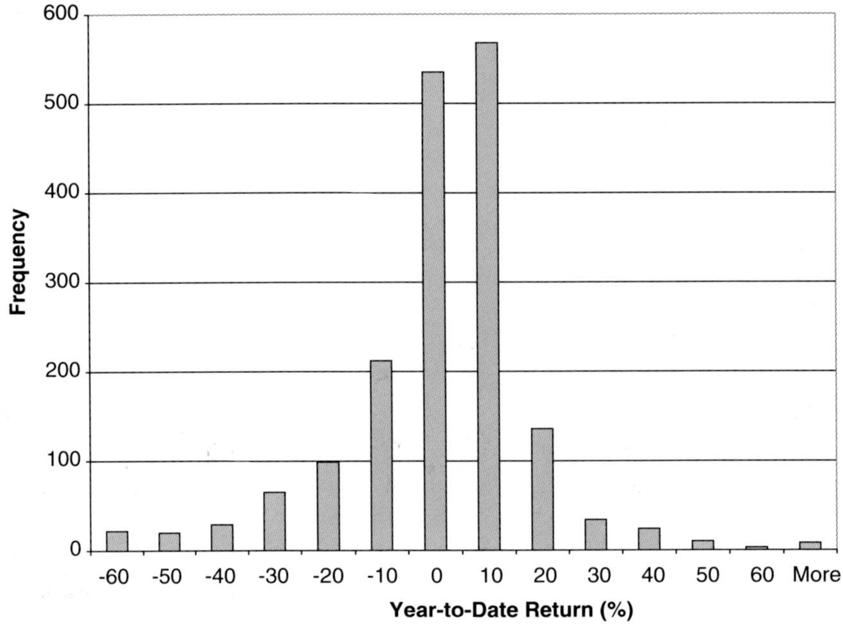

Figure 3 Histogram of year-to-date return at the time of liquidation of hedge funds in the TASS Graveyard database, January 1994 to August 2004.

Serial correlation of monthly returns—the correlation between one month's return and a previous month's return—has been proposed as a measure of smoothed returns and illiquidity exposure by Lo (2001, 2002) and Getmansky, Lo, and Makarov (2004), and there is considerable variation in the first-order serial correlation coefficient across the categories in the Combined database. The six categories with the highest averages are Convertible Arbitrage (31.4%), Fund of Funds (19.6%), Event Driven (18.4%), Emerging Markets (16.5%), Fixed-Income Arbitrage (16.2%), and Multi-Strategy (14.7%). Given the descriptions of these categories provided by TASS (see the appendix) and the fact that they involve some of the most illiquid securities traded, positive serial correlation does seem to be a reasonable proxy for valuation and illiquidity risk (see Section 5 for a more detailed analysis). In contrast, equities and futures are among the most liquid securities in which hedge funds invest, and not surprisingly, the average first-order serial correlations for Equity Market Neutral, Long/Short Equity, and Managed Futures categories are 5.1%, 9.5%, and –0.6%, respectively. Dedicated Shortseller funds also have a low average first-order autocorrelation, 5.9%, which is consistent with the high degree of liquidity that often characterizes shortsellers (by definition, the ability to short a security implies a certain degree of liquidity). We shall return to illiquidity risk in Section 5, where we consider some surprising differences in serial correlation between Live and Graveyard funds.

Finally, Figure 4 provides a summary of two key characteristics of the Graveyard funds: the age distribution of funds at the time of liquidation, and the distribution of their assets under management. The median age of Graveyard funds is 45 months, hence half of all liquidated funds never reached their fourth anniversary. The mode of the distribution is 36 months. The median assets under management for funds in the Graveyard database is $6.3 million, not an uncommon size for the typical startup hedge fund.

In the next two sections, we shall turn to more specific aspects of liquidated funds: attrition rates in Section 4 and valuation and illiquidity risk in Section 5.

4 Attrition Rates

To develop a sense for the dynamics of the TASS database and the birth and death rates of hedge funds over the past decade,[15] in Table 5 we report annual frequency counts of the funds in the database at the start of each year, funds entering the Live database during the year, funds exiting during the year and moving to the Graveyard database, and funds entering and exiting within the year. The panel labelled "All Funds" contains frequency counts for all funds, and the remaining 11 panels contain the same statistics for each category. Also included in Table 5 are attrition rates, defined as the ratio of funds exiting in a given year to the number of existing funds at the start of the year, and the performance of the category as measured by the annual compound return of the CSFB/Tremont Index for that category.

For the unfiltered sample of all funds in the TASS database, and over the sample period from 1994 to 2003, the average attrition rate is 8.8%.[16] This is similar to the 8.5% attrition rate obtained by Liang (2001) for the 1994–1999 sample period. The aggregate attrition rate rises in 1998, partly due to LTCM's demise and the dislocation caused by its aftermath. The attrition rate increases to a peak of 11.4% in 2001, mostly due to the Long/Short Equity category—presumably the result of the bursting of the technology bubble.

Although 8.8% is the average attrition rate for the entire TASS database, there is considerable variation in average attrition rates across categories. Averaging the annual attrition rates from 1994 to 2003 within each category yields the following:

Convertible Arbitrage	5.2%	Global Macro	12.6%
Dedicated Shortseller	8.0%	Long/Short Equity	7.6%
Emerging Markets	9.2%	Managed Futures	14.4%
Equity Market Neutral	8.0%	Multi-Strategy	8.2%
Event Driven	5.4%	Fund of Funds	6.9%
Fixed Income Arbitrage	10.6%		

These averages illustrate the different risks involved in each of the 11 investment styles. At 5.2%, Convertible Arbitrage enjoys the lowest average attrition rate, which is not surprising since this category has the second-lowest average return volatility of 5.89% (see Table 4). The highest average attrition rate is 14.4% for Managed Futures, which is also consistent with the 18.55% average volatility of this category, the highest among all 11 categories.

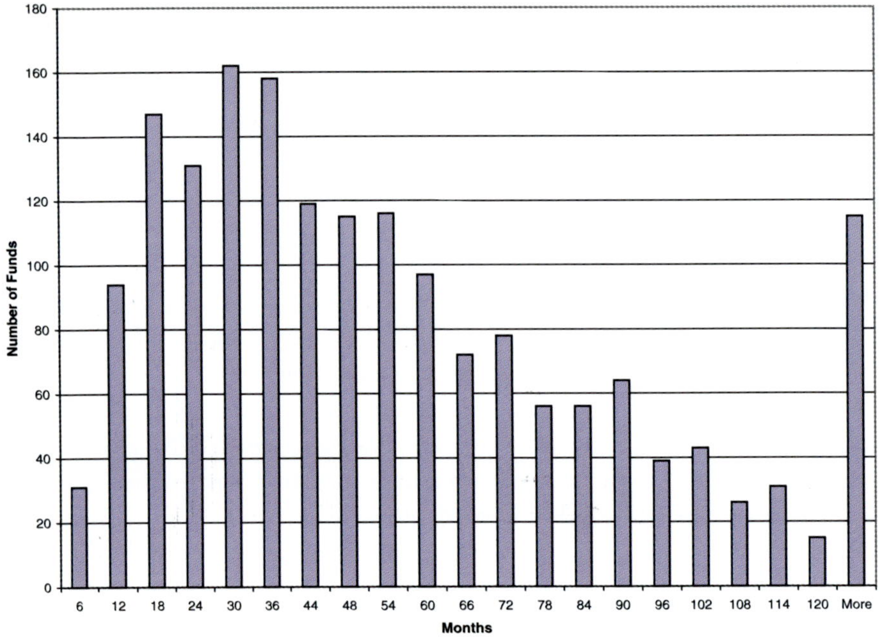

(a) Age distribution

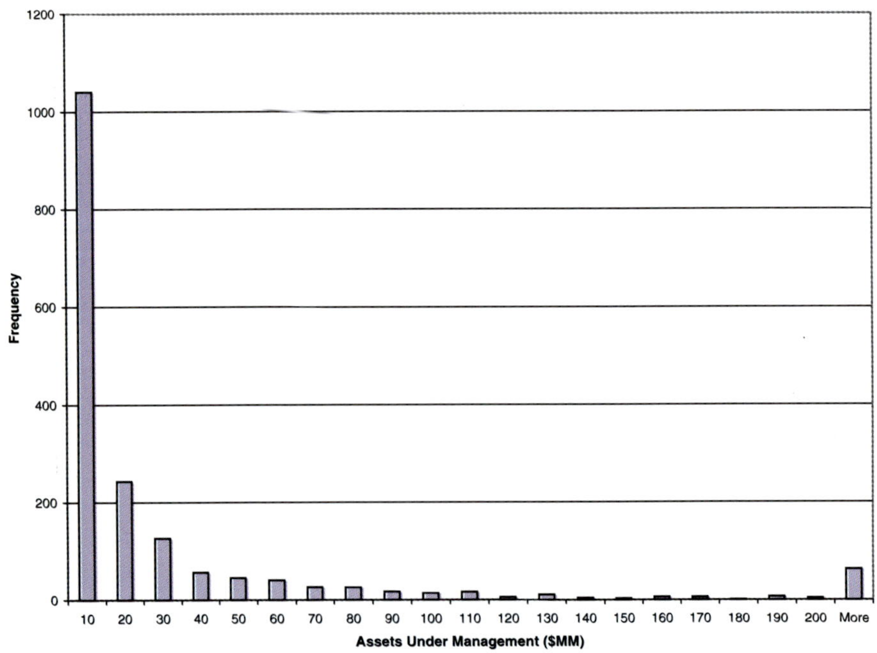

(b) Assets under management

Figure 4 Histograms of age distribution and assets under management at the time of liquidation for funds in the TASS Graveyard database, January 1994 to August 2004.

Table 5 Attrition rates for all hedge funds in the TASS Hedge Fund database, and within each style category, from January 1994 to August 2004. Index returns are annual compound returns of the CSFB/Tremont Hedge-Fund Indexes.

Year	Existing funds	New entries	New exits	Intra-year entry and exit	Total funds	Attrition rate (%)	Index return (%)	Existing funds	New entries	New exits	Intra-year entry and exit	Total funds	Attrition rate (%)	Index return (%)	Existing funds	New entries	New exits	Intra-year entry and exit	Total funds	Attrition rate (%)	Index return (%)
	All funds							Equity Markets Neutral							Long/Short Equity						
1994	769	251	23	2	997	3.0	−4.4	12	7	1	0	18	8.3	−2.0	168	52	2	0	218	1.2	−8.1
1995	997	299	61	1	1,235	6.1	21.7	18	10	0	0	28	0.0	11.0	218	74	7	0	285	3.2	23.0
1996	1,235	332	120	9	1,447	9.7	22.2	28	10	0	0	38	0.0	16.6	285	116	21	2	380	7.4	17.1
1997	1,447	356	100	6	1,703	6.9	25.9	38	14	0	0	52	0.0	14.8	380	118	15	2	483	3.9	21.5
1998	1,703	346	162	9	1,887	9.5	−0.4	52	29	2	2	79	3.8	13.3	483	117	33	2	567	6.8	17.2
1999	1,887	403	183	7	2,107	9.7	23.4	79	36	14	1	101	17.7	15.3	567	159	42	3	684	7.4	47.2
2000	2,107	391	234	9	2,264	11.1	4.8	101	17	13	0	105	12.9	15.0	684	186	55	5	815	8.0	2.1
2001	2,264	460	257	6	2,467	11.4	4.4	105	49	9	0	145	8.6	9.3	815	156	109	3	862	13.4	−3.7
2002	2,467	432	246	9	2,653	10.0	3.0	145	41	14	2	172	9.7	7.4	862	137	107	5	892	12.4	−1.6
2003	2,653	325	285	12	2,693	10.7	15.5	172	23	32	0	163	18.6	7.1	892	83	110	2	865	12.3	17.3
2004	2,693	1	87	1	2,607	3.2	2.7	163	0	5	0	158	3.1	4.7	865	0	27	0	838	3.1	1.5
	Convertible Arbitrage							Event Driven							Managed Futures						
1994	26	13	0	0	39	0.0	−8.1	71	16	0	0	87	0.0	0.7	181	52	8	1	225	4.4	11.9
1995	39	12	0	0	51	0.0	16.6	87	27	1	0	113	1.1	18.4	225	41	30	0	236	13.3	−7.1
1996	51	14	7	0	58	13.7	17.9	113	29	3	0	139	2.7	23.0	236	42	49	2	229	20.8	12.0
1997	58	10	3	0	65	5.2	14.5	139	31	3	0	167	2.2	20.0	229	37	36	1	230	15.7	3.1
1998	65	14	5	0	74	7.7	−4.4	167	28	2	1	193	1.2	−4.9	230	25	37	0	218	16.1	20.7
1999	74	10	3	0	81	4.1	16.0	193	29	19	1	203	9.8	22.3	218	35	40	1	213	18.3	−4.7
2000	81	17	3	0	95	3.7	25.6	203	38	15	0	226	7.4	7.2	213	13	35	0	191	16.4	4.3
2001	95	25	5	0	115	5.3	14.6	226	34	19	3	241	8.4	11.5	191	18	19	0	190	9.9	1.9
2002	115	22	6	0	131	5.2	4.0	241	40	30	2	251	12.4	0.2	190	22	32	0	180	16.8	18.3
2003	131	11	10	0	132	7.6	12.9	251	21	23	1	249	9.2	20.0	180	23	21	2	182	11.7	14.2
2004	132	0	10	0	122	7.6	0.6	249	0	15	0	234	6.0	5.7	182	0	5	0	177	2.7	−7.0

Table 5 (*Continued*)

Year	Existing funds	New entries	New exits	Intra-year entry and exit	Total funds	Attrition rate (%)	Index return (%)	Existing funds	New entries	New exits	Intra-year entry and exit	Total funds	Attrition rate (%)	Index return (%)	Existing funds	New entries	New exits	Intra-year entry and exit	Total funds	Attrition rate (%)	Index return (%)
	Dedicated Shortseller							Fixed Income Arbitrage							Multi-Strategy						
1994	11	1	0	0	12	0.0	14.9	22	16	3	0	35	13.6	0.3	17	5	3	1	19	17.6	—
1995	12	0	1	0	11	8.3	−7.4	35	12	2	0	45	5.7	12.5	19	7	2	0	24	10.5	11.9
1996	11	3	1	0	13	9.1	−5.5	45	16	4	0	57	8.9	15.9	24	14	1	0	37	4.2	14.0
1997	13	3	1	0	15	7.7	0.4	57	15	4	1	68	7.0	9.4	37	13	3	0	47	8.1	18.3
1998	15	1	0	0	16	0.0	−6.0	68	16	14	0	70	20.6	−8.2	47	8	5	1	50	10.6	7.7
1999	16	4	1	0	19	6.3	−14.2	70	13	8	0	75	11.4	12.1	50	10	2	0	58	4.0	9.4
2000	19	2	1	0	20	5.3	15.8	75	9	11	0	73	14.7	6.3	58	10	2	1	66	3.4	11.2
2001	20	1	6	0	15	30.0	−3.6	73	20	7	0	86	9.6	8.0	66	16	1	0	81	1.5	5.5
2002	15	1	1	0	15	6.7	18.2	86	23	5	0	104	5.8	5.7	81	14	5	0	90	6.2	6.3
2003	15	1	1	0	15	6.7	−32.6	104	12	9	0	107	8.7	8.0	90	14	14	4	90	15.6	15.0
2004	15	0	2	0	13	13.3	9.1	107	0	4	0	103	3.7	4.7	90	0	0	0	90	0.0	2.8
	Emerging Markets							Global Macro							Fund of Funds						
1994	44	25	0	0	69	0.0	12.5	50	11	3	0	58	6.0	−5.7	167	53	3	0	217	1.8	—
1995	69	34	1	0	102	1.4	−16.9	58	19	5	0	72	8.6	30.7	217	63	12	1	268	5.5	—
1996	102	25	4	0	123	3.9	34.5	72	16	13	4	75	18.1	25.6	268	47	17	1	298	6.3	—
1997	123	40	8	0	155	6.5	26.6	75	19	6	1	88	8.0	37.1	298	56	21	1	333	7.0	—
1998	155	22	25	1	152	16.1	−37.7	88	20	7	2	101	8.0	−3.6	333	66	32	0	367	9.6	—
1999	152	26	18	0	160	11.8	44.8	101	12	15	1	98	14.9	5.8	367	69	21	0	415	5.7	—
2000	160	20	25	2	155	15.6	−5.5	98	18	33	0	83	33.7	11.7	415	61	41	1	435	9.9	—
2001	155	5	28	0	132	18.1	5.8	83	15	9	0	89	10.8	18.4	435	121	45	0	511	10.3	—
2002	132	4	11	0	125	8.3	7.4	89	26	9	0	106	10.1	14.7	511	102	26	0	587	5.1	—
2003	125	12	13	1	124	10.4	28.7	106	15	8	1	113	7.5	18.0	587	110	44	1	653	7.5	—
2004	124	0	1	0	123	0.8	3.1	113	0	1	0	112	0.9	4.4	653	1	17	1	637	2.6	—

Note: Attrition rates for 2004 are severely downward-biased because TASS typically waits 8 to 10 months before moving a non-reporting fund from the Live to the Graveyard database; therefore, as of August 2004, many non-reporting funds in the Live database have not yet been moved to the Graveyard.

Within each category, the year-to-year attrition rates exhibit different patterns, partly attributable to the relative performance of the categories. For example, Emerging Markets experienced a 16.1% attrition rate in 1998, no doubt because of the turmoil in emerging markets in 1997 and 1998, which is reflected in the −37.7% return in the CSFB/Tremont Index Emerging Markets Index for 1998. The opposite pattern is also present—during periods of unusually good performance, attrition rates decline, as in the case of Long/Short Equity from 1995 to 2000 where attrition rates were 3.2%, 7.4%, 3.9%, 6.8%, 7.4%, and 8.0%, respectively. Of course, in the three years following the bursting of the technology bubble—2001–2003—the attrition rates for Long/Short Equity shot up to 13.4%, 12.4%, and 12.3%, respectively. These patterns are consistent with the basic economics of the hedge-fund industry: good performance begets more assets under management, greater business leverage, and staying power; poor performance leads to the Graveyard.

To develop a better sense of the relative magnitudes of attrition across categories, Table 6 and Figure 5(a) provide a decomposition by category where the attrition rates in each category are renormalized so that when they are summed across categories in a given year, the result equals the aggregate attrition rate for that year. From these renormalized figures, it is apparent that there is an increase in the proportion of the total attrition rate due to Long/Short Equity funds beginning in 2001. In fact, Table 6 shows that of the total attrition rates of 11.4%, 10.0%, and 10.7% in the years 2001–2003, the Long/Short Equity category was responsible for 4.8, 4.3, and 4.1 percentage points of those totals, respectively. Despite the fact that the average attrition rate for the Long/Short Equity category is only 7.6% from 1994 to 2003, the funds in this category are more numerous, hence they contribute more to the aggregate attrition rate. Figure 5(b) provides a measure of the impact of these attrition rates on the industry by plotting the total assets under management of funds in the TASS database along with the relative proportions in each category. Long/Short Equity funds are indeed a significant fraction of the industry, hence the increase in their attrition rates in recent years may be a cause for some concern.

5 Valuation and Illiquidity Risk

One of the most pressing issues facing the hedge-fund industry is the valuation of funds, particularly those containing assets that do not always have readily available market prices with which to mark portfolios to market. Feffer and Kundro (2003) conclude that one of the most common manifestations of fraud—which accounts for over 50% of the hedge-fund liquidations in their sample—involves the misrepresentation of investments, defined by Feffer and Kundro (2003, p. 5) as "The act of creating or causing the generation of reports and valuations with false and misleading information." Valuation is so central to the proper functioning of financial institutions that the International Association of Financial Engineers—a not-for-profit organization of investment professionals in quantitative finance—convened a special committee to formulate guidelines for best-practices valuation procedures, outlined in a June 2004 white paper (Metzger *et al.*, 2004). The importance of valuation procedures has been underscored recently by

Table 6 Decomposition of attrition rates by category for all hedge funds in the TASS Hedge Fund database, from January 1994 to August 2004, and corresponding CSFB/Tremont Hedge-Fund Index returns, and assets under management.

Year	All Funds	Convert Arb	Ded Short	Emrg Mkts	EqMkt Neutral	Event Driven	Fixed Income Arb	Global Macro	L/S Equity	Man Futures	Multi-Strategy	Fund of Funds
Total attrition rates and components by category (in %)												
1994	3.0	0.0	0.0	0.0	0.1	0.0	0.4	0.4	0.3	1.0	0.4	0.4
1995	6.1	0.0	0.1	0.1	0.0	0.1	0.2	0.5	0.7	3.0	0.2	1.2
1996	9.7	0.6	0.1	0.3	0.0	0.2	0.3	1.1	1.7	4.0	0.1	1.4
1997	6.9	0.2	0.1	0.6	0.0	0.2	0.3	0.4	1.0	2.5	0.2	1.5
1998	9.5	0.3	0.0	1.5	0.1	0.1	0.8	0.4	1.9	2.2	0.3	1.9
1999	9.7	0.2	0.1	1.0	0.7	1.0	0.4	0.8	2.2	2.1	0.1	1.1
2000	11.1	0.1	0.0	1.2	0.6	0.7	0.5	1.6	2.6	1.7	0.1	1.9
2001	11.4	0.2	0.3	1.2	0.4	0.8	0.3	0.4	4.8	0.8	0.0	2.0
2002	10.0	0.2	0.0	0.4	0.6	1.2	0.2	0.4	4.3	1.3	0.2	1.1
2003	10.7	0.4	0.0	0.5	1.2	0.9	0.3	0.3	4.1	0.8	0.5	1.7
2004	3.2	0.4	0.1	0.0	0.2	0.6	0.1	0.0	1.0	0.2	0.0	0.6
Mean	8.8	0.2	0.1	0.7	0.4	0.5	0.4	0.6	2.4	1.9	0.2	1.4
SD	2.7	0.2	0.1	0.5	0.4	0.4	0.2	0.4	1.6	1.0	0.2	0.5
Annual returns of CSFB/Tremont Hedge-Fund Indexes by category (in %)												
1994	−4.4	−8.1	14.9	12.5	−2.0	0.7	0.3	−5.7	−8.1	11.9	—	—
1995	21.7	16.6	−7.4	−16.9	11.0	18.4	12.5	30.7	23.0	−7.1	11.9	—
1996	22.2	17.9	−5.5	34.5	16.6	23.0	15.9	25.6	17.1	12.0	14.0	—
1997	25.9	14.5	0.4	26.6	14.8	20.0	9.4	37.1	21.5	3.1	18.3	—

Table 6 *(Continued)*

Year	All Funds	Convert Arb	Ded Short	Emrg Mkts	EqMkt Neutral	Event Driven	Fixed Income Arb	Global Macro	L/S Equity	Man Futures	Multi-Strategy	Fund of Funds
1998	−0.4	−4.4	−6.0	−37.7	13.3	−4.9	−8.2	−3.6	17.2	20.7	7.7	—
1999	23.4	16.0	−14.2	44.8	15.3	22.3	12.1	5.8	47.2	−4.7	9.4	—
2000	4.8	25.6	15.8	−5.5	15.0	7.2	6.3	11.7	2.1	4.3	11.2	—
2001	4.4	14.6	−3.6	5.8	9.3	11.5	8.0	18.4	−3.7	1.9	5.5	—
2002	3.0	4.0	18.2	7.4	7.4	0.2	5.7	14.7	−1.6	18.3	6.3	—
2003	15.5	12.9	−32.6	28.7	7.1	20.0	8.0	18.0	17.3	14.2	15.0	—
2004	2.7	0.6	9.1	3.1	4.7	5.7	4.7	4.4	1.5	−7.0	2.8	—
Mean	11.6	11.0	−2.0	10.0	10.8	11.8	7.0	15.3	13.2	7.5	11.0	—
SD	11.3	10.5	15.5	25.2	5.6	10.4	6.8	13.9	16.5	9.4	4.3	—
Total assets under management (in $MM) and percent breakdown by category (in %)												
1994	57,684	3.8	0.7	9.3	1.0	9.5	3.9	20.5	20.7	5.1	7.5	18.0
1995	69,477	3.9	0.5	8.1	1.3	10.0	4.7	18.5	22.9	4.0	9.2	17.0
1996	92,513	4.2	0.4	8.7	2.3	10.1	5.9	17.9	23.4	3.2	7.8	16.1
1997	137,814	4.7	0.4	8.9	2.7	10.4	6.7	18.8	21.9	2.7	7.5	15.3
1998	142,669	5.5	0.6	4.0	4.4	12.5	5.7	16.8	24.4	3.3	6.8	16.0
1999	175,223	5.3	0.6	4.6	5.2	11.7	4.6	9.1	34.5	2.8	6.6	15.1
2000	197,120	5.4	0.5	2.5	5.5	10.6	3.3	1.9	31.1	1.9	4.4	12.7
2001	246,695	8.1	0.3	2.8	7.4	13.9	4.7	2.3	35.3	3.0	5.5	16.6
2002	277,695	8.5	0.3	3.1	7.2	13.0	6.2	3.1	30.2	3.9	6.1	18.4
2003	389,965	8.8	0.1	4.3	6.0	13.0	6.2	5.4	25.7	5.0	5.8	19.7
2004	403,974	8.8	0.2	4.2	5.9	13.5	7.1	6.6	26.3	5.3	6.8	15.3
Mean	178,685	5.8	0.5	5.6	4.3	11.5	5.2	11.4	27.0	3.5	6.7	16.5
SD	103,484	1.9	0.2	2.8	2.4	1.5	1.1	7.8	5.3	1.0	1.4	2.0

Note: Attrition rates for 2004 are severely downwarc-biased because TASS typically waits 8–10 months before moving a non-reporting fund from the Live to the Graveyard database; therefore, as of August 2004, many non-reporting funds in the Live database have not yet been moved to the Graveyard. Consequently, the reported means and standard deviations in all three panels computed over the 1994–2003 period.

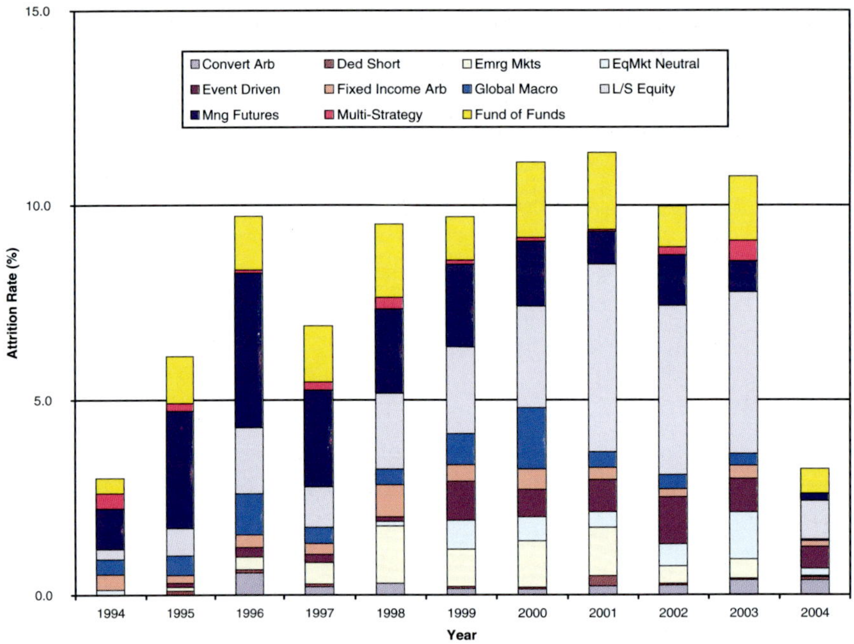

(a) Attrition rates

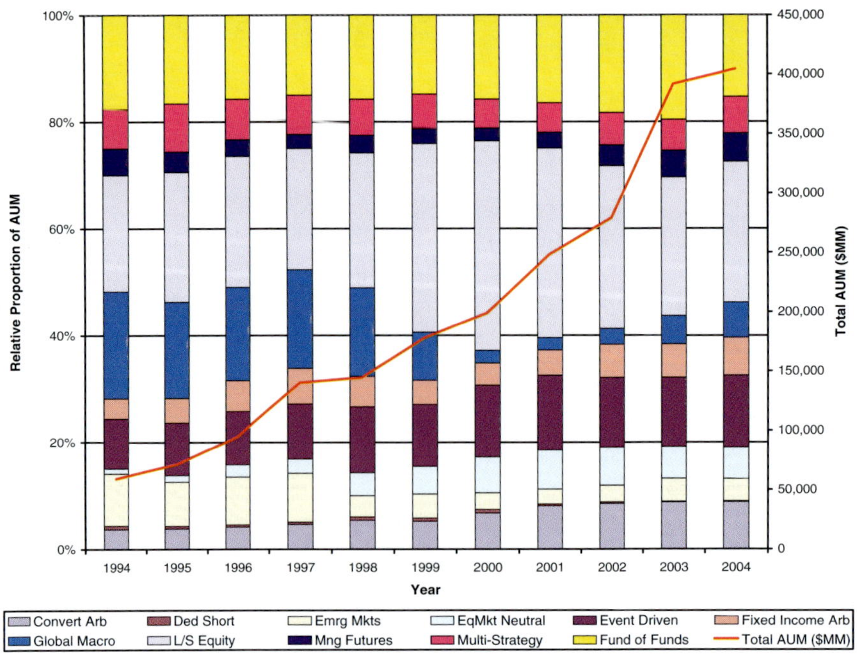

(b) Assets under management

Figure 5 Attrition rates and total assets under management for funds in the TASS Live and Graveyard database from January 1994 to August 2004. Note: the data for 2004 is incomplete, and attrition rates for this year are severely downward biased because of a 8- to 10-month lag in transferring non-reporting funds from the Live to the Graveyard database.

the mutual-fund market-timing scandal in which certain investment companies were successfully prosecuted and fined for allowing open-end mutual-fund transactions to occur at stale prices.[17] By engaging in such transactions, these investment companies were effectively permitting outright wealth transfers from a fund's buy-and-hold shareholders to those engaged in opportunistic buying and selling of shares based on more current information regarding the fund's daily NAVs.

Valuation issues arise mainly when a fund is invested in illiquid assets, i.e., assets that do not trade frequently and cannot easily be traded in large quantities without significant price concessions. For portfolios of illiquid assets, a hedge-fund manager often has considerable discretion in marking the portfolio's value at the end of each month to arrive at the fund's net asset value. Given the nature of hedge-fund compensation contracts and performance statistics, managers may have an incentive to "smooth" their returns by marking their portfolios to less than their actual value in months with large positive returns so as to create a "cushion" for those months with lower returns. Such return-smoothing behavior yields a more consistent set of returns over time, with lower volatility, lower market beta, and a higher Sharpe ratio, but it also produces positive serial correlation as a side effect.[18] In fact, it is the magnitudes of the serial correlation coefficients of certain types of hedge funds that led Getmansky, Lo, and Makarov (2004) to develop their econometric model of smoothed returns and illiquidity exposure. After considering other potential sources of serial correlation—time-varying expected returns, time-varying leverage, and the presence of incentive fees and high-water marks—they conclude that the most plausible explanation is illiquidity exposure and smoothed returns.[19]

We hasten to add that some manager discretion is appropriate and necessary in valuing portfolios, and Getmansky, Lo, and Makarov (2004) describe several other sources of serial correlation in the presence of illiquidity, none of which is motivated by deceit. For example, a common method for determining the fair market value for illiquid assets is to extrapolate linearly from the most recent transaction price (which, in the case of emerging-market debt, might be several months ago), yielding a price path that is a straight line or, at best, a piecewise-linear trajectory. Returns computed from such marks will be smoother, exhibiting lower volatility and higher serial correlation than true economic returns, i.e., returns computed from mark-to-market prices where the market is sufficiently active to allow all available current information to be impounded in the price of the security. For assets that are more easily traded and with deeper markets, mark-to-market prices are more readily available, extrapolated marks are not necessary, and serial correlation is therefore less of an issue. But for assets that are thinly traded, or not traded at all for extended periods of time, marking to market is often an expensive and time-consuming procedure that cannot easily be performed frequently.

Even if a hedge-fund manager does not make use of any form of linear extrapolation to mark the assets in his portfolio, he may still be subject to smoothed returns if he obtains marks from broker-dealers that engage in such extrapolation. For example, consider the case of a conscientious hedge-fund manager attempting to obtain the most accurate mark for his portfolio at month end by getting bid/offer quotes from three independent broker-dealers for every asset in his portfolio, and then marking each asset at the average of the three quote midpoints. By averaging the quote midpoints, the manager is inadvertently downward-biasing price volatility, and if broker-dealers employ linear extrapolation in formulating their quotes (and many do, through sheer necessity because they have little else to go on for the most illiquid assets), or if they fail to update their quotes because of light volume, serial correlation will also be induced in reported returns.

Apart from performance-smoothing concerns, investing in illiquid assets yields additional risk exposures, those involving credit crunches and "flight-to-quality" events. Although liquidity and credit are separate sources of risk exposures for hedge funds and their investors—one type of risk can exist without the other—nevertheless, they have been inextricably intertwined because of the problems encountered by LTCM and many other fixed-income relative-value hedge funds in August and September of 1998.

The basic mechanisms driving liquidity and credit are now familiar to most hedge-fund managers and investors. Because many hedge funds rely on leverage, the size of the positions are often considerably larger than the amount of collateral posted to support those positions. Leverage has the effect of a magnifying glass, expanding small profit opportunities into larger ones, but also expanding small losses into larger losses. When adverse changes in market prices reduces the market value of collateral, credit is withdrawn quickly, and the subsequent forced liquidation of large positions over short periods of time can lead to widespread financial panic, as in the aftermath of the default of Russian government debt in August 1998. Along with the many benefits of a truly global financial system is the cost that a financial crisis in one country can have dramatic repercussions in several others.

To quantify the impact of illiquidity risk and smoothed returns, Getmansky, Lo, and Makarov (2004) start by asserting that a fund's true economic returns in month t is given by R_t, which represents the sum total of all the relevant information that would determine the equilibrium value of the fund's securities in a frictionless market. However, they assume that true economic returns are not observed. Instead, R_t^o denotes the reported or observed return in period t, and let

$$R_t^o = \theta_0 R_t + \theta_1 R_{t-1} + \cdots + \theta_k R_{t-k} \tag{1}$$

$$\theta_j \in [0, 1], \quad j = 0, \ldots, k \tag{2}$$

$$1 = \theta_0 + \theta_1 + \cdots + \theta_k \tag{3}$$

which is a weighted average of the fund's true returns R_t over the most recent $k + 1$ periods, including the current period. This averaging process captures the essence of smoothed returns in several respects. From the perspective of illiquidity-driven smoothing, (1) is consistent with several models in the nonsynchronous trading literature (see Getmansky, Lo, and Makarov, 2004). Alternatively, (1) can be viewed as the outcome of marking portfolios to simple linear extrapolations of acquisition prices when market prices are unavailable, or "mark-to-model" returns where the pricing model is slowly varying through time. And, of course, (1) also captures the intentional smoothing of performance.

The constraint (3) that the weights sum to 1 implies that the information driving the fund's performance in period t will eventually be fully reflected in observed returns, but this process could take up to $k + 1$ periods from the time the information is generated. This is a plausible restriction in the current context of hedge funds for several reasons. Even the most illiquid security will trade eventually, and when it does, all of the cumulative information affecting that security will be fully impounded into its transaction price. Therefore, the parameter k should be selected to match the kind of illiquidity of the fund—a fund comprised mostly of exchange-traded US equities would require a much lower value of k than a private equity fund. Alternatively, in the case of intentional smoothing of performance, the necessity of periodic external audits of fund performance imposes a finite limit on the extent to which deliberate smoothing can persist.[20]

Under the smoothing mechanism (1), Getmansky, Lo, and Makarov (2004) show that observed returns have lower variances, lower market betas, and higher Sharpe ratios than true returns. Smoothed returns also exhibit positive serial correlation up to order k, and the magnitude of the effect is determined by the pattern of weights $\{\theta_j\}$. If, for example, the weights are disproportionately centered on a small number of lags, relatively little serial correlation will be induced. However, if the weights are evenly distributed among many lags, this will result in higher serial correlation. A useful summary statistic for measuring the concentration of weights is

$$\xi \equiv \sum_{j=0}^{k} \theta_j^2 \in [0, 1] \tag{4}$$

This measure is well known in the industrial organization literature as the *Herfindahl index*, a measure of the concentration of firms in a given industry where θ_j represents the market share of firm j. Because $\theta_j \in [0, 1]$, ξ is also confined to the unit interval, and is minimized when all the θ_j are identical, which implies a value of $1/(k+1)$ for ξ, and is maximized when one coefficient is 1 and the rest are 0, in which case $\xi = 1$. In the context of smoothed returns, a lower value of ξ implies more smoothing, and the upper bound of 1 implies no smoothing; hence we shall refer to ξ as a "smoothing index."

Using the method of maximum-likelihood, Getmansky, Lo, and Makarov (2004) estimate the smoothing model (1)–(3) by estimating an MA(2) process for observed returns assuming normally distributed errors, with the additional constraint that the MA coefficients sum to 1, and we apply the same procedure to our updated and enlarged sample of funds in the TASS Combined hedge-fund database from February 1977 to August 2004. For purposes of estimating (1), we impose an additional filter on our data, eliminating funds with less than five years of non-missing monthly returns. This leaves a sample of 1,840 funds for which we estimate the MA(2) smoothing model. The maximum-likelihood estimation procedure did not converge for three of these funds, indicating some sort of misspecification or data error, hence we have results for 1,837 funds: 1,226 in the Live database and 611 in the Graveyard database.[21]

Table 7 contains summary statistics for the maximum-likelihood estimate of the smoothing parameters $(\theta_0, \theta_1, \theta_2)$ and smoothing index ξ for both databases. Five categories have smaller average values of ξ than the others in the Live database: Convertible Arbitrage (0.635), Emerging Markets (0.723), Event Driven (0.665), Fixed Income Arbitrage (0.686), Long/Short Equity (0.838), and Multi-Strategy (0.663). To determine the statistical significance of these averages, Table 7 reports z-statistics which are asymptotically standard normal under the null hypothesis that $\xi = 1$; hence, values greater than 1.96 indicate significance at the 95% level,[22] and these six categories yield average smoothing indexes that are statistically significant at the 99% level. These results coincide with common intuition about the nature of these five categories—they do invest in rather illiquid securities, in contrast to funds in the other categories such as Dedicated Shortsellers and Managed Futures, both of which involve particularly liquid securities by the nature of their investment mandate.[23]

Table 7 shows that similar patterns hold for funds in the Graveyard database. Five out of the six categories exhibit statistically significant smoothing indexes, the exception being the last category, Multi-Strategy, with an average smoothing index of 0.960 for Graveyard funds versus 0.663 for Live funds. However, there are only eight funds of this type in the Graveyard database as compared to 39 funds in the Live database, hence the sample may be too small to draw inferences with any degree of confidence.

A comparison of the degree of smoothing between Live and Graveyard funds in these five categories yields mixed results: for Emerging Markets, Event Driven, and Long/Short Equity, the Live funds yield smaller smoothing indexes, but for Convertible Arbitrage and Fixed-Income Arbitrage, the Graveyard funds exhibit a somewhat greater degree of average smoothing. A scatterplot of smoothing-index estimates for Live and Graveyard funds is given in Figure 6, and a visual comparison suggests that there is little difference in illiquidity risk across Live and Graveyard funds. However, the histograms of smoothing indexes ξ and smoothing coefficients θ_0 in Figure 7 tell a very different story. These histograms show that the distributions of the two smoothing measures for Live funds are more heavily weighted in the left tails than for Graveyard funds.

There are at least three possible explanations for this difference. One is that Live funds are, by definition, more successful at controlling risk and, as a result, do tend to have smoother returns. Another interpretation is that funds with smoother returns are more attractive to investors and, therefore, have greater staying power. A third possibility is that funds with more illiquidity risk are, on average, compensated for bearing such risk, which in turn implies stronger performance and greater asset-gathering abilities. With additional information about the specific investment process of a given fund, e.g., the fund prospectus and an investment due-diligence meeting, it may be possible for an investor to determine which one of these three explanations is most likely to apply on a case-by-case basis.

Of course, in contrast to cases of fraud, there is nothing inappropriate about hedge funds taking on illiquidity risk as long as such risk is properly disclosed. In fact, from

Table 7 Means and standard deviations of maximum likelihood estimates of MA(2) smoothing process $R_t^o = \theta_0 R_t + \theta_1 R_{t-1} + \theta_2 R_{t-2}$, $\xi \equiv \theta_0^2 + \theta_1^2 + \theta_2^2$, for hedge funds in the TASS Live and Graveyard databases with at least five years of returns history during the period from November 1977 to August 2004. z-statistics are asymptotically standard normal under the null hypotheses that $\theta_0 = 1$, $\theta_1 = 0$, $\theta_2 = 0$, and $\xi = 1$.

	Live funds									Graveyard funds								
	Sample	θ_0		θ_1		θ_2		ξ		Sample	θ_0		θ_1		θ_2		ξ	
Category	size	Mean	z-Stat	Mean	z-Stat	Mean	z-Stat	Mean	z-Stat	size	Mean	z-Stat	Mean	z-Stat	Mean	z-Stat	Mean	z-Stat
Convertible Arbitrage	57	0.724	12.15	0.201	9.16	0.076	5.67	0.635	7.42	22	0.705	10.54	0.203	10.52	0.092	4.11	0.582	11.91
Dedicated Shortseller	8	0.960	1.66	0.091	8.22	−0.051	−1.73	0.944	1.12	8	1.180	−0.74	0.000	0.00	−0.179	−1.09	2.073	−0.95
Emerging Markets	87	0.818	14.99	0.157	17.56	0.025	2.43	0.723	14.15	49	0.868	4.98	0.126	7.54	0.006	0.34	0.831	2.94
Equity Market Neutral	49	0.887	3.88	0.034	1.17	0.079	3.93	0.894	1.80	16	0.902	1.86	0.089	2.40	0.009	0.31	0.897	1.17
Event Driven	128	0.774	19.63	0.158	16.75	0.068	8.61	0.665	18.68	55	0.812	8.34	0.158	11.37	0.029	1.75	0.739	6.65
Fixed Income Arbitrage	43	0.789	9.80	0.144	9.67	0.067	4.36	0.686	10.06	22	0.749	5.49	0.151	6.10	0.100	3.11	0.672	4.09
Global Macro	48	0.989	0.44	0.053	2.80	−0.042	−2.04	1.048	−0.86	40	1.012	−0.31	0.041	1.35	−0.053	−2.15	1.140	−1.45
Long/Short Equity	389	0.871	14.08	0.099	15.78	0.030	4.06	0.838	7.68	143	0.905	6.60	0.072	6.83	0.023	2.09	0.887	3.93
Managed Futures	104	1.090	−5.16	0.009	0.74	−0.099	−8.51	1.257	−5.99	126	1.131	−4.58	−0.066	−3.21	−0.065	−3.84	1.479	−4.47
Multi-Strategy	39	0.777	10.45	0.130	7.47	0.093	7.93	0.663	10.31	8	0.944	0.80	0.031	0.47	0.026	1.17	0.960	0.28
Fund of Funds	274	0.856	3.18	0.104	3.87	0.040	1.98	1.610	−0.77	122	0.913	3.76	0.099	7.43	−0.012	−0.81	0.958	0.74
All	1,226	0.865	12.04	0.106	15.34	0.029	5.15	1.011	−0.06	611	0.940	5.47	0.065	9.12	−0.006	−0.85	1.020	−0.61

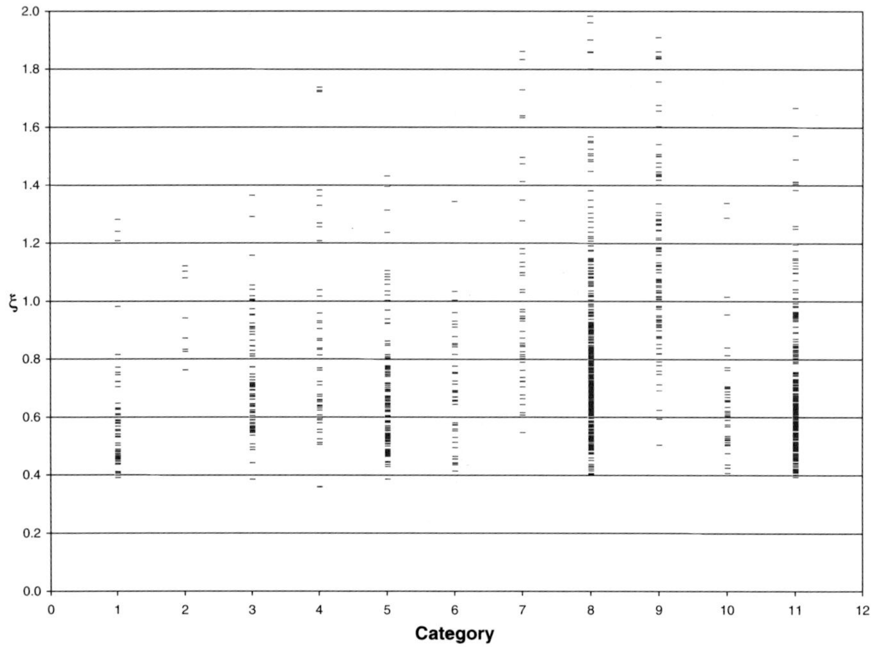

(a) Smoothing index ξ for Live funds

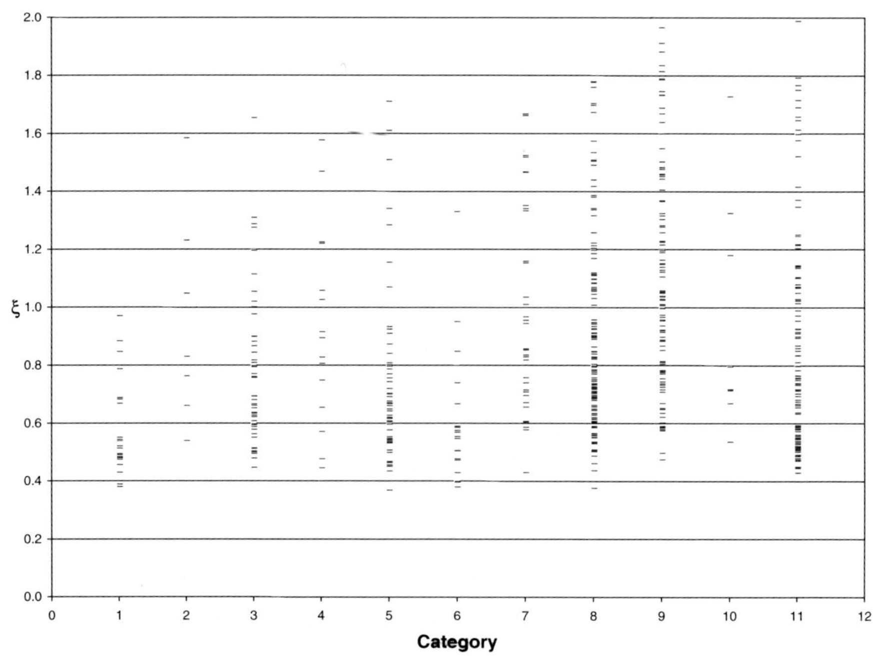

(b) Smoothing index ξ for Graveyard funds

Figure 6 Smoothing index estimates ξ by category for hedge funds in the TASS Live and Graveyard databases with at least five years of returns history during the period from November 1977 to August 2004. Category definitions: 1 = Convertible Arbitrage, 2 = Dedicated Short Bias, 3 = Emerging Markets, 4 = Equity Market-Neutral, 5 = Event Driven, 6 = Fixed-Income Arbitrage, 7 = Global Macro, 8 = Long/Short Equity, 9 = Managed Futures, 10 = Multi-Strategy, 11 = Fund of Funds.

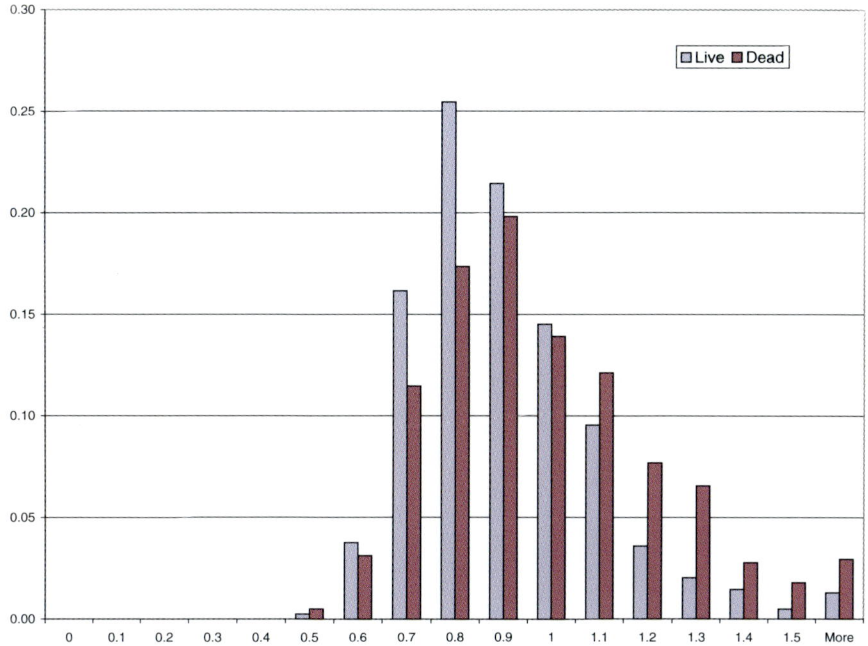

(a) Smoothing parameter θ_0

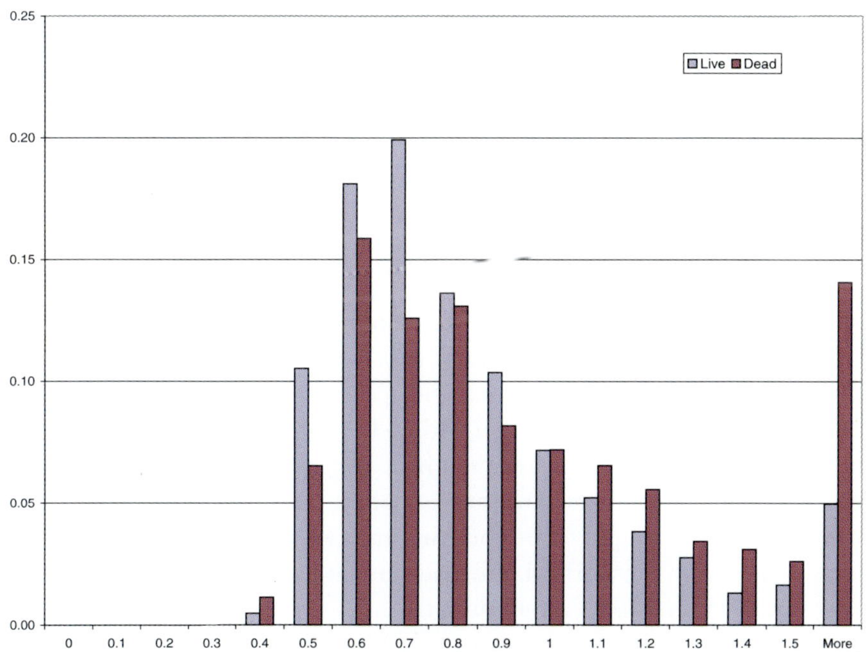

(b) Smoothing index ξ

Figure 7 Histograms of estimated smoothing parameters θ_0 and smoothing indexes ξ for hedge funds in the TASS Live and Graveyard databases with at least five years of returns history during the period from November 1977 to August 2004.

both theoretical and empirical perspectives, significant rewards accrue to investors willing to bear illiquidity risk (see, for example: Ibbotson Associates, 2004; Lo, Mamaysky, and Wang, 2004). Moreover, the willingness of certain investors to bear such risks has created considerable social value in allowing those who cannot afford such risks to shed them at reasonable cost. However, proper disclosure is critical in this case because the nuances of illiquidity risk are more subtle than traditional market risks, and not all investors are fully equipped to evaluate them. Despite considerable progress in the recent literature in modeling both credit and illiquidity risk,[24] the complex network of creditor/obligor relationships, revolving credit agreements, and other financial interconnections is largely unmapped. Perhaps some of the newly developed techniques in the mathematical theory of networks will allow us to construct systemic measures for liquidity and credit exposures and the robustness of the global financial system to idiosyncratic shocks. The "small-world" networks considered by Watts and Strogatz (1998) and Watts (1999) seem to be particularly promising starting points.

6 Conclusions

The TASS Graveyard database reminds us that not too long ago, hedge funds were a cottage industry, with rapid turnover and many small startups—half of all liquidated funds never reach their fourth anniversary, and the median assets under management for funds in the Graveyard is just over $6 million. Performance is a significant driver of liquidations, with Graveyard funds generally exhibiting lower average returns and higher volatilities. Graveyard funds also seem to exhibit less illiquidity exposure as measured by serial correlation and the MA(2) smoothed-returns model of Getmansky, Lo, and Makarov (2004). Certain investment styles such as Managed Futures and Global Macro are prone to higher attrition rates, presumably because of their higher risk levels, and the recent increase in attrition rates for Long/Short Equity funds is a potential source of concern because of the large number of funds in this category and the amount of assets involved. More generally, the apparent inverse relation between performance and attrition rates implies some interesting patterns in the dynamics of the hedge-fund industry, where strategies and hedge-fund style-categories will wax and wane according to strategy returns, with potentially significant implications for market efficiency, as outlined in Farmer and Lo (1999) and Lo (2004). Whether these dynamics are intrinsic to the markets in which hedge funds invest, or created by the repercussions of major fund flows into and out of the industry, is still an open question. But in either case, they imply serious business risks for managers and investors alike.

Despite the wealth of statistical information that the TASS database provides, it is silent on a great many issues surrounding the liquidation of hedge funds. For example, unlike the hand-collected sample of funds in Feffer and Kundro's (2003) study, we do not know the details of each Graveyard fund's liquidation, hence we cannot tell whether macroeconomic events are more important than operational risks in determining a hedge fund's fate. The historical lack of transparency of the hedge-fund industry, coupled with the fact that it is still largely unregulated, suggests that a comprehensive analysis of hedge-fund liquidations is difficult to complete in the near term. The great heterogeneity of the hedge-fund industry, even within a particular style category, makes it all the more challenging to draw specific inferences from existing data sources.

However, there is reason to be cautiously optimistic. The recent influx of assets from institutional investors—who require greater transparency to carry out their fiduciary obligations—is inducing hedge funds to be more forthcoming. Also, the regulatory environment is shifting rapidly. In particular, the US Securities and Exchange Commission (SEC) recently voted to require hedge funds to register as investment advisers under the Investment Advisers Act of 1940 (Rule 203(b)(3)-2). This proposal has generated considerable controversy, with compelling arguments on both sides of the debate and a 3-to-2 split vote among the commissioners. While registration might provide an additional layer of protection for investors, the costs of registration are substantial—both for the SEC and for many smaller hedge funds—which may stifle the growth of this vibrant industry.

Nevertheless, registering hedge funds may not be sufficient, especially if the goal is to protect the general public and promote the long-run health of the financial services industry. Registration requires filing certain information with the SEC on a regular basis and being subject to periodic on-site examinations, but the kind of information required does not necessarily address the main concern that hedge funds pose for the financial system: are hedge funds engaged in activities that can destabilize financial markets and cause widespread dislocation throughout the industry? This concern was first brought to public awareness in August 1998 when the default of Russian government debt triggered a global "flight to quality" that caught many hedge funds by surprise. One of the most significant players in this market, LTCM, lost most of its multi-billion-dollar capital base in a matter of weeks. Ultimately, LTCM was bailed out by a consortium organized by the Federal Reserve Bank of New York because its collapse might have set off a chain reaction of failures of other major financial institutions.

The possibility of a "domino effect" in the hedge-fund industry is one of the most important revelations to have come out of the LTCM debacle.

Prior to August 1998, vulnerabilities in the global financial system involved stock market crashes, bank runs, and hyperinflation—otherwise known as "systemic risk"—were largely the province of central bankers and finance ministers. Such events were rare but generally well understood, as in the case of the Asian Crisis of 1997 in which over-leveraged financial institutions and weak corporate governance led to a series of currency devaluations, stock market crashes, and defaults in Korea, Thailand, Indonesia, and other Asian countries. However, with the collapse of LTCM, a new source of systemic risk was born: the hedge fund. Given how little is known about these unregulated entities, a natural reaction to August 1998 is to regulate them. However, the specific information about LTCM's activities that might have helped regulators and investors to avoid the stunning losses of 1998—the fund's leverage, the number of credit lines available to the fund, the vulnerability of those credit lines during extreme market conditions, and the degree to which other funds had similar positions—is currently not required of registered investment advisers.

Apart from the costs and benefits of requiring hedge funds to register, it is clear that a different approach is needed to address the larger issue of systemic risk posed by hedge funds. We propose two specific innovations: a database of more detailed information about hedge funds and associated financial institutions to be collected and maintained by the SEC, and a separate unit within the SEC charged with the responsibility of conducting forensic examinations and providing publicly available summary reports in the wake of unintentional hedge-fund liquidations.

Without data, it is virtually impossible for regulators to engage in any meaningful over-sight of the hedge-fund industry. An example of the importance of data for regulatory oversight is event analysis—one of the most powerful tools for detecting insider trading—in which the statistical properties of stock-price movements are compared before, during, and after the release of material information regarding the stock. Unusual price movements prior to the release of material information sometimes signals an information leak, which can then be verified or refuted by a more detailed investigation. Without historical price data, the SEC's Division of Enforcement would lose its ability to monitor thousands of publicly traded securities simultaneously and in a timely fashion, making it virtually impossible for the SEC to enforce insider-trading laws broadly given the current size of its staff.

Regulators should have access to the following information from all hedge funds: monthly returns, leverage, assets under management, fees, instruments traded, and all brokerage, financing, and credit relationships. In addition, regulators should collect similar information from prime brokers, banks, and other hedge-fund counterparties, as well as information about the capital adequacy of these financial institutions, as they are likely to be among the first casualties in any systemic event involving hedge funds. This information should be archived so that over time, a complete historical database is developed and the dynamics of each entity and the industry can be tracked and measured.

There is, of course, a privacy issue regarding such highly confidential data that must be properly addressed. Unlike publicly traded companies such as mutual funds, which are required to disclose a great deal of information because they are selling their securities to the general public, hedge funds are private partnerships that can solicit only a limited clientele: investors who are deemed to be sophisticated and able to tolerate significant financial risks. As a result, managers willing to provide greater disclosure may choose a public offering such as a mutual fund, and those preferring opacity may choose instead to form a hedge fund. This menu of choices has great social benefits in providing a wider range of alternatives to suit different preferences and markets, and should not be limited. However, it is possible to collect and analyze hedge-fund data while protecting the confidentiality of all parties concerned, as illustrated by the relationship between US banks and the Office of the Comptroller of the Currency.

In addition to serving as a repository for hedge-fund data, the SEC can play an even more valuable role in reducing systemic risk by investigating and producing public reports of hedge-fund liquidations. Although there may be common themes in the demise of many hedge funds—too much leverage, too concentrated a portfolio, operational failures, securities fraud, or insufficient assets under management—each liquidation has its own unique circumstances and is an opportunity for the hedge-fund industry to learn and improve. We need look no further than the National Transportation Safety Board (NTSB) for an excellent and practical role model of an investigative unit specifically designed to provide greater transparency and improve public safety.

In the event of an airplane crash, the NTSB assembles a team of engineers and flight-safety experts who are immediately dispatched to the crash site to conduct a thorough investigation, including interviewing witnesses, poring over historical flight logs and maintenance records, and sifting through the wreckage to recover the flight recorder or "black box" and, if necessary, reassembling the aircraft from its parts so as to determine the ultimate cause of the crash. Once its work is completed, the NTSB publishes a report summarizing the team's investigation, concluding with specific recommendations for avoiding future occurrences of this type of accident. The report is entered into a searchable database that is available to the general public (see http://www.ntsb.gov/ntsb/query.asp) and this has been one of the major factors underlying the remarkable safety record of commercial air travel.

For example, it is now current practice to spray airplanes with de-icing fluid just prior to take-off when the temperature is near freezing and it is raining or snowing. This procedure was instituted in the aftermath of USAir Flight 405's crash on March 22, 1992. Flight 405 stalled just after becoming airborne because of ice on its wings, despite the fact that de-icing fluid was applied before it left its gate. Apparently, Flight 405's take-off was delayed because of air traffic, and ice re-accumulated on its wings while it waited for a departure slot on the runway in the freezing rain. The NTSB Aircraft Accident Report AAR-93/02—published on February 17, 1993 and available through several internet sites—contains a sobering summary of the NTSB's findings (Report AAR-93/02, page *vi*):

> The National Transportation Safety Board determines that the probable cause of this accident were the failure of the airline industry and the Federal Aviation Administration to provide flightcrews with procedures, requirements, and criteria compatible with departure delays in conditions conducive to airframe icing and the decision by the flightcrew to take off without positive assurance that the airplane's wings were free of ice accumulation after 35 minutes of exposure to precipitation following de-icing. The ice contamination on the wings resulted in an aerodynamic stall and loss of control after liftoff. Contributing to the cause of the accident were the inappropriate procedures used by, and inadequate coordination between, the flightcrew that led to a takeoff rotation at a lower than prescribed air speed.
>
> The safety issues in this report focused on the weather affecting the flight, USAir's de-icing procedures, industry airframe de-icing practices, air traffic control aspects affecting the flight, USAir's takeoff and preflight procedures, and flightcrew qualifications and training. The dynamics of the airplane's impact with the ground, postaccident survivability, and crash/fire/rescue activities were also analyzed.

Current de-icing procedures have no doubt saved many lives thanks to NTSB Report AAR-93/02, but this particular innovation was paid for by the lives of the 27 individuals who did not survive the crash of Flight 405. Imagine the waste if the NTSB did not investigate this tragedy and produce concrete recommendations to prevent this from happening again.

Hedge-fund liquidations are, of course, considerably less dire, generally involving no loss of life. However, as more pension funds make allocations to hedge funds, and as the "retailization" of hedge funds continues, losses in the hedge-fund industry may have more signifficant implications for individual investors, in some cases threatening retirement wealth and basic living standards. Moreover, the spillover effects of an industry-wide shock to hedge funds should not be under-estimated, as the events surrounding LTCM in the Fall of 1998 illustrated. For these reasons, an SEC-sponsored organization dedicated to investigating, reporting, and archiving the "accidents" of the hedge-fund industry—and the financial services sector, more generally—may yield significant social benefits in much the same way that the NTSB has improved transportation safety enormously for all air travellers. By maintaining teams of experienced professionals—forensic accountants, financial engineers from industry and academia, and securities and tax attorneys—that work together on a regular basis to investigate a number of hedge-fund liquidations, the SEC would be able to determine quickly and accurately how each liquidation came about, and the resulting reports would be an invaluable source of ideas for improving financial markets and avoiding future liquidations of a similar nature.[25]

The establishment of an NTSB-like organization within the SEC will not be inexpensive. Currently, the SEC is understaffed and overburdened, and this is likely to worsen now that all hedge funds are required to register under the Investment Advisers Act of 1940. In addition, the lure of the private sector makes it challenging for government agencies to attract and retain individuals with expertise in these highly employable fields. Individuals trained in forensic accounting, financial engineering, and securities law now command substantial premiums on Wall Street over government pay scales. Although the typical SEC employee is likely to be motivated more by civic duty than financial gain, it would be unrealistic to build an organization on altruism alone.

The cost of an SEC-based "Capital Markets Safety Board" is more than justified by the valuable lessons that would be garnered from a systematic analysis of financial incidents and the public dissemination of recommendations by seasoned professionals that review multiple cases each year. The benefits would accrue not only to the wealthy—which is currently how the hedge-fund industry is tilted—but would also flow to retail investors in the form of more stable financial markets, greater liquidity, reduced borrowing and lending costs as a result of decreased systemic risk exposures, and a wider variety of investment choices available to a larger segment of the population because of increased transparency, oversight, and, ultimately, financial security. It is unrealistic to expect that market crashes, panics, collapses, and fraud will ever be completely eliminated from our capital markets, but we should avoid compounding our mistakes by failing to learn from them.

Acknowledgments

Research support from AlphaSimplex Group and the MIT Laboratory for Financial Engineering is gratefully acknowledged. We thank Gifford Fong and Svetlana Sussman for helpful comments and Sunil Aggarwal, Neil Desai, and Maria Simona Jelescu for research assistance.

Appendix

The following is a list of category descriptions, taken directly from TASS documentation, that define the criteria used by TASS in assigning funds in their database to one of 11 possible categories:

Convertible Arbitrage This strategy is identified by hedge investing in the convertible securities of a company. A typical investment is to be long the convertible bond and short the common stock of the same company. Positions are designed to generate profits from the fixed income security as well as the short sale of stock, while protecting principal from market moves.

Dedicated Shortseller Dedicated shortsellers were once a robust category of hedge funds before the long bull market rendered the strategy difficult to implement. A new category, short biased, has emerged. The strategy is to maintain net short as opposed to pure short exposure. Short biased managers take short positions in mostly equities and derivatives. The short bias of a manager's portfolio must be constantly greater than zero to be classified in this category.

Emerging Markets This strategy involves equity or fixed income investing in emerging markets around the world. Because many emerging markets do not allow shortselling, nor offer viable futures or other derivative products with which to hedge, emerging market investing often employs a long-only strategy.

Equity Market Neutral This investment strategy is designed to exploit equity market inefficiencies and usually involves being simultaneously long and short matched equity portfolios of the same size within a country. Market neutral portfolios are designed to be either beta or currency neutral, or both. Well-designed portfolios typically control for industry, sector, market capitalization, and other exposures. Leverage is often applied to enhance returns.

Event Driven This strategy is defined as "special situations" investing designed to capture price movement generated by a significant pending corporate event such as a merger, corporate restructuring, liquidation, bankruptcy or reorganization. There are three popular sub-categories in event-driven strategies: risk (merger) arbitrage, distressed/high yield securities, and Regulation D.

Fixed Income Arbitrage The fixed income arbitrageur aims to profit from price anomalies between related interest rate securities. Most managers trade globally with a goal of generating steady returns with low volatility. This category includes interest rate swap arbitrage, US and non-US government bond arbitrage, forward yield curve arbitrage, and mortgage-backed securities arbitrage. The mortgage-backed market is primarily US-based, over-the-counter and particularly complex.

Global Macro Global macro managers carry long and short positions in any of the world's major capital or derivative markets. These positions reflect their views on overall market direction as influenced by major economic trends and/or events. The portfolios of these funds can include stocks, bonds, currencies, and commodities in the form of cash or derivatives instruments. Most funds invest globally in both developed and emerging markets.

Long/Short Equity This directional strategy involves equity-oriented investing on both the long and short sides of the market. The objective is not to be market neutral. Managers have the ability to shift from value to growth, from small to medium to large capitalization stocks, and from a net long position to a net short position. Managers may use futures and options to hedge. The focus may be regional, such as long/short US or European equity, or sector specific, such as long and short technology or healthcare stocks. Long/short equity funds tend to build and hold portfolios that are substantially more concentrated than those of traditional stock funds.

Managed Futures This strategy invests in listed financial and commodity futures markets and currency markets around the world. The managers are usually referred to as Commodity Trading Advisors, or CTAs. Trading disciplines are generally systematic or discretionary. Systematic traders tend to use price and market specific information (often technical) to make trading decisions, while discretionary managers use a judgmental approach.

Multi-Strategy The funds in this category are characterized by their ability to dynamically allocate capital among strategies falling within several traditional hedge fund disciplines. The use of many strategies, and the ability to reallocate capital between them in response to market opportunities, means that such funds are not easily assigned to any traditional category.

The Multi-Strategy category also includes funds employing unique strategies that do not fall under any of the other descriptions.

Fund of Funds A "Multi Manager" fund will employ the services of two or more trading advisors or Hedge Funds who will be allocated cash by the Trading Manager to trade on behalf of the fund.

Notes

1 See Armitstead (2004).

2 See Atkins and Hays (2004).

3 Using merged data from three vendors—TASS, HFR, and ZCM/MAR—from 1994 to 2000, Agarwal, Daniel, and Naik (2004, Figure 1) show that only 10% of their sample of 1776 live and 1655 inactive funds are common to all three databases.

4 These databases typically refer requests for prospectuses to the funds themselves so that each fund is responsible for discharging its legal responsibility to determine whether or not an individual requesting fund documents is indeed a "qualified investor."

5 Each fund is assigned a numerical code, and only qualified investors are given the mapping from codes to fund names.

6 These studies use different databases, which may explain the variation in their estimates. However, Liang (2000) and Agarwal, Daniel, and Naik (2004) show that several of these databases do have some funds in common (see note 3).

7 The lack of transparency and the unregulated status of most hedge funds are significant barriers to any systematic data collection effort, hence it is difficult to draw inferences about industry norms.

8 For further information about these data, see http://www.tremont.com.

9 TASS has adopted a policy of transferring funds from the Live to the Graveyard database if they do not report returns for an 8- to 10-month period.

10 For studies attempting to quantify the degree and impact of survivorship bias, see Baquero, Horst, and Verbeek (2002), Brown *et al.* (1992) and Brown, Goetzmann, and Park (1999, 2001a,b), Carpenter and Lynch (1999), Fung and Hsieh (1997b, 2000), Horst, Nijman, and Verbeek (2001), Hendricks, Patel, and Zeckhauser (1997), and Schneeweis and Spurgin (1996).

11 TASS defines returns as the change in net asset value during the month (assuming the reinvestment of any distributions on the reinvestment date used by the fund) divided by the net asset value at the beginning of the month, net of management fees, incentive fees, and other fund expenses. Therefore, these reported returns should approximate the returns realized by investors. TASS also converts all foreign-currency denominated returns to US-dollar returns using the appropriate exchange rates.

12 See the references in note 10.

13 Of the 1,765 funds in the Graveyard database, four funds did not have status codes assigned; hence we coded them as 9's ("Unknown"). They are 3,882 (Fund of Funds), 34053 (Managed Futures), 34053 (Managed Futures), 34054 (Managed Futures), 34904 (Long/Short Equity).

14 The kth order autocorrelation or "serial correlation" coefficient ρ_k is defined as $\rho_k \equiv \text{Cov}[R_t, R_{t-k}]/Var[R_t]$, which is simply the correlation coefficient between month t's return and month $t-k$'s return.

15 Recall that TASS launched their Graveyard database in 1994, hence this is the beginning of our sample for Table 5.

16 We do not include 2004 in this average because TASS typically waits 8 to 10 months before moving a non-reporting fund from the Live to the Graveyard database. Therefore, the attrition rate is severely downward biased for 2004 since the year is not yet complete, and many non-reporting funds in the Live database have not yet been classified as Graveyard funds. Also, note that there is only one new fund in 2004—this figure is grossly downward-biased as well. Hedge funds often go through an "incubation period" where managers trade with limited resources to develop a track record. If successful, the manager will provide the return stream to a database vendor like TASS, and the vendor usually enters the entire track record into the database, providing the fund with an "instant history." According to Fung and Hsieh (2000), the average incubation period—from a fund's inception to its entry into the TASS database—is one year.

17 See Boudoukh *et al.* (2002) for a more detailed discussion of the mutual-fund timing issue.

18 Asness, Krail, and Liew (2001) were perhaps the first to document the fact that certain "market neutral" hedge funds had significant beta exposure but with respect to lagged market returns. Getmansky, Lo, and Makarov (2004) show that this phenomenon is consistent with illiquidity exposure and smoothed returns.

[19] Although illiquidity and smoothed returns are two distinct phenomena, one facilitates the other—for highly liquid securities, both theory and empirical evidence suggest their returns are unlikely to be very smooth. Indeed, as a practical matter, if the assets in the manager's portfolio are actively traded, the manager has little discretion in marking the portfolio. The more illiquid the portfolio, the more latitude the manager has in determining its value, e.g., discretionary accruals for unregistered private placements and venture capital investments. In fact, Chandar and Bricker (2002) conclude that managers of certain closed-end mutual funds use accounting discretion to manage fund returns around a passive benchmark.

[20] In fact, if a fund allows investors to invest and withdraw capital only at pre-specified intervals, imposing lock-ups in between, and external audits are conducted at these same pre-specified intervals, then it may be argued that performance smoothing is irrelevant. For example, no investor should be disadvantaged by investing in a fund that offers annual liquidity and engages in annual external audits with which the fund's net-asset-value is determined by a disinterested third party for purposes of redemptions and new investments. However, there are at least two additional concerns that remain—historical track records and estimates of a fund's liquidity exposure are both affected by smoothed returns—and they are important factors in the typical hedge-fund investor's overall investment process. Moreover, given the questions surrounding the role that the auditors at Arthur Andersen played in the Enron affair, there is the further concern of whether third-party auditors are truly objective and free of all conflicts of interest.

[21] The reference numbers for the funds that did not yield maximum-likelihood estimates are 1018, 1405, and 4201.

[22] Specifically, if $\bar{\xi}$ is the average smoothing index for all funds in a given category, then $z \equiv (1-\bar{\xi})/\text{se}(\bar{\xi})$ where $\text{se}(\bar{\xi})$ is the standard error of $\bar{\xi}$, given by the cross-sectional standard deviation of all the individual estimates of ξ divided by the square root of the number of funds in the sample. This assumes that the individual estimates of ξ are independently and identically distributed, which may not be a good approximation for funds within a given category. In these cases, robust standard errors can be computed. Nevertheless, the relative rankings of the z-statistics across categories may still contain useful information.

[23] Futures contracts are, by definition, more liquid than the underlying spot, and the ability to shortsell a security implicitly requires a certain degree of liquidity.

[24] See, for example, Bookstaber (1999, 2000) and Kao (2000), and their citations.

[25] Formal government investigations of major financial events do occur from time to time, as in the April 1999 *Report of the President's Working Group in Financial Markets on Hedge Funds, Leverage, and the Lessons of Long-Term Capital Management*. However, this inter-agency report was put together on an *ad hoc* basis with committee members that had not worked together previously and regularly on forensic investigations of this kind. With multiple agencies involved, and none in charge of the investigation, the administrative overhead becomes more significant. Although any thorough investigation of the financial services sector is likely to involve the SEC, the CFTC, the US Treasury, and the Federal Reserve—and inter-agency cooperation should be promoted—there are important operational advantages in tasking a single office with the responsibility for coordinating all such investigations and serving as a repository for the expertise in conducting forensic examinations of financial incidents.

References

Ackermann, C., McEnally, R., and Ravenscraft, D. (1999). "The Performance of Hedge Funds: Risk, Return, and Incentives." *Journal of Finance* **54**, 833–874.

Agarwal, V. and Naik, N. (2000a). "Performance Evaluation of Hedge Funds with Buy-and-Hold and Option-Based Strategies." Hedge Fund Centre Working Paper No. HF–003, London Business School.

Agarwal, V. and Naik, N. (2000b). "On Taking the 'Alternative' Route: The Risks, Rewards, and Performance Persistence of Hedge Funds." *Journal of Alternative Investments* **2**, 6–23.

Agarwal, V. and Naik, N. (2000c). "Multi-Period Performance Persistence Analysis of Hedge Funds Source." *Journal of Financial and Quantitative Analysis* **35**, 327–342.

Agarwal, V. and Naik, N. (2000d). "Generalized Style Analysis of Hedge Funds." *Journal of Asset Management* **1**, 93–109.

Agarwal, V. and Naik, N. (2004). "Risks and Portfolio Decisions Involving Hedge Funds." *Review of Financial Studies* **17**, 63–98.

Agarwal, V., Daniel, N., and Naik, N. (2004). "Flows, Performance, and Managerial Incentives in the Hedge Fund Industry." Working Paper, Georgia State University.

Amin, G. and Kat, H. (2003a). "Hedge Fund Performance 1990–2000: Do the Money Machines Really Add Value?" *Journal of Financial and Quantitative Analysis* **38**, 251–274.

Amin, G. and Kat, H. (2003b). "Welcome to the Dark Side: Hedge Fund Attrition and Survivorship Bias over the Period 1994–2001." *Journal of Alternative Investments* **6**, 57–73.

Amin, G. and Kat, H. (2003c). "Stocks, Bonds, and Hedge Funds." *Journal of Portfolio Management* **29**, 113–119.

Armitstead, L. (2004). "Dalman Stakes His Own Cash on Hedge Fund." *UK Sunday Times*, Business Section, October 10.

Asness, C., Krail, R., and Liew, J. (2001). "Do Hedge Funds Hedge?" *The Journal of Portfolio Management* **28**, 6–19.

Atkins, T. and Hays, S. (2004). "Worries Rise About Indebted Funds of Hedge Funds." *Reuters*, October 15.

Bares, P., Gibson, R., and Gyger, S. (2003). "Style Consistency and Survival Probability in the Hedge Funds Industry." Working Paper, University of Zurich.

Baquero, G., Horst, J., and Verbeek, M. (2002). "Survival, Look-Ahead Bias and the Performance of Hedge Funds." Working Paper, Erasmus University, Rotterdam.

Bookstaber, R (1999). "A Framework for Understanding Market Crisis." In: *Risk Management: Principles and Practices*. Charlottesville, VA: Association for Investment Management and Research.

Bookstaber, R. (2000). "Understanding and Monitoring the Liquidity Crisis Cycle." *Financial Analysts Journal*, 17–22.

Boudoukh, J., Richardson, M., Subrahmanyam, M., and Whitelaw, R. (2002). "Stale Prices and Strategies for Trading Mutual Funds." *Financial Analysts Journal* **58**, 53–71.

Boyson, N. (2002). "How Are Hedge Fund Manager Characteristics Related to Performance, Volatility and Survival." Working Paper, Ohio State University.

Brooks, C. and Kat, H. (2002). "The Statistical Properties of Hedge Fund Index Returns and Their Implications for Investors." *Journal of Alternative Investments* **5**(2), 25–44.

Brown, S. and Goetzmann, W. (2003). "Hedge Funds With Style." *Journal of Portfolio Management* **29**, 101–112.

Brown, S., Goetzmann, W., Ibbotson, R., and Ross, S. (1992). "Survivorship Bias in Performance Studies." *Review of Financial Studies* **5**, 553–580.

Brown, S., Goetzmann, W., and Ibbotson, R. (1999). "Offshore Hedge Funds: Survival and Performance 1989–1995." *Journal of Business* **72**, 91–118.

Brown, S., Goetzmann, W., and Liang, B. (2002). "Fees on Fees in Funds of Funds." Yale ICF Work Paper No. 02–33.

Brown, S., Goetzmann, W., and Park, J. (2000). "Hedge Funds and the Asian Currency Crisis." *Journal of Portfolio Management* **26**, 95–101.

Brown, S., Goetzmann, W., and Park, J. (2001a). "Conditions for Survival: Changing Risk and the Performance of Hedge Fund Managers and CTAs." Yale School of Management Working Paper No. F–59.

Brown, S., Goetzmann, W., and Park, J. (2001b). "Careers and Survival: Competition and Risks in the Hedge Fund and CTA Industry." *Journal of Finance* **56**, 1869–1886.

Carpenter, J. and Lynch, A. (1999). "Survivorship Bias and Attrition Effects in Measures of Performance Persistence." *Journal of Financial Economics* **54**, 337–374.

Chan, N., Getmansky, M., Haas, S., and Lo, A. (2004). "Systemic Risk and Hedge Funds." In: M. Carey and R. Stulz (eds.), *The Risks of Financial Institutions and the Financial Sector*. Chicago, IL: University of Chicago Press (in press).

Chandar, N. and Bricker, R. (2002). "Incentives, Discretion, and Asset Valuation in Closed-End Mutual Funds." *Journal of Accounting Research* **40**, 1037–1070.

Edwards, F. and Caglayan, M. (2001). "Hedge Fund and Commodity Fund Investments in Bull and Bear Markets." *The Journal of Portfolio Management* **27**, 97–108.

Farmer, D. (2002). "Market Force, Ecology and Evolution." *Industrial and Corporate Change* **11**, 895–953.

Farmer, D. and Lo, A. (1999). "Frontiers of Finance: Evolution and Efficient Markets." *Proceedings of the National Academy of Sciences* **96**, 9991–9992.

Feffer, S. and Kundro, C. (2003). "Understanding and Mitigating Operational Risk in Hedge Fund Investments." Working Paper, The Capital Markets Company Ltd.

Fung, W. and Hsieh, D. (1997a). "Empirical Characteristics of Dynamic Trading Strategies: The Case of Hedge Funds." *Review of Financial Studies* **10**, 275–302.

Fung, W. and Hsieh, D. (1997b). "Investment Style and Survivorship Bias in the Returns of CTAs: The Information Content of Track Records." *Journal of Portfolio Management* **24**, 30–41.

Fung, W. and Hsieh, D. (1999). "A Primer on Hedge Funds." *Journal of Empirical Finance* **6**, 309–31.

Fung, W. and Hsieh, D. (2000). "Performance Characteristics of Hedge Funds and Commodity Funds: Natural versus Spurious Biases." *Journal of Financial and Quantitative Analysis* **35**, 291–307.

Fung, W. and Hsieh, D. (2001). "The Risk in Hedge Fund Strategies: Theory and Evidence from Trend Followers." *Review of Financial Studies* **14**, 313–341.

Fung, W. and Hsieh, D. (2002a). "Asset-Based Style Factors for Hedge Funds." *Financial Analysts Journal* **58**, 16–27.

Fung, W. and Hsieh, D. (2002b). "Benchmarks of Hedge Fund Performance: Information Content and Measurement Biases." *Journal of Alternative Investments* **58**, 22–34.

Getmansky, M. (2004). "The Life Cycle of Hedge Funds: Fund Flows, Size and Performance." Unpublished Working Paper, MIT Laboratory for Financial Engineering.

Getmansky, M. and Lo, A. (2003). "A System Dynamics Model of the Hedge Fund Industry." Unpublished Working Paper, MIT Laboratory for Financial Engineering.

Getmansky, M., Lo, A., and Makarov, I. (2004). "An Econometric Analysis of Serial Correlation and Illiquidity in Hedge-Fund Returns." *Journal of Financial Economics* (in press).

Goetzmann, W., Ingersoll, J., and Ross, S. (2003). "High Water Marks and Hedge Fund Management Contracts." *Journal of Finance* **58**, 1685–1718.

Gregoriou, G. (2002). "Hedge Fund Survival Lifetimes." *Journal of Asset Management* **3**, 237–252.

Greenspan, A. (1998). "Statement before the Committee on Banking and Financial Services, U.S. House of Representatives." *Federal Reserve Bulletin* **84**, 1046–1050.

Hendricks, D., Patel, J., and Zeckhauser, R. (1997). "The J-Shape of Performance Persistence Given Survivorship Bias." *Review of Economics and Statistics* **79**, 161–170.

Horst, J., Nijman, T., and Verbeek, M. (2001). "Eliminating Look-Ahead Bias in Evaluating Persistence in Mutual Fund Performance." *Journal of Empirical Finance* **8**, 345–373.

Howell, M.J. (2001). "Fund Age and Performance." *Journal of Alternative Investments* 4(2), 57–60.
Ibbotson Associates (2004). *Stocks, Bonds, Bills, and Inflation 2004 Yearbook.* Chicago, IL: Ibbotson Associates.
Ineichen, A. (2001). "The Myth of Hedge Funds: Are Hedge Funds The Fireflies Ahead of the Storm?" *Journal of Global Financial Markets* 2(4), 34–46.
Jen, P., Heasman, C., and Boyatt, K. (2001). "Alternative Asset Strategies: Early Performance in Hedge Fund Managers." Internal Document, Lazard Asset Management, London (http://www.aima.org).
Kao, D. (2000). "Estimating and Pricing Credit Risk: An Overview." *Financial Analysts Journal* **56**, 50–66.
Kao, D. (2002). "Battle for Alphas: Hedge Funds versus Long-Only Portfolios." *Financial Analysts Journal* **58**, 16–36.
Kramer, D. (2001). "Hedge Fund Disasters: Avoiding the Next Catastrophe." *Alternative Investment Quarterly* 1.
Liang, B. (1999). "On the Performance of Hedge Funds." *Financial Analysts Journal* **55**, 72–85.
Liang, B. (2000). "Hedge Funds: The Living and the Dead." *Journal of Financial and Quantitative Analysis* **35**, 309–326.
Liang, B. (2001). "Hedge Fund Performance: 1990–1999." *Financial Analysts Journal* **57**, 11–18.
Liang, B. (2003). "The Accuracy of Hedge Fund Returns." *Journal of Portfolio Management* **29**, 111–122.
Lo, A. (1999). "The Three P's of Total Risk Management." *Financial Analysts Journal* **55**, 87–129.
Lo, A. (2001). "Risk Management for Hedge Funds: Introduction and Overview." *Financial Analysts Journal* **57**, 16–33.
Lo, A. (2002). "The Statistics of Sharpe Ratios." *Financial Analysts Journal* **58**, 36–50.
Lo, A. (2004). "The Adaptive Markets Hypothesis: Market Efficiency from an Evolutionary Perspective." *Journal of Portfolio Management* **30**, 15–29.
Lo, A., Mamaysky, H., and Wang, J. (2004). "Asset Prices and Trading Volume Under Fixed Transactions Costs." *Journal of Political Economy* **112**, 1054–1090.
Lochoff, R. (2002). "Hedge Funds and Hope." *The Journal of Portfolio Management* **28**, 92–99.
MacKenzie, D. (2003). "Long-Term Capital Management and the Sociology of Arbitrage." *Economy and Society* **32**, 349–380.
McDonough, W. (1998). "Statement before the Committe on Banking and Financial Services, U.S. House of Representatives." *Federal Reserve Bulletin* **84**, 1050–1054.
Metzger, L. and The IAFE Investor Risk Committee (2004). "Valuation Concepts for Investment Companies and Financial Institutions and Their Stakeholders." Investor Risk Committee White Paper, International Association of Financial Engineers.
Pérold, A. (1999). *Long-Term Capital Management, L.P. (A-D) Harvard Case Study.* Boston, MA: Harvard Business School Press.
President's Working Group on Financial Markets (1999). *Hedge Funds, Leverage, and the Lessons of Long-Term Capital Management.*
Schneeweis, T. and Spurgin, R. (1996). "Survivor Bias in Commodity Trading Advisor Performance." *Journal of Futures Markets* **16**, 757–772.
Watts, D. and Strogatz, S. (1998). "Collective Dynamics of 'Small-World' Networks." *Nature* **393**, 440–442.
Watts, D. (1999). *Small Worlds: The Dynamics of Networks between Order and Randomness.* Princeton, NJ: Princeton University Press.

Keywords: Hedge funds; risk management; liquidity

Journal of Investment Management
Vol. 2, No. 4 (2004), pp. 94–105

THE DANGERS OF MECHANICAL INVESTMENT DECISION-MAKING: THE CASE OF HEDGE FUNDS

*Harry M. Kat**

Over the last 20 years, investors have come to approach investment decision-making in an increasingly mechanical manner. Optimizers are filled up with historical return data and the "optimal" portfolio follows almost automatically. In this paper, we argue that such an approach can be extremely dangerous, especially when alternative investments such as hedge funds are involved. Proper hedge fund investing requires a much more elaborate approach to investment decision-making than currently in use by most investors. The available data on hedge funds should not be taken at face value, but should first be corrected for various types of biases and autocorrelation. Tools like mean–variance analysis and the Sharpe ratio that many investors have become accustomed to over the years are no longer appropriate when hedge funds are involved as they concentrate on the good part while completely skipping over the bad part of the hedge fund story. Investors also have to find a way to figure in the long lock-up and advance notice periods, which makes hedge fund investments highly illiquid. In addition, investors will have to give weight to the fact that without more insight in the way in which hedge funds generate their returns it is very hard to say something sensible about hedge funds' future longer-run performance. The tools to accomplish this formally are not all there yet, meaning that more than ever investors will have to rely on common sense and doing their homework.

1 Introduction

Hedge funds are on their way to becoming the next big thing in investment management. New funds start up every day, hedge funds are marketed aggressively to institutions, and, under pressure to make up for recent losses, many institutional investors are showing serious interest. The amount of assets under management by hedge funds has grown from around $40 billion in 1990 to an estimated $800 billion in 2004. In line with this, the number of hedge funds worldwide has grown to around 6000. In the early days not much was known about hedge funds. Since 1994, however, a number of data vendors, hedge fund advisors, and fund of hedge funds operators have been collecting performance and other data on hedge funds. This has allowed researchers to take a more serious look at hedge funds. Although research in

*Professor of Risk Management and Director Alternative Investment Research Centre, Cass Business School, City University, 106 Bunhill Row, London, EC2Y 8TZ, United Kingdom. Tel.: +44 –20-70408677; e-mail: harry@harrykat.com

this area is still in its infancy, it has become clear that hedge funds are a lot more complicated than common stocks and investment-grade bonds and may not be as phenomenally attractive as many hedge fund managers and marketers want investors to believe. Hedge fund investing requires a much more elaborate approach to investment decision-making than what most investors are used to. Mechanically applying the same decision-making processes as typically used for stock and bond investments may lead to some very nasty surprises.

2 Modern Portfolio Theory in Action

Before the arrival of finance theory as we known it today, finance was a very practical discipline. Finance students would spend their time studying accounting, taxation, law, and the writings of Benjamin Graham and others. With the arrival of Harry Markowitz's mean–variance analysis, Bill Sharpe's CAPM, and Gene Fama's efficient market hypothesis things changed, however. From a practical discipline, finance very quickly reinvented itself as a branch of neoclassical price theory, concentrating on the analysis of abstract little "toy worlds" where most of what makes life complicated is simply assumed away in an attempt to come to the essence of things. At the same time, computers and databases started to evolve up to a point where nowadays every investor has access to extensive computing power and market data. All this has had a profound impact on the way investment decisions are being taken. Mean–variance optimizers play an important part in modern investment management and essentially take over a substantial portion of the responsibility for the asset allocation decision. Likewise, performance evaluation relies heavily on theoretical concepts such as the Sharpe ratio and Jensen's alpha. All these tools have become so common that many investors tend to apply them in a purely mechanical fashion, giving little or no thought to their underlying assumptions. The same is true for the required inputs. Often, means and especially variances and correlation coefficients are simply calculated from downloaded historical return data with little or no consideration for the sometimes very specific factors that generated the data in question.

The way in which the basic concepts of modern finance are used in practice leaves a lot to be desired. Despite this, their application in the stock and bond markets does not appear to be without some merit. There are a number of reasons for this. First, return data on stocks and bonds often cover a long time period and tend to be of good quality. Second, stock and bond returns tend to exhibit statistical characteristics that are very much in line with what is assumed in theory. Third, stock and bond markets typically tend to offer relatively good liquidity. When we move away from stocks and bonds and into the realm of alternative investments then the situation changes dramatically. Serious data problems, complex return generating processes, non-normal return distributions, low transparancy, and substantial illiquidity all have to be taken into account properly. If not, investors risk self-deception. They will see miracles where there are none and vice versa. In the sections that follow we will discuss these matters in greater detail focusing on hedge funds and the typical way in which "sophisticated" investors look at them.

3 Hedge Fund Data

With the hedge fund industry still in its infancy and hedge funds under no formal obligation to disclose their results, gaining insight into the performance characteristics of hedge funds is not straightforward. Fortunately, many funds nowadays release performance as well as other administrative data to attract new investors and to accommodate existing investors. These data are collected by a number of data vendors and fund advisors, some of whom make their data available to qualifying investors and researchers. The available data on hedge funds are not without problems though. Some of the problems are given below.

3.1 An unknown universe

Most hedge funds only report into one or two databases. As a result, every database covers a different subset of the hedge fund universe and different researchers may arrive at quite different conclusions simply because different databases were used.

3.2 No independent auditing

Most databases are of relatively low quality as most data vendors simply pass on the data supplied by the fund managers and their administrators without any independent verification. This means that before any serious research can take place, one must check the data for a number of possible errors and either correct these or delete the funds in question altogether.

3.3 Backfill bias

Hedge fund databases tend to be backfilled, that is, although typically funds only start reporting to a database some time after their actual start-up, when they do, their full track record is included in the database. Since only funds with good track records will eventually decide to report, this means that the available data sets are overly optimistic about hedge fund performance. As shown in Posthuma and Van der Sluis (2003), on average actual hedge fund returns may be 4% per annum lower than reported.

3.4 Survivorship bias

Most data vendors only supply data on funds that are still in operation. However, disappointing performance is a major reason for hedge funds to close down. As shown in Amin and Kat (2003), this means that the data available to investors will overestimate the returns that investors can realistically expect from investing in hedge funds by 2–4% per annum. In addition, concentrating on survivors only will lead investors to underestimate the risk of hedge funds by 10–20%.

3.5 Marking-to-market problems

Since many hedge funds invest in illiquid assets, their administrators have great difficulty generating up-to-date valuations of their positions. When confronted with this problem, administrators will either use the last reported transaction price or a conservative estimate of the current market price, which creates artificial lags in the evolution of these funds' net asset values. As we will discuss in more detail in Section 4, this will lead to very substantial underestimation of hedge fund risk, sometimes by as much as 30–40%.

3.6 Limited data

Since most data vendors only started collecting data on hedge funds around 1994, the available data set on hedge funds is very limited. The available data on hedge funds also span a very special period: the bull market of the 1990s and the various crises that followed combined with the spectacular growth of the hedge fund industry itself. This sharply contrasts with the situation for stocks and bonds. Not only do we have return data over differencing intervals much shorter than 1 month, we also have those data available over a period that extends over many business cycles. This has allowed us to gain insight into the main factors behind stock and bond returns and also allows us to distinguish between normal and abnormal market behaviors. The return generating process behind hedge funds, on the other hand, is still very much a mystery and so far we have little idea what constitutes normal behavior and what not.

With institutional interest in hedge funds on the increase another question that arises is when the hedge fund industry will reach capacity. While the industry has experienced strong growth over the last 5 years in terms of assets under management, hedge funds themselves are showing lower returns every year. This could be an indication that there are no longer enough opportunities in the global capital markets to allow hedge funds to continue to deliver the sort of returns that we have seen so far.

4 Hedge Fund Risk

Marking-to-market problems tend to create lags in the evolution of hedge funds' net asset values, which statistically shows up as autocorrelation in hedge funds' returns. As discussed in Brooks and Kat (2002), for example, this autocorrelation causes estimates of the standard deviation of hedge fund returns to exhibit a systematic downward bias. The second column in Table 1 shows the average 1-month autocorrelation found in the returns of individual hedge funds in some of the usual strategy groups over the period 1994–2001. The table shows that the problem is especially acute for convertible arbitrage and distressed securities funds, which makes sense as these funds' assets will typically be the most difficult to value. One way to correct for the observed autocorrelation is to "unsmooth" the observed returns by creating a new set of returns that are more volatile but whose other characteristics are unchanged. One method to do so stems from the real estate finance literature, where due to smoothing in appraisals and infrequent valuations of properties, the returns of direct property investment indexes suffer from similar problems as hedge fund returns (see Geltner, 1991, 1993). The third and fourth columns of Table 1 show the average standard deviations of the original as well as the unsmoothed returns on individual hedge funds belonging to the different

Table 1 Average 1-month autocorrelation and standard deviations of original and unsmoothed individual hedge fund returns.

	AC (1)	Original SD	Unsmoothed SD
Merger arbitrage	0.13	1.75	2.02
Distressed securities	0.25	2.37	3.05
Equity mkt. neutral	0.08	2.70	3.04
Convertible arbitrage	0.30	3.01	4.00
Global macro	0.03	5.23	5.37
Long/short equity	0.09	5.83	6.37
Emerging markets	0.15	8.33	9.75

strategy groups. From the table we see that the difference between the observed and the true standard deviation can be very substantial. For distressed securities funds the true standard deviation is almost 30% higher than observed. For convertible arbitrage funds the difference is even higher.

A second reason why many investors think hedge funds are less risky than they really are results from the use of the standard deviation as the sole measure of risk. Generally speaking, risk is one word, but not one number. The returns on portfolios of stocks and bonds risk are more or less normally distributed. Because normal distributions are fully described by their mean and standard deviation, the risk of such portfolios can indeed be measured with one number. Confronted with non-normal distributions, however, it is no longer appropriate to use the standard deviation as the sole measure of risk. In that case investors should also look at the degree of symmetry of the distribution, as measured by its so-called "skewness," and the probability of extreme positive or negative outcomes, as measured by the distribution's "kurtosis." A symmetrical distribution will have a skewness equal to zero, while a distribution that implies a relatively high probability of a large loss (gain) is said to exhibit negative (positive) skewness. A normal distribution has a kurtosis of 3, while a kurtosis higher than 3 indicates a relatively high probability of a large loss or gain. Since most investors are in it for the longer run, they strongly rely on compounding effects. This means that negative skewness and high kurtosis are extremely undesirable features as one big loss may destroy years of careful compounding

Table 2 shows the average skewness and kurtosis found in the returns of individual hedge funds from various strategy groups. From the table it is clear that the average hedge fund's returns tend to be far from normally distributed and may exhibit significant negative skewness as well as substantial kurtosis. Put another way, hedge fund returns may exhibit relatively low standard deviations but they also tend to provide skewness and kurtosis attributes that are exactly opposite to what investors desire. It is this whole package that constitutes hedge fund risk, not just the standard deviation.

The skewness and kurtosis properties of hedge funds should not come as a complete surprise. If we delve deeper into the return generating process it becomes obvious that most spread trading and pseudo-arbitrage will generate these features by their very

Table 2 Average skewness and kurtosis of individual hedge fund returns.

	Skewness	Kurtosis
Merger arbitrage	−0.50	7.60
Distressed securities	−0.77	8.92
Equity mkt. neutral	−0.40	5.58
Convertible arbitrage	−1.12	8.51
Global macro	1.04	10.12
Long/short equity	0.00	6.08
Emerging markets	−0.36	7.83

nature as the profit potential of trades will typically be a lot smaller that their loss potential. Consider a merger arbitrage fund for example. When a takeover bid is announced the share price of the target will jump towards the bid. It is at this price that the fund will buy the stock. When the takeover proceeds as planned the fund will make a limited profit equal to the difference between the relatively high price at which it bought the stock and the bid price. When the takeover fails, however, the stock price falls back to its initial level, generating a loss that may be many times bigger than the highest possible profit. Spread traders are confronted with a similar payoff profile. When the spread moves back to its perceived equilibrium value they make a limited profit, but when the market moves against them they could be confronted with a much larger loss. This is why strategies like this are sometimes referred to as "picking up nickels in front of a steamroller." Of course, there is no reason why a trader could not get lucky and avoid getting hit by the steamroller for a long period of time. This does not mean that the risk was never there, however. It always was. It just never materialized so it does not show from the trader's track record.

5 Hedge Fund Sharpe Ratios

To evaluate hedge fund performance many investors use the Sharpe ratio, which is calculated as the ratio of the average excess return and the return standard deviation of the fund being evaluated. When applied to raw hedge fund return data, the relatively high means and low standard deviations offered by hedge funds lead to Sharpe ratios that are considerably higher than those of most benchmarks. Whilst this type of analysis is widely used, it is not without problems. First, survivorship bias, backfill bias, and autocorrelation will cause investors to overestimate the mean and underestimate the standard deviation. Second, the Sharpe ratio does not take account of the negative skewness and excess kurtosis observed in hedge fund returns. This means that the Sharpe ratio will tend to systematically overstate true hedge fund performance. There tends to be a clear relationship between a fund's Sharpe ratio and the skewness and kurtosis of that fund's return distribution. High Sharpe ratios tend to go together with negative skewness and high kurtosis. This means that the relatively high mean and low standard deviation offered by hedge funds is not a free lunch. Investors simply pay

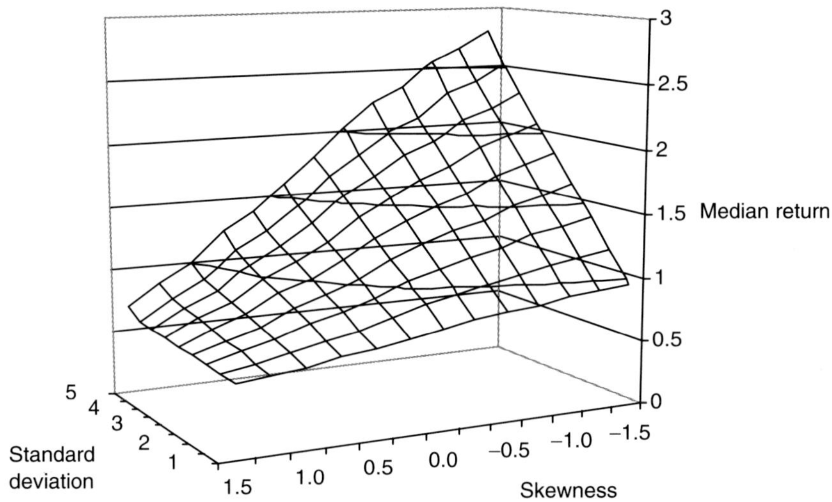

Figure 1 Trade-off between median, standard deviation, and skewness.

for a more attractive Sharpe ratio in the form of more negative skewness and higher kurtosis.

Another way to look at this is to use ordinary put and call options to create distributions that have exceedingly non-normal characteristics. Starting with the (approximately normal) return distribution of the index we can increase the skewness of that distribution by buying puts on that index for example. Likewise, we can reduce skewness by selling calls on that index. When we calculate the median (for skewed distributions this is a better measure of location than the mean), standard deviation, and skewness of such distributions and plot those graphically we obtain a graph as in Figure 1, which shows the median return as a function of the standard deviation and skewness. From the graph we see that for a given level of standard deviation lower (higher) skewness produces a higher (lower) median. Alternatively, we could, of course, say that for a given median lower skewness produces a lower standard deviation and vice versa. From the graph in Figure 1 we can derive (median-based) Sharpe ratios for different skewness levels. The result is shown in Figure 2, where the slope of each line equals the Sharpe ratio for the given level of skewness. Obviously, the lower the skewness level, the higher the Sharpe ratio will be. This shows how wrong it can be to evaluate fund managers who produce returns with different degrees of skewness with the same benchmark Sharpe ratio. Different skewness levels require different benchmark Sharpe ratios, higher when skewness is negative and lower when skewness is positive. If not, the good guys, who produce positively skewed returns, will end up being punished while the bad guys are rewarded.

6 Hedge Fund Alphas

Another performance measure often used is Jensen's alpha. The idea behind alpha is to first construct a portfolio that replicates the sensitivities of a fund to the relevant

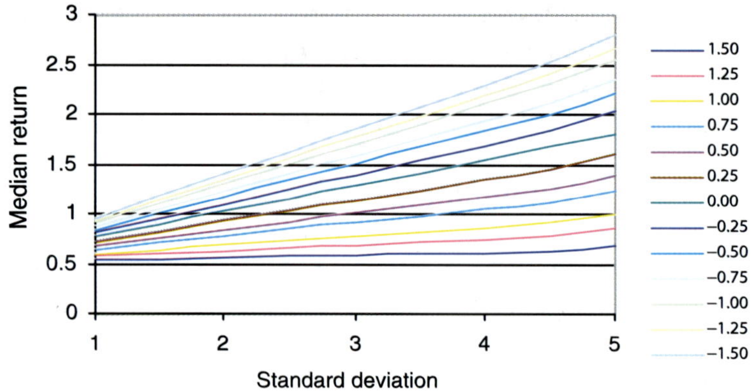

Figure 2 Sharpe ratios for different skewness levels.

return generating factors and then compare the fund return with the return on that portfolio. If the fund produces a higher average return, this can be interpreted as superior performance since both share the same return generating factors. The main problem with this approach lies in the choice of return generating factors. As mentioned earlier, we have little idea what factors really generate hedge fund returns. As a result, investors who calculate hedge funds' alphas are likely to leave out one or more relevant risk factors. This will produce excess return where in reality there is none. Good examples of often forgotten but extremely important risks are credit and liquidity risks. So far, no study of hedge fund performance has correctly figured in credit or liquidity risk as a source of return, despite the fact that some hedge funds virtually live of it.

Providing liquidity can be expected to be compensated by a higher average return. However, when this is not taken into account, we will find alpha where there is in fact none. Table 3 provides a simple example. For individual funds in the various strategy groups, Table 3 shows (a) the average alpha assuming the stock and bond markets are the only relevant risk factors, and (b) the average 1-month autocorrelation coefficient found in these funds monthly returns. Since the autocorrelation found in hedge fund returns primarily stems from marking-to-market problems in illiquid markets, we can

Table 3 Regression individual hedge fund alphas on autocorrelation coefficients.

	Average alpha	Average AC (1)	Regression coefficient
Merger arbitrage	1.20	0.13	1.1356
Distressed securities	0.89	0.25	0.8720
Equity mkt. neutral	0.40	0.08	0.3112
Convertible arbitrage	0.97	0.30	1.2975
Global macro	0.26	0.03	0.2864
Long/short equity	0.94	0.09	0.8954
Emerging markets	0.33	0.15	0.3680

use the autocorrelation coefficient as a measure of the liquidity risk taken on by a fund. From the table we see that there tends to be a positive relationship between alpha and autocorrelation. This is also confirmed by the last column, which shows the results of regressing individual funds' alphas on their autocorrelation coefficients. All regression coefficients are positive and significant (t-values not reported), meaning that in every category the funds that take most liquidity risk also tend to be the funds with the highest alphas.

The above makes it very clear that when it comes to hedge funds, traditional performance evaluation methods like the Sharpe ratio and alpha can be extremely misleading. A high Sharpe ratio or alpha should not be interpreted as an indication of superior manager skill, but first and foremost as an indication that further research is required. One can only speak of superior performance if such research shows that the manager in question generates the observed excess return without taking any unusual and/or catastrophic risks. Unfortunately, simply studying a manager's past returns will not be enough. Apart from the fact that most hedge fund managers do not have much of a track record to study, extreme events only occur infrequently so that it is hard if not impossible to identify the presence of catastrophic risk from a relatively small sample of returns. Consider the following example. A substantial portion of the outstanding supply of catastrophe-linked bonds is held by hedge funds. These bonds pay an exceptionally high coupon in return for the bondholder putting (part of) his principal at risk. Since the world has not seen a major catastrophe for some time now, these bonds have performed very well and the available return series show little skewness. However, this does not give an accurate indication of the actual degree of skewness as when a catastrophe does eventually occur, these bonds will produce very large losses.

There are no shortcuts to hedge fund selection. After properly controlling for the risks involved, small funds do not perform better than larger funds, young funds do not perform better than older funds, closed funds do not perform better than open funds, etc. Proper hedge fund selection is first and foremost a matter of asking the right questions and doing one's homework. There are various due diligence question lists available on the internet and more and more institutions develop their own. The use of such lists harbors its own risks, however. First, it may lead to a more and more mechanical application where getting all the questions answered becomes more important than correctly interpreting the answers. Second, in an attempt to offload as much responsibility and job risk as possible, especially institutional investors will add more and more questions to the list, thereby wasting more and more of hedge fund managers' time. When setting up a due diligence procedure, investors must remember that one of the most important goals is to obtain proper insight in the true risk–return profile (including the relationship with other asset classes) of the strategy followed. This means asking a lot of detailed questions about the strategy and risk management procedures followed, going home and studying the latter under many different scenarios. Common sense and doing one's homework are crucial in alternative investments.

Table 4 Individual hedge fund and hedge fund portfolio risks.

	Individual hedge funds			Portfolio of hedge funds		
	Standard deviation	Skewness	Corr S&P 500	Standard deviation	Skewness	Corr S&P 500
Merger arbitrage	1.75	−0.50	0.47	1.04	−2.19	0.56
Distressed securities	2.37	−0.77	0.37	1.54	−2.60	0.47
Equity mkt. neutral	2.70	−0.40	0.07	1.14	−0.41	0.19
Convertible arbitrage	3.01	−1.12	0.19	1.64	−1.35	0.38
Global macro	5.23	1.04	0.14	2.43	0.87	0.37
Long/short equity	5.83	0.00	0.35	2.95	−0.29	0.63
Emerging markets	8.33	−0.36	0.44	6.15	−0.65	0.67

7 Hedge Fund Diversification

For risk-averse investors, diversification is often said to be the only true free lunch in finance. Unfortunately, this does not include hedge funds. Although combining hedge funds into a basket will substantially reduce the standard deviation of the return on that portfolio, it can also be expected to lower the skewness and raise the correlation with the stock market.

Table 4 shows the standard deviation, skewness, and correlation with the S&P 500 of the average individual hedge fund in the various strategy groups as well as an equally weighted portfolio of all funds in each group. From the table we see that forming portfolios leads to a very substantial reduction in standard deviation. With the exception of emerging market funds, the portfolio standard deviations are approximately half the standard deviations of the average individual fund. This signals that the degree of correlation between funds in the same strategy group must be quite low. Apparently, there are many different ways in which the same general strategy can be executed. Contrary to standard deviation, skewness is not diversified away and actually drops further as portfolios are formed. With the exception of equity market neutral funds, the portfolio skewness figures are lower than for the average individual fund, with especially merger arbitrage and distressed securities funds standing out. Despite the lack of overall correlation, it appears that when markets are bad for one hedge fund, they tend to be bad for other funds as well. Finally, comparing the correlation with the S&P 500 of individual funds and portfolios we clearly see that the returns on portfolios of hedge funds tend to be much more correlated with the stock market than the returns on individual funds. Although individual hedge funds may be more or less market neutral, the portfolios of hedge funds that most investors actually invest in definitely are not.

8 Hedge Funds and Equity

It is often argued that given their relatively weak correlation with other asset classes, hedge funds can play an important role in risk reduction and yield enhancement strategies. Again, this diversification service does not come for free, however. Although the

Table 5 Effects of combining hedge funds with stocks and bonds.

% HF	SD	Skewness	Kurtosis
0	2.49	−0.33	2.97
5	2.43	−0.40	3.02
10	2.38	−0.46	3.08
15	2.33	−0.53	3.17
20	2.29	−0.60	3.28
25	2.25	−0.66	3.42
30	2.22	−0.72	3.58
35	2.20	−0.78	3.77
40	2.18	−0.82	3.97
45	2.17	−0.85	4.19
50	2.16	−0.87	4.41

inclusion of hedge funds in a portfolio may significantly improve that portfolio's mean–variance characteristics, it can also be expected to lead to significantly lower skewness as well as higher kurtosis. Table 5 shows what happens to the standard deviation, skewness, and kurtosis of the portfolio return distribution if, starting with 50% stocks and 50% bonds, we introduce hedge funds (modeled by the average equally weighted random portfolio of 20 funds) in a traditional stock–bond portfolio. As expected, when hedge funds are introduced the standard deviation drops significantly. This represents the relatively low correlation of hedge funds with stocks and bonds. This is the good news. The bad news, however, is that a similar drop is observed in the skewness of the portfolio return. In addition, we also observe a rise in kurtosis.

Especially the skewness effect goes far beyond what one might expect given the hedge fund skewness results in Table 4. When things go wrong in the stock market, they also tend to go wrong for hedge funds. Not necessarily because of what happens to stock prices (after all, many hedge funds do not invest in equity), but because a significant drop in stock prices will often be accompanied by a widening of credit spreads, a significant drop in market liquidity, higher volatility, etc. Since hedge funds are highly sensitive to such factors, when the stock market drops, hedge funds can be expected to show relatively bad performance as well. Recent experience provides a good example. Over the year 2002, the S&P 500 dropped by more than 20% with relatively high volatility and substantially widening credit spreads. Distressed debt funds, at the start of 2002 seen by many investors as one of the most promising sectors, suffered substantially from the widening of credit spreads. Credit spreads also had a negative impact on convertible arbitrage funds. Stock market volatility worked in their favor, however. Managers focusing on volatility trading generally fared best, while managers actively taking credit exposure did worst. Equity market neutral funds suffered greatly from a lack of liquidity, while long/short equity funds with low net exposure outperformed managers who remained net long throughout the year. As a result, overall hedge fund performance in 2002 as measured by the main hedge fund indexes was more or less flat.

9 Hedge Funds and Mean–Variance Analysis

When studied in a mean–variance framework, the inclusion of hedge funds in a portfolio appears to pay off impressive dividends: equity-like returns with bond-like risk. Since mean–variance analysis only looks at the mean and standard deviation, however, it skips over the fact that with hedge funds more attractive mean–variance attributes tend to go hand in hand with less-attractive skewness and kurtosis properties. In addition, it skips over the significant co-skewness between hedge funds and equity.

We performed two standard mean–variance optimizations: one with only stocks and bonds, and one with stocks, bonds and hedge funds as the available asset classes. The results of both optimizations can be found in Table 6. Starting with the case without hedge funds (top panel), we see that moving upwards over the efficient frontier results in a straightforward exchange of bonds for stocks. Since stocks have a higher mean than bonds, the mean goes up. While this happens, the skewness of the return distribution drops in a more or less linear fashion as stock returns are more negatively skewed than bond returns. The kurtosis of the return distribution remains more or less unchanged. Next, we added hedge funds and recalculated the efficient frontier (bottom panel). Moving over the efficient frontier, we see that at first bonds are exchanged for stocks while the hedge fund allocation remains more or less constant. When the bond allocation is depleted, the equity allocation continues to grow but now at the expense of the hedge fund allocation. Similar to the case without hedge funds, if we increase the standard deviation, the mean goes up, while the skewness of the return distribution goes down. Unlike what we saw before, however, skewness drops as long as bonds are being replaced by equity but rises again as hedge funds start to be replaced by equity. The lowest level of skewness is reached when the bond allocation reaches 0%, which is in line with our earlier observation that in terms of skewness hedge funds and equity are not a good mix.

Comparing the case with and without hedge funds we see a significant improvement in the mean, especially for lower standard deviations. However, we also see a major

Table 6 Mean–variance optimal portfolios.

Std. dev.	Mean	% Stocks	% Bonds	% HFund	Skew	Kurtosis
Stocks and bonds only						
2	0.77	32.79	67.21		0.04	3.23
2.5	0.95	50.31	49.69		−0.34	2.97
3	1.10	64.68	35.32		−0.55	3.24
3.5	1.23	77.86	22.14		−0.68	3.57
4	1.36	90.44	9.56		−0.77	3.86
Stocks, bonds, and hedge funds						
2	0.92	18.07	26.81	55.12	−0.82	4.39
2.5	1.06	29.95	10.75	59.30	−0.99	5.26
3	1.20	45.07	0	54.93	−1.07	5.47
3.5	1.30	67.08	0	32.92	−1.00	4.81
4	1.39	86.14	0	13.86	−0.89	4.32

deterioration in skewness and kurtosis, with the largest change taking place exactly there where the mean improves most. From this it is painfully clear that standard mean–variance portfolio decision-making is not appropriate when hedge funds are involved as it completely ignores these effects. When hedge funds are involved investors need a decision-making framework that also incorporates the skewness and kurtosis of the portfolio return distribution. Since portfolios with low skewness will tend to exhibit the most attractive mean–variance properties, mean–variance optimizers are essentially nothing more than skewness minimizers.

When bringing together different assets or asset classes in a mean–variance framework, we implicitly assume that these are comparable in terms of liquidity and the quality of the inputs used. With stocks and bonds this assumption is often justified. When alternative investments are introduced, however, this is no longer true. Many hedge funds employ long lock-up and advance notice periods. Such restrictions are not only meant to reduce management costs and cash holdings but also allow managers to aim for longer-term horizons and invest in relatively illiquid securities. As a result, hedge fund investments are substantially less liquid than stocks or bonds. In addition, since the available hedge fund data cover such a short and exceptional period we have little idea what the return generating process behind hedge funds looks like and what constitutes normal behavior and what not. This illiquidity and additional uncertainty should be properly incorporated in the portfolio optimization process. If not, hedge funds are artificially made to look good and consequently too much money will be allocated to them.

10 Conclusions

Proper hedge fund investing requires a much more elaborate approach to investment decision-making than currently in use by most investors. The available data on hedge funds should not be taken at face value, but should first be corrected for various types of biases and autocorrelation. Tools like mean–variance analysis and the Sharpe ratio that many investors have become accustomed to over the years are no longer appropriate when hedge funds are involved as they concentrate on the good part while completely skipping over the bad part of the hedge fund story. Investors also have to find a way to figure in the long lock-up and advance notice periods, which make hedge fund investments highly illiquid. In addition, investors will have to give weight to the fact that without more insight in the way in which hedge funds generate their returns it is very hard to say something sensible about hedge funds' future longer-run performance. The tools to accomplish this formally are not there, meaning that more than ever investors will have to rely on good old-fashioned common sense and doing their homework. Given the lemming-like behavior of especially institutional investors, however, for most this may well turn out to be too much to ask for.

It has also become clear that hedge funds are not the miracle cure that many investors think or have been told they are. Again, this boils down to a matter of common sense. Anyone who is well calibrated to the world we live in will have extreme difficulty believing that there is a significant (and growing) number of people who are able to systematically beat the market to such an extent that even after deducting "2 plus 20" or even more the investor is left with a superior return. Hedge funds offer investors a way to obtain a lower standard deviation and/or higher expected return but only at the cost of lower skewness and higher kurtosis. Whether the resulting portfolio makes for a more attractive investment than the original is purely a matter of taste, not a general rule.

References

Amin, G. and Kat, H. (2003). "Welcome to the Dark Side: Hedge Fund Attrition and Survivorship Bias 1994–2001." *Journal of Alternative Investments* **Summer**, 57–73.

Brooks, C. and Kat, H. (2002). "The Statistical Properties of Hedge Fund Index Returns and their Implications for Investors." *Journal of Alternative Investments* **Fall**, 26–44.

Geltner, D. (1991). "Smoothing in Appraisal-Based Returns." *Journal of Real Estate Finance and Economics* **4**, 327–345.

Geltner, D. (1993). "Estimating Market Values from Appraised Values without Assuming an Efficient Market." *Journal of Real Estate Research* **8**, 325–345.

Posthuma, N. and Van der Sluis, P. (2003). "A Reality Check on Hedge Fund Returns." Working Paper, ABP Investments.

Keywords: Hedge funds; portfolio management; mean-variance analysis; Sharpe ratio; alpha

Journal of Investment Management
Vol. 1, No. 1 (2003), pp. 94–134

UNDERSTANDING MUTUAL FUND AND HEDGE FUND STYLES USING RETURN-BASED STYLE ANALYSIS

Arik Ben Dor, Ravi Jagannathan†, and Iwan Meier**

We illustrate the use of return-based style analysis in practice using several examples. We demonstrate the importance of selecting the right style benchmarks and how the use of inappropriate style benchmarks may lead to wrong conclusions. For example, when style analysis is applied to sector-oriented funds, the set of benchmarks should include sector or industry indexes. We show how asset turnover and style graphs over time can be used to ensure right inference about the effective style of a fund, and how to extend return-based style analysis to analyze hedge fund styles. In the examples we consider, return-based style analysis provides insights not available through commonly used peer evaluation alone.

1 Introduction

During the past three decades, the direct holdings of corporate equities by individuals has come down and the holdings through money management institutions has correspondingly increased. Mutual funds and pension funds held almost 40% of US corporate equities by the end of 2001, more than three times the 14% they held in 1970.[1] Mutual funds, in particular, have become an attractive vehicle for individual investors for investing in financial assets. An estimated 52% of US households invest in mutual funds. While in 1990 mutual funds as a group were holding assets worth $1 trillion, the number reached $7 trillion in 2001. Approximately half of this was accounted for by equity funds.[2] The 8307 mutual funds in December 2001 held 21 percent of the $13.9 trillion of outstanding, publicly traded US equities.[3]

By holding stocks through institutions managed by professional money managers, individual investors and plan sponsors have been able to reap the benefits of diversification and specialization. However, this benefit is not without cost. Indirect holding of equities by relying on fund managers introduces invisible agency costs in addition to visible fees. This is due to the need to monitor the actions of fund managers to ensure compliance with stated objectives and to evaluate their performance.

The menu of mutual funds available to an investor is large, ranging from domestic real-estate stock funds, international funds invested in emerging markets, to municipal bond funds designed for investors who are subject to federal income tax. For example, Morningstar, a prominent source of information on

*Kellogg School of Management at Northwestern University.

†Kellogg School of Management and National Bureau of Economic Research.

mutual funds, reports returns on four broad categories (domestic stock funds, international stock funds, fixed-income funds, and municipal bond funds) which are further divided into 48 sub-categories. The Investment Company Institute enumerates 33 investment objective categories. These classifications by themselves, however, are not very helpful in deciding how to allocate the money across the different fund categories.

When allocating capital among several fund managers, individual investors and plan sponsors have to ensure that their investment objectives are met, the bets taken by the different managers do not cancel out, and management fees that they pay are related to performance. The large number of fund categories and the diversity in investment objectives even within narrow fund categories makes it difficult to understand how the returns on different funds interact with each other. Hence, there is a need for a conceptual framework that helps individual investors and plan sponsors understand what a fund manager is doing. Sharpe (1988, 1992a) provides one framework, "return-based style analysis," that is attractive for that purpose. In this paper, we show how return-based style analysis can provide information not available through commonly used peer-group comparisons alone. We discuss common pitfalls that a user of return-based style analysis should be aware of. We also provide guidelines for choosing the right style benchmarks, interpreting estimated style changes, and checking robustness of the style characterization based on the use of different optimization criteria.

To the casual observer, it may appear that portfolio-composition-based style analysis would convey more information about the style of an actively managed fund than return-based style analysis. This need not be true. To see why, consider a manager who provides portfolio insurance by synthetically creating a put option on the market index through active trading. An investor would be able to identify that the manager is indeed providing a put option based on return-based style analysis using appropriately chosen benchmarks and judiciously chosen options on the benchmarks. It may be difficult to arrive at that conclusion based on an examination of the manager's portfolio holdings at different points, even for an analyst who is trained in derivative mathematics. In our view, portfolio-composition-based and return-based style analyses are complements rather than substitutes.

Many popular hedge fund strategies generate returns that exhibit low average correlations with stock and bond returns. However, the correlations could be high under certain market conditions, especially periods associated with large movements in stock and bond prices. Therefore, return-based style analysis using standard asset classes will have difficulty in characterizing the risks in hedge fund strategies with sufficient accuracy. We discuss the modifications that are necessary to apply return-based style analysis to hedge funds.

The rest of the paper is organized as follows. Section 2 contains a review of the methodology of return-based style analysis. Section 3 shows how the technique can be used in practice. Some common pitfalls are discussed in Section 4. In Section 5, we show how to modify the methodology to examine hedge funds. We summarize and conclude in Section 6.

2 Methodology

2.1 Linear factor models and return-based style analysis

Linear factor models are commonly used in investment analysis for generating inputs for portfolio optimization. Consider the linear N-factor model given below that decomposes the return $r_{i,t}$ on security i in period t into two parts: the first is a linear function of the factors and the second is orthogonal to the first part.

$$r_{i,t} = a_{i,0} + a_{i,1}f_{1,t} + a_{i,2}f_{2,t} + \cdots + a_{i,N}f_{N,t} + \varepsilon_{i,t} \tag{1}$$

The coefficients $a_{i,n}$, $n = 1, 2, \ldots, N$, measure the sensitivity of the return on security i, $r_{i,t}$, to the nth factor, $f_{n,t}$, and $\varepsilon_{i,t}$ is the component of $r_{i,t}$ that cannot be explained by the N factors. In addition, the residual (non-factor component), $\varepsilon_{i,t}$, for asset i is uncorrelated with that for asset j. This last property is what distinguishes the linear factor model given in Eq. (1) from a standard multiple regression exercise. Commonly used factors include returns on asset classes and unexpected changes in macroeconomic variables. In Sharpe's (1988) return-based style analysis, there is no intercept term, $a_{i,0}$, every factor is a return on some asset class, and the coefficients sum to unity.

Consider an active portfolio manager who is restricted to investing a fraction $b_{p,n}$ of the amount given to him in asset class $n = 1, 2, \ldots, N$. The only discretion allowed is to pick securities from within each asset class. An investor can either give the funds to the active portfolio manager or hold a passive portfolio with fractions $b_{p,n}$ invested in the nth asset class index, $x_{n,t}$. The returns on the two strategies will not, in general, be the same. The difference, $e_{p,t} = r_{p,t} - [b_{p,1}x_{1,t} + b_{p,2}x_{2,t} + \cdots + b_{p,N}x_{N,t}]$, arises from the manager selecting to weight securities within a given asset class differently than the corresponding asset class index. Knowing the properties of the *selection* component, $e_{p,t}$, will be helpful to an investor who is considering allocating the funds to the active portfolio manager. In general, a portfolio manager will have some flexibility regarding the fraction $b_{p,n}$ invested in each asset class, n. Hence, the investor who allocates funds to the active portfolio manager would also be interested in finding out how the manager distributed the funds across the different asset classes in addition to picking securities within each asset class. Sharpe's (1988) return-based style analysis helps identify the effective style of the active portfolio manager given by the asset class exposures, $b_{p,n}$, $n = 1, 2, \ldots, N$, and separate the selection component, $e_{p,t}$, from the return provided by the manager, $r_{p,t}$.

The *effective style* of a fund manager are those asset class coefficients, $b_{p,1}, \ldots, b_{p,N}$, that minimize the variance of the error terms $e_{p,t}$ in the asset class factor model given in Eq. (2a) subject to the constraints (2b) and (2c):

$$r_{p,t} = [b_{p,1}x_{1,t} + b_{p,2}x_{2,t} + \cdots + b_{p,N}x_{N,t}] + e_{p,t} \quad \text{for } t = 1, 2, \ldots, T \tag{2a}$$

$$\text{s.t. } b_{p,n} \geq 0 \quad \text{for } n = 1, 2, \ldots, N \tag{2b}$$

$$b_{p,1} + b_{p,2} + \cdots + b_{p,N} = 1 \tag{2c}$$

where $r_{p,t}$ is the return on the managed fund, the factor $x_{n,t}$, $n = 1, 2, \ldots, N$, is the period t return on the nth asset class—often called nth *style benchmark index*—and the portfolio weights $b_{p,n}$ are constrained to be positive and add up to unity. When applying return-based style analysis to hedge funds in Section 5, we will eliminate constraint (2b) and allow the manager to take short positions.[4]

Inserting the optimal weights $b_{p,n}$ in Eq. (2a) and rearranging, we can express the excess return of the portfolio over the style benchmark as

$$e_{p,t} = r_{p,t} - [b_{p,1}x_{1,t} + b_{p,2}x_{2,t} + \cdots + b_{p,N}x_{N,t}] \qquad (3)$$

The component $[b_{p,1}x_{1,t} + b_{p,2}x_{2,t} + \cdots + b_{p,N}x_{N,t}]$ is that part of the return, $r_{p,t}$, that is due to the manager's effective style, also referred to as the *style benchmark return*. The difference between the return and the manager's effective style, $e_{p,t}$, given on the left-hand side is referred to as the selection component of the manager's return. The standard deviation of the selection component is the *style benchmark tracking error* of the fund.[5]

2.2 *Role of adjusted R^2 measure in choosing style weights*

Return-based style analysis estimates the weights for the N given style benchmarks by minimizing the variance of the tracking error, subject to the constraints (2b) and (2c). Let R^2, a measure of the goodness-of-fit, be given by

$$R^2 = 1 - \frac{\text{var}(e_p)}{\text{var}(r_p)} \qquad (4a)$$

R^2 equals 1 minus the ratio of the variance of the tracking error to the variance of the return on the managed portfolio. Note that the statistic will equal 1 if the model fits perfectly, that is, there is no tracking error. Then, minimizing the variance of the tracking error is the same as maximizing the R^2 measure given in Eq. (4a).[6]

Typically, one would let the data determine the appropriate number and type of style benchmarks to use in a particular application. Increasing the number of style benchmarks will reduce the tracking error in any given sample. However, the style coefficients will be estimated with less precision reducing the confidence one can have on the estimates. One way to take this effect into account would be to adjust the measured R^2 downward by a penalty that increases with the number of style benchmarks used. The commonly used *adjusted* R^2 measure of the goodness-of-fit is given by

$$\text{Adjusted } R^2 = 1 - \left(\frac{T-1}{T-N}\right) \times \frac{\text{var}(e_p)}{\text{var}(r_p)} \qquad (4b)$$

where N is the number of asset classes and T the number of observations. Var(e_p) is the variance of excess returns of the fund over the style benchmark.

2.3 *An alternative: the Akaike information criterion*

An alternative to choosing style weights that maximize adjusted R^2 would be to choose style weights that minimize the *Akaike information criterion* (AIC), especially in situations where the number of asset classes is large.[7] The AIC is given below:

$$\mathrm{AIC} = T \times \log\left[\frac{\mathrm{var}(e_p)}{T}\right] + 2N. \tag{4c}$$

For every subset of the N asset classes the value of the above criterion is calculated. The subset that produces the smallest information criterion is selected. The use of the AIC is obviously computationally more complex but can eliminate asset classes that do not contribute much to the fit of the model. The AIC penalizes additional variables more heavily than the adjusted R^2 measure. Our default criterion is R^2 and whenever the adjusted R^2 or AIC is used it is indicated in the text.

2.4 The effective style of a multi-manager portfolio

An attractive property of return-based style analysis is the straightforward extension from a single manager to a multi-manager portfolio as shown by Sharpe (1988). Consider the example of a plan sponsor who allocates the available funds across several money managers. Denote by w_p the proportion of money allocated to manager p. In total, there are $p = 1, 2, \ldots, P$ portfolio managers and R_t is the plan sponsor's overall portfolio return. The aggregation involves two steps. First, identify the style of each manager separately. Second, sum up the exposures of all managers for each asset class, weighted by the fraction of money allocated to each manager. Formally, the *effective mix* of the overall portfolio is described by

$$\begin{aligned} R_t = \sum_{p=1}^{P} w_p r_{p,t} &= \left[\sum_p w_p b_{p,1}\right] x_{1,t} + \left[\sum_p w_p b_{p,2}\right] x_{2,t} + \cdots \\ &+ \left[\sum_p w_p b_{p,N}\right] x_{N,t} + \left[\sum_p w_p e_{p,t}\right] \end{aligned} \tag{5}$$

The brackets are the money-weighted exposures to the asset classes. Consider the first asset class with returns $x_{1,t}$. Each portfolio manager p has an exposure of $b_{p,1}$ to asset class 1. Manager p has a weight w_p in the overall portfolio. The summation over all managers measures the exposure of the plan sponsor to the first asset class.

3 Return-Based Style Analysis in Practice

3.1 Data and asset class specifications

For illustrating the use of return-based style analysis in practice, we use monthly return data for open-end mutual funds (net-of-fee) from the Morningstar database along with the StyleAdvisor® software of Zephyr Associates Inc.[8]

We follow standard practice and use the 3-month Treasury bills as the cash equivalent.[9] Intermediate-(maturities between 1 and 10 years) and long-term Treasury bonds (with maturities beyond 10 years) are represented using two Salomon Brothers

Treasury indexes: SSB Treasury 1–10 yr and SSB Treasury 10+ yr. Level shifts and twists in the shape of the term structure affect longer maturities differently. The SSB Corporate Bond index serves as the benchmark for US corporate bonds. It captures the dynamics of credit spreads over Treasury bonds that compensate investors for incurring default risk.

We use returns on the Russell 3000 index, produced by the Frank Russell Company, to measure the performance of publicly traded common stocks incorporated in the US and its territories. The index includes the 3000 largest US companies (based on market capitalization) and represents approximately 98% of the publicly traded US equity. The Russell 3000 constituents are ranked annually and split into two subsets. The largest 1000 stocks constitute the Russell 1000 index and the remaining companies comprise the Russell 2000 index. The companies in each index are further assigned to value and growth subindexes. Russell uses a combination of the price-to-book ratio and xthe consensus forecast for the long-term growth from I/B/E/S (Institutional Brokers Estimate System) to classify the stocks into value and growth. Stocks with high price-to-book or price-to-earnings ratios are classified as growth stocks since a high P/E ratio indicates high expected rates of earnings growth in the future, whereas stocks with low price-to-book or price-to-earnings ratios define value stocks.

The value and growth part of the different indexes typically earn different returns over time and appear to respond differently to economy-wide, pervasive shocks. The interested reader is referred to Siegel (1998) who provides an in-depth discussion of the distribution of value and growth stocks among different index aggregates and reviews the performance patterns in the past; and Dimson *et al.* (2002) who extend the analysis of historic returns to the last 101 years for 16 countries. The four Russell 3000 subindexes seem to fulfill Sharpe's (1988, 1992a) desirable properties: (i) market-capitalized, (ii) exhaustive, (iii) mutually exclusive,[10] and (iv) replicable. They also represent the typical four quadrants used to visualize the style of a domestic equity manager in a style box.

To cover the performance of foreign investments we include three global equity Morgan Stanley Composite Indexes (MSCI). The MSCI EASEA index represents Europe, Australasia, and the Far East, excluding Japan. For Japan, the MCSI country index is added separately. The MSCI Emerging Markets Free (EMF) proxies for equity investments in emerging countries—currently (April 2002) 27 countries are covered. The add-on "Free" indicates that the index accounts for country-specific restrictions on share ownership by foreigners. The Lehman non-US bond index is designed to measure the performance of fixed-income investments outside the US. Appendix A provides a detailed description of the selected indexes.

3.2 An example: Vanguard Windsor

We use monthly return data on the Vanguard Windsor fund (ticker VWNDX) for the period January 1988 to December 2001 to illustrate the application of return-based style analysis. Morningstar classifies the fund as a large-cap value fund. In the annual report of October 2001, Vanguard declares the Russell 1000 Value index as the "best fit"

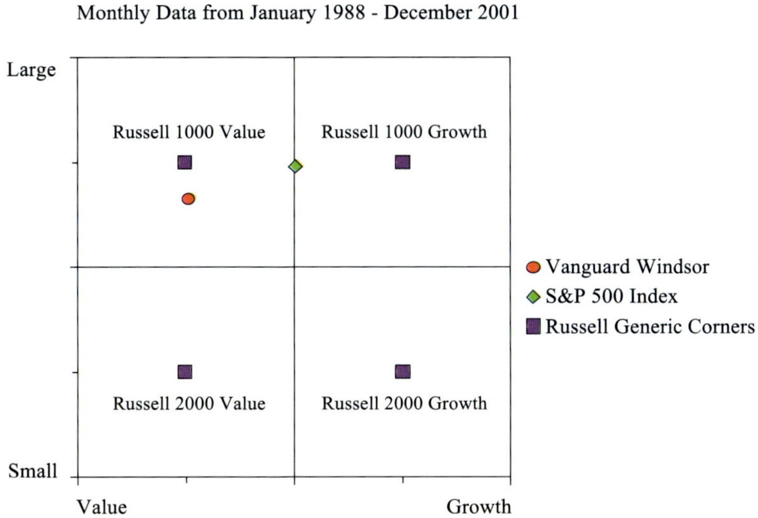

Figure 1 Vanguard Windsor style box.

Table 1 Style box for Vanguard Windsor.

Generic Corners	Coordinates	Value −1	Growth +1	Sum
Large	+1	0.812	0.000	0.812
Small	−1	0.160	0.000	−0.160
	Sum	−0.972	0.000	−0.972/0.652

The exposures are from the return-based style analysis results in Figure 2. The rows and columns labeled "Sum" take the sum weighted by the coordinate (+1 or −1). The lower right cell displays the position in the style box.

for the Windsor fund. In the investment objective, they position themselves as a value fund that primarily "invests in large- and mid-capitalization common stocks [. . .]."

The *style box* in Figure 1 provides a first snapshot of the nature of Windsor's investment style.[11] StyleAdvisor uses by default four quadrants to classify an investor along the two dimensions value/growth and small-cap/large-cap.[12] The four Russell 3000 subindexes form the *style basis*. They span the range of the axis coordinates from −1 to 1 and mark the midpoints of the quadrants. Table 1 illustrates the calculations to determine the position of Vanguard Windsor within the style box. The four cells in the center contain the exposures from return-based style analysis. Then, sum up the exposures for each of the two columns (value and growth) and rows (large and small) and weight by the coordinate value of the four groups (+1 or −1). The resulting position is shown in the lower right cell: value/growth = −0.972 and size = 0.652. The style box indeed classifies the fund as a mostly large-cap value fund.

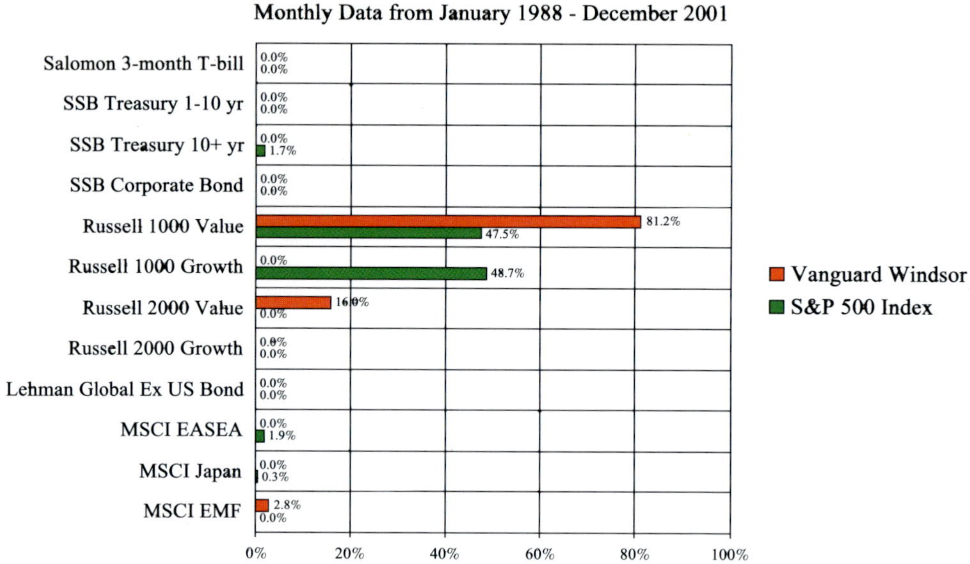

Figure 2 Return-based style analysis for Vanguard Windsor.

The results of return-based style analysis in Figure 2 provide more details. A passive portfolio with 81.2% invested in the Russell 1000 Value and 16.0% invested in the Russell 2000 Value—plus a fraction of 2.8% in MSCI Emerging Markets—characterizes the style of Windsor best over the given period. The small exposure to the MSCI Emerging Market index may pick up some of the deviations due to different weighting of stocks when compared to the Russell 1000 Value and Russell 2000 Value subindexes, stock picking, or changing style over time. We will address changing styles later in Section 4.5. The 12 asset classes explain 85.6% of the monthly returns of Windsor as measured by the R^2 and depicted in the pie chart in Figure 3. Excluding the last four indexes that are not relevant for a US domestic equity fund, the weights are 82.1% for the Russell 1000 Value and 17.9% for the Russell 2000 Value index. The explanatory power remains approximately the same with $R^2 = 85.5\%$. Alternatively, we could use the full set of twelve assets and minimize the AIC criterion instead of R^2. As a result of the imposed penalty for additional parameters, the optimization assigns a zero exposure to the MSCI Emerging Markets index and the exposures to the two Russell value indexes are exactly the same as if we exclude the indexes measuring exposure to foreign investments.

Using the S&P 500, a commonly used benchmark for large-cap funds, instead of the style benchmark explains only 65.9% of the variation in returns of Vanguard Windsor. Return-based style analysis conveys additional information on the typical asset-mix of the fund. The effective style of the S&P 500 benchmark is substantially different from that of Vanguard Windsor. A style benchmark with 47.5% in the Russell 1000 Value, 48.7% in the Russell 1000 Growth, with the balance split between MSCI EASEA, SSB Treasury 10+ yr and MSCI Japan, explains 99.1% of the return variance in the S&P 500. In terms of effective style, Vanguard Windsor is mostly a large-cap

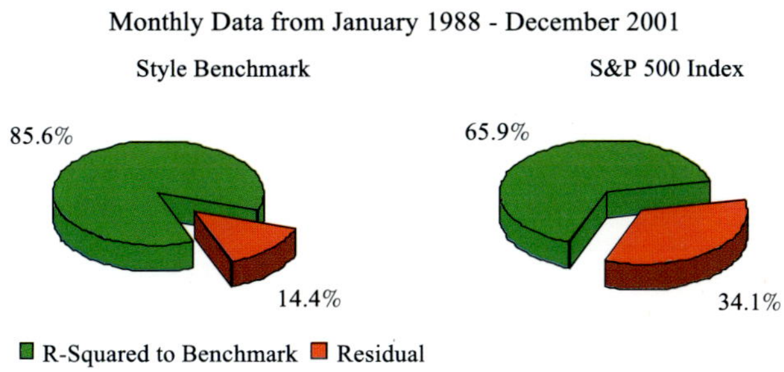

Figure 3 Performance attribution for Vanguard Windsor.

value fund whereas the S&P 500 gives equal weighting to large-cap value and growth. The low R^2 in the return-based style analysis for Vanguard Windsor, when compared to the S&P 500, suggests substantial active management.

3.3 Performance analysis

Next, we analyze potential *style changes* over time following Sharpe (1992a). As discussed above, we apply the methodology to monthly returns on the Vanguard Windsor fund from January 1988 to December 2001. For each month, we use the past 60 monthly returns to determine the style. Thus, the first calculation uses data from January 1988 to December 1992 to assess the style on December 1992. The 60-month window is then moved forward by 1 month and the style is recalculated.

The dynamics of the changes in style for Vanguard Windsor are portrayed in Figure 4. Each shaded area represents the percentage contribution of the asset class to the style. At the start of 1994, the exposure to the Russell 2000 Value reached almost 40%, the remaining 60% were attributed to the Russell 1000 Value. The exposure to the small-cap value index was gradually substituted until 1997. During the period from 1998 to 2000, the fund developed some exposure (up to 11.3% in October 1998) to the Russell 2000 Growth. From October 1997 onwards, the fund began investing a substantial amount (3–12%) in securities whose returns can be best described by the MSCI EMF index.

Given the changes in style over time, the question arises how to assess the performance of the fund. We apply the following out-of-sample performance procedure. As described above, we calculate the style of the fund each month. To evaluate the performance in month t, we use the style benchmark calculated using data from $t-60$ to $t-1$. We then compare the return the style benchmark would have yielded during month t and compare it to the actual return of the fund. The difference is the performance of the fund due to selection.

Figure 5 depicts the return differences between Vanguard Windsor and two benchmarks: the S&P 500 and the style benchmark. Each data point describes the return difference between the fund and the benchmark over the past 60 months. The graph reveals that Vanguard outperformed the S&P 500 initially. During the late 1990s, the performance was less favorable, with a dip of -12.0% in early 2000. If we use the style

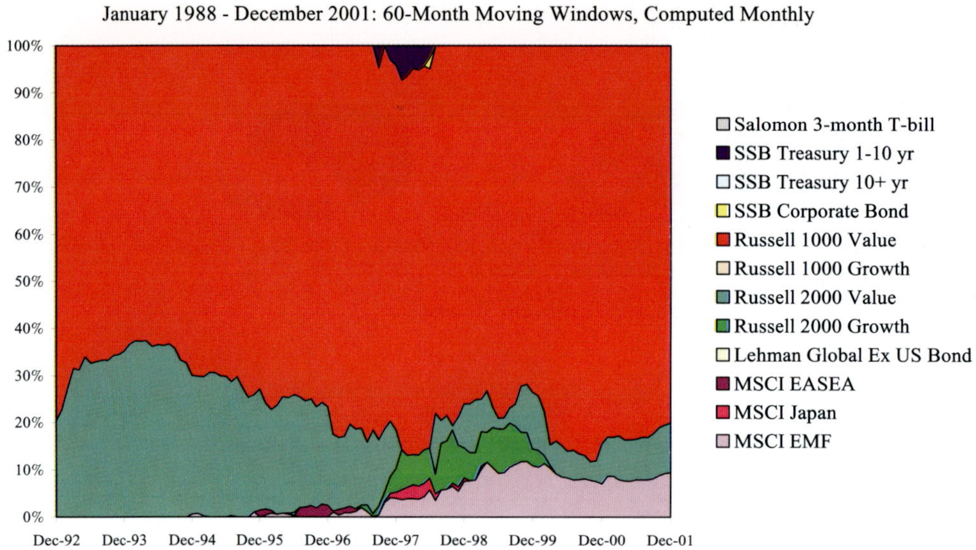

Figure 4 Style changes of Vanguard Windsor.

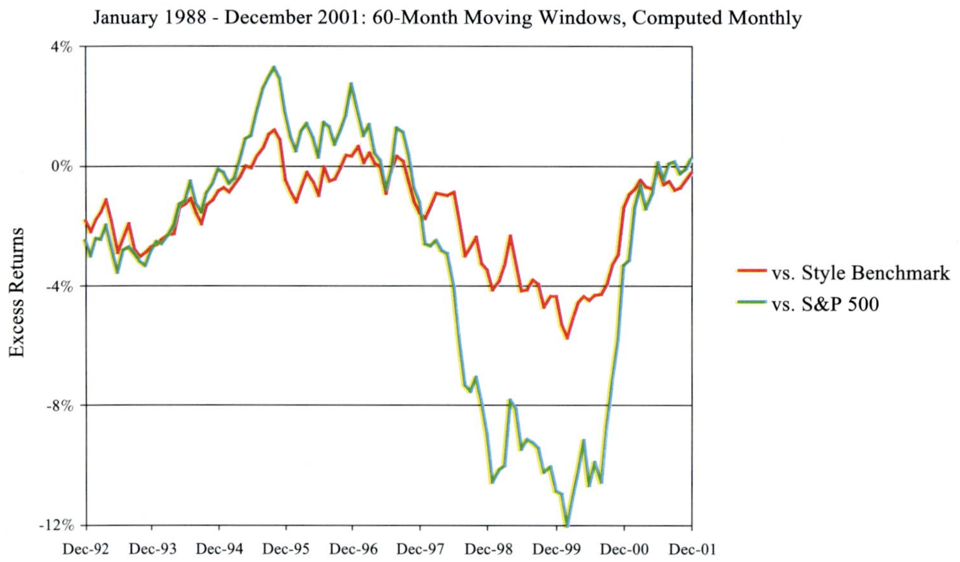

Figure 5 Vanguard Windsor versus style and market benchmark.

benchmark instead, the deviations are less pronounced in both directions, confirming that the fund more closely tracks the style benchmark than the S&P 500. The performance of the fund relative to the style benchmark looks worse than when compared to the S&P 500. The annualized average excess return of the fund is −0.64% against the style benchmark and −0.49% against the S&P 500. The cumulative excess return over the 9 years is −50.14% and −38.06%, respectively.

3.4 Growth and income funds

In this section, we demonstrate how return-based style analysis reveals incremental information beyond the fund's self-stated classification and investment policy as described in the prospectus.[13] We compare the style of four domestic funds with an identical name (growth and income): The Alliance Growth & Income (ticker CABDX), Goldman Sachs Growth and Income Fund (GSGRX), Putnam Fund for Growth and Income (PGRWX), and the Vanguard Growth and Income Fund (VQNPX).[14] In the prospectus, all funds declare that they aim to seek long-term growth of capital and income by picking currently undervalued stocks as their target. The funds focus on common stocks of established companies with the potential for growth and that are expected to pay dividends—the income component. They use a bottom–up approach and fundamentals to determine undervalued companies and do not take any sector or market timing bets. Appendix B summarizes the funds' objectives, size, and fee structure based on the prospectuses as of December 2001. Based on this information, it is a difficult task for the investor to perceive stylistic differences. Morningstar classifies the funds as large-cap value funds, with the exception of Vanguard that is considered to be a blend of large-cap value and growth stocks.

Alliance Capital annotates that their Growth and Income fund selects "stocks of good quality" and "may also invest in fixed-income and convertible securities." The style analysis in Figure 6 shows that the fund primarily invests in large-cap value stocks (76.8% Russell 1000 Value) but has also a considerable exposure of 17.5% to large-cap growth stocks (Russell 1000 Growth). There is no evidence that the fund actually holds a position in fixed-income or convertible securities that would also manifest in positive weights for fixed-income asset classes.

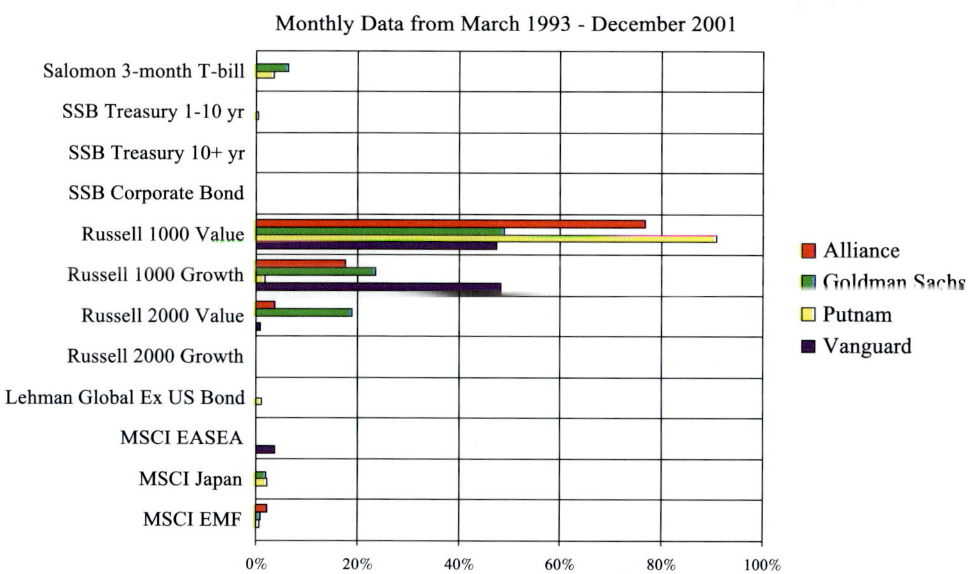

Figure 6 Growth and income funds.

For the Goldman Sachs Growth and Income Fund, 6.3% is attributed to short-term T-bills. This complies with the statement in the prospectus that "the fund may also invest up to 35% of its total assets in fixed-income securities." Their self-declared investment style is value, which is only partially confirmed by the style analysis with a total exposure to large and small-cap value stocks of 67.6% (48.8% Russell 1000 Value and 18.8% Russell 2000 Value). The fund faces a substantial exposure of 23.4% to the Russell 1000 Growth index. According to the prospectus, Goldman Sachs may invest up to 25% in foreign markets. Style analysis indicates that the total allocation to foreign assets is only 2.7% (1.8% MSCI Japan and 0.9% MSCI EMF).

The Putnam fund invests mainly in common stock of large US companies with a "focus on value stocks." This is confirmed by Figure 6. As the classification of Morningstar suggests, the Vanguard fund provides a blend of large value and growth stocks. The exposure of 95.6% to the two Russell 1000 indexes shows that the fund likely exceeds the lower bound of 65% invested in S&P 500 stocks as declared in the prospectus. Activity in the fixed-income segment that would be allowed to a limited extent cannot be detected.

Despite similar objectives, the strategy implementations differ substantially. Fund names together with the prospectus do not necessarily deliver a concise description of the investment style. The literature has addressed the problem of misclassification. During the period from 1972 to 1992, Brown and Goetzmann (1997) found 237 funds that switched their fund objective. They propose a classification algorithm that identifies funds that are either strategically or unintentionally assigned to an incorrect category. Using a different methodology, DiBartolomeo and Witkowski (1997) conclude that 9% of the 748 equity funds in their study are seriously misclassified and 31% somewhat misclassified; mostly funds within the categories small-cap and aggressive growth. They show that their reclassification is robust out-of-sample. From the switches in the Morningstar classification, Indro *et al.* (1998) infer that 57% of the 770 actively managed funds changed their investment orientation (value/growth/blend, large-/medium-/small-cap) over the 3-year period 1993–1995.

Kim *et al.* (2002) add fund characteristics similar to the ones outlined in portfolio-composition-based style analysis (see Section 3.6) to past returns and screen a sample of 1043 funds from December 1993 to December 1996. They find that more than half are not consistent with their self-declared objective and "over 33% of the funds depart severely from their stated objectives." Deviations occur most frequently in the categories income, growth, or growth and income—the category we used as an example. The empirical evidence in Michaud (1998) indicates that even categorizing stocks into value and growth using the price-to-book ratio may be problematic. He demonstrates that at least three distinct factors are required to identify value stocks, that is, the value style attribute itself is multidimensional.

3.5 *Active versus passive portfolio management*

The difference $(1 - R^2)$ is often used as a measure of the degree of active management of a fund. A passively managed fund performs no research and fundamental analysis and tracks a benchmark trying to keep transaction costs low and consequently has a high R^2. Depending on the composition of the benchmark, the passive manager thus provides a portfolio with a particular style.

Active management of mutual funds can take different forms: a manager can (i) hold different securities within each asset class, or even outside any asset class, and (ii) deviate from the asset class weights for the style benchmark from time to time, depending on market conditions. The style is then no longer able to mimic the returns of the fund and the excess returns—whether positive or negative—become larger in conjunction with a lower R^2 statistic. If the deviations are the result of (i), these excess returns are called the *selection* component of the fund's return; (ii) is referred to as *timing*. The selection component can result from, for example, industry concentration, stock picking, or a different degree of diversification due to a limited number of assets.

The numbers for R^2 in Figure 7 indicate that Goldman Sachs employed the most active management strategy, whereas Putnam and Vanguard more closely tracked a passive asset mix.[15] This conclusion is consistent with the funds' fee structure (Appendix B). The *expense ratio* expresses the operating costs that are periodically deducted from the fund's assets as a percentage of total assets under management. Active management may explain the relatively high expense ratio of 1.19% for the Goldman Sachs Growth and Income fund when compared to the 0.38% of Vanguard.[16] With the exception of Vanguard, the other three funds charge a commission or sales charge, called front(-end) load, which is paid when the shares are purchased (4.25%–5.75%).[17]

3.6 *Comparison with portfolio-composition-based style analysis*

Instead of relying exclusively on past returns, portfolio-composition-based style analysis builds the characteristics of the managed portfolio from knowledge of the characteristics

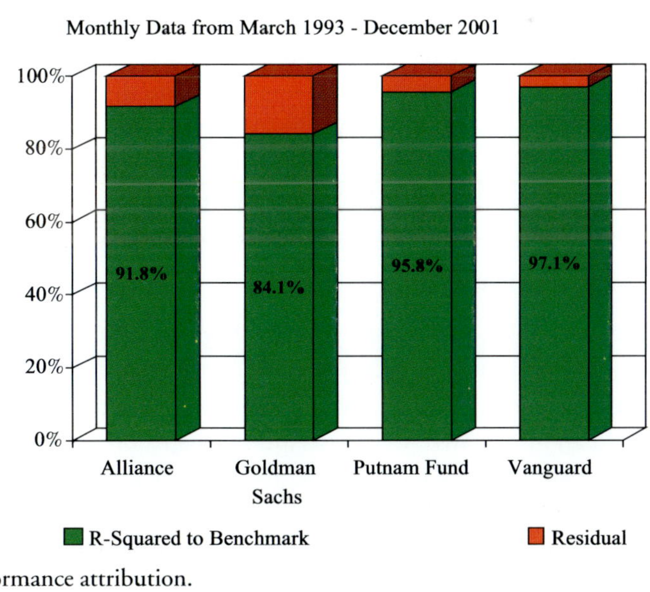

Figure 7 Performance attribution.

of individual securities that make up the portfolio. The following characteristics are typically used for stocks: market capitalization, book-to-market ratio, historic earnings growth rate, dividend yield, and industry or economic sector to which the stock belongs. Duration and credit rating are some of the commonly used characteristics for fixed-income securities. Aggregating the information explains the typical average characteristics of the portfolio. The return on the managed fund can be analyzed by examining how the manager deviated from the performance benchmark.

In what follows, we consider the Goldman Sachs Growth and Income Fund in order to illustrate the use of portfolio-composition-based style analysis. The reader who is interested in more examples is referred to the BARRA fundamental analysis for the AT&T Pension fund that is described in Sharpe (1992b).

Table 2 (Panel A) contains the characteristics of the fund when compared with the S&P 500. The fund holds 95 stocks with a median market capitalization of $27.8 billion, which is roughly half of the median market capitalization of the S&P 500. The price-to-earnings and price/cash flow ratios are lower than these for the S&P 500. The price-to-book ratio is higher as one would expect. This confirms the conclusion reached from return-based style analysis and the Morningstar classification that the Goldman Sachs Growth and Income Fund resembles a value/growth blend. Consistent with an income fund, the long-term earnings are higher than for the S&P 500. The fund is a pure equity fund with no bond holdings and a minor cash position. The results of return-based style analysis found a moderate exposure to foreign equity, which is confirmed by the portfolio weight for foreign holdings of 4.9% at the end of January 2002. Panel B of Table 2 shows the sector breakdown and Panel C the top 10 holdings. When compared to the S&P 500, the fund's weights are tilted towards financials and services and away from retail, technology, and health.

A limitation of return-based style analysis is that the style we calculate represents an average of the styles employed by the fund in the past. While portfolio-composition-based analysis has the advantage that it provides an estimate of the style going forward, it requires information that may be difficult to gather. Whereas asset class returns are easily available on a daily basis, updates of fundamentals may be delayed. Another advantage of return-based style analysis is that the conclusions are less sensitive to window dressing and, hence, less subject to manipulations by managers. In some situations, it is advisable to use a combination of the two methods.

4 Choosing Style Benchmarks

In this section, we discuss the importance of choosing the right style benchmark asset classes as well as some common pitfalls one should be aware of while implementing return-based style analysis in practice. An appropriate choice of the asset classes is important to obtain an informative style description, map a broad spectrum of portfolios, and draw correct conclusions about the degree of active management. We find that certain sector funds, like utilities, require the addition of sector indexes to the basic asset classes. Using Fidelity Magellan as an example, we illustrate how to interpret the results for an actively managed fund and compare the information content to peer evaluation.

Table 2 Portfolio-composition-based style analysis: Goldman Sachs Growth and Income Fund (GSGRX).

A: Fundamentals

	GSGRX	S&P 500
Number of stocks	95	500
Median market capitalization (billions)	$27.8	$58.0
Price/earnings ratio	25.1	30.3
Price/book ratio	4.2	3.7
Price/cash flow	13.2	18.9
Long-term earnings	16.2%	14.2%
Cash investments	0.1%	—
Bond holdings	0.0%	—
Foreign holdings	4.9%	—
Turnover ratio (fiscal year)	40.0%	—

B: Industry weightings

Sector breakdown (% of common stock)	GSGRX	S&P 500	Difference
Financials	36.2	17.8	18.4
Staples	11.0	8.9	2.1
Services	10.8	4.9	5.9
Industrials	10.4	11.0	–0.6
Energy	10.0	6.4	3.6
Technology	7.3	16.8	–9.5
Utilities	6.4	2.9	3.5
Health	6.3	14.9	–8.6
Retail	1.0	13.6	–12.6

C: Top 10 holdings

	Name	Sector	% Net assets	P/E	YTD return %
1	Exxon Mobil	Energy	3.35	17.64	–0.19
2	Citigroup	Financials	3.32	16.00	–13.50
3	Chevron Texaco	Energy	2.87	26.54	–8.00
4	Bank of America	Financials	2.70	12.36	–2.81
5	ConAgra	Staples	2.46	18.71	–0.66
6	Merck	Health	2.43	19.51	4.18
7	Philip Morris	Staples	2.26	13.43	13.35
8	Freddie Mac	Financials	2.18	11.18	–3.44
9	Heinz HJ	Staples	2.08	28.99	1.53
10	XL Capital	Financials	2.05	23.48	3.04

Informations based on the Morningstar website as of January 31, 2002.

4.1 *Asset class misspecification*

In this section, we demonstrate that an inadequate choice of indexes to represent asset classes can seriously distort the outcome of return-based style analysis. Buetow and Ratner (2000) combine the S&P 500 Barra Value and Growth with the Russell 2000 Value and Growth indexes to span the US equity universe. In one example, they apply return-based style analysis to the Vanguard Strategic Equity Fund and find that the results are inconsistent with the investment objectives and fundamentals of the fund. Atkinson *et al.* (2001) point out that by using these stock indexes the authors omit approximately 500 mid-cap companies—the ones accounted for by the Russell 1000 but not the S&P 500. They demonstrate that when the four Russell 3000 subindexes are used (and the adjusted R^2 as the optimization criterion), the outcome of the style analysis accurately matches the stated investment objectives of the fund.

While increasing the number of asset classes, it is important to keep in mind that some of the asset classes may be redundant. It may be possible to approximate the return on an asset class by the return on a portfolio of the other asset classes with sufficient degree of accuracy. Ignoring this introduces what is commonly known as multicollinearity among asset classes. The correlation pattern among our 12 asset classes is shown in Table 3. The three longer-term bond indexes, the SSB Treasury 1–10 yr, SSB Treasury 10+ yr and the SSB Corporate Bond index, exhibit the highest cross-correlations. Within each of the two size subindexes—the Russell 1000 and Russell 2000—the value and growth indexes have correlation coefficients of 0.72 and 0.80, respectively. The value and growth indexes are also correlated across the size classes, namely 0.72 between the Russell 1000 Value and Russell 2000 Value and 0.78 for the growth subindexes. If asset classes are highly correlated, the optimization algorithm will have difficulty in finding the loadings for the asset classes. Attributions may oscillate over time between two highly correlated asset classes and make the exposures uninformative and interpretations difficult. One way to guard against this would be to leave out asset classes when including them does not lead to a significant increase in the adjusted R^2 or a significant decrease in the AIC. We discuss the "number of asset classes" further in Section 4.2.

It is also necessary to exercise caution while constructing style benchmark asset class portfolios by subdividing major stock indexes. The collection of assets representing an asset class can critically depend on the order in which major indexes are subdivided and grouped. The following stylized example provides an illustration. Assume the universe of securities consists of four stocks with the following size ($ billions) and P/E ratios—A: with size 40 and P/E ratio 10, B: 30/15, C: 20/20, and D: 10/25. The broad stock market index consists of the four stocks with weights equal to their relative market capitalization. The total market capitalization is 100, the median market capitalization 25, and the P/E ratio 15.[18] Consider subdividing this index into value and growth. The value index will consist of A and B with a median capitalization of 35 and a P/E ratio of 12.1.[19] The characteristics of the growth index are 15/21.7. When we first divide the universe of the four securities into large and small stocks, we get the following characteristics: large (A and B) 35/12.1 and small (C and D) 15/21.7. The value and growth subindexes then have the following characteristics: large/value (consisting only of stock A) 40/10, large/growth (B) 30/15, small/value (C) 20/20, and small/growth (D) 10/25; that is, the P/E ratio of small/value is bigger compared to the large/growth subindex. Of course, this is an extremely simplified example. However, it

Table 3 Correlations.

	Salomon 3-month T-bill	SSB Treasury 1−10 yr	SSB Treasury 10+ yr	SSB Corporate Bond	Russell 1000 Value	Russell 1000 Growth	Russell 2000 Value	Russell 2000 Growth	Lehman Global Ex US Bond	MSCI EASEA	MSCI Japan
Salomon 3-month T-bill	1.00										
SSB Treasury 1−10 yr	0.19	1.00									
SSB Treasury 10+ yr	0.11	0.90	1.00								
SSB Corporate Bond	0.13	0.91	0.91	1.00							
Russell 1000 Value	0.02	0.24	0.28	0.40	1.00						
Russell 1000 Growth	0.04	0.16	0.20	0.32	0.72	1.00					
Russell 2000 Value	−0.08	0.08	0.15	0.29	0.72	0.60	1.00				
Russell 2000 Growth	−0.04	−0.02	0.04	0.18	0.53	0.78	0.80	1.00			
Lehman Global Ex US Bond	0.01	0.36	0.25	0.24	0.04	0.07	−0.08	−0.02	1.00		
MSCI EASEA	0.02	0.11	0.12	0.21	0.58	0.65	0.50	0.55	0.40	1.00	
MSCI Japan	−0.07	0.07	0.04	0.08	0.29	0.37	0.20	0.31	0.41	0.52	1.00
MSCI EMF	−0.01	−0.09	20.10	0.08	0.49	0.55	0.55	0.60	0.00	0.56	0.37

The correlation matrix is based on monthly returns from January 1988 to December 2001. The 12 asset classes are described in Appendix A.

illustrates that if value and growth stocks are not evenly distributed among size classes, subdividing an index may categorize a stock in a different style class.[20]

Specific sectors are dominated either by value or growth stocks. Typical value stock sectors are financials, energy, and, as we will see in Section 4.3, most utilities. Growth stocks are more widespread in high-tech industries like drugs, telecommunications, and computers. Siegel (1998) shows that at the end of 1996 the S&P 500 growth stocks outnumber value stocks, eight out of the largest 10 companies fall in the category growth, and the average market capitalization of value stocks is smaller.

Thus, it matters what universe is considered and what criteria are used to define the constituents of value and growth subindexes. Standard & Poor's divides the market capitalization of the S&P 500 equally into S&P 500/Barra Value and S&P 500/Barra Growth. After the rebalancing on November 6, 2002, the S&P 500/Barra Value covers approximately twice as many companies as the S&P 500/Barra Growth, more precisely 336 versus 164.[21] The style subindexes of the Russell 1000 and Russell 2000 are also subdivided such that approximately 50% of the market capitalization is assigned to value and 50% to growth. The breakpoints for the Russell 1000 in 2001 are a price-to-book ratio of 0.192 and the I/B/E/S long-term growth forecast of 14.4%. For the Russell 2000 both breakpoints are substantially higher, namely 0.418 and 18.0%.[22]

4.2 Number of asset classes

Our 12 asset classes include two size classes, large-cap and small-cap stocks, and a subdivision into value and growth.[23] Since 1997, Morningstar maps a fund in a style box by assigning stocks to one of three size classes and to one of three value/growth categories (value, growth, and a blend between value and growth).[24] The MSCI Emerging Market index could be further subdivided into Africa, Asia, Eastern Europe, and Latin America. An international investor who is seriously exposed to currency risk may consider adding currencies as additional asset classes.

While a larger number of assets automatically increases the explanatory power of the style benchmark, measured by R^2, it also introduces noise. An extensive set of asset classes contains more likely highly correlated asset classes and the optimization procedure may have difficulty to attribute exposures to asset classes. Even though the in-sample tracking improves, the interpretation of the results may become more difficult and the parameters less robust.

In some instances, an asset class that does not explicitly appear in the model can be closely represented by a combination of other asset classes. For example, Sharpe (1992a) pointed out that no additional, distinct asset class is needed when applying return-based style analysis to a fund with the focus on convertible securities. Convertible securities are most often bonds that entitle the holder to exchange each bond for a number of shares of common stock. For valuation, a convertible bond can be separated into a straight bond and call options. A call option, on the other hand, is a derivative security and can be replicated by dynamically rebalancing a portfolio of riskfree assets and stocks. When the share price of common stock is relatively low (high), the value of the call option is low (high) and the convertible bond behaves more like a straight bond (stock).

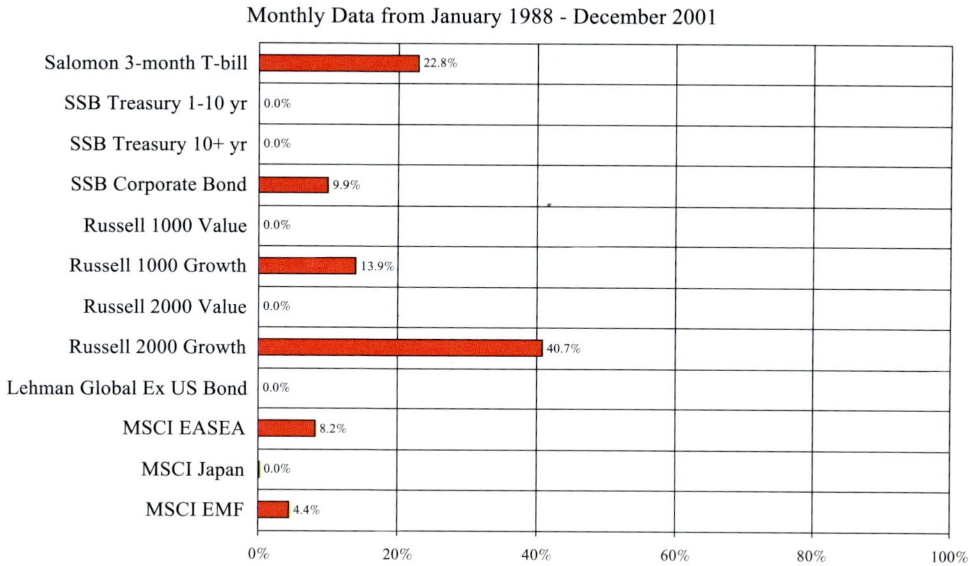

Figure 8 Fidelity Convertible Securities.

We use the Fidelity Convertible Securities Fund (FCVSX) for illustrative purposes. The Fidelity Convertible Fund "normally invests at least 80% of assets in convertible securities, which are often lower-quality debt securities [. . .]." The issuers may be domestic or foreign.[25] The style analysis captures a large fraction of the monthly variation in the fund's returns, namely $R^2 = 86.9\%$. The most pervasive factors are domestic fixed-income securities, domestic growth stocks, and, to a smaller extent, foreign equity (Figure 8). The large attribution to the Russell 2000 Growth index may reflect the strategy to buy lower-quality debt securities that are typically bonds of smaller companies. Most remarkably, the fund is characterized as a combination of fixed-income and stock exposure.

4.3 Sector indexes

The Putnam Utilities Growth and Income Fund (ticker PUGIX) defines utilities as companies that "[. . .] derive at least 50% of their assets, revenues or profits from producing or distributing electric, gas, or other types of energy, supplying water, or providing telecommunications services such as telephone, microwave or other media (but not public broadcasting)."[26]

The column labeled "Basic model" in Panel B of Table 4 reports the results of return-based style analysis when using our 12 standard asset classes. The fact that the fund primarily invests in large companies is reflected by the large attribution to the Russell 1000 Value index. At first sight, the large exposure to Treasury bonds and the zero exposure to domestic corporate bonds might be surprising. However, many utility companies still operate in highly regulated markets or investors may assume that the government will back up these companies in distressed situations. Sharpe (1992a) remarks that utility stocks display features of bonds and stocks as "revenues are

Table 4 Putnam Utilities Growth and Income Fund.

A: Correlations

Asset class	Dow US Energy	Dow US Telecoms	Dow US Utilities
Salomon 3-month T-bill	−0.03	−0.08	0.06
SSB Treasury 1−10 yr	0.14	0.12	0.20
SSB Treasury 10+ yr	0.12	0.10	0.29
SSB Corporate Bond	0.19	0.20	0.24
Russell 1000 Value	0.53	0.47	0.38
Russell 1000 Growth	0.32	0.50	0.07
Russell 2000 Value	0.36	0.20	0.22
Russell 2000 Growth	0.29	0.30	0.01
Lehman Global Ex US Bond Index	0.18	0.06	0.03
MCSI EASEA	0.35	0.28	0.10
MSCI Japan	0.25	0.20	−0.06
MSCI EMF	0.29	0.22	−0.02
Dow United States Energy	1.00	0.17	0.49
Dow United States Telecommunications	0.17	1.00	0.10
Dow United States Utilities	0.49	0.10	1.00

B: Return-based style analysis

Asset class	Basic model		Extended model	
Optimization criterion	R^2 (%)	AIC (%)	R^2 (%)	AIC (%)
Salomon 3-month T-bill	4.0	—	4.7	—
SSB Treasury 1−10 yr	7.4	—	—	—
SSB Treasury 10+ yr	20.7	26.4	—	—
SSB Corporate Bond	—	—	—	—
Russell 1000 Value	56.5	57.9	14.1	14.6
Russell 1000 Growth	—	—	—	—
Russell 2000 Value	—	—	3.2	4.0
Russell 2000 Growth	—	—	—	—
Lehman Global Ex US Bond	11.4	15.7	10.8	14.0
MCSI EASEA	—	—	—	—
MSCI Japan	—	—	—	—
MSCI EMF	—	—	—	—
Dow United States Energy			6.1	5.5
Dow United States Telecommunications			16.9	17.0
Dow United States Utilities			44.2	44.8
R^2	60.4		92.4	
Adjusted R^2	56.4	59.5	91.4	92.0

Panel A of the table shows the correlations between the three Dow Jones sector indexes and the original 12 asset classes, plus the cross–correlations in the last three rows. Panel B contains the results of return-based style analysis with the basic 12 asset classes (Basic model) and when the three sector indexes are included (Extended model). Each version is estimated using the two optimization criteria standard R^2 and the Akaike information criterion (AIC). The data is monthly from January 1992 to December 2001.

'sticky' because of the regulatory process." The Californian energy crisis disclosed the complexity of the market environment. The attempt to deregulate the power industry in California peaked in financial difficulties of two of the state's largest electric utilities, Southern California Edison and Pacific Gas & Electric Co. (filed for bankruptcy in

April 2001) and power outages. One of the reasons was the freely fluctuating wholesale prices that soared due to increasing demand while retail prices remained fixed and thus prohibited utility companies to pass the higher costs on to customers. The state of California eventually entered the energy market buying electricity.

The exposure to foreign bonds can either result from direct investments in foreign companies or American companies that are globally active. Examples are Verizon, a worldwide provider of communications services, or the UK based Vodafone Group PLC which rank among the top 10 equity holdings in October 2001. The fund targets investment-grade bonds; that is, bonds rated BBB and above or Baa and above, with intermediate- to long-term maturity. Most remarkably, the R^2 value for the analysis is very low with 60.4%.

In a second step, we perform style analysis by augmenting the asset classes by three sector indexes. We use the Dow Jones indexes for the sectors energy, telecommunications, and utilities. Panel A of Table 4 demonstrates that the correlations of the sector indexes with the other asset classes are, in general, moderate. The three cross-correlations are 0.10, 0.17, and 0.49, the latter between the Dow US Energy and Dow US Utilities. Adding the three indexes improves the adjusted R^2 dramatically from 56.4 to 91.4%. This confirms that the fund does not employ a highly active management strategy but the return pattern of utilities cannot be properly replicated by a mix of bonds and large-cap stocks. Note the exposure to bills, which results from occasionally large positions in short-term interest rate securities. As of October 2001, the fund reported holding 5.7% of its net assets in cash.[27] The cash position varies over time explaining why it is discarded when using the AIC criterion.

4.4 *Low R^2 as an indicator of active management*

The difference $(1 - R^2)$ is often used as an indicator of the level of active management. This is only true when the asset classes used for the style benchmark are correctly specified, as we have seen in the example of the Putnam Utilities Growth and Income Fund above. An incomplete or inadequate set of asset classes will lead to a low R^2 and could be misinterpreted as an indication of active management.

Going back to the initial Vanguard Windsor example illustrates this point. If in Figure 2 we use the S&P 500, a commonly used performance benchmark for large-cap funds, only 65.9% of the variation in the fund returns can be explained. The low R^2 in this case does not imply a high degree of active management. As the style box (Figure 1) indicates, the S&P 500 divides the 500 largest US companies in approximately 50% growth and 50% value. It is not the appropriate index to replicate the bias of Windsor towards value and medium-cap stocks. The asset class specification further determines what would be a low or high value for R^2. We replicate the R^2-table in Buetow, Johnson and Runkle (2000) and report the R^2s for Morningstar equity, fixed-income, hybrid, international and specialty equity indexes from January 1988 to December 2001. The values in Table 5 represent typical R^2s we would expect for a fund within a particular category. Overall, the results in the table indicate that our 12 asset classes are not suited to analyze municipal bonds and high-yield bonds.

Table 5 R^2 by fund type.

A: Bond and equity indexes

Bond indexes

Name	R^2
Short-term government	96.6
Intermediate-term government	97.4
Long-term government	97.9
Muni short-term	62.7
Muni national intermediate-term	65.3
Muni national long-term	64.7
Ultrashort-term bond	69.3
Short-term bond	95.8
Intermediate-term bond	98.7
Long-term bond	96.6
High-yield bond	46.0

Equity indexes

Name	R^2
Large value	97.9
Large blend	99.2
Large growth	97.7
Mid-cap value	94.3
Mid-cap blend	97.2
Mid-cap growth	96.1
Small value	94.2
Small blend	97.0
Small growth	96.9

B: Hybrid, international and specialty indexes

Hybrid/international indexes

Name	R^2
Convertibles	91.8
Domestic hybrid	99.1
International hybrid	94.6
World stock	96.4
Diversified Pacific/Asia	80.4
Foreign stock	94.8
Japan stock	87.8

Specialty indexes

Name	R^2
Specialty-communications	83.1
Specialty-financial	83.1
Specialty-gealth	65.7
Specialty-natural resources	48.4
Specialty-precious metals	14.8
Specialty-real estate	53.1
Specialty-technology	81.7
Specialty-utilities	63.9

The R^2 values of return-based style analysis applied to 35 Morningstar indexes are given. The calculations are based on monthly returns from January 1988 to December 2001 and the 12 asset classes described in Appendix A.

As Fung and Hsieh (1997a) remark, we could include a municipal bond index to represent non-taxable bond returns. This is particularly relevant for individual investors holding 75% of the municipal bonds that are exempted from federal income tax (see Fabozzi, 1997, chapter 9). The set of asset classes is biased towards domestic US investments and should be adapted to study international funds with a substantial exposure to currency risks. This explains the relatively low R^2s for Diversified Pacific/Asia and Japan stock funds. As we already pointed out, for sector funds the basic 12 classes should be augmented by sector indexes. In particular, we do not account for commodities, like precious metals or natural resources, and the asset classes will perform poorly when examining the exposures of REITs (Real Estate Investment Trust) or any portfolio related to real estate. Sharpe (1992a) added a mortgage index to cover this fund category.

Another indicator of active management is the turnover ratio. A low turnover ratio combined with a low R^2 is likely the result of ill-specified benchmark asset classes. A high turnover ratio or expense ratio are indicators for an actively managed fund.[28] A turnover ratio of 100% means that on average assets stay in the portfolio for 1 year.

High turnover ratios are linked to larger trading activity whereas low turnover ratios of 20–30% are typical for buy-and-hold strategies. The passive Vanguard 500 Index fund (VFINX), for example, has an extremely low turnover of 4%. According to the prospectus, the average annual turnover from 1996 to 2001 for Vanguard Windsor is 45%. The asset turnover if we would have invested in the style benchmark for this fund (Figure 4) is 4.31%.

4.5 Style consistency and changes in management

To review whether the fund has changed its style in the past, we roll a 60-month window through time. It has been previously stressed (see e.g. Sharpe, 1992a and Buetow *et al.*, 2000) that return-based style analysis always portrays the average style over the recent history. The Vanguard Balanced Index Fund (VBINX) targets a 60 : 40 allocation to two indexed portfolios of stocks and bonds. Figure 9 shows the analysis for the period from October 1992 to December 2001. The first 60 monthly returns are used to determine the style benchmark as of September 1997. Every month the analysis is repeated and the window of the past 60 monthly returns is shifted by 1 month.

Figure 9 portrays only minor changes in the exposures to the 12 asset classes. The style of the Vanguard Balanced Index Fund is truly balanced and consistent over time. The sums of the exposures to US stocks (54.8%) and bonds (43.8%) closely match the fund's self-declared investment objective. Even though Vanguard tracks different aggregates, namely the Wilshire 5000 Equity Index and the Lehman Brothers Aggregate Bond Index, the style mapping to our 12 asset classes is stable over time. The explanatory power of the style benchmark, R^2, is 99.3%, supporting the conclusion of Buetow *et al.* (2000) that return-based style analysis is especially successful where the fund strategy allocates assets to indexed asset classes.

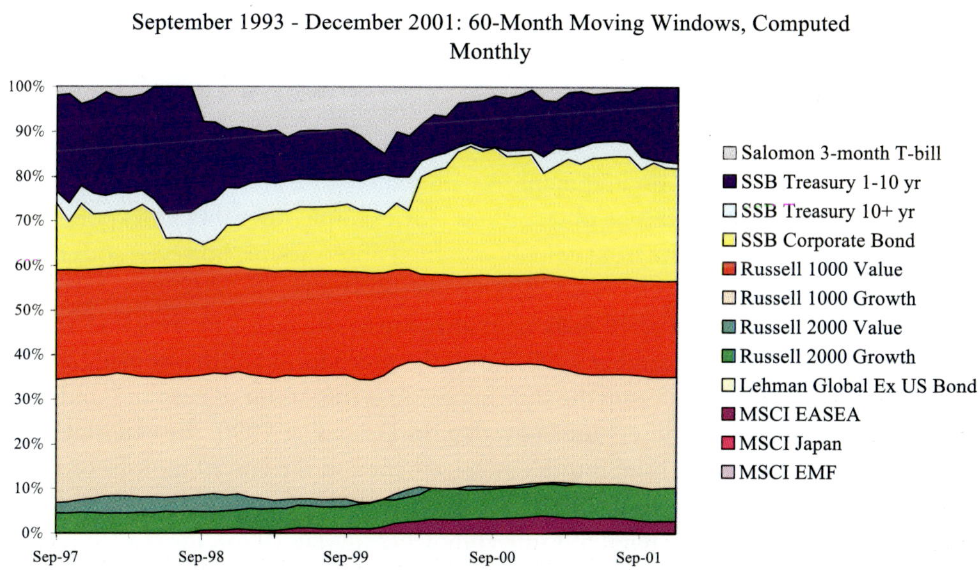

Figure 9 Style changes of Vanguard Balanced Index.

Characterizing the style of an actively managed fund poses a serious challenge and reveals the limits of return-based style analysis. For example, consider the Fidelity Magellan Fund (FMAGX). It was launched in 1963 and named after the Portuguese explorer Ferdinand Magellan who was leading the first expedition to circumnavigate the globe in 1519–22. In the prospectus (May 2002), the investment objective is outlined as seeking capital appreciation. The fund is "not constrained by any particular investment style" and switching between value and growth strategies may occur at any time. Fidelity Magellan is the world's largest actively managed fund with six million investors and $80 billion assets under management as of December 2001.

Table 6 breaks the monthly observations from January 1988 to December 2001 into the different management periods. Panel A exhibits the exposures to the basic 12 asset classes identified by return-based style analysis. The table only covers the last 2.5 years of Peter Lynch's tenure that started in May 1979. His successor, Morris Smith, pursued a similar investment philosophy although he narrowed the number of stocks from 1300 in March 1990, when Lynch announced his resignation, to about 800. He added non-bank financial stocks like insurance and money management firms.[29] Financials are typically large-cap value stocks, which may explain the increased exposure to the Russell 1000 Value. The main shift occurred from small-cap value to small-cap growth stocks.

Jeffrey Vinik's portfolio management style has been described as making sweeping sector bets like technology, holding stocks of all market capitalization, trading frenetically, and trying to time the market. He completely eliminated the exposure to large-cap growth companies and instead developed a position in large-cap value stocks. The sector bet on technology shows up in the substantial exposure to the Russell 2000 Growth index. The comparatively low R^2 of 74.1% confirms the high turnover strategy. Robert Stansky, on the other hand, trimmed the number of stocks to 250–350 and reduced the annual turnover below 40%. He favors big companies and significantly increased the average market capitalization. The average exposure to the Russell 1000 until the end of 2001 was 90.7% (37.0% Russell 1000 Value and 53.7% Russell 1000 Growth).

Next, in Figure 10 we analyze the change in style under each management using a 36-month rolling window. There is no answer on theoretical grounds as to what is the optimal length of the trailing window. Similar to the choice of the optimization criterion the window length is based on judgment. An alternative to a shorter window size is to put more weight on most recent observations, for example, by using an exponential weighting scheme. Departure from equally weighted observations, however, adds noise to the optimization process.

The vertical lines in Figure 10 indicate management changes. The time line on the horizontal axis begins in December 1990, 7 months after Morris Smith assumed control of Fidelity Magellan. In analyzing the style history, it is important to keep in mind that from month to month 35 observations overlap. In December 1990, the exposures are calculated from the 7 months of Smith's management and the last 29 months of Peter Lynch's tenure. The switch from Smith to Jeffrey Vinik demonstrates the effect of the trailing window. During the reign of Vinik (July 1992 to May 1996), the shaded region denoting exposure to the Russell 1000 Growth index is large. However, 3 years—the

Table 6 Management changes of Fidelity Magellan.

	Sample	Full	Lynch	Smith	Vinik	Stansky
	From	01/88	01/88	06/90	07/92	06/96
	To	12/01	05/90	06/92	05/96	12/01
A: Manager styles						
Asset class						
Salomon 3-month T-bill		—	—	—	—	—
SSB Treasury 1−10 yr		—	—	—	—	—
SSB Treasury 10+ yr		—	—	—	2.4%	—
SSB Corporate Bond		—	—	—	—	5.5%
Russell 1000 Value		38.4%	29.0%	37.0%	46.0%	37.0%
Russell 1000 Growth		44.3%	47.0%	45.6%	—	53.7%
Russell 2000 Value		2.3%	14.9%	—	—	—
Russell 2000 Growth		7.8%	7.7%	17.4%	29.9%	3.8%
Lehman Global Ex US Bond		—	—	—	2.8%	—
MCSI EASEA Index		4.2%	—	—	14.8%	—
MSCI Japan		3.1%	1.2%	—	3.2%	—
MSCI EMF		—	0.3%	—	0.9%	—
R-squared		93.1%	97.1%	98.3%	74.1%	96.9%
B: Excess returns						
Monthly average excess returns over 3-month T-bills						
Style benchmark		0.69	0.97	0.34	0.99	0.50
Selection		0.17	0.36	0.34	0.01	0.13
Fidelity Magellan		0.86	1.32	0.68	1.00	0.63
S&P 500		0.77	1.06	0.38	0.96	0.65
Standard deviation of excess returns over 3-month T-bills						
Style benchmark		4.13	3.59	4.50	2.21	5.18
Selection		1.15	0.77	0.82	1.67	0.94
Fidelity Magellan		4.39	3.74	5.04	2.92	5.24
S&P 500		4.08	3.76	4.36	2.23	5.05
Sharpe ratio						
Style benchmark		0.17	0.27	0.08	0.45	0.10
Selection		0.14	0.46	0.41	0.01	0.13
Fidelity Magellan		0.20	0.35	0.14	0.34	0.12
S&P 500		0.19	0.28	0.09	0.43	0.13

Panel A shows the results of return-based style analysis for the full sample and the subperiods for the four managers between January 1988 and December 2001: Peter Lynch (his tenure started in May 1979 and the table covers only the last 29 months), Morris Smith, Jeffrey Vinik, and Robert Stansky. Panel B compares the performance over the different subperiods. The mean, standard deviation, and Sharpe ratio of the monthly excess returns is divided into a style benchmark and selection component. The three statistics are also reported for the S&P 500.

length of the time window—after Vinik took over the management the attribution to the large-cap growth index vanishes. Thus, the gradually declining exposure to the Russell 1000 Growth index is a mere result of the periods overlapping with the Smith period (June 1990 to June 1992). The actual shift in the portfolio style is shown more drastically in Table 6. Considering only the observations of Vinik's period, the attribution to large-cap growth stocks is zero. During the last year of his tenure, Vinik invested in the bond market and put 19% of the fund into long-term US Treasury bonds, a bet that likely accelerated his exit as stock markets went up. The spike can be

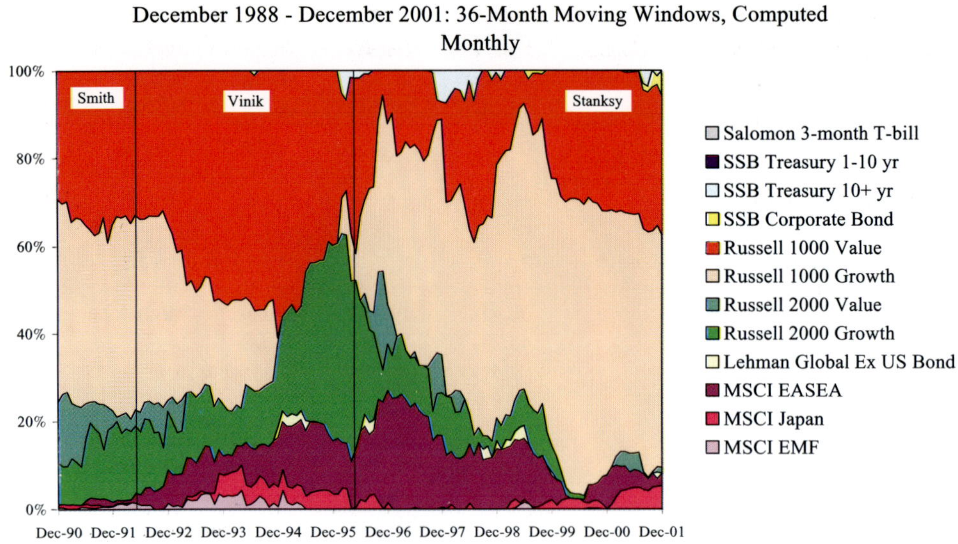

Figure 10 Style changes in Fidelity Magellan.

seen at the top of the graph. At the end of March 1996, the top three holdings were long-term (10 and 30-year) Treasury bonds.[30]

Robert Stansky quickly moved into large-growth stocks, computer companies like Cisco, Dell, and Oracle, health care, and retail.[31] His style is described as picking blue-chip companies and preferring growth stocks—before his engagement with Magellan he managed the Fidelity Growth Fund. Stansky made one of the biggest bets starting in August 1998. Technology stock prices were corrected downwards during the summer and "he went on a buying spree" as the succeeding sharp increase in the weight of the Russell 1000 Growth index shows. By the end of 1998, the position in tech stocks reached 25.8% of the assets.[32] The style history visualizes the large exposure to large-cap growth stocks. Consistent with the finding of Table 6, the attribution to the Russell 2000 Growth quickly passed out of the trailing window.

Panel B of Table 6 describes the risk-return tradeoff for Fidelity Magellan over the full sample and for each management period separately. The mean and standard deviation of the monthly excess returns are broken down into the fraction that can be explained by the style benchmark and the selection component. As a reference point, the last row reports the corresponding value for the S&P 500.

Besides average returns and standard deviations, the table contains the average Sharpe ratio over time. The Sharpe ratio of the selection component of Lynch (during the last 2.5 years) and Smith is better than for the other two. The market during Vinik's period is characterized by high average returns, low volatility, and a high Sharpe ratio of 0.43 for the S&P 500. However, his value for the selection component is the lowest among all four managers. The consistently positive Sharpe ratios for the selection components documents the success of Fidelity Magellan over the 13 years.

In his critique of return-based style analysis, Christopherson (1995) raises the point that the style based on historic data is misleading. It is correct that due to the rolling window there is a delay until a permanent shift in the style becomes apparent. As Trzcinka (1995) replies, in this case the addition of portfolio data can be valuable to detect a shift earlier. However, data describing firm characteristics may become available later, whereas returns for the asset classes are easily available on a daily basis at low cost. Using weekly or daily data and comparing the deviations of the fund from what you would expect from the style can also indicate substantial departures from the style in a timely manner.

4.6 Manager universes and peer evaluation

Funds often reference their position within a manager universe. "Based on the portfolio statistics and compositions over the past 3 years," Morningstar assigns five stars if a fund is within the top 10% of similar funds. Lipper Index Service provides more than 85 indexes to classify and rank fund performance relative to their peers.[33]

The peer evaluation in the prospectus of Fidelity Magellan (May 22, 2002) raises some questions. The fund is compared to the Lipper Large-Cap Core Funds Average and the Lipper Large-Cap Supergroup Average over the past 1, 5, and 10-years. The Large-Cap Core Funds covers mutual funds with similar portfolio characteristics and capitalization and the Large-Cap Supergroup is only based on comparable capitalization. Given the big changes in Fidelity Magellan's investment style, a 10-year return comparison with the two manager universes is not informative. As we have seen in Table 6, during the tenure of Jeffrey Vinik from July 1992 to May 1996, the average exposure to the Russell 2000 Growth—measuring small-cap companies—was 29.9%. At the end of 2001, the Vanguard Growth & Income Fund we analyzed in Figure 6 also ranked among the 30 funds constituting the Lipper Large-Cap Core Funds Index. As we have seen, a balanced mix of Russell 1000 Value and Growth is a good proxy for this fund.

Bailey (1992) argues that peer evaluation violates key assumptions of a good benchmark and the median manager is only specifiable *ex post*. It is well documented that manager universe averages are upwardly biased due to survivorship bias. Poorly performing funds are eliminated from the database or cease operation. The results on the survivorship bias by Grinblatt and Titman (1989), Brown *et al.* (1995), and Malkiel (1995) indicate that mutual fund returns are overstated by 0.1–1.4%.

5 Style Analysis of Hedge Funds

Hedge funds are less regulated than mutual funds. They are typically available only to institutional investors and individual investors who meet certain minimum wealth constraints.[34] Unlike mutual funds that follow a defined investment strategy and are limited to investing in specific asset classes, hedge funds have substantial amount of freedom to choose from among a variety of investment strategies. For example, hedge funds can take short positions in securities and trade in derivative assets whereas most mutual funds cannot do so. In order to align the incentives of hedge fund managers who have more flexibility in terms of what investment strategy to choose with that of investors, hedge fund managers are compensated with an incentive fee of 15–20% in addition to a 1–2% management fee (see Fung and Hsieh, 1999; Liang, 2000).[35] Hedge fund managers also have a substantial amount of their own wealth invested in the funds they manage.

The importance of hedge funds as an investment vehicle has increased in the recent past. TASS Management Limited (TASS), based on reports from 2722 funds, estimates that hedge funds as a group had between $450 and $500 billion under management in 2001.[36] For tax reasons many hedge funds are domiciled offshore. According to Brown *et al.* (1999), at the end of 1996, hedge funds reporting to Managed Account Reports (MAR) had $68 billion assets under management and $31.7 billion managed by offshore entities. The variety of hedge funds is almost unlimited. TASS assigns hedge funds to nine major categories, with long/short equity hedge funds totaling 44%. The Hedge Fund Research Inc. (HFR) classifies hedge fund styles into 33 categories.

Performing return-based style analysis using traditional asset classes is unsuitable for determining the effective style of hedge funds due to their low correlations with returns on traditional asset classes. For example, using eight traditional asset classes, Fung and Hsieh (1997a) find that 48% of the hedge funds had R^2s of less than 25%, whereas more than half of the mutual funds had R^2s above 75%. Unlike mutual funds that have mainly positive exposures to asset classes and relatively large exposures to US stocks and bonds, hedge funds have significant exposure to most asset classes, with 25% of the exposures being negative.

Traditional mutual funds follow well-defined investment strategies. A typical mutual fund manager is mainly engaged in selection, that is, selects mispriced securities that belong to some pre-specified asset classes. In contrast, a hedge fund manager will often time the market, sectors, and countries by actively moving the money around, invest in derivative securities, and engage in dynamic trading strategies that exploit relative mispricing among securities. In that case, return-based style analysis will, in general, not be able to capture the manager's effective style. For example, consider a portfolio of short positions in puts and calls on the S&P 500 index. The return on the position will depend on the return on the S&P 500 in a nonlinear way. The position will result in losses for large changes in the index value and will result in gains otherwise. However, the position can be formed in such a way that its beta as well as its R^2 in return-based style analysis is zero. Clearly, return-based style analysis using standard asset classes is of little value in this case.

Even when a hedge fund does not directly invest in derivative securities, its returns may exhibit option-like features because of active changing of positions across asset classes.[37] Merger arbitrage, a commonly employed hedge fund investment strategy, would be an example that exhibits an option-like payoff structure even though the strategy does not involve derivative securities. When a merger or an acquisition is announced and there is no uncertainty regarding the deal going through, the target firm's stock price should trade at the price it is offered by the acquirer. This need not be the case when there is substantial deal uncertainty. Typically, target firms trade at a discount to their value based on the offer price. Merger arbitrage attempts to capture the spread between the target's price and the offering price by taking a long position in the target and a short position in the acquirer. Mitchell and Pulvino (2001) demonstrate that merger arbitrage strategy returns are "positively correlated with market returns in severely depreciating markets but uncorrelated with market returns in appreciating markets." They conclude that the return to merger arbitrage resembles the return on uncovered puts on the market index. Hence, return-based style analysis using traditional asset classes will not be able to capture the risk associated with the return on merger arbitrage strategies. In what follows, we discuss these issues further and show how return-based style analysis can be modified.

5.1 Additional asset classes for return-based style analysis of hedge funds

It would be difficult to capture the effective style of a hedge fund manager just by increasing the number of style benchmarks by additional standard asset classes. As Glosten and Jagannathan (1994) point out, the returns on portfolios managed using active strategies—as is the case with hedge funds—would exhibit option-like features. Fung and Hsieh (2001) and Mitchell and Pulvino (2001) empirically demonstrate that returns generated by hedge fund strategies do indeed exhibit significant nonlinear, option-like patterns. The nonlinear return pattern results from the use of derivatives, either explicitly or implicitly through the use of dynamic trading.

When a manager's return is related to the benchmark returns in a nonlinear manner, it would be difficult to identify the selection component of the manager's return using linear factor models, of which return-based style analysis is a special case. For example, Jagannathan and Korajczyk (1986) and Grinblatt and Titman (1989) showed that if investors were to evaluate the performance of a manager by measures like Jensen's alpha or the Treynor–Black appraisal ratio, then a manager selling call options on a standard benchmark will appear to be falsely classified as a superior performer. Merton (1981) and Dybvig and Ross (1985) noted that portfolios managed with superior information would typically result in returns that exhibit option-like features even when the managers do not explicitly trade in options.

Glosten and Jagannathan (1994) suggested augmenting the return on style benchmark indexes with returns on selected options on the style benchmark indexes in order to capture the investment style of portfolio managers who employ dynamic trading strategies. Instead, we suggest following a two-step approach when analyzing hedge funds using return-based style analysis. In the first step, we augment the traditional asset classes with a set of selected hedge fund style benchmark indexes for characterizing the effective style of an individual fund. An example of such a style benchmark index would be the return on a portfolio of hedge funds that specialize in merger arbitrage.[38] One would need a collection of such benchmarks, one for every commonly used hedge fund strategy. In the second step, we analyze the nature of the risks in these benchmarks using return-based style analysis after augmenting traditional asset classes with a collection of options on those asset classes, as we demonstrate later on.

This two-step approach has the following advantage. On average, the hedge fund industry is young and the data history of hedge funds is short. Many hedge fund strategies are characterized by significant left-tail risk, that is, the fund's return becomes largely negative in the event of a sharp unexpected drop in asset class returns. These events are rare and may not appear often enough in the sample to be captured with sufficient accuracy using options on standard asset classes. Once we have identified the effective style of a hedge fund using the pure strategy benchmarks we discussed earlier, we can go back in history to evaluate the risk in those pure strategies using options on asset classes with a larger time series of data. The use of a longer time series will facilitate better appreciation of the risk in these pure strategies that arises due to excessive exposure to extreme events.

Suppose these additional, pure strategies so identified are investable. Then, we can augment our standard asset classes with these benchmark hedge fund strategies or styles. Denote the additional style benchmark returns that are necessary to capture the effective style of hedge funds by y_n and their loadings by c_n. Then, Eq. (2a) becomes:

$$\begin{aligned} r_{p,t} = {} & [b_{p,1}x_{1,t} + \cdots + b_{p,N}x_{N,t}] + [c_{p,1}y_{1,t} + \cdots \\ & + c_{p,N}y_{N,t}] + e_{p,t} \quad \text{for } t = 1, 2, \ldots, T \end{aligned} \tag{2a$'$}$$

As of now, a set of such benchmarks is not available. In its absence we will use the indexes constructed by the Hedge Fund Research Institute (HFR) for illustrative purposes. In what follows, we show that including HFR indexes as additional style benchmarks does improve the R^2 in style regressions when analyzing individual hedge funds. For that purpose we use the Hudson Valley fund classified in TASS as a fund employing an event-driven strategy. Since hedge funds can take short positions, we do not restrict the coefficients in return-based style analysis to be positive when analyzing hedge funds.[39]

The results are given in Table 7. Style analysis using standard asset classes gives an R^2 of 21.8%. When AIC is used to screen out redundant asset classes we are left only with three asset classes: 83.0% weight on Salomon 3-month T-bills, 14.3% weight on the Russell 2000 Value index, and 2.7% weight on the MSCI Japanese stock index. The 18.4% adjusted R^2 for the style regression with these three asset classes is higher than the 15.3% adjusted R^2 when all 12 traditional asset classes are used, indicating that the other traditional asset classes are not required. The adjusted R^2 increases from 18.4 to 72.1% (with the AIC as the optimization criterion) when the HFR Merger Arbitrage index is included as a style benchmark. The substantial increase confirms the need to add additional style benchmarks when analyzing hedge funds. The merger arbitrage index gets a weight of 96.2%, indicating that the Hudson Valley hedge fund is primarily a one-strategy fund. We now go on to characterize the risk in the HFR Merger Arbitrage index we used to augment the traditional asset classes.

5.2 *Characterizing the risk in two hedge fund strategies: merger arbitrage and market timing*

Academic research has identified the payoff pattern for a few hedge fund strategies: market timing, equity non-hedge and short selling are directional strategies; merger arbitrage (at least in its pure form) and equity hedge aim to have low correlation with the market and make non-directional bets by providing liquidity where it is needed and

Table 7 Analysis of an individual event-driven hedge fund.

Asset classes	Basic		Basic plus HFR Merger Arbitrage Index	
Optimization criterion	R^2 (%)	AIC (%)	R^2 (%)	AIC (%)
Salomon 3-month T-bill	108.6	83.0	18.3	8.9
SSB Treasury 1—10 yr	−31.8	—	−6.3	—
SSB Treasury 10+ yr	8.5	—	5.1	—
SSB Corporate Bond	0.7	—	−11.6	—
Russell 1000 Value	6.2	—	0.8	—
Russell 1000 Growth	−0.2	—	2.2	—
Russell 2000 Value	8.2	14.3	−2.7	—
Russell 2000 Growth	2.4	—	0.5	—
Lehman Global Ex US Bond	−3.2	—	−3.8	−6.0
MCSI EASEA	−1.8	—	−1.8	—
MSCI Japan	3.1	2.7	2.2	2.6
MSCI EMF	−0.6	—	−1.3	−1.7
HFR Merger Arbitrage			98.4	96.2
R^2	21.8		73.8	
Adjusted R^2	15.3	18.4	71.4	72.1

The results of return-based style analysis using different sets of asset classes are provided. The monthly returns for Hudson Valley Partners LP are from January 1990 to December 2001.

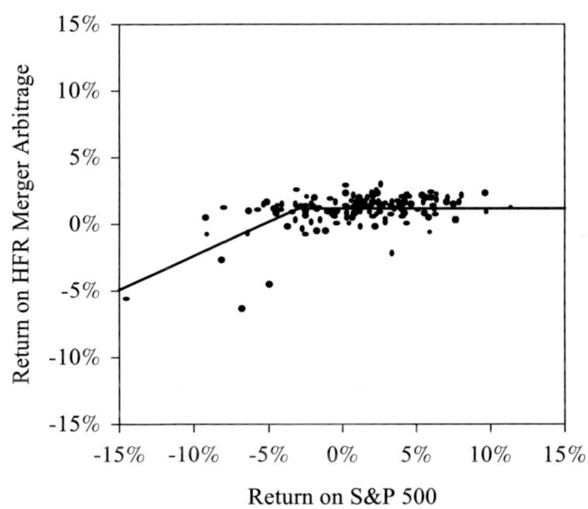

Figure 11 HFR Merger Arbitrage.

exploit relative mispricing of securities. In this section, we examine merger arbitrage and market timing. We will discuss the three equity-oriented strategies, equity non-hedge, equity hedge, and short selling, in Section 5.4.

We use monthly data from January 1990 to December 2001 of the HFR Merger Arbitrage and Market Timing indexes (for a description see Appendix C). Figures 11 and 12 show the returns of the two strategies against the S&P 500. We fit the payoff of a short put option and a straddle to these strategies.[40] The kinked line in the left scatter plot (Figure 11) shows a put option payoff diagram fitted to the data. Going short a put

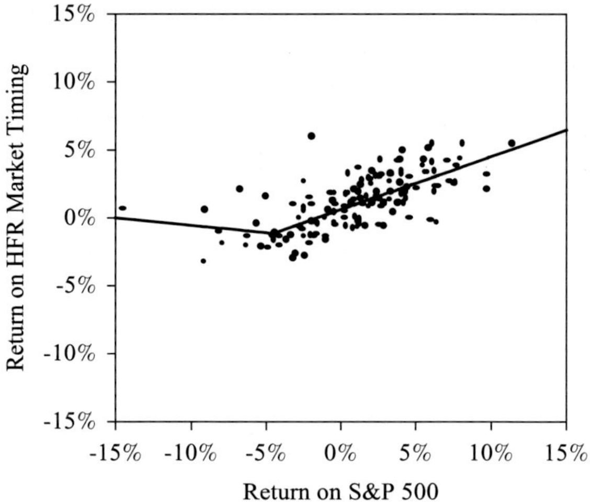

Figure 12 HFR Market Timing.

option on the S&P 500 will earn the premium if the market is above the exercise price. The kink (exercise price) is at −3.0% and the level to the right at 1.2%. The slope on the downside is 0.509. Fitting a straddle to the HFR Market Timing index in Figure 12 positions the kink at −4.5%. As expected, the slope to the right is positive 0.391 and negative −0.012 to the left. For a perfect market timer we would definitely expect a more symmetric pattern. There are many possible reasons why this is not the case: some hedge funds in the category "market timing" try only to time appreciating markets and otherwise hold positions in the money market (which agrees with the description of the HFR Market Timing index in Appendix C), shorting certain securities is more difficult than being long, and the funds in the index are after all not perfect market timers. However, both diagrams confirm the option-like payoff patterns.

In the next step, we incorporate traded options that mimic these payoffs into return-based style analysis. We use data on option returns calculated from at-the-money (ATM) and out-of-the-money (OTM) call and put options on the S&P 500 Composite Index provided by Agarwal and Naik (2002). In addition, we drop the restriction (2b) of the classic return-based style analysis and allow for short positions. The negative weights make it possible to create new artificial return series as linear combinations of the existing ones. For example, a combination of long and short positions in the three classes of Treasury securities will, in general, help capture the interest rate exposure of the hedge fund strategy using return-based style analysis more accurately. However, as can be seen from Figure 13, when we use the AIC that penalizes strongly additional variables the wildly fluctuating long and short positions in the three Treasury securities classes disappear, but the adjusted R^2 remains about the same. Mitchell and Pulvino (2001) observe that in the sample of mergers and acquisitions that they examine the target firm is typically smaller than the acquirer. Agarwal and Naik (2002) find evidence that more often the acquirer is a large growth firm and the target is a smaller value firm. The results in Figure 13 are consistent with these findings. To exploit risk arbitrage an

January 1990 - December 2001, Calculated Using the Akaike Criterion

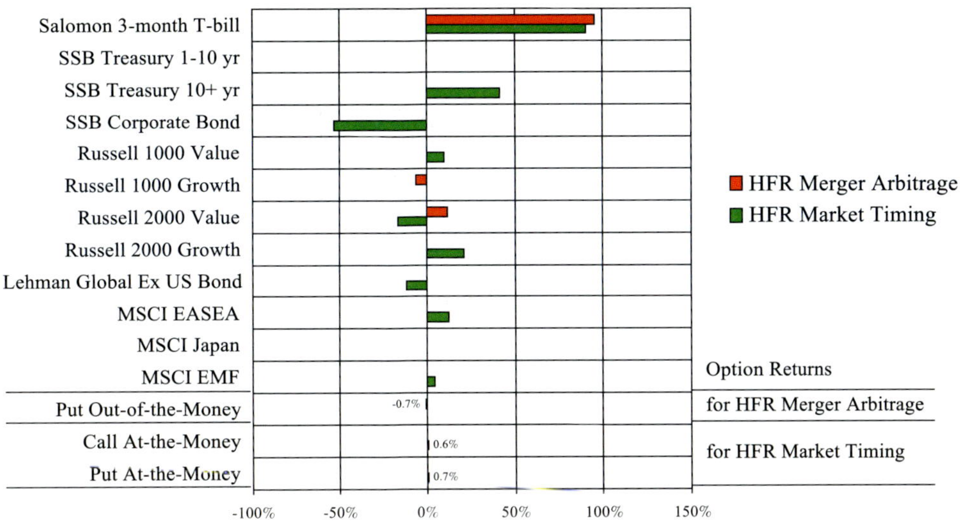

Figure 13 Style analysis with options.

investor would on average go short the acquiring firm, that is, Russell 1000 Growth, and long the target firm, that is, Russell 2000 Value.

The weight of −0.7% on the put options for merger arbitrage appears to be small. However, we have to keep in mind that even when the weight attached to a written option position is small, it can have significant amount of sensitivity to tail events. For example, consider investing $100 in cash and writing 1.2 index put options with an exercise price of $90 and 3 months to maturity when the current index value is $100. Suppose the interest rate is 5% per year and the index volatility is 20% per year. Then, the Black-Scholes put option value will be $0.55. The portfolio will have $100 in T-bills and −$0.66 in index put options, that is, 100.7% of the funds invested in T-bills and −0.7% invested in out-of-the-money index put options. Suppose the index value drops steeply to $80 right after forming the position, that is, a 20% drop. The position will lose $12, that is, a 12% drop. Hence, the position can lose a significant amount in severely depreciating markets even though most of the money is in T-bills.

We have to be careful in interpreting R^2 values—even when the R^2 is relatively low, there can be significant tail event risk. For merger arbitrage and market timing the adjusted R^2 increases from 29.9 and 60.8%, respectively, to 38.8 and 64.6%, when option returns are included (Figure 13). Figure 14 shows the style changes for the HFR Merger Arbitrage index over time. The negative exposures are displayed below the horizontal axis. In order to make the OTM put option position visible, it is scaled up by a factor of 10, that is, the exposure to put options with 1/10 of the return are shown. Spikes represent drastic changes as each data point represents an average exposure over the past 36 observations. Taking into account that this figure plots the style shifts for an index, where idiosyncratic risk is averaged out, we get an idea of the dynamics of the strategies hedge funds implement.

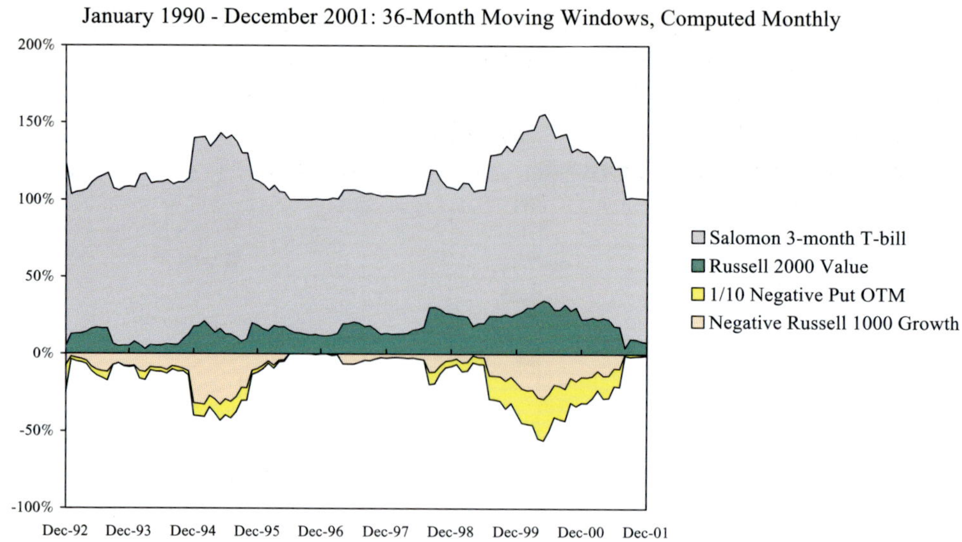

Figure 14 Style changes of HFR Merger Arbitrage.

5.3 *Index choice and survivorship bias*

There are three major providers for hedge fund indexes. (i) Credit Suisse First Boston/Tremont (CT) provides indexes that are value-weighted and based on the TASS database. Only funds with at least $10 million in assets and audited financial statements are included in the indexes. (ii) In contrast, Hedge Fund Research (HFR) indexes are equally-weighted without any minimum asset size requirements. Due to legal arrangements the constituents of the HFR indexes are not disclosed. (iii) Managed Account Reports (MAR) indexes correspond to the performance of the median manager within the investment style class and are available beginning January 1994.[41] Note that the correlations among the three indexes for some hedge fund strategies are low. For example, the correlations for the strategy named "market neutral" are between 0.26 and 0.37 among the three indexes. This is an indication that hedge funds most often follow a mixture of strategies. It is difficult to form a fixed-weight portfolio of these funds that accurately represents a particular pure hedge fund strategy. Hence, the conclusions reached using one set of indexes may be reversed when another set of indexes is used, highlighting the need for caution in interpreting the results from return-based style analysis.

When evaluating managers using indexes it is important to keep in mind that the way funds are included in the index may bias the conclusions. In many cases index providers include hedge funds after they already existed for some time. At the time of inclusion the history of returns is backfilled in the database. The average return on such funds will in general overstate what investors expected since these funds ended up successfully and survived. Fung and Hsieh (2000b) discuss the biases that arise due to this practice. The survivorship bias can be large. For example, in the sample of Brown, Goetzmann, and Ibbotson (1999), only 25 out of 108 hedge funds survived over the 7 years from 1989 to 1995. Survivorship rates also vary across databases.

Ackerman, McEnally, and Ravenscraft (1999), Fung and Hsieh (2000b), and Liang (2000) report higher attrition rates in TASS than HFR. Fung and Hsieh (1997b) discuss the survivorship bias for CTAs and argue that it can substantially overstate the benchmark return. Based on a sample of offshore hedge funds Brown, Goetzmann, and Ibbotson (1999) find a survivorship bias of approximately 3% per year, similar to the bias found by Fung and Hsieh (2000b) for the hedge funds reporting to TASS. Due to the lack of data on defunct hedge funds the quality of the databases is low during the period prior to 1994 (see Fung and Hsieh, 2000b, 2002).

5.4 Equity-oriented strategies

We saw earlier that the hedge fund strategy "merger arbitrage," while in general uncorrelated with the market, loses money when the market sharply depreciates. In that sense, the payoff from the strategy resembles selling disaster insurance. The strategy rarely loses money, but when it does, the amount of the loss can be large and the associated risk is systematic and not diversifiable. Several hedge fund strategies involve this type of excessive sensitivity to tail events. In the history of returns available to the investor, such events may not have taken place with sufficient regularity to accurately assess the probability of their occurrence. In that case, the coefficients for index options included as additional asset classes when analyzing benchmark hedge fund strategies may not be significant; and the investor is left to analyze the risks associated with those strategies through introspection.

For example, consider equity-oriented strategies. According to TASS, 44% of the hedge funds can be classified as equity-oriented strategies. These hedge funds try to time the market and take short and long positions in overvalued and undervalued stocks, respectively. HFR differentiates between three equity-oriented strategies: equity non-hedge, equity hedge, and short selling (for a description see Appendix C). Equity non-hedge funds predominantly hold long positions in equities. Equity-hedge funds eliminate part of the systematic risk in the bets they take by using short positions, stock options, and index options, depending on market conditions. Hedge funds in the short selling category sell securities they do not own and consider to be overvalued. They anticipate a price decline and expect to buy the securities back at a future date at a lower price. These types of hedge funds still have substantial correlations with the standard asset classes. The correlation for equity non-hedge with the S&P 500 is 0.86, for equity hedge still 0.64, and for short selling −0.69.

Figure 15 shows the exposures for the three equity-oriented strategies using the AIC criterion. The estimated effective style for the HFR Short Selling index has a 167.2% long position in the Salomon 3-month T-bill index and a combined 90.8% short position in Russell 2000 Growth and MSCI Japan (plus a 24.8% long position in the Russell 2000 Value), with an associated adjusted R^2 of 81.3%. The finding that the short selling strategy has no negative exposure to the MSCI EMF confirms the observation that in many emerging markets short selling is prohibited. Even in the most advanced stock exchanges, like Hong Kong, restricted short selling was allowed only recently (see Frank and Jagannathan, 1998).

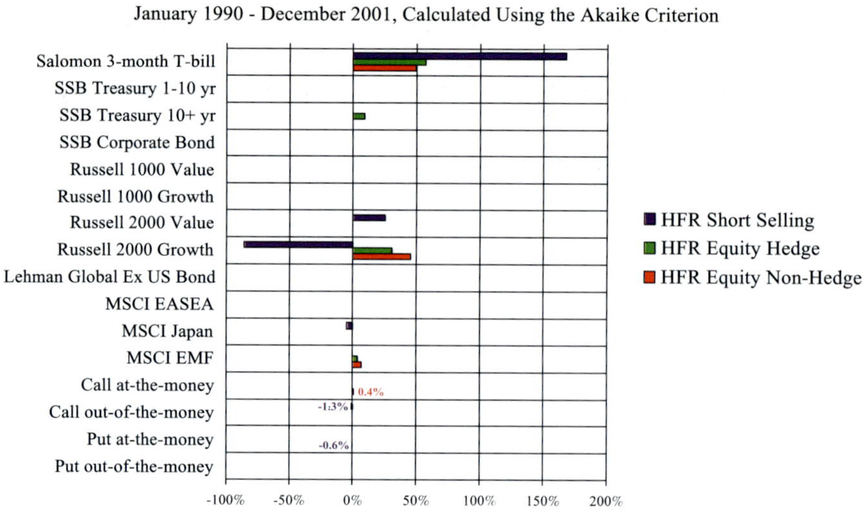

Figure 15 Style analysis for equity-oriented hedge fund strategies.

The effective style for HFR Equity Hedge consists of a portfolio of Salomon 3-month T-bills, SSB Treasury 10+ yr, Russell 2000 Growth, and MSCI EMF with an adjusted R^2 of 73.9%. The HFR Equity Non-Hedge exhibits a major exposure to the Russell 2000 Growth and also to the MSCI EMF with an associated adjusted R^2 in the style regression of 91.6%. The portfolio is tilted towards small and growth equities, which is consistent with the view that small growth companies are more likely to be mispriced. For example, Bogle (1998) finds that out of the nine style classes in the Morningstar style box only for the small-cap growth category the average actively managed funds outperformed a passive index. The exposure to the MSCI EMF is in line with Agarwal and Naik (2002) who use stepwise regression in their analysis.

The coefficients for index options are small for all three strategies (between -1.3 and $+0.4\%$), even though one may suspect that index options may be relevant. For example, the equity hedge strategy may involve taking simultaneous long and short positions in two stocks in the Russell 1000 Value index resulting in zero exposure to Russell 1000 Value. While the two stocks may have similar sensitivity to small market moves, they may have different sensitivity to the market for large moves. If sharp moves in the market occur over a short period of time, the position may show large gains or losses similar to a portfolio of out-of-the-money options. In the data used for return-based style analysis there may be no such large sharp price movements but that does not mean that such a move may not occur in the future.

A word of caution is in order when using return-based style analysis, especially for hedge funds. Given the flexibility allowed to hedge fund managers, an individual hedge fund manager may choose strategies in the future that may be very different from the ones employed in the past. Hence, the risks and rewards from any given individual fund may be vastly different from that indicated by return-based style analysis. An investigation of individual hedge funds in the TASS database indicates that the R^2s can be low. This suggests that a given fund may be following strategies that are difficult to capture sufficiently accurately using the style benchmark asset classes we discussed. Therefore, an investor will have to obtain additional information regarding a fund's strategies through discussions with the hedge fund manager and arrive at the right collection of asset classes to use in return-based style analysis of that fund.

5.5 *Stepwise regression to identify major exposures*

In our examples we used the AIC to select which style benchmarks to leave out in return-based style analysis. Stepwise regression is another commonly used technique that would be useful for that purpose. It has been applied in the hedge fund literature by Liang (1999), Fung and Hsieh (2000b), and Agarwal and Naik (2002), to determine pervasive factors. The forward stepwise regression starts with a constant term on the right hand side. At each step, the most significant term, that is, the one with the highest F-statistic, is added to the model. We use a 5% significance level as the threshold for the inclusion of an additional parameter. The model is re-estimated and it is tested whether any variable can be removed without loss of much explanatory power. Note that the R^2 values in stepwise regressions tend to be upwardly biased and the standard significance tests of the coefficients do not apply.

The results obtained using stepwise regression are given in Table 8. We did not impose the constraint that the coefficients sum to one in the stepwise regressions. Instead we normalize the coefficients by dividing by the absolute value of the sum of the coefficients. We compare the results of the stepwise regression in Table 8 to Figures 14 and 15. The striking result is that the adjusted R^2 values do not change much when the stepwise regression approach is used even though we did not impose the constraint that the coefficients sum to one. The coefficients for the different asset classes differ by a large amount, suggesting that there are several equivalent ways to describe the effective style using these asset classes. The set of coefficients we pick by imposing the constraint that they must sum to one in return-based style analysis appears more reasonable given the strategies implied by the style names. When the R^2 is low, this indeterminacy may indicate the difficulties associated with replicating the returns by any fixed-weight portfolio of the style benchmark asset classes.

6 Conclusions

Return-based style analysis helps investors understand the effective style of funds in which they invest in, monitor and evaluate managers to whom they entrust their money, and ensure that their asset allocation is consistent with their investment objectives. Return-based analysis is easy to implement and interpret and is a useful precursor to more detailed analysis based on the actual portfolio holdings.

Proper use of the technique requires correct specification of the style benchmark asset classes. Inappropriate or inadequate choice of style benchmarks can lead to wrong characterization of the effective style of the portfolio manager and the level of active management. The use of the Akaike information criterion helps narrow down the number of asset classes required for capturing the effective style of a manager.

Table 8 Stepwise regression analysis.

Asset class	Merger Arbitrage	Market Timing	Short Selling	Equity Hedge	Equity Non-Hedge
Constant/Salomon 3-month T-Bill	13.3%	5.9%	1.4%	3.8%	1.7%
SSB Treasury 1–10 yr	—	—	—	—	—
SSB Treasury 10 +yr	—	—	—	—	—
SSB Corporate Bond	—	—	—	—	—
Russell 1000 Value	—	—	—	—	—
Russell 1000 Growth	❸ −99.8%	—	—	—	—
Russell 2000 Value	❶ 197.7%	❹ −62.7%	❸ 42.1%	—	—
Russell 2000 Growth	—	❷ 95.1%	❶ −141.3%	❶ 96.2%	❶ 85.8%
MCSI EASEA	—	—	—	—	—
MSCI Japan	—	❸ 57.8%	—	—	—
MSCI EMF	—	—	—	—	❸ 12.8%
Call ATM		❶ 3.9%	—	—	❹ 0.8%
Call OTM			❷ −2.2%	—	—
Put ATM		—	—	—	❷ −1.2%
Put OTM	❷ −11.2%		—	—	—
Adjusted R^2	37.4%	60.6%	82.0%	73.0%	91.7%

Estimation results for HFR Merger Arbitrage, Market Timing, and the three equity-oriented indexes Equity Non-Hedge, Equity Hedge and Short Selling. The corresponding columns contain the results of a forward-stepwise regression on the twelve asset classes and the additional options. The numbers indicate the order in which the variables are added. The threshold significance levels for adding and removing variables are 5% and 10%, respectively.

Return-based style analysis characterizes the average style of a manager over a period of time. While it is possible to detect style rotation to some extent using return-based style analysis, the procedure may not be able to detect short-lived style deviations even when they are large in magnitude. As is the case with all analysis that relies on historical data, it is necessary to exercise caution in making forecasts about the future based on past performance.

The method can be modified to examine the effective style of hedge fund managers by augmenting traditional asset classes with benchmark hedge fund style indexes, each of which represents the return on a particular pure hedge fund strategy. Return-based style analysis using traditional asset classes augmented by carefully chosen index options can then be used to characterize the risks in the pure hedge fund strategies that the hedge fund style indexes represent. Given that hedge fund managers are typically reluctant to disclose their holdings, portfolio-composition-based style analysis may not be feasible for hedge funds.

Acknowledgments

We thank David A. Hsieh for providing the hedge fund returns, Vikas Agarwal and Narayan Naik for the options strategy returns, and Gordon Alexander, Tom Idzorek, and Laurens Swinkels for helpful comments.

Appendix A: Asset classes

Asset class	Description
Salomon 3-month T-bill	Salomon Brothers 3-month Treasury bill index
SSB Treasury 1−10 yr	Intermediate Treasury notes and bonds with maturities between 1 and 10 years
SSB Treasury 10+ yr	Long-term Treasury bonds with maturities over 10 years
SSB Corporate Bond	Corporate bonds with ratings of at least BB
Russell 1000 Value	The Russell 3000® Index measures the performance of the 3000 largest US companies based on
Russell 1000 Growth	total market capitalization, which represents approximately 98% of the investable US equity
Russell 2000 Value	market
Russell 2000 Growth	The Russell 1000® Index measures the performance of the 1000 largest companies in the Russell 3000 Index, which represents approximately 92% of the total market capitalization of the Russell 3000 Index. As of May 31, 2002, the average market capitalization was approximately $11 billion; the median market capitalization was approximately $3.5 billion. The index had a total market capitalization range of approximately $309 billion to $1.3 billion The Russell 2000® Index measures the performance of the 2000 smallest companies in the Russell 3000 Index. As of May 31, 2002, the average market capitalization was approximately $490 million; the median market capitalization was approximately $395 million. The index had a total market capitalization range of approximately $1.3 billion to $128 million Each stock in the Russell 1000 and Russell 2000 is ranked by two variables, the price-to-book ratio and the I/B/E/S forecast long-term growth mean. Variables are combined to create a composite value score for each stock. Stocks are ranked by the composite value score and a non-linear probability algorithm is applied to the distribution to determine style membership weights. 70% are classified as all value or all growth and 30% are weighted proportionally to both value and growth. *Source*: www.russell.com
Lehman Global Ex US Bond	All issues in the Lehman Global Index must be fixed rate, non-convertible debt and have at least 1 year remaining to maturity. Securities from countries classified as emerging markets are excluded. The country components are weighted according to market capitalization, except for Japan, which is weighted according to the market capitalization of the 40 largest Japanese government bonds. For accuracy in pricing, some illiquid issues are also excluded. *Source*: www.styleadvisor.com
MSCI EASEA	MSCI EASEA (MSCI EAFE excluding Japan). The MSCI EAFE® Index (Europe, Australasia, Far East) is a free float-adjusted market capitalization index that is designed to measure developed market equity performance, excluding the US and Canada. As of April 2002, the MSCI EAFE Index consisted of the following 21 developed market country indexes: Australia, Austria, Belgium, Denmark, Finland, France, Germany, Greece, Hong Kong, Ireland, Italy, Japan, the Netherlands, New Zealand, Norway, Portugal, Singapore, Spain, Sweden, Switzerland, and the United Kingdom
MSCI Japan	Country composite index targets 60% coverage of the market capitalization. Selection criteria include: size, long- and short-term volume, cross-ownership and float

Appendix A: *Continued*

Asset class	Description
MSCI EMF	The MSCI EMF (Emerging Markets Free) Index^{SM} is a free float-adjusted market capitalization index that is designed to measure equity market performance in the global emerging markets. As of April 2002, the MSCI EMF Index consisted of the following 26 emerging market country indexes: Argentina, Brazil, Chile, China, Colombia, Czech Republic, Egypt, Hungary, India, Indonesia, Israel, Jordan, Korea, Malaysia, Mexico, Morocco, Pakistan, Peru, Philippines, Poland, Russia, South Africa, Taiwan, Thailand, Turkey and Venezuela. *Source*: www.msci.com

Appendix B: Growth and income funds—objective and investment strategy

The information is based on the funds' prospectuses as of December 2001.

Alliance Capital Growth & Income
Objective: The fund seeks to provide income and capital appreciation
Primary investment strategies: The fund primarily invests in dividend-paying common stocks of good quality. It may also invest in fixed-income and convertible securities. The fund tries to maintain a defensive dividend yield and price-to-earnings ratio, a fully invested posture, and a high degree of sector and industry diversification. The fund invests in quality companies that trade at undeserved discounts to their peers. The fund does not make sector or market timing bets, but instead emphasizes intensive, bottom-up research and careful stock selection.
Size: $3.2 billions, Front load: 4.25%, Expense ratio: 0.91%

Goldman Sachs Growth & Income
Objective: This fund seeks long-term growth of capital and growth of income through investments in equity securities of well-established companies that are considered to have favorable prospects for capital appreciation and/or dividend-paying ability
Primary investment strategies: Based on a research-intensive approach, the fund employs a value investing strategy that emphasizes stocks they believe to be inexpensive relative to the fund's estimate of their actual worth. The fund maintains a long-term investment horizon with low turnover
Size: $335 millions, Front load: 5.50%, Expense ratio: 1.19%

Putnam Fund for Growth & Income
Objective: The fund seeks to provide capital growth and current income by investing primarily in common stocks that offer the potential for capital growth while also providing current income
Primary investment strategies: The fund invests mainly in common stocks of US companies, with a focus on value stocks that offer the potential for capital growth, current income, or both. Value stocks are those that we believe are currently undervalued by the market. We look for companies undergoing positive change. If we are correct and other investors recognize the value of the company, the price of the stock may rise. We invest mainly in large companies
Size: $18.6 billions, Front load: 5.75%, Expense ratio: 0.81%

Vanguard Growth & Income
Objective: The fund seeks to provide a total return (capital appreciation plus dividend income) greater than the return of the Standard & Poor's 500 Index
Primary investment strategies: The fund's adviser uses computer models to select a broadly diversified group of stocks that, as a whole, have investment characteristics similar to those of the S&P 500 index, but are expected to provide a higher total return than that of the index. At least 65% (and typically more than 90%) of the fund's assets will be invested in stocks that are included in the index. Most of the stocks held by the fund provide dividend income as well as the potential for capital appreciation
Size: $6.6 billions, Front load: –, Expense ratio: 0.38%

Appendix C: HFR hedge fund classes

Merger arbitrage	Sometimes called risk arbitrage, involves investment in event-driven situations such as leveraged buy-outs, mergers, and hostile takeovers. Normally, the stock of an acquisition target appreciates while the acquiring company's stock decreases in value. These strategies generate returns by purchasing stock of the company being acquired, and in some instances, selling short the stock of the acquiring company. Managers may employ the use of equity options as a low-risk alternative to the outright purchase or sale of common stock. Most merger arbitrage funds hedge against market risk by purchasing S&P put options or put option spreads
Market timing	Involves allocating assets among investments by switching into investments that appear to be beginning an uptrend, and switching out of investments that appear to be starting a downtrend. This primarily consists of switching between mutual funds and money markets. Typically, technical trend-following indicators are used to determine the direction of a fund and identify buy and sell signals. In an up move "buy signal," money is transferred from a money market fund into a mutual fund in an attempt to capture a capital gain. In a down move "sell signal," the assets in the mutual fund are sold and moved back into the money market for safe keeping until the next up move. The goal is to avoid being invested in mutual funds during a market decline
Equity non-hedge	Predominately long equities although they have the ability to hedge with short sales of stocks and/or stock index options. These funds are commonly known as "stock-pickers." Some funds employ leverage to enhance returns. When market conditions warrant, managers may implement a hedge in the portfolio. Funds may also opportunistically short individual stocks. The important distinction between equity non-hedge funds and equity hedge funds is equity non-hedge funds do not always have a hedge in place. In addition to equities, some funds may have limited assets invested in other types of securities.
Equity hedge	Investing consists of a core holding of long equities hedged at all times with short sales of stocks and/or stock index options. Some managers maintain a substantial portion of assets within a hedged structure and commonly employ leverage. Where short sales are used, hedged assets may be comprised of an equal dollar value of long and short stock positions. Other variations use short sales unrelated to long holdings and/or puts on the S&P 500 index and put spreads. Conservative funds mitigate market risk by maintaining market exposure from 0 to 100%. Aggressive funds may magnify market risk by exceeding 100% exposure and, in some instances, maintain a short exposure. In addition to equities, some funds may have limited assets invested in other types of securities
Short selling	Involves the sale of a security not owned by the seller; a technique used to take advantage of an anticipated price decline. To effect a short sale, the seller borrows securities from a third party in order to make delivery to the purchaser. The seller returns the borrowed securities to the lender by purchasing the securities in the open market. If the seller can buy that stock back at a lower price, a profit results. If the price rises, however, a loss results. A short seller must generally pledge other securities or cash with the lender in an amount equal to the market price of the borrowed securities. This deposit may be increased or decreased in response to changes in the market price of the borrowed securities. *Source*: www.hfr.com

Notes

[1] *Source:* Flow of Funds Accounts of the United States, Board of Governors of the Federal Reserve System.

2 Equity funds had a market value of $3.4 trillion, followed by money market funds ($2.3 trillion), bond ($0.9 trillion), and hybrid funds ($0.3 trillion) that are invested in equity, bonds, and derivatives.

3 *Source: Mutual Fund Fact Book*, Investment Company Institute, 2001 (www.ici.org, "About Mutual Funds").

4 The reader is referred to Kim *et al.* (2000) for a discussion of the issues involved in calculating the standard errors.

5 Fund managers are typically evaluated by comparing the return on their portfolio with that of a performance benchmark index. The standard deviation of the excess return of the fund over the performance benchmark is referred to as the *performance benchmark tracking error*.

6 Since the style coefficients are estimated after imposing the constraints, the estimated value of $\mathrm{var}(r_p)$ will not in general equal the estimated value of $\mathrm{var}(b_{p,1}x_{1,t} + b_{p,2}x_{2,t} + \cdots + b_{p,N}x_{N,t})$ + the estimated value of $\mathrm{var}(e_p)$. Hence the R^2 computed using Eq. (4a) will not in general equal R^2 computed using the standard formula given by $R^2 = \mathrm{var}(b_{p,1}x_{1,t} + b_{p,2}x_{2,t} + \cdots + b_{p,N}x_{N,t})/\mathrm{var}(e_p)$.

7 A number of other criteria have been proposed in the literature to adjust for the loss of degrees of freedom due to the use of a larger number of explanatory variables. For a discussion and justification of these criteria, see, e.g. Amemiya (1985).

8 StyleAdvisor is a registered trademark, Zephyr Associates Inc. For more information see www.styleadvisor.com.

9 Salomon 3-month US Treasury bill index.

10 The joint of price-to-book ratio and analysts' growth forecasts used by Russell allows to classify about 70% of the stocks as purely value or growth, the remaining 30% are "weighted proportionally to both value and growth" (see www.russell.com, "US Equity Indexes: Construction & Methodology"). The weights always sum to 100% to ensure mutual exclusivity. For example, 20% of a stock may be in the value index and 80% in the growth index.

11 The style box was introduced by Sharpe (1988) and Tierney and Winston (1991).

12 Morningstar separates funds into three size classes and value, blend, and growth stocks, totaling nine quadrants (see www.morningstar.com, "Style Box: Help"). Since June 2002, Morningstar's market overview is summarized by 16 indexes. The new methodology assigns stocks to the different style orientations based on 10 variables (www.morningstar.com, "Morningstar Market Indexes").

13 The SEC requires a prospectus to include the fund's goal, fees, and expenses, and a description of the investment strategies and risks.

14 We select investor shares, class A, for all funds.

15 This observation is consistent with the style changes over time. We will address style changes in Section 4.5. The exposures to the different asset classes of the Goldman Sachs Growth and Income, and to a lesser extent the Alliance Growth & Income fund, shift much more than for the comparable funds of Putnam and Vanguard.

16 The expense ratio includes all operating expenses incurred by the fund. The ranking using management fees alone is: 0.70% Goldman Sachs, 0.48% Alliance, 0.42% Putnam, and 0.36% Vanguard (*Source*: Morningstar).

17 For selling shares, none of the funds imposes a back(-end) load, or named formally "contingent deferred sales charge."

18 $(40/100) \times 10 + (30/100) \times 15 + (20/100) \times 20 + (10/100) \times 25 = 15$.

19 The total market capitalization of the value index is 70 and the P/E ratio is calculated as $(40/70) \times 10 + (30/70) \times 15 = 12.1$.

20 Buetow *et al.* (2000) replace the Russell 2000 with the BGI Small Cap indexes and use them in conjunction with the S&P Mid Cap and S&P 500. The correlation between the Russell 2000 and the BGI Small Cap indexes is 0.98 for the data period from January 1988 to December 2001. Analyzing the Fidelity Select Technology fund, the authors find a large increase in the exposure to the S&P Midcap 400 and S&P/Barra 500 Growth index over time when the Russell 2000 Growth index is replaced with the BGI Small Cap index. Using our 12 asset classes and substituting the Russell 2000 with the BGI Small Cap indexes and setting the size of the trailing window to 3 months, we cannot confirm this result.

21 *Source*: www.spglobal.com, "S&P U.S. Indexes: Constituents and Data."

22 *Source*: www.russell.com, "Russell Indexes: Construction and Methodology Details."

23 An alternative approach to span the US equity styles pursued by Agarwal and Naik (2002) is to add the Fama-French size and value factors to the Russell 3000.

24 The Frank Russell Company, for example, offers the Russell Top 200 Value and Growth index and the Russell 800 Midcap Value and Growth that add up to the Russell 1000.

25 Based on the prospectus from January 2002, p. 3.

26 See prospectus dated February 2002, p. 2.

27 Information on holdings is taken from the fund's annual report, October 31, 2001.

28 Morningstar takes the lesser of purchases or sales (excluding all securities with maturities of less than 1 year) in the nominator and the average monthly net assets in the denominator.

29 "Quarterly review of mutual funds: decade's star Magellan likes financial stocks." *The Wall Street Journal*, July 7, 1990.

30 "Magellan: what to expect from Stansky." *Business Week*, June 14, 1996; "Vinik quits Magellan as Stansky steps aboard." *The Wall Street Journal*, June 24, 1996.

31 "Fidelity Magellan shifts investments, as net redemption rate slows down." *The Wall Street Journal*, September 6, 1996.

32 "Sailing past the S&P 500." *Business Week*, February 1, 1999; "Magellan sails into uncharted waters." *The Wall Street Journal*, July 15, 1999.

33 Lipper's US Diversified Equity (USDE) classification system, introduced in September 1999, classifies funds by the stocks they hold rather than their stated objectives. For details, see "Lipper U.S. Diversified Equity Fund Classification Source Document." *Lipper*, 2002; www.lipperweb.com, "USA Client Services: Fund Definitions."

34 Most hedge funds are organized as private limited partnerships. The minimum investment level is often \$1 million, whereas for 83% of the mutual funds the minimum investment requirement is \$5000 or lower. Source: *Mutual Fund Fact Book*, Investment Company Institute, 2001.

35 Many hedge funds have the so-called high water mark provisions. For example, suppose a manager has an incentive fee of 20% and he incurs a loss of \$100 000 in year 1 and gains \$300 000 in year 2. The fund first has to cross the high water mark before the fund manager participates in the gains. In year 2, he will earn $20\% \times (300\,000 - 100\,000) = \$40\,000$. The asymmetric fee structure, where managers enjoy a percentage of the earnings but do not have to rebate fees when losses occur, is not allowed in mutual funds. Fung and Hsieh (1999) discuss the legal differences between mutual and hedge funds and the history of regulations in detail.

36 "Asset flow report, fourth quarter." *Tremont TASS Research*, 2001; www.tremontadvisers.com, "Research Library: Reports."

[37] Several papers have pointed out that returns on actively managed portfolios will have option-like features. The interested reader is referred to Merton (1981), Dybvig and Ross (1985), Jagannathan and Korajczyk (1986), and Glosten and Jagannathan (1994).

[38] Another approach to identify common factors in hedge fund returns is through principal component analysis of the returns on a large collection of hedge funds as in Fung and Hsieh (1997a). From a data set of 320 hedge funds and 89 commodity trading advisor pools (CTA) they extract five principal components, that is, five common investment styles. Two of the investment styles have high correlations with traditional asset classes. The R^2 is 70% for the style that involves buying undervalued stocks and 56% for the style that involves investments in distressed companies. The style "distressed" can be captured by returns on high-yield corporate bonds, reducing the set of relevant, additional style factors to three. Using a distinct data set of 901 CTAs, Fung and Hsieh (1997b) find one dominant style factor, a strategy described as "trend-following." Note that the styles identified this way correspond to returns on some portfolios of hedge funds used in the principal component analysis.

[39] Agarwal and Naik (2000) allow for negative weights and investigate the impact of constraining the weights to add up to one. For a sample of eight HFR indexes from January 1994 to September 1998, they conclude that the R^2 increases by 1–16% if the constraint is dropped, with a bigger effect on non-directional strategies than directional strategies.

[40] We choose the slope, the kink, and the level of the horizontal right leg of the payoff diagram such that the squared deviations are minimized. An alternative is to run a linear spline regression [see e.g. Greene (1999) for an introduction] and choose a threshold value that maximizes the R^2. For merger arbitrage, the spline regression allows the segment to the right of the kink to have a nonzero slope. Using data from 1963 to 1998, Mitchell and Pulvino (2001) find a slightly positive slope coefficient to the right of the kink, but not significant at the 1% level.

[41] *Source*: www.marhedge.com.

References

Ackermann, C., McEnally, R., and Ravenscraft, D. (1999). "The Performance of Hedge Funds: Risk, Return, and Incentives." *Journal of Finance* **54**(3), 833–874.

Agarwal, V. and Naik, N. Y. (2000). "Generalised Style Analysis of Hedge Funds." *Journal of Asset Management* **1**(1), 93–109

Agarwal, V. and Naik, N. Y. (2002). "Risks and Portfolio Decisions Involving Hedge Funds." *Review of Financial Studies* (in press).

Amemiya, T. (1985). *Advanced Econometrics*. Cambridge, MA: Harvard University Press.

Atkinson, B., Averill, K., and Hardy, S. (2001). "The Dangers of Misusing Returns Based Style Analysis." www.styleadvisor.com, Resources: Research Articles.

Bailey, J. V. (1992). "Are Manager Universes Acceptable Performance Benchmarks?" *Journal of Portfolio Management* **18**(3), 9–13.

Bogle, J. C. (1998). "The Implications of Style Analysis for Mutual Fund Performance Evaluation." *Journal of Portfolio Management* **24**(4), 34–42.

Brown, S. J. and Goetzmann, W. N. (1997). "Mutual Fund Styles." *Journal of Financial Economics* **43**(3), 373–399.

Brown, S. J., Goetzmann, W. N., and Ibbotson, R. G. (1999). "Offshore Hedge Funds: Survival and Performance, 1989–95." *Journal of Business* **72**(1), 91–117.

Brown, S. J., Goetzmann, W. N., and Ross, S. A. (1995). "Survival." *Journal of Finance* **50**(3), 853–873.

Buetow, G. W., Johnson, R. R., and Runkle, D. E. (2000). "The Inconsistency of Return-Based Style Analysis." *Journal of Portfolio Management* **26**(3), 61–77.
Buetow, G. W. and Ratner, H. (2000). "The Dangers in Using Return Based Style Analysis in Asset Allocation." *Journal of Wealth Management* **3**(2), 26–38.
Christopherson, J. A. (1995). "Equity Style Classification." *Journal of Portfolio Management* **21**(3), 32–43.
DiBartolomeo, D. and Witkowski, E. (1997). "Mutual Fund Misclassification: Evidence Based on Style Analysis." *Financial Analysts Journal* **53**(5), 32–43.
Dimson, E., Marsh, P., and Staunton, M. (2002). *Triumph of the Optimists: 101 Years of Global Investment Returns*. Princeton University Press, Princeton, NJ.
Dybvig, P. H. and Ross, S. A. (1985). "Differential Information and Performance Measurement Using a Security Market Line." *Journal of Finance* **40**(2), 383–399.
Fabozzi, F. J. (1997). *The Handbook of Fixed-Income Securities*, 5th edn. New York, NY: McGraw-Hill.
Frank, M. and Jagannathan, R. (1998). "Why Do Stock Prices Drop by Less Than the Value of the Dividend? Evidence from a Country Without Taxes." *Journal of Financial Economics* **47**, 161–188.
Fung, W. and Hsieh, D. A. (1997a). "Empirical Characteristics of Dynamic Trading Strategies: The Case of Hedge Funds." *Review of Financial Studies* **10**(2), 275–302.
Fung, W. and Hsieh, D. A. (1997b). "Survivorship Bias and Investment Style in the Returns of CTAs." *Journal of Portfolio Management* **24**(1), 30–41.
Fung, W. and Hsieh, D. A. (1999). "A Primer on Hedge Funds." *Journal of Empirical Finance* **6**(3), 309–331.
Fung, W. and Hsieh, D. A. (2000a). "Measuring the Market Impact of Hedge Funds." *Journal of Empirical Finance* 7(1), 1–36.
Fung, W. and Hsieh, D. A. (2000b). "Performance Characteristics of Hedge Funds and CTA Funds: Natural Versus Spurious Biases." *Journal of Quantitative and Financial Analysis* **35**(3), 291–307.
Fung, W. and Hsieh, D. A. (2001). "The Risk in Hedge Fund Strategies: Theory and Evidence from Trend Followers." *Review of Financial Studies* **14**(2), 313–341.
Fung, W. and Hsieh, D. A. (2002). "Hedge Fund Benchmarks: Information Content and Biases." *Financial Analysts Journal* **58**(1), 22–34.
Glosten, L. R. and Jagannathan, R. (1994). "A Contingent Claim Approach to Performance Evaluation." *Journal of Empirical Finance* **1**, 133–160.
Greene, W. H. (1999). *Econometric Analysis*, 4th edn. Englewood Cliffs, NJ: Prentice-Hall.
Grinblatt, M. and Titman, S. (1989). "Mutual Fund Performance: An Analysis of Quarterly Portfolio Holdings." *Journal of Business* **62**(3), 393–416.
Jagannathan, R. and Korajczyk, R. A. (1986). "Assessing the Market Timing Performance of Managed Portfolios." *Journal of Business* **59**, 217–236.
Indro, D. C., Jiang, C. X., Hu, M. Y. and Lee, W. Y. (1998). "Mutual Fund Performance: A Question of Style." *Journal of Investing* 7(2), 46–53.
Kim, M., Shukla, R., and Tomas, M. (2000). "Mutual Fund Objective Misclassification." *Journal of Economics and Business* **52**, 309–323.
Kim, T., Stone, D., and White, H. (2000). "Asymptotic and Bayesian Confidence Intervals for Sharpe Style Weights." Discussion Paper 2000–27, *University of San Diego*, Department of Economics,
Liang, B. (1999). "On the Performance of Hedge Funds." *Financial Analysts Journal* **55**(4), 72-85.
Liang, B. (2000). "Hedge Funds: The Living and the Dead." *Journal of Financial and Quantitative Analysis* **35**(3), 309–326.
Malkiel, B. G. (1995). "Returns from Investing in Equity Mutual Funds 1971 to 1991." *Journal of Finance* **50**(2), 549–572.
Merton, R. C. (1981). "On Market Timing and Investment Performance I: An Equilibrium Theory of Values for Market Forecasts." *Journal of Business* **54**(3), 363–406.
Michaud, R. O. (1998). "Is Value Multidimensional? Implications for Style Management and Global Stock Selection." *Journal of Investing* 7, 61–65.

Mitchell, M. and Pulvino, T. (2001). "Characteristics of Risk and Return in Risk Arbitrage." *Journal of Finance* **56**(6), 2135–2175.
Sharpe, W. F. (1988). "Determining a Fund's Effective Asset Mix." *Investment Management Review*, 59–69.
Sharpe, W. F. (1992a). "Asset Allocation: Management Style and Performance Measurement." *Journal of Portfolio Management* **18**(2), 7–19.
Sharpe, W. F. (1992b). "The AT&T Pension Fund." Graduate School of Business, Stanford University, Case.
Siegel, J. J. (1998). *Stocks for the Long Run*, 2nd edn. New York, NY: McGraw-Hill.
Tierney, D. E. and Winston, K. (1991). "Using Generic Benchmarks to Present Manager Styles." *Journal of Portfolio Management* **17**(4), 33–36.
Trzcinka, C. A. (1995). "Equity Style Classifications: Comment." *Journal of Portfolio Management* **21**(3), 44–46.

Journal of Investment Management
Vol. 2, No. 4 (2004), pp. 76–93

ALTERNATIVE INVESTMENTS: CTAs, HEDGE FUNDS, AND FUNDS-OF-FUNDS

*Bing Liang**

In this paper, we study alternative investment vehicles such as hedge funds, funds-of-funds, and commodity trading advisors (CTAs) by investigating their performance, risk, and fund characteristics. Considering them as three distinctive investment classes, we study them not only on a stand-alone basis but also on a portfolio basis. We find several interesting results. First, CTAs differ from hedge funds and funds-of-funds in terms of trading strategies, liquidity, and correlation structures. Second, during the period 1994–2001, hedge funds outperform funds-of-funds, which in turn outperform CTAs on a stand-alone basis. These results can be explained by the double fee structure but not survivorship bias. Third, correlation structures for alternative investment vehicles are different under different market conditions. Hedge funds are highly correlated to each other and are not well hedged in the down markets with liquidity squeeze. The negative correlations with other instruments make CTAs suitable hedging instruments for insuring downside risk. When adding CTAs to the hedge fund portfolio or the fund-of-fund portfolio, investors can benefit significantly from the risk-return trade-off.

1 Introduction

Alternative investments differ from traditional investments in low correlation with traditional asset classes, managers' involvement in their personal wealth, dynamic trading strategies, and use of a wide range of techniques and instruments. Hungry for positive returns in the recent bear markets, institutional investors such as investment banks, insurance companies, pension funds, and even university endowments are flocking to the alternative investment markets. Due to the special features, lack of regulatory oversight, and demands from both wealthy and institutional investors, alternative investment vehicles have gained popularity lately. Alternative investments include, but are not limited to, hedge funds, fund-of-hedge funds, commodity trading advisors (CTAs), private equity, partnerships, and venture capital. In this paper, we focus on three major alternative investment vehicles: hedge funds, funds-of-funds, and CTAs. In fact, major data vendors such as TASS Management Ltd. and Center for International Securities and Derivatives Markets (CISDM) at the University of Massachusetts collect data for all three categories.[1] There are certainly similarities among these three investment classes.

However, a hedge fund is different from a fund-of-funds. A hedge fund charges a management fee and incentive fee while a fund-of-funds not only charges these

*Isenberg School of Management, University of Massachusetts, Amherst, MA 01003, USA. Tel. +1-413-545-3180; fax: +1-413-545-3858; e-mail: bliang@som.umass.edu

fees at the fund-of-fund level but also passes on hedge fund level fees in the form of after fee returns to the fund-of-fund investors. In fact, underlying hedge fund fees will be transferred to the fund-of-fund investors regardless of whether the funds-of-funds makes a profit or not. As a result, total fees from a fund-of-fund can exceed the total realized return on the fund. Brown *et al.* (2004) examine this issue and propose an alternative fee arrangement for funds-of-funds, under which the fund-of-fund managers will absorb the underlying hedge funds fees and establish their own incentive fees at the fund-of-fund level. This will provide a better incentive for fund-of-fund managers and reduce the dead-loss costs for investors under the current fee arrangement. Because of the above issues, we need to separate funds-of-funds from hedge funds in order to study the differences in performance, risk, and fee structures.

Although there are certain similarities between hedge funds and CTAs, such as management and incentive fee structures, high initial investment requirements, use of leverage and derivatives, systematic differences can also exist. For example, hedge funds are involved in varieties of dynamic trading strategies using different financial instruments in different markets while CTAs mainly consist of technical trading strategies in commodity and financial futures markets. Investing in different instruments from different markets can result in differences in risk and returns. In addition, CTAs must register with the Commodity Futures Trading Commission (CFTC) while hedge funds are largely exempt from government regulations.[2] Most importantly, correlations among various hedge fund styles are relatively high while correlations among CTAs and hedge fund styles are very low. This correlation structure of CTAs with others may make them an excellent candidate for hedging downside risk. Therefore, it is necessary to distinguish CTAs from hedge funds or funds-of-funds.

In this paper, we simultaneously evaluate these three major alternative investment vehicles in terms of performance, risk, and fee structures. We separate the three groups as three distinctive investment classes. By doing so, we can investigate the similarities and differences among them and further explore the investment strategies that are employed by fund managers. In addition, our study is conducted not only on a stand-alone basis but also on a portfolio basis of adding one investment class to another. In particular, we study the relationship among different investment strategies under different market environments in order to see how market conditions impact fund returns and risks and how investors can benefit from combining CTAs with their hedge fund or fund-of-fund portfolios.

We find several interesting results. First, although funds-of-funds are linked to hedge funds through some common asset class factors, they underperform their hedge fund components, due to the double fee structure and incomplete coverage (hence ineffective diversification) of the hedge fund universe.[3] Some superior hedge funds may be closed to investment so funds-of-funds will not be able to access them. Because of these, investors who invested in funds-of-funds will face inferior risk-return trade-off than that of hedge funds. Second, CTA styles are slightly or negatively correlated with hedge fund styles or funds-of-funds depending on the general market conditions. Asset class factor analysis also indicates that CTAs follow very different trading strategies from those of hedge funds or funds-of-funds. Especially, the only significant factors to explain CTA returns are the option trading factors, which cannot explain hedge fund or fund-of-fund returns. Finally, we find that correlation structures are different in the up markets from those in the down markets. Hedge funds and funds-of-funds are highly correlated with each other in the down markets, they are not well hedged. Because of the negative correlation with other instruments, CTAs are suitable candidates for hedging the downside risk. Adding CTAs to the hedge fund portfolio or the fund-of-fund portfolio, investors can significantly benefit from the risk-return trade-off.

2 Data

The data are provided by Zurich Capital Markets Inc. (Zurich), which is now owned by CISDM at the University of Massachusetts. As of March 2002, there are 2357 hedge funds (1164 live funds and 1193 defunct funds), 597 funds-of-funds (including 349 live and 248 defunct), and 1510 CTAs (294 live CTAs and 1216 defunct CTAs).[4] CISDM classifies CTAs into live CTAs and CTAs and defines a hedge fund or a fund-of-funds defunct if it fails to report to the data vendor in three consecutive months or more.

Table 1 shows the basic statistics of the data. The median management fees for hedge funds, funds-of-funds, and CTAs are 1, 1, and 2%, respectively. Apparently, hedge funds charge the least amount of management fees, compared with funds-of-funds and CTAs. Note that a fund-of-fund invests in different hedge funds and hence charges two-tier fees: a fee that is indirectly paid to the individual hedge fund (1% on average) in which the funds-of-funds invest and a fee that is paid directly to the funds-of-funds (1% on average). The two-tier fees are all borne by investors in the form of after fee returns. All things being equal, returns from hedge funds will be higher than returns from funds-of-funds since lower management fees are charged. Apart from the management fee, the median incentive fees for hedge funds, funds-of-funds, and CTAs are all 20%. Again, a fund-of-funds may deliver lower after fee returns than a hedge fund due to the two-tier fee structure.

The median minimum investment for hedge funds, funds-of-funds, and CTAs are \$300,000, \$250,000, and \$250,000, respectively. They are all designed for accredited investors or institutional investors. As of December 2001, the median fund assets for hedge funds, funds-of-funds, and CTAs are \$36, \$34, and \$13 million, respectively. Hence, most funds or CTAs are relatively small. It seems that the average size for a CTA is smaller than those of hedge funds or funds-of-funds. Consistent with the small asset base, Table 1 also indicates that on average a CTA has only four employees. The median fund ages (of both live and defunct funds) for the three portfolio groups are 44, 52, and 46 months. Fund-of-funds has the longest average life because of the diversification effect across different hedge fund components. If one or more hedge funds die in the fund-of-fund portfolio, other hedge funds can still remain in the portfolio and funds-of-funds managers can easily switch to other hedge funds to replace the defunct ones.

Table 1 Basic statistics of hedge funds, funds-of-funds, and CTAs.

	Hedge funds				Funds-of-funds				CTA			
	N	Mean	Std dev.	Median	*N*	Mean	Std dev.	Median	*N*	Mean	Std dev.	Median
Mfee	2357	0.910	0.737	1.00	597	0.908	0.786	1.00	1510	2.295	1.494	2.00
Ifee	2357	12.764	9.844	20.00	597	14.497	7.591	20.00	1510	19.340	5.879	20.00
Min	2357	670,339	2,369,825	300,000	597	573,798	1,955,354	250,000	1510	998,754	2,706,656	250,000
Staff	N/A	N/A	N/A	N/A	N/A	N/A	N/A	N/A	1170	10.32	88.11	4.00
Asset[a]	1118	116.489	279.491	36.315	346	111.042	243.829	34.265	297	106.928	323.736	13.14
Age	2297	53.256	38.611	44.00	580	59.545	40.060	52.00	1508	59.942	49.415	46.00

As of March 2002, there are 2357 hedge funds (1164 live funds and 1193 defunct funds), 597 funds-of-funds (349 live and 248 defunct), and 1510 CTAs (294 live and 1216 defunct). Mfee is the management fee in percentage, Ifee is the incentive fee in percentage, Min is the minimum dollar investment, and staff is the number of staff for a CTA. Assets are in millions of dollars. Age is the number of months from a fund's inception or the time when the first monthly return is recorded (whichever is the latter).

[a] As of December 2001.

3 Performance, Risk, and Fee Structures

3.1 Performance and risk

One of the conventional measures for hedge fund returns and risks is Sharpe ratio. However, recent studies have challenged the effectiveness of using Sharpe ratio to evaluate hedge fund performance when returns are negatively skewed, have high kurtosis, and show strong autocorrelations. Lo (2002) documents that the positive autocorrelation in hedge fund returns can overstate the Sharpe ratio. He recommends using the autocorrelation adjusted Sharpe ratio instead of the regular Sharpe ratios in the following way:

$$\eta(q)\ \mathrm{SR} \quad \text{with } \eta(q) = \frac{q}{\sqrt{q + 2\sum_{k=1}^{q-1}(q-k)\rho_k}} \tag{1}$$

where SR is the regular Sharpe ratio on a monthly basis, ρ_k is the kth autocorrelation for hedge fund returns, and $\eta(q)$ SR is the annualized autocorrelation adjusted Sharpe ratio with $q = 12$. Note when returns are independently and identically distributed (i.i.d.), the annualize Sharpe ratio is $\sqrt{12}$ SR, which may overstate the true Sharpe ratio if the returns are positively autocorrelated as $\eta(q)$ in (1) is less than $\sqrt{q}$.

We estimate the autocorrelation coefficients up to lag 11 by using a rolling 24-month window. For example, for the year 1994, we estimate autocorrelations using the data from 1994 to 1995, and so on.[5] Table 2 displays raw returns, standard deviations, $\sqrt{12}$ SR and the autocorrelation adjusted Sharpe ratios $\eta(q)$ SR over a 7-year period from 1994 to 2000. There are several interesting findings. First, hedge funds outperform funds-of-funds in six out of seven years when performance is measured by raw returns (all of the t-statistics for return differences are significant at the 1% level). This proportion falls to 5 out of 7 years when the autocorrelation adjusted Sharpe ratio is used. Hence, we conclude that hedge funds outperform funds-of-funds during this 7-year period on both a risk-adjusted and a non-adjusted basis. Note that the $\sqrt{12}$ SRs are different from the $\eta(q)$ SRs, reflecting the nature of non-normality and non i.i.d. distribution in hedge fund returns. There are 4 out of 7 years when hedge funds outperform funds-of-funds, compared with 5 out of 7 years when $\Delta\eta(12)$ SR is used.

We can attribute the outperformance to the two-tier fee structure of funds-of-funds, which reduces the after fee performances. This argument is consistent with Brown *et al.* (2004). Although a fund-of-funds offers diversification it comes with a cost: the fees may not justify the diversification effect. Fung and Hsieh (2000) argue that the underperformance of funds-of-funds can be largely attributed to the survivorship bias. However, the difference in the survivorship between hedge funds and funds-of-funds is only 0.093% on a monthly basis while the return difference between the two is 0.4108%, much higher than the survivorship difference.[6] Second, hedge funds also outperform CTAs during the same time period. When raw return is used, hedge funds earn higher returns than CTAs in 4 out of 7 years (all t-statistics are significant at the 1% level) while CTA is the winner in only 1 out of 7 years (significant at the 10% level only). When the autocorrelation adjusted Sharpe ratio is used, the result is very

Table 2 Performance and risk for hedge funds, funds-of-funds, and CTAs.

	Hedge funds					Funds-of-funds					CTA				
Year	No.	Return	Std dev.	$\sqrt{12}$ SR	$\eta(12)$ SR	No.	Return	Std dev.	$\sqrt{12}$ SR	$\eta(12)$ SR	No.	Return	Std dev.	$\sqrt{12}$ SR	$\eta(12)$ SR
1994	716	0.29	3.39	0.32	0.25	203	−0.37	0.94	−1.39	−0.97	712	0.47	3.57	−0.59	−1.02
1995	870	1.52	2.45	1.89	3.54	253	0.83	1.35	1.58	2.14	718	1.16	2.86	−0.14	−0.31
1996	1062	1.71	2.29	3.54	6.85	299	1.32	0.87	2.69	5.04	675	1.03	3.12	−0.72	−1.44
1997	1277	1.68	2.71	1.52	1.57	356	1.33	1.42	1.76	1.48	617	1.23	2.84	0.35	0.62
1998	1421	0.48	3.04	0.56	0.48	384	−0.01	1.78	−0.12	−0.10	564	0.78	3.33	−1.33	−1.69
1999	1476	2.76	4.15	2.06	1.96	404	2.00	1.80	2.28	2.23	503	0.24	2.11	−0.41	−0.45
2000	1451	0.64	3.19	0.76	1.17	430	0.58	1.31	0.79	1.28	433	0.68	2.61	−0.13	−0.24

	HF − FOF			HF − CTA			FOF − CTA		
Year	t-Return	$\Delta\sqrt{12}$ SR	$\Delta\eta(12)$ SR	t-Return	$\Delta\sqrt{12}$ SR	$\Delta\eta(12)$ SR	t-Return	$\Delta\sqrt{12}$ SR	$\Delta\eta(12)$ SR
1994	4.59***	1.71	1.22	−0.98	0.91	1.27	−5.61***	−0.80	0.05
1995	5.82***	0.31	1.40	2.66***	2.03	3.85	−2.43**	1.72	2.44
1996	4.55***	0.86	1.81	4.87***	4.26	8.29	2.17**	3.40	6.48
1997	3.30***	−0.24	0.09	3.30***	1.17	0.96	0.73	1.40	0.87
1998	3.99***	0.68	0.57	−1.89*	1.89	2.16	−4.73***	1.21	1.59
1999	5.46***	−0.21	−0.27	17.64***	2.47	2.42	13.56***	2.68	2.68
2000	0.65	−0.03	−0.11	−0.26	0.89	1.41	−0.77	0.92	1.52

As of March 2002, there are 2357 hedge funds (1164 live funds and 1193 defunct funds), 597 funds-of-funds (349 live and 248 defunct), and 1510 CTAs (294 live and 1216 defunct). $\sqrt{12}$ SR is the annualized Sharpe ratio when returns are i.i.d. while $\eta(12)$ SR is the autocorrelation adjusted Sharpe ratio on an annual basis. $\Delta\sqrt{12}$ SR is the difference between the two $\sqrt{12}$ SRs and $\Delta\eta(12)$ SR is the difference between the two $\eta(12)$SRs.

***Significant at the 1% level.
**Significant at the 5% level.
*Significant at the 10% level.

dramatic: CTAs underperform hedge funds in all seven years no matter whether we use $\Delta\sqrt{12}$ SR or $\Delta\eta(q)$ SR. We may attribute this underperformance to high attrition rate and survivorship bias, high fees, relatively less diversified positions/high volatility, and high leverage of CTAs. Third, CTAs even underperform funds-of-funds. When the autocorrelation adjusted Sharpe ratio is used, CTAs underperform funds-of-funds in all 7 years. The results are similar when $\sqrt{12}$ SR is used although the results from raw returns are mixed.

In summary, according the risk-return analysis, we rank hedge funds the highest, funds-of-funds are the second, and CTAs the lowest on a stand-alone basis. This ranking order may have to do with the fee structures, risks, and the autocorrelation structures of these different investment classes. We know that hedge funds charge fewer fees than those of funds-of-funds and CTAs and that CTAs are mostly likely trend followers while hedge funds are different arbitragers.

3.2 *The asset class factor model*

For performance attribution and evaluation of these investment vehicles, we adopt a multi-asset class factor model and regress asset returns on several asset class factors and risk factors. Similar kinds of analyses have been conducted by Sharpe (1992) for mutual funds, Fung and Hsieh (1997a), Ackermann *et al.* (1999), and Liang (1999) for hedge funds. Recently, Agarwal and Naik (2004) document that adding the Fama-French factors and the option-based trading factors can significantly enhance the power of explaining hedge fund returns. Therefore, we adopt a similar setting as Agarwal and Naik. First, we have eight basic asset class factors that are the same as those used in the previous studies. In particular, we use the S&P 500 index for the US equity market, Morgan Stanley Capital International's (MSCI) developed country index for other developed equity markets, MSCI emerging market index for emerging markets, Salomon Brothers world government bond index and Salomon Brothers Broad Investment Grade (BIG) index for government bond and broad bond markets, Federal Reserve Bank trade-weighted dollar index for currency, gold price for commodities, and one-month US dollar deposit for cash. In addition, we have added the Fama–French's (1993) size (small-minus-big or SMB) and value/book-to-market (high-minus-low or HML) factors on top of the eight basic factors. Finally, four option-based risk factors are added; they are the highly liquid at-the-money (ATM) and out-of-the money (OTM) European call and put options on the S&P 500 index trading on the Chicago Mercantile Exchange. These option factors are exactly the same as those of Agarwal and Naik (2004). They are designed to capture the non-linearity in fund returns. As a result, the asset class factor model can be expressed as[7]:

$$R_{it} = \alpha_k + \sum_{k=1}^{N} \beta_k F_{kt} + \varepsilon_{it}. \qquad (2)$$

To test the different roles of various factors and check the robustness of the model, we run several regressions for each of the three investment classes. These regressions include either the full 14 factors or a subset of these factors. The model with only the eight basic asset class factors is called the base model. The model with the eight factors, two Fama–French factors, and four option factors is called the full model. We also have the basic factor plus the Fama–French factor model and the basic factor plus the option factor model. As a result, we have four regressions for each of the three investment classes.

Table 3 reports these regression results. For the results of hedge funds, across four different regression models, returns are significantly related to MSCI developed country index (excluding US), MSCI emerging market index, Salomon Brothers world government bond index, the BIG index, and the Fama–French size factor. Apparently, hedge funds invest in both the equity and bond markets. Especially, hedge funds long securities in the developed equity and emerging equity markets, short government bonds and long broad investment grade bonds, and long small stocks while going short on large stocks during the time period we study. We know that many hedge funds have net long equity positions that will benefit from up equity markets in general. Note that the coefficients on the two bond factors have opposite signs; we can interpret the reverse signs as something such as fixed income arbitrage: long the broad investment grade bonds and short sell government bonds. This is based on betting that the credit spread between the two will converge, which is a popular bond trading strategy during that time period. The adjusted R^2s for the four models range from 72.9 to 91.6%, indicating very high explanatory powers of the model. Interestingly, the marginal benefit of adding the Fama–French size and value factors to the base model is highly significant, reflected by the increased R^2 from 74.5 to 91%. Hedge funds may long small stocks while short selling large stocks, and long growth stocks and short selling value stocks to make arbitrage profits. In contrast, the marginal benefit of adding the four option-based factors to the base model is not significant; the adjusted R^2 is actually declined from 74.5 to 72.9%. This is in contrast to the results by Agarwal and Naik (2004), who find that option factors are significant for different hedge fund strategies. While Agarwal and Naik examine hedge fund factor loadings at each style, we focus on hedge funds as one investment class as our interest is to distinguish hedge funds from CTAs at the aggregate level. In addition, we run several regressions to check the robustness of the results.

The regression results for funds-of-funds are similar to those for hedge funds although the regressions are not as strong: the models pick up exactly the same asset class factors and the estimates have the same signs as those for hedge funds. This is not surprising because funds-of-funds invest in different hedge funds, they should cover similar investment styles on average. The adjusted R^2s for the fund-of-fund regressions range from 65.4 to 79.4%, lower than those of the hedge funds. Again, the marginal benefits of adding the Fama–French factors and the option factors to the base model are very similar to those of hedge funds.

In a strong contrast, the models have very low explanatory powers for CTAs. The adjusted R^2s range from -7.2 to 14.3%. Comparisons across three groups indicate that CTAs follow very different investment strategies from hedge funds or funds-of-funds.

Table 3 Asset class factor regressions for hedge funds, funds-of-funds, and CTAs.

	Full model			Base + optn			Base + FF			Base model		
Variable	HF	FOF	CTA	HF	FOF	CTA	HF	FOF	CTA	HF	FOF	CTA
Intercept	1.10***	0.81***	0.88	0.83**	0.61*	0.87*	0.94***	0.63**	0.54	0.66*	0.43	0.55
SPret	0.01	−0.35	−0.63	−0.60*	−0.75***	−0.51	0.03	−0.14	−0.06	−0.43**	−0.46***	−0.05
Developed	0.21	0.28	−0.07	0.66***	0.57***	−0.17	0.25*	0.31*	−0.22	0.68***	0.61***	−0.22
Emerging	0.10**	0.10*	0.18	0.23***	0.18***	0.15	0.10**	0.09	0.10	0.22***	0.17***	0.10
Deposit	−0.02	−0.02	−0.14	−0.10	−0.06	−0.12	−0.04	−0.02	−0.05	−0.10	−0.06	−0.05
Fed	−0.41	−0.23	0.55	−0.17	−0.10	0.41	−0.36	−0.23	0.06	−0.14	−0.08	0.08
Gold	−0.09*	−0.13**	−0.06	−0.03	−0.09	−0.08	−0.06	−0.08	−0.06	0.01	−0.03	−0.06
Gov	−0.55**	−0.42*	0.72	−0.64*	−0.50	0.68	−0.56***	−0.52**	0.31	−0.74**	−0.65**	0.32
BIG	0.68**	0.68*	0.31	1.26**	1.08**	0.26	0.69**	0.63*	0.63	1.30**	1.05**	0.61
SMB	0.28***	0.20***	0.01				0.26***	0.19***	−0.02			
HML	−0.05	−0.02	0.05				−0.07	−0.04	−0.01			
ATMC	−0.01	0.00	0.03*	0.00	0.00	0.02*						
OTMC	0.01	0.01	−0.01	0.00	0.00	−0.01						
ATMP	−0.04*	−0.03	−0.09*	−0.05	−0.04	−0.08*						
OTMP	0.03*	0.03	0.07*	0.04	0.03	0.07*						
R^2	94.98	87.62	44.90	82.19	77.28	43.68	93.59	85.15	23.43	80.36	73.66	23.39
Adj R^2	91.64	79.37	8.16	72.90	65.42	14.30	91.03	79.21	−7.20	74.54	65.85	0.69

As of March 2002, there are 2357 hedge funds (1164 live funds and 1193 defunct funds), 597 funds-of-funds (349 live and 248 defucnt), and 1510 CTAs (294 live and 1216 defunct). The dependent variable is the average monthly returns from 1998 to 2000. The independent variables are the S&P 500 index (S&P), MSCI developed country index (Developed), MSCI emerging market index (Emerging), Salomon Brothers world government bond index (Gov) and Salomon Brothers Broad Investment Grade (BIG) index, Federal Reserve Bank trade-weighted dollar index (Fed), gold price (Gold), 1-month US dollar deposit rate (Deposit), Fama–French size factor (SMB) and Book-to-Market factor (HML), Agarwal–Naik at-the-money (ATMC) and out-of-money (OTMC) European call option factors, and at-the-money (ATMP) and out-of-money (OTMP) European put option factors.

***Significant at the 1% level.
**Significant at the 5% level.
*Significant at the 10% level.

The signs of factor loadings for CTAs are very different from those of the other two classes. It is well known that CTAs mainly invest in futures markets and often are used for hedging equity market risk. This can be reflected from the negative signs of the S&P 500 index and the MSCI developed market index. In addition, CTAs are long and short timers in commodities or financial futures, which may result in no correlation with the commodity index as long and short positions can cancel each other out. This can explain why the coefficient on factor "gold" is insignificant. The Fama–French size and value factors are not significant, reflecting that CTAs are generally not arbitragers in the equity markets. The only significant factors for CTAs are the three out of four option factors, which are insignificant for hedge funds and funds-of-funds. Although CTAs may not trade in the option markets directly, their returns may show non-linear or option-like patterns due to some long–short combinations. As a result, CTA returns may be relatively high under extreme market conditions than the normal conditions, which will lead to concavity in returns. In fact, our result here is consistent with Fung and Hsieh (1997b) that CTAs exhibit option-like conditional return patterns with respect to equity markets.

Once again, across all three panels we can see that hedge funds outperform the other two classes: the intercept term or the unexplained return from the full factor model is 1.1% per month and significant at the 1% level for hedge funds, it is 0.81% per month for funds-of-funds and significant at the 1% level while the intercept term for CTAs is not significantly different from zero. These results are consistent with the Sharpe ratio analyses that are reported in Table 2.

In summary, we find that CTAs are different from hedge funds or fund-of-funds in trading strategies. The only significant factors for CTAs are option-related factors while equity market and bond market factors are picked up by hedge fund or fund-of-fund styles. On a stand-alone basis, the pecking order of performance is hedge funds, funds-of-funds, and CTAs.

4 Performance Evaluation in a Portfolio Framework and under Different Market Environments

The above section indicates that CTAs are different from either hedge funds or funds-of-funds in investment strategies. In this section, we further study the correlation structures among hedge funds, funds-of-funds, CTAs, and the market index. We conduct the simple correlation analysis not only in the up markets but also in the down markets. We run piecewise regressions for non-linearities in fund returns.

It is important to distinguish the correlation structure in the up markets from that of the down markets. This is because of the following reasons. First, due to the option-like payoff or fee structures, CTAs exhibit return complexity rather than linearity with respect to equity market returns. Hedge fund returns may also show non-linearity due to the option-like fee structures and the derivative securities involved. Second, if the market is doing well, there should be plenty of instruments and strategies available for fund managers to maneuver, active trading and dynamic strategies will produce varieties of trading positions, and different timing skills will further make these positions less correlated. In contrast, if the market is down, the supply of liquidity can quickly vanish, fund managers may not have much room to maneuver and they are forced to invest in limited securities and follow similar strategies. Therefore correlations among different funds even different styles can be very high. For example, during the Russian debt crisis in 1998, managers of fixed income arbitrage funds are driven to liquid government securities and escape the illiquid debt instruments. This herding behavior makes fixed income arbitrage funds highly correlated among each other. Kyle (1985) summarizes market liquidity by using three components: "tightness" (the cost of turning around a position during a short period), "depth" (the size of an order flow innovation required to change prices by a given amount), and "resiliency" (the speed with which prices can recover from a random shock). Third, it is well known that CTAs offer natural hedges for traditional investment vehicles such as bonds and stocks. In the up markets, CTAs may be less attractive to hedge fund investors due to inferior returns to bonds or stocks. However, in the down markets, CTAs may be desired due to the negative correlations with other asset classes and relative sound performance compared to the others. Therefore, in the following analysis, we will study correlation structures in both up and down markets.

4.1 Non-linearities in fund returns

We use the following model to capture the non-linearity of fund returns with respect to the S&P 500 index:

$$R_{it} = \alpha_i + \beta_i^+ I_t^+ + \beta_i^- I_t^- + \varepsilon_{it}, \tag{3}$$

where $I_t^+ = R_{mt}$, if $R_{mt} > 0$ and $I_t^+ = 0$ otherwise, $I_t^- = R_{mt}$, if $R_{mt} \leq 0$ and $I_t^- = 0$ otherwise, and R_{mt} is the monthly return on the S&P 500 index.

From Table 4 we observe several results. First, beta asymmetry in the up and down markets is very obvious. In Panel A, the up market betas are generally insignificantly different from zero except for the global established, long only, and short selling styles. Note that they are directional strategies, which are related to the stock markets directly. The non-directional strategies may offer a certain hedge so that the market exposure is not significant. In Panel B, the only significant beta for CTAs is from the stock trading program. In a strong contrast, the 15 down market betas are all significant at the conventional level except for CTA's currency program. Second, the down market betas are all positive for hedge fund or fund-of-fund styles (except for the short selling strategy) while they are all significantly negative for the CTA styles (except for the stock trading program). In other words, hedge funds or funds-of-funds are positively related to the S&P 500 index in the down market while the CTAs are negatively related to the index. This confirms our earlier conjecture of liquidity squeeze in the down markets. Note that the market neutral hedge funds are "market neutral" only in the up market with a zero beta; the 0.19 beta in the down market is significantly different from zero. Therefore, hedge funds are not well hedged in the down markets as in the up markets. This is particularly true for emerging market, long only, and sector funds, all having betas higher than one. Again, they are all directional strategies. Third, the R^2s

Table 4 Piecewise regression results in the up and down markets.

Style	alpha	*t*-alpha	beta+	*t*(beta+)	beta−	*t*(beta−)	Adj R^2
Panel A: HF/FOF							
Event driven	1.88	3.74***	−0.03	−0.30	0.62	5.40***	0.50
Global macro	1.44	2.44**	0.06	0.46	0.47	3.50***	0.32
Global emerging	1.80	1.13	0.42	1.18	1.41	3.89***	0.43
Global established	1.86	2.11**	0.50	2.54**	0.94	4.76***	0.60
Global international	1.55	2.26**	0.20	1.32	0.50	3.19***	0.36
Long-only	1.62	1.07	0.75	2.20**	1.36	3.95***	0.51
Market neutral	1.45	4.53***	0.00	0.02	0.19	2.61***	0.17
Sector	3.50	2.71***	0.40	1.37	1.29	4.41***	0.49
Short	−0.04	−0.02	−0.68	−1.65*	−1.58	−3.77***	0.45
FOF	1.77	2.87***	0.17	1.26	0.63	4.54***	0.50
Panel B: CTA							
Agriculture	0.15	0.20	0.02	0.14	−0.44	−2.60***	0.16
Currency	1.36	2.63***	−0.13	−1.11	0.15	1.31	0.00
Diversified	−0.20	−0.22	0.09	0.46	−0.56	−2.68***	0.15
Financial	−0.43	−0.57	0.20	1.22	−0.46	−2.74***	0.14
Stock	1.41	3.03***	0.19	1.79*	0.18	1.72*	0.23

Alphas and Betas are estimated from the following regression: $R_{it} = \alpha_i + \beta_i^+ I_t^+ + \beta_i^- I_t^- + \varepsilon_{it}$, where $I_t^+ = R_{mt}$, if $R_{mt} > 0$ and $I_t^+ = 0$ otherwise; $I_t^- = R_{mt}$, if $R_{mt} \leq 0$ and $I_t^- = 0$ otherwise. R_{mt} is the monthly return on the S&P 500 index. As of March 2002, there are 2357 hedge funds (1164 live funds and 1193 defunct funds), 597 funds-of-funds (349 live and 248 defunct), and 1510 CTAs (294 live and 1216 defunct). The regression is conducted from 1998 to 2000 using 36 monthly returns.

*Significant at 10% level.
**Significant at 5% level.
***Significant at 1% level.

are higher for the hedge fund or fund-of-fund styles than those of CTA styles. This reinforces the notion that CTAs are generally not invested in the equity markets and they are different from hedge funds and funds-of-funds in trading strategies, which generally long equities and bonds. This pattern of beta asymmetry supports Mitchell and Pulvino (2001) who show that most risk arbitrage funds are positively correlated with the markets returns in the down markets but uncorrelated with the market returns in the up markets.

4.2 Correlations at the investment style level

Although Table 4 offers equity market betas in both the up and down markets, it does tell us the cross correlations among different fund styles. Because of this, in Table 5 we report the simple correlation coefficients across ten hedge fund or fund-of-fund styles and across five CTA styles in the up markets.[8] We define up market when the S&P 500 index has positive returns. We also report the cross correlation among hedge funds, funds-of-funds, and CTAs. Across hedge fund styles, we observe two results: first, all styles are moderately to highly correlated, with coefficients ranging from a low of 0.306 to a high of 0.926.[9] All 36 coefficients except for four (all four from the short selling style) are significant at the 5% level. This can be explained by two possible

Table 5 Correlation coefficients across hedge fund, fund-of-fund, and CTA styles in up and down markets.

	EV	MA	EM	ES	IN	LO	NE	SE	SH	FF	AG	CU	DI	FI	ST
Up markets															
EV	1.000	0.672*	0.565*	0.616*	0.720*	0.485*	0.802*	0.520*	−0.354	0.769*	0.432	−0.033	0.120	−0.166	0.092
MA		1.000	0.555*	0.676*	0.711*	0.475*	0.784*	0.580*	−0.306	0.799*	0.206	0.164	0.389	0.134	0.274
EM			1.000	0.725*	0.870*	0.636*	0.684*	0.543*	−0.453*	0.853*	−0.076	−0.206	−0.053	−0.180	0.109
ES				1.000	0.779*	0.781*	0.761*	0.838*	−0.727*	0.926*	0.252	−0.128	0.072	−0.072	0.317
IN					1.000	0.594*	0.873*	0.489*	−0.463*	0.913*	0.180	−0.132	0.020	−0.209	0.026
LO						1.000	0.558*	0.797*	−0.779	0.745*	0.183	−0.394	0.001	−0.158	0.186
NE							1.000	0.539*	−0.401	0.890*	0.459*	−0.174	0.126	−0.203	0.114
SE								1.000	−0.731*	0.766*	0.122	−0.099	0.089	−0.006	0.326
SH									1.000	−0.577*	−0.135	0.203	0.023	0.144	−0.017
FF										1.000	0.230	−0.139	0.081	−0.140	0.240
AG											1.000	−0.311	−0.157	−0.312	−0.088
CU												1.000	0.648*	0.710*	−0.081
DI													1.000	0.882*	−0.045
FI														1.000	0.014
ST															1.000
Down markets															
EV	1.000	0.737*	0.889*	0.924*	0.886*	0.842*	0.894*	0.891*	−0.816	0.960*	−0.497*	−0.111	−0.770*	−0.730*	0.443
MA		1.000	0.670*	0.878*	0.677*	0.853*	0.753*	0.823*	−0.905	0.853*	−0.216	−0.040	−0.446	−0.497*	0.699*
EM			1.000	0.802*	0.897*	0.692*	0.760*	0.752*	−0.734*	0.880*	−0.281	−0.108	−0.688*	−0.661*	0.344
ES				1.000	0.789*	0.962*	0.923*	0.975*	−0.950*	0.985*	−0.477	−0.110	−0.643*	−0.650*	0.581*
IN					1.000	0.690*	0.827*	0.732*	−0.745*	0.866*	−0.225	−0.114	−0.510*	−0.507*	0.383
LO						1.000	0.877*	0.965*	−0.916	0.930*	−0.439	−0.120	−0.561*	−0.618*	0.588*
NE							1.000	0.917*	−0.870	0.936*	−0.394	−0.192	−0.539*	−0.514*	0.481
SE								1.000	−0.917*	0.960*	−0.486	−0.182	−0.629*	−0.644*	0.565*
SH									1.000	−0.926*	0.266	0.118	0.419	0.429	−0.705*
FF										1.000	−0.435	−0.127	−0.670*	−0.663*	0.554*
AG											1.000	0.215	0.728*	0.727*	0.091
CU												1.000	0.115	0.142	0.204
DI													1.000	0.938*	−0.049
FI														1.000	−0.050
ST															1.000

EV, event driven; MA, global macro; EM, global emerging market; ES, global established markets; IN, global international markets; LO, long only; NE, market neutral; SE, sector; SH, short sale; FF, funds-of-funds. Strategy code for CTAs: DIV, diversified trading program; CUR, currency trading program; AG, agricultural trading program; STX, stock trading program; FI, financial trading program.

*Significant at the 5% level.

reasons: aggregation at each style level reduces variability of an individual fund and, different funds correlate through some net long positions in the equity markets or bond markets. Styles may also be connected through some common factors that affect equity markets or bond markets. This is confirmed by the significant equity market factor and bond market factor loadings in Table 3. Second, the style short sale is negatively correlated with other styles, indicating an opposite bet on the direction of asset price movement. For funds-of-funds, the correlation is positive with all hedge fund styles except for short sale. Again, this is consistent with the notion that funds-of-funds invest in different hedge funds. Across CTA styles, there are some correlations among diversified trading programs and financial trading programs. However, the remaining styles are not significantly correlated.

Across hedge funds, funds-of-funds, and CTAs, all 50 correlation coefficients except for one are not significant (inside the box). This forms a very strong contrast with the high correlations among hedge fund styles. This result is consistent with the analysis from the asset class factor regression in the previous section, where we show that CTAs are different from hedge funds or funds-of-funds in asset class factors. The low correlation between CTAs and hedge fund or fund-of-fund styles may have strong implications for portfolio managers' investment decisions and asset allocation decisions: adding CTAs to hedge funds or funds-of-funds may increase the diversification effect hence improve the risk-return trade-off of an investor's portfolio. We will discuss this further in the next section.

In the down markets, we can find that the magnitudes of correlations in the down markets are higher than those in the up markets, consistent with our conjecture of limited liquidity supplies in the down markets. Across hedge fund styles, all 36 correlation coefficients except for four (again from the short selling style) are higher than the corresponding numbers in up markets. They are ranging from a low of 0.67 to a high of 0.985 (comparing with 0.306–0.926 in up markets). Among hedge funds, funds-of-funds, and CTAs, agriculture, currency, diversified, and financial trading programs are all negatively correlated with hedge fund or fund-of-fund styles except for the short selling strategy. Stock trading program is positively correlated with hedge fund styles. Twenty-four out of 50 coefficients are significant, compared with only one significant coefficient in up markets. Note that most coefficients under diversified, financial, and stock trading programs are significantly different from zero.

In summary, combining the non-linear piecewise regression analysis with the simple correlation analysis in both up and down markets, we find that all funds exhibit beta asymmetry in different market environments. They are related to the market index more in the down markets than in the up markets. In particular, hedge funds and funds-of-funds are highly correlated each other, which is especially true in the down markets. Hedge funds and funds-of-funds have highly positive betas with respect to the S&P 500 index in the down market. CTAs have zero correlation with hedge funds or funds-of-funds in the up markets but have significantly negative correlations in the down markets. CTAs also have significantly negative market betas (and relatively high in magnitude) in the down markets. This correlation structure can make CTAs a suitable hedging instrument for other alternative investment vehicles, especially in the down markets.

4.3 Benefits of adding CTAs to other investment classes

The performance analysis in the previous section only focuses on a stand-alone basis: we do not mix one investment class with another. Poor stand-alone performance from CTAs does not prevent them from becoming good candidates for adding to other investment portfolios, especially when CTAs and other portfolios have negative or low correlations as indicated previously. As a matter of fact, CTAs may be very well suited for excellent hedging instruments for the other investment classes. It is well known that CTAs or commodity funds offer good hedges against the equity and bond market downturns (see Sharpe *et al.* 1999; Irwin *et al.* 1993).

With the low or negative correlations between CTAs and others in mind, we now build portfolios of CTAs and hedge funds, and portfolios between CTAs and funds-of-funds. Because we need the autocorrelation adjusted Sharpe ratios to measure performance and risk, we focus on four consecutive years: the bull markets from 1998 to 1999 and the bear markets from 2000 to 2001. In Panel A of Table 6, we report the regular Sharpe ratios, $\sqrt{12}$ SRs, and the autocorrelation adjusted Sharpe ratios of hedge fund, fund-of-fund, and CTA portfolios. Although the pecking order of performance during the up markets is hedge funds, funds-of-funds, and CTAs, this order is totally reversed in the down markets. Actually, CTAs offer higher Sharpe ratios in the down markets than those in the up markets. In the down markets, funds-of-funds may offer better diversification than the individual hedge funds, which can help reduce risk significantly. The negative correlation between CTAs and the others can certainly play an important role in achieving higher risk adjusted performance for CTAs in the market downturn.

We also report these Sharpe ratios of various portfolio combinations between CTAs and hedge funds, and between CTAs and funds-of-funds in Panels B and C. Interestingly, adding CTAs to hedge funds or funds-of-funds can improve the Sharpe ratios in a majority of the portfolio combinations. For example, in the up market, when we add CTAs to hedge funds (with the stand-alone Sharpe ratios 0.44 and 1.07 for the two groups, respectively), the combined Sharpe ratios in Panel B are higher than both of the stand-alone hedge fund Sharpe ratios and the CTA Sharpe ratios for all but the 10/90 combination. Investors can benefit from combining the two investment classes. Amazingly, CTAs can add benefits to funds-of-funds for all portfolio combinations in the up markets. The results in Panel C show that the combined Sharpe ratios are all higher than 0.63, the stand-alone Sharpe ratio for funds-of-funds. The optimal portfolio combination for hedge funds and CTAs is 30% hedge funds and 70% CTAs (with the highest Sharpe ratio 2.08) while the optimal combination for funds-of-funds and CTAs is 40% funds-of-funds and 60% CTAs with a Sharpe ratio 1.74.

The results for the down markets are similar to those of the up markets. Hedge fund investors will benefit from adding CTAs to their portfolios in all portfolio combinations

Table 6 Sharpe ratios of hedge funds, funds-of-funds, CTAs, and portfolio combinations.

	Bull market 1998–1999			Bear market 2000–2001		
Portfolio	Sharpe	$\sqrt{12}$ SR	$\eta(12)$ SR	Sharpe	$\sqrt{12}$ SR	$\eta(12)$ SR
Panel A: three groups						
Hedge funds	0.36	1.25	1.07	0.03	0.09	0.14
Funds-of-funds	0.23	0.80	0.63	0.03	0.12	0.20
CTAs	0.10	0.35	0.44	0.09	0.31	0.55
Panel B: HF + CTA						
0.1/0.9	0.17	0.59	0.85	0.09	0.32[a]	0.63[a]
0.2/0.8	0.26	0.90	1.49[a]	0.09	0.33[a]	0.71[a]
0.3/0.7	0.36	1.23	2.08[a,b]	0.09	0.33[a]	0.80[a]
0.4/0.6	0.43	1.48[a]	2.03[a]	0.09	0.31[a]	0.83[a,b]
0.5/0.5	0.45	1.57[a]	1.74[a]	0.08	0.29	0.73[a]
0.6/0.4	0.45	1.54[a]	1.50[a]	0.07	0.25	0.56[a]
0.7/0.3	0.42	1.47[a]	1.34[a]	0.06	0.21	0.40
0.8/0.2	0.40	1.39[a]	1.22[a]	0.05	0.16	0.29
0.9/0.1	0.38	1.31[a]	1.14[a]	0.04	0.12	0.20
Panel C: FOF + CTA						
0.1/0.9	0.14	0.48	0.69[a]	0.09	0.32[a]	0.60[a]
0.2/0.8	0.19	0.64	1.13[a]	0.09	0.32[a]	0.64[a]
0.3/0.7	0.24	0.83[a]	1.72[a]	0.09	0.33[a]	0.70[a]
0.4/0.6	0.29	1.01[a]	1.74[a,b]	0.09	0.33[a]	0.74[a]
0.5/0.5	0.32	1.10[a]	1.34[a]	0.09	0.32[a]	0.79[a,b]
0.6/0.4	0.32	1.09[a]	1.06[a]	0.09	0.30	0.74[a]
0.7/0.3	0.30	1.02[a]	0.88[a]	0.08	0.27	0.60[a]
0.8/0.2	0.27	0.94[a]	0.77[a]	0.06	0.22	0.45
0.9/0.1	0.25	0.87[a]	0.69[a]	0.05	0.17	0.30

[a] Improvement on Sharpe ratios when adding CTAs to the portfolio.
[b] Indicate the highest autocorrelation adjusted Sharpe ratio.
As of March 2002, there are 2357 hedge funds (1164 live funds and 1193 defunct funds), 597 funds-of-funds (349 live and 248 defunct), and 1510 CTAs (294 live and 1216 defunct). Every month, we calculate portfolio returns as the equally weighted average of all funds in the portfolio. Different portfolios are formed between hedge funds and CTAs, and between funds-of-funds and CTAs. A 0.1/0.9 combination represents for a 10% investment in hedge funds/funds-of-funds and a 90% investment in CTAs. Up markets are from 1998 to 1999 while down markets are from 2000 to 2001. Sharpe ratios are estimated using 24 monthly return observations in the up and down markets, respectively. $\sqrt{12}$ SR is the annualized Sharpe ratio when returns are i.i.d. while $\eta(12)$ SR is the autocorrelation adjusted Sharpe ratio on an annualized basis where

$$\eta(12) = \frac{12}{\sqrt{12 + 2\sum_{k=1}^{11} (12 - k)\rho_k}}$$

is used for calculating the autocorrelation adjusted Sharpe ratios.

with 40% or more allocations in CTAs. Similarly, fund-of-fund investors can benefit from adding CTAs with a portfolio weight 30% or more in CTAs. The optimal portfolio combination for hedge funds and CTAs is 40% hedge funds and 60% CTAs (the highest Sharpe ratio is 0.83) while the optimal combination for funds-of-funds and CTAs is 50% funds-of-funds and 50% CTAs with a Sharpe ratio of 0.79.

These results can be explained by the low or negative correlation between CTAs and other investment classes, by different investment strategies, and by the different autocorrelation structures of these investment vehicles. The results are robust no matter whether we use $\eta(12)$ SRs or $\sqrt{12}$ SRs for comparison. Actually, the autocorrelation adjusted Sharpe ratios can only make our results stronger.

5 Conclusion

Using a large database on hedge funds, funds-of-funds, and CTAs, we study the issues of risk, return, and fee structures of these alternative investment vehicles. By comprehensively evaluating all these investment vehicles, we distinguish one investment class from the other in order to study the differences and similarities. We examine these investment classes not only on a stand-alone basis but also on a portfolio basis of combining one class with another. The following are our results.

First, hedge funds and funds-of-funds are linked through some common asset class factors. These factors are MSCI developed country index, MSCI emerging market index, Salomon Brothers world government bond index, Salomon Brothers BIG index, and the Fama–French size factor. Apparently, hedge funds primarily invest in equity markets or bond markets. However, due to the double fee structure of funds-of-funds, funds-of-funds under perform hedge funds during the period from 1994 to 2001. This underperformance is unlikely to be explained by survivorship bias. Unlike the previous findings (see Agarwal and Naik 2004), we find only the Fama–French factors can add significantly to the power of explaining hedge fund returns; the option strategy factors cannot.

Second, CTAs differ from the other two asset classes in several ways. The only significant factor loadings for CTA returns are the option-based factors, not equity or bond factors. This reflects the option-like payoffs (or concavity in returns) with respect to the equity markets and the fact that CTAs generally do not invest in equity or bond markets. In addition, CTAs have zero or negative correlation with the other two investment classes and with the equity market index.

Third, correlation coefficients and equity market betas from piecewise regressions in the up markets are generally lower than those in the down markets. This can be explained by the drain of liquidity supply during market crisis, when fund managers do not have much flexibility to maneuver and have to herd. Hedge funds or funds-of-funds offer lower risk-return trade-off than CTAs in the down markets. Therefore, hedge funds are not well hedged in the down markets; rather they are highly correlated with each other and with the market index. In contrast, CTA styles are not or only negatively correlated with hedge funds, funds-of-funds, and the market index.

Fourth, on a stand-alone basis, CTAs trail behind hedge funds and funds-of-funds during the same time period. This underperformance can be attributed to high management fees, high attrition rate and survivorship bias, under-diversified portfolio positions in futures markets, and high leverage in futures contracts. However, due to the negative correlation, CTAs provide significant diversification benefits to other investment classes: adding CTAs to investors' hedge fund portfolio or fund-of-fund portfolio can significantly improve their risk-return trade-off. In other words, CTAs are good hedging instruments for hedge funds, funds-of-funds, and the equity markets when the others are not well hedged. This is especially true in the down markets.

Acknowledgments

The author acknowledges a research grant from the Foundation for Managed Derivatives Research. The author is obligated to Stephen Brown for his encouragement of this project and for suggestions that have significantly improved the paper. I would like to thank Sanjay Nawalkha, Will Goetzmann, Hossein Kazemi, Nelson Lacey, Dick Oberuc, Tom Schneeweis, Paul Weller, and seminar participants at London School of Economics, University of Massachusetts, and University of Warwick for their comments. I am grateful to Zurich Capital Markets Inc. for providing the data and to Vikas Agarwal and Narayan Naik for providing the options strategy data.

Notes

[1] Previously, the data was owned by Zurich Capital Markets, Inc. It was also known as the Managed Accounts Reports (MARs) data.

[2] Although some CTAs have switched names to hedge funds in order to avoid regulation, this nominal change does not affect their fundamental trading strategies.

[3] Our survey indicates that an average fund-of-funds invests in only 13 hedge funds. However, Park and Staum (1998) indicate that well diversified funds-of-funds need more hedge funds.

[4] There are three ways in which investors can invest in managed futures. Public commodity funds are similar to equity or bond mutual funds except they invest in commodity or financial futures. Privately placed funds pool investors' money and hire one or more CTAs to manage the pooled funds. Finally, investors can have one or more CTAs directly manage their money on an individual basis. Therefore, a CTA can engage in both public and private funds. To avoid double counting, we only use the CTA sample from CISDM.

[5] We only report the adjusted Sharpe ratios from 1994 to 2000 (not 2001) because we need the data in 2001 to estimate the autocorrelation structures for year 2000.

[6] Survivorship bias is calculated as the difference between the portfolio of live funds and the portfolio of all funds. The annual survivorship biases for hedge funds, funds-of-funds, and CTAs are 2.32, 1.18, and 5.89%, respectively.

[7] We have also tried the yield spread factor (Baa corporate bond yield minus the 10-year Treasury yield), but it is insignificant for any of the four models so that we do not include it in the results.

[8] The sample period from 1998 to 2000 includes both the bull and bear markets. We require all funds having 36 monthly consecutive returns to calculate the correlation. We separate the up markets from the down markets to deal with the non-linearity problem.

[9] Other studies such as Ackermann *et al.* (1999) and Liang (1999) have found much lower correlations. The difference comes from different datasets and different time periods used. For example, based on CISDM data, the average positive correlation coefficient during the 1992–1994 and 1995–1997 periods are 0.5007 and 0.6714, respectively, compared with 0.8296 in the 1998–2000 period. It seems that there is an increasing correlation pattern among hedge fund styles over these time periods.

References

Ackermann, C., McEnally, R., and Ravenscraft, D. (1999). "The Performance of Hedge Funds: Risk, Return and Incentives." *Journal of Finance* **54**, 833–874.

Agarwal, V. and Naik, N. (2004). "Risks and Portfolio Decisions Involving Hedge Funds." *Review of Financial Studies* **17**, 63–98.

Brown, S. J., Goetzmann, W. N., and Liang, B. (2004). "Fees on Fees in Funds-of-Funds." *Journal of Investment Management* **2**, 39–56.

Fung, W. and Hsieh, D. A. (1997a). "Empirical Characteristics of Dynamic Trading Strategies: The Case of Hedge Funds." *The Review of Financial Studies* **10**, 275–302.

Fung, W. and Hsieh, D. A. (1997b). "Survivorship Bias and Investment Style in the Returns of CTAs." *The Journal of Portfolio Management* **24**, 30–41.

Fung, W. and Hsieh, D. A. (2000). "Performance Characteristics of Hedge Funds and Commodity Funds: Natural vs. Spurious Biases." *Journal of Financial and Quantitative Analysis* **35**, 291–307.

Getmansky, M., Lo, A. W., and Makarov, I. (2004). "An Econometric Model of Serial Correlation and Illiquidity in Hedge Fund Returns." *Journal of Financial Economics*, forthcoming.

Irwin, S. H., Krukemyer, T. R., and Zulauf, C. R. (1993). "Investment Performance of Public Commodity Pools: 1979–1990." *The Journal of Futures Markets* **13**, 799–820.

Kyle, A. (1985). "Continuous Auctions and Insider Trading." *Econometrica* **53**, 1315–1335.

Liang, B. (1999). "On the Performance of Hedge Funds." *Financial Analysts Journal* **55**, 72–85.

Liang, B. (2000). "Hedge Funds: The Living and the Dead." *Journal of Financial and Quantitative Analysis* **35**, 309–326.

Lo, A. (2002). "The Statistics of Sharpe Ratios." *Financial Analysts Journal* **58**, 36–52.

Mitchell, M. and Pulvino, T. (2001). "Characteristics of Risk in Risk Arbitrage." *Journal of Finance* **56**, 2135–2175.

Park, J. M. and Staum, J. C. (1998). "Fund of Fund Diversification: How Much Is Enough?" *The Journal of Alternative Investments* **1**, 39–42.

Sharpe, W. F. (1992). "Asset Allocation: Management Style and Performance Measurement." *Journal of Portfolio Management* **18**, 7–19.

Sharpe, W. F., Alexander, G. J., and Bailey, J. V. (1999). *Investments*, 6th edn. Englewood cliffs, NJ: Prentice-Hall.

Keywords: Hedge funds; funds-of-funds; commodity trading advisors

Journal of Investment Management
Vol. 2, No. 1 (2004), pp. 32–40

MANAGED FUTURES AND HEDGE FUNDS: A MATCH MADE IN HEAVEN

Harry M. Kat

In this paper we study the possible role of managed futures in portfolios of stocks, bonds, and hedge funds. We find that allocating to managed futures allows investors to achieve a very substantial degree of overall risk reduction at, in terms of expected return, relatively limited costs. Apart from their lower expected return, managed futures appear to be more effective diversifiers than hedge funds. Adding managed futures to a portfolio of stocks and bonds will reduce that portfolio's standard deviation more and quicker than hedge funds will, and without the undesirable side effects on skewness and kurtosis. The overall portfolio standard deviation can be reduced further by combining both hedge funds and managed futures with stocks and bonds. As long as at least 45–50% of the alternatives allocation is allocated to managed futures, this will have no negative side effects on skewness and kurtosis.

1 Introduction

Hedge funds are often said to provide investors with the best of both worlds: an expected return similar to equity combined with a risk similar to that of bonds. When past returns are simply extrapolated and risk is defined as the standard deviation of the fund return, this is indeed true. Recent research, however, has shown that the risk and dependence characteristics of hedge funds are substantially more complex than those of stocks and bonds. Amin and Kat (2003), for example, show that although including hedge funds in a traditional investment portfolio may significantly improve that portfolio's mean–variance characteristics, it can also be expected to lead to significantly lower skewness. The additional negative skewness that arises when hedge funds are introduced in a portfolio of stocks and bonds forms a major risk as one large negative return can destroy years of careful compounding. To hedge this risk, investors will have to expand their horizon beyond stocks and bonds. In Kat (2003) it was shown how stock index put options may be used to hedge against the unwanted skewness effect of hedge funds. In Kat (2002) it was shown that put options on (baskets of) hedge funds may perform a similar task.

Of course, the list of possible remedies does not end here. Any asset or asset class that has suitable (co-)skewness characteristics can be used. One obvious candidate is managed futures. Managed futures programs are often trend-following in nature. In essence, what these programs do is somewhat similar to what option traders will do to hedge a short call position. When the market moves up, they increase exposure and

Cass Business School, City University, 106 Bunhill Row, London, EC2Y 8TZ, UK. Tel.: +44.(0)20.70408677; e-mail: harry@harrykat.com vice versa. By moving out of the market when it comes down, managed futures programs avoid being pulled in. As a result, the (co-)skewness characteristics of managed futures programs can be expected to be more or less opposite to those of many hedge funds.

In this paper, we investigate how managed futures mix with stocks, bonds, and hedge funds and how they can be used to control the undesirable skewness effects that arise when adding hedge funds to portfolios of stocks and bonds. We find that managed futures combine extremely well with stocks and bonds as well as hedge funds and that the combination allows investors to significantly improve the overall risk characteristics of their portfolio without, under the assumptions made, giving up much in terms of expected return.

2 Managed Futures

The asset class "managed futures" refers to professional money managers known as commodity trading advisors or CTAs who manage assets using the global futures and options markets as their investment universe. Managed futures have been available for investment since 1948 when the first public futures fund started trading. The industry did not take off until the late 1970s though. Since then the sector has seen a fair amount of growth with, currently, an estimated $40–45 billion under management.

There are three ways in which investors can get into managed futures. First, investors can buy shares in a public commodity (or futures) fund, in much the same way as they would invest in a stock or bond mutual funds. Second, investors can place funds privately with a commodity pool operator (CPO) who pools investors' money and employs one or more CTAs to manage the pooled funds. Third, investors can retain one or more CTAs directly to manage their money on an individual basis or hire a manager of managers (MOM) to select CTAs for them. The minimum investment required by funds, pools, and CTAs varies considerably, with the direct CTA route open only to investors that want to make a substantial investment. CTAs charge management and incentive fees comparable to those charged by hedge funds, i.e. 2% management fee plus 20% incentive fee. Similar to funds of hedge funds, funds and pools charge an additional fee on top of that.

Initially, CTAs were limited to trading commodity futures (which explains terms such as public commodity fund, CTA, and CPO). With the introduction of futures on currencies, interest rates, bonds, and stock indexes in the 1980s, however, the trading spectrum widened substantially. Nowadays, CTAs trade both commodity and financial futures. Many take a very technical, systematic approach to trading, but others opt for a more fundamental, discretionary approach. Some concentrate on particular futures markets, such as agricultural, currencies, or metals, but most diversify over different types of markets.

For our purposes, one of the most important features of managed futures is their trend-following nature. That CTA returns have a strong trend-following component can be shown by calculating the correlation between managed futures returns and the returns on a purely mechanical trend-following strategy. One such strategy is the one underlying the Mount Lucas Management (MLM) index. The latter reflects the results of a purely mechanical, moving average based trading strategy in 25 different, commodity and financial, futures markets. Estimates of the correlation between the MLM index and CTA returns are typically positive and highly significant.

3 Data

We distinguish between four different asset classes: stocks, bonds, hedge funds, and managed futures. Stocks are represented by the S&P 500 index and bonds by the 10-year Salomon Brothers Government Bond index. Hedge fund return data were obtained from Tremont TASS, which is one of the largest hedge fund databases currently available. After eliminating funds with incomplete and ambiguous data as well as funds of funds, per May 2001 the database at our disposal contained monthly net of fee returns on 1195 live and 526 dead funds. To avoid survivorship bias, we created 455 7-year monthly return series by, starting off with the 455 funds that were alive in June 1994, replacing every fund that closed down during the sample period by a fund randomly selected from the set of funds alive at the time of closure, following the same type of strategy and of similar age and size. Next, we used random sampling to create 500 different equally-weighted portfolios containing 20 hedge funds each. From the monthly returns on these portfolios we calculated the mean, standard deviation, skewness, and kurtosis and determined the median value of each of these statistics. Subsequently, we selected the portfolio whose sample statistics came closest to the latter median values. We use this "median portfolio" to represent hedge funds.

Managed futures are represented by the Stark 300 index. This asset-weighted index is compiled using the top 300 trading programs from the Daniel B. Stark & Co. database.[1] The top 300 trading programs are determined quarterly, based on assets under management. When a trading program closes down, the index does not get adjusted backwards, which takes care of survivorship bias issues. All 300 of the CTAs in the index are classified by their trading approach and market category. Currently, the index contains 248 systematic and 52 discretionary traders, which split up into 169 diversified, 111 financial only, 9 financial and metals, and 11 non-financial trading programs.

Throughout we use monthly return data over the period June 1994 to May 2001. For bonds, hedge funds, and managed futures we use the sample mean as our estimate of the expected future return. For stocks, however, we assume an expected return of 1% per month as it would be unrealistic to assume an immediate repeat of the 1990s bull market. Under these assumptions, the basic return statistics for our four asset classes are shown in Table 1. The table shows that managed futures returns have a lower mean and a higher standard deviation than hedge fund returns. However, managed futures also exhibit positive instead of negative skewness and much lower kurtosis.[2] From the correlation matrix we see that the correlation of managed futures with stocks and hedge funds, especially, is extremely low. This means that, as long as there are no negative side effects such as lower skewness or higher kurtosis, for example, managed futures will make very good diversifiers. This is what we investigate in more detail next.

Table 1 Basic statistics S&P 500, bonds, hedge funds, and managed futures.

	S&P 500	Bonds	Hedge funds	Managed futures
Mean	1.00	0.45	0.99	0.70
Standard deviation	4.39	1.77	2.44	2.89
Skewness	−0.82	0.58	−0.47	0.45
Excess kurtosis	1.05	1.45	2.67	0.21
Correlations				
S&P 500	1			
Bonds	0.15	1		
HF	0.63	−0.05	1	
MF	−0.07	0.20	−0.14	1

4 Stocks, Bonds, Plus Hedge Funds or Managed Futures

Given the complexity of the relationship between hedge fund and equity returns, we study the impact of hedge funds and managed futures for two different types of investors. The first are what we will refer to as "50/50 investors." These are investors that always invest an equal amount in stocks and bonds. When adding hedge funds and/or managed futures to their portfolio, 50/50 investors will reduce their stock and bond holdings by the same amount. This gives rise to portfolios like 45% stocks, 45% bonds, and 10% hedge funds, or 40% stocks, 40% bonds, and 20% managed futures. The second type of investors are what we will call "33/66 investors." These investors always divide the money invested in stocks and bonds in such a way that $\frac{1}{3}$ is invested in stocks and $\frac{2}{3}$ is invested in bonds.

The first step in our analysis is to see whether there are any significant differences in the way in which hedge funds and managed futures combine with stocks and bonds. We, therefore, form portfolios of stocks, bonds, and hedge funds, as well as stocks, bonds, and managed futures. Table 2 shows the basic return statistics for

Table 2 Return statistics 50/50 portfolios of stocks, bonds, and hedge funds or managed futures.

	Hedge funds					Managed futures			
% HF	Mean	SD	Skew	Kurt	% MF	Mean	SD	Skew	Kurt
0	0.72	2.49	−0.33	−0.03	0	0.72	2.49	−0.33	−0.03
5	0.73	2.43	−0.40	0.02	5	0.71	2.37	−0.28	−0.18
10	0.74	2.38	−0.46	0.08	10	0.71	2.26	−0.21	−0.30
15	0.76	2.33	−0.53	0.17	15	0.71	2.16	−0.14	−0.39
20	0.77	2.29	−0.60	0.28	20	0.71	2.08	−0.06	−0.42
25	0.78	2.25	−0.66	0.42	25	0.71	2.00	0.02	−0.40
30	0.80	2.22	−0.72	0.58	30	0.71	1.95	0.10	−0.32
35	0.81	2.20	−0.78	0.77	35	0.71	1.91	0.18	−0.20
40	0.82	2.18	−0.82	0.97	40	0.71	1.89	0.24	−0.06
45	0.84	2.17	−0.85	1.19	45	0.71	1.89	0.30	0.08
50	0.85	2.16	−0.87	1.41	50	0.71	1.91	0.34	0.19

Table 3 Return statistics 33/66 portfolios of stocks, bonds, and hedge funds or managed futures.

	Hedge funds					Managed futures			
% HF	Mean	SD	Skew	Kurt	% MF	Mean	SD	Skew	Kurt
0	0.62	2.01	0.03	0.21	0	0.62	2.01	0.03	0.21
5	0.64	1.97	−0.05	0.13	5	0.62	1.93	0.09	0.17
10	0.66	1.93	−0.14	0.08	10	0.63	1.85	0.15	0.14
15	0.68	1.90	−0.24	0.04	15	0.63	1.79	0.22	0.15
20	0.69	1.87	−0.34	0.04	20	0.64	1.75	0.28	0.18
25	0.71	1.86	−0.43	0.09	25	0.64	1.71	0.34	0.24
30	0.73	1.85	−0.52	0.17	30	0.65	1.70	0.39	0.30
35	0.75	1.84	−0.60	0.31	35	0.65	1.70	0.42	0.36
40	0.77	1.85	−0.66	0.49	40	0.65	1.72	0.45	0.41
45	0.79	1.86	−0.71	0.70	45	0.66	1.76	0.47	0.43
50	0.80	1.89	−0.75	0.94	50	0.66	1.81	0.48	0.42

50/50 investors. Table 3 shows the same for 33/66 investors. From Table 2 we see that if the hedge fund allocation increases, both the standard deviation and the skewness of the portfolio return distribution drop substantially, while at the same time the return distribution's kurtosis increases. A similar picture emerges from Table 3 for 33/66 investors, except that the drop in skewness is much more pronounced. With managed futures the picture is different. If the managed futures allocation increases, the standard deviation drops faster than with hedge funds. More remarkably, skewness rises instead of dropping, while the reverse is true for kurtosis. Although (under the assumptions made) hedge funds offer a somewhat higher expected return, from an overall risk perspective, managed futures appear to be better diversifiers than hedge funds.

5 Hedge Funds Plus Managed Futures

The next step is to study how hedge funds and managed futures combine with each other. This is shown in Table 4. Adding managed futures to a hedge fund portfolio will

Table 4 Return statistics portfolios of hedge funds and managed futures.

% MF	Mean	SD	Skew	Kurt
0	0.99	2.44	−0.47	2.67
5	0.97	2.31	−0.37	2.31
10	0.96	2.18	−0.27	1.91
15	0.94	2.06	−0.15	1.46
20	0.93	1.96	−0.03	1.01
25	0.92	1.88	0.09	0.59
30	0.90	1.81	0.20	0.23
35	0.89	1.76	0.29	−0.01
40	0.87	1.74	0.36	−0.14
45	0.86	1.74	0.39	−0.17
50	0.85	1.76	0.39	−0.15

put downward pressure on the portfolio's expected return, as the expected return on managed futures is lower than that of hedge funds. From a risk perspective, however, the benefits of managed futures are again very substantial. From the table we see that adding managed futures to a portfolio of hedge funds will lead to a very significant drop in the portfolio return's standard deviation. With 40% invested in managed futures the standard deviation comes down from 2.44% to 1.74%. Skewness rises quickly as well; from −0.47 without to 0.39 when 45% is invested in managed futures. In addition, kurtosis exhibits a strong drop; from 2.67 without to −0.17 when 45% is invested in managed futures. Giving up 10–15 basis points per month in expected return does not seem an unrealistic price to pay for such a substantial improvement in overall risk profile.

6 Stocks, Bonds, Hedge Funds, and Managed Futures

The final step in our analysis is to bring all four asset classes together in one portfolio. We do so in two steps. First, we combine hedge funds and managed futures into what we will call the "alternatives portfolio." Secondly, we combine the alternatives portfolio with stocks and bonds. We vary the managed futures allocation in the alternatives portfolio as well as the alternatives allocation in the overall portfolio from 0% to 100% in 5% steps.

Without managed futures, increasing the alternatives allocation will significantly raise the expected return. When the managed futures allocation increases, however, the expected return will drop. This follows directly from the assumption that the expected return on hedge funds is 0.99%, but only 0.7% on managed futures. On the risk front, the picture is a lot more interesting. Figures 1 and 2 show that investing in alternatives can substantially reduce the overall portfolio return's standard deviation, for 50/50 as well as 33/66 investors. The drop, however, is heavily dependent on the percentage of

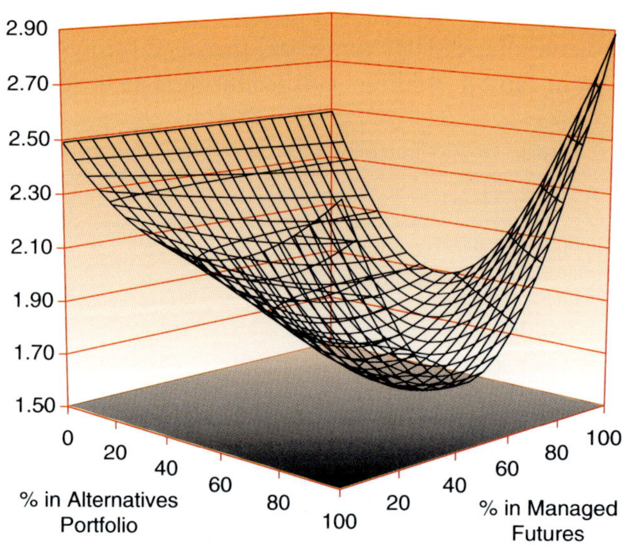

Figure 1 Standard deviation 50/50 portfolios of stocks, bonds, HF, and MF.

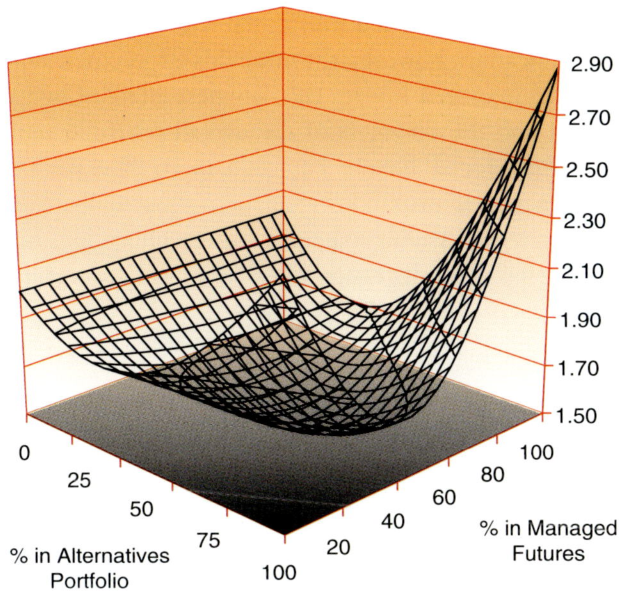

Figure 2 Standard deviation 33/66 portfolios of stocks, bonds, HF, and MF.

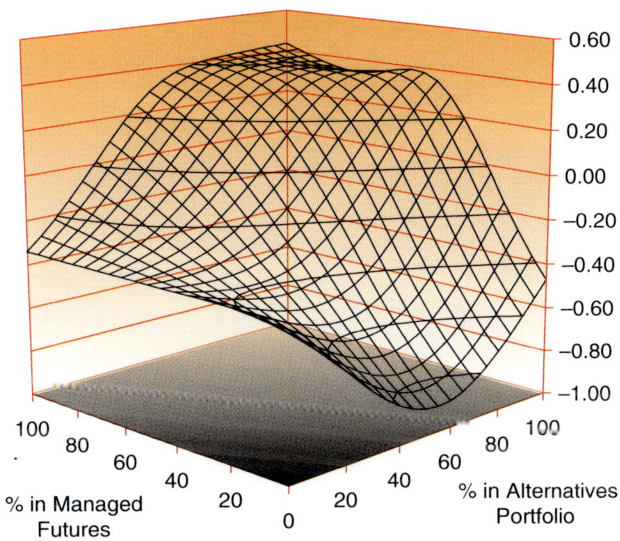

Figure 3 Skewness 50/50 portfolios of stocks, bonds, HF, and MF.

managed futures in the alternatives portfolio. Surprisingly, for allocations to alternatives between 0% and 20% the lowest standard deviations are obtained without hedge funds, i.e. when 100% is invested in managed futures. For higher alternatives allocations, however, it pays to also include some hedge funds in the alternatives portfolio. This makes sense, as for the alternatives portfolio itself the lowest standard deviation is found when 40–45% is invested in managed futures. We saw that before in Table 4.

Figures 3 and 4 show the skewness results for 50/50 and 33/66 investors, respectively. From these graphs we see once more that, without managed futures increasing, the alternatives allocation will lead to a substantial reduction in skewness. The higher the managed futures allocation, however, the more this effect is neutralized. When more than 50% is invested in managed futures the skewness effect of hedge funds is (more than) fully eliminated and the skewness of the overall portfolio return actually rises when alternatives are introduced. Finally, Figures 5 and 6 show the results on kurtosis. With 0% allocated to managed futures, kurtosis rises substantially when the alternatives allocation is increased. With a sizable managed futures allocation, however, this is no longer the case and kurtosis actually drops when more weight is given to alternatives.

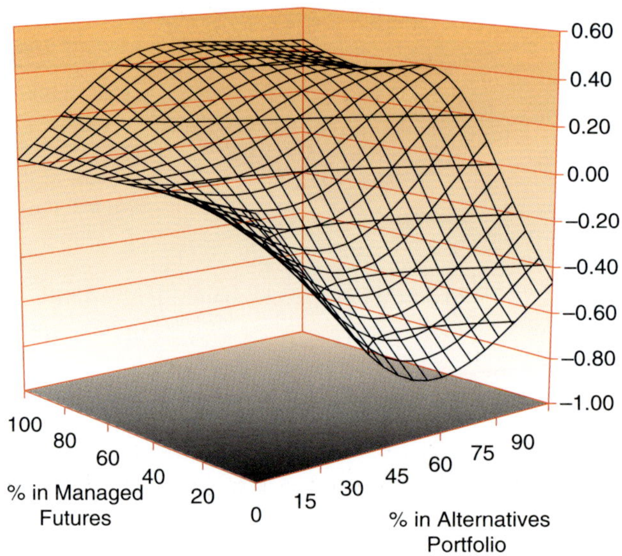

Figure 4 Skewness 33/66 portfolios of stocks, bonds, HF, and MF.

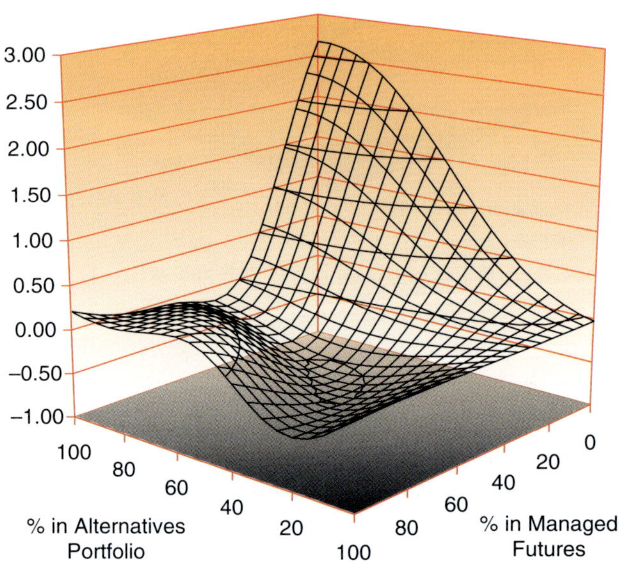

Figure 5 Kurtosis 50/50 portfolios of stocks, bonds, HF, and MF.

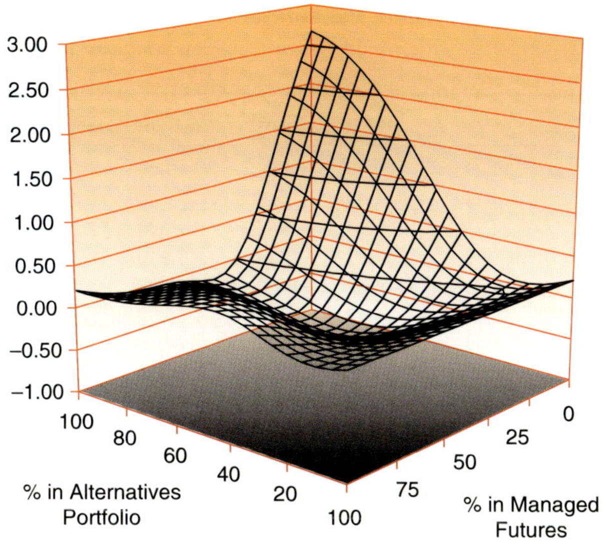

Figure 6 Kurtosis 33/66 portfolios of stocks, bonds, HF, and MF.

In sum, Figures 1–6 show that *investing in managed futures can improve the overall risk profile of a portfolio far beyond what can be achieved with hedge funds alone*. Making an allocation to managed futures not only neutralizes the unwanted side effects of hedge funds but also leads to further risk reduction. Assuming managed futures offer an acceptable expected return, all of this comes at quite a low price in terms of expected return foregone.

To make sure that the above findings have general validity, i.e., are not simply due to the particular choice of index, we repeated the above procedure with a number of other CTA indexes, including various indexes calculated by The Barclay Group. In all cases the results were very similar to what we found above, meaning that our results are robust with respect to the choice of the managed futures index.

7 Skewness Reduction with Managed Futures

The above leads us to the question as to what the exact costs are of using managed futures to eliminate the negative skewness effects of introducing hedge funds in a traditional portfolio of stocks and bonds. To answer this question, we follow the same procedure as in Kat (2003). First, we determine the managed futures allocation required to bring the overall portfolio skewness back to its level before the addition of hedge funds, which is −0.33 for 50/50 investors and 0.03 for 33/66 investors. Subsequently, we leverage (assuming 4% interest) the resulting portfolio to restore the standard deviation. The resulting overall portfolio allocations and the accompanying changes in expected return (on a per annum basis) and kurtosis are shown in Tables 5 and 6. From the latter we see that the optimal portfolios are quite straightforward. In essence, the bulk of the managed futures holdings is financed by borrowing, without changing much about the stock, bond, and hedge fund allocations. It is interesting to see that for smaller

Table 5 Allocations and change in mean and kurtosis 50/50 portfolios of stocks, bonds, hedge funds, managed futures, and cash with −0.33 skewness and standard deviations as in third column in Table 2.

Initial % HF	% Stocks	% Bonds	% HF	% MF	% Cash	Gain mean pa	Change kurt
0	50.00	50.00	0.00	0.00	0.00	0.00	0.00
5	47.42	47.42	4.99	5.48	−5.30	0.66	−0.18
10	44.71	44.71	9.94	9.95	−9.30	1.15	−0.34
15	41.99	41.99	14.82	13.60	−12.40	1.53	−0.50
20	39.34	39.34	19.67	16.55	−14.90	1.83	−0.66
25	36.67	36.67	24.45	18.91	−16.70	2.05	−0.82
30	34.09	34.09	29.22	20.80	−18.20	2.23	−0.98
35	31.55	31.55	33.98	22.33	−19.40	2.37	−1.15
40	29.06	29.06	38.75	23.32	−20.20	2.46	−1.31
45	26.61	26.61	43.54	24.04	−20.80	2.53	−1.46
50	24.25	24.25	48.50	24.40	−21.40	2.60	−1.59

Table 6 Allocations and change in mean and kurtosis 33/66 portfolios of stocks, bonds, hedge funds, managed futures, and cash with 0.03 skewness and standard deviations as in third column in Table 3.

Initial % HF	% Stocks	% Bonds	% HF	% MF	% Cash	Gain mean pa	Change kurt
0	33.33	66.67	0.00	0.00	0.00	0.00	0.00
5	32.08	64.16	5.07	6.70	−8.00	0.98	−0.07
10	30.54	61.07	10.18	12.71	−14.50	1.79	−0.15
15	28.83	57.66	15.26	17.96	−19.70	2.44	−0.22
20	26.99	53.99	20.25	22.37	−23.60	2.93	−0.31
25	25.11	50.22	25.11	26.06	−26.50	3.29	−0.42
30	23.21	46.41	29.84	29.04	−28.50	3.53	−0.56
35	21.32	42.63	34.44	31.41	−29.80	3.69	−0.73
40	19.47	38.94	38.94	33.15	−30.50	3.76	−0.93
45	17.65	35.29	43.31	34.35	−30.60	3.76	−1.15
50	15.85	31.71	47.56	35.18	−30.30	3.70	−1.38

initial hedge fund allocations the optimal hedge fund and managed futures allocation are more or less equal. This is true for 50/50 as well as 33/66 investors.

Looking at the change in expected return, we see that as a result of the addition of managed futures and the subsequent leverage the expected return actually increases instead of drops. From the last column we also see that this rise in expected return is accompanied by a significant drop in kurtosis. This compares very favorably with the results in Kat (2002, 2003) where it is shown that the costs of skewness reduction through stock index or hedge fund puts can be quite significant.

8 Conclusion

In this paper we have studied the possible role of managed futures in portfolios of stocks, bonds, and hedge funds. We found that allocating to managed futures allows investors to achieve a very substantial degree of overall risk reduction at limited costs. Apart from their lower expected return, managed futures appear to be more effective diversifiers than hedge funds. Adding managed futures to a portfolio of stocks and bonds will reduce that portfolio's standard deviation more and quicker than hedge funds will, and without the undesirable side effects on skewness and kurtosis. This does not mean that hedge funds are superfluous though. Overall portfolio standard deviation can be reduced further by combining both hedge funds and managed futures with stocks and bonds. As long as at least 45–50% of the alternatives allocation is allocated to managed futures, this again will not have any negative side effects on skewness and kurtosis. Assuming that, on average, hedge funds will continue to provide higher returns than managed futures, the inclusion of hedge funds will also boost the portfolio's expected return somewhat.

Acknowledgments

I would like to thank Daniel Stark (Daniel B. Stark & Co.) and Sol Waksman (The Barclay Group) for helpful comments as well as for providing the managed futures index return series used.

Notes

[1] Note that contrary to the MLM index, the Stark 300 is a true CTA index.

[2] Over the sample period the MLM index has a mean of 0.89%, a standard deviation of 1.63%, a skewness of −0.81 and a kurtosis of 3.42. The Stark 300 index, therefore, has fundamentally different skewness and kurtosis properties than the MLM index as well.

References

Amin, G. and Kat, H. (2003). "Stocks, Bonds and Hedge Funds: Not a Free Lunch!" *Journal of Portfolio Management* **Summer**, 113–120.

Kat, H. (2002). "In Search of the Optimal Fund of Hedge Funds." Working Paper, Alternative Investment Research Centre, Cass Business School (downloadable from www.cass.city.ac.uk/airc).

Kat, H. (2003). "Taking the Sting Out of Hedge Funds." *Journal of Wealth Management* **Winter**, 67–76.

Keywords: Hedge funds; managed futures; CTAs (Portfolio) diversification; skewness

Journal of Investment Management
Vol. 2, No. 4 (2004), pp. 39–56

FEES ON FEES IN FUNDS OF FUNDS

Stephen J. Brown[a,*], *William N. Goetzmann*[b], *and Bing Liang*[c]

Funds of funds are an increasingly popular avenue for hedge fund investment. Despite the increasing interest in hedge funds as an alternative asset class, the high degree of fund-specific risk and the lack of transparency may give fiduciaries pause. In addition, many of the most attractive hedge funds are closed to new investment. Funds of funds resolve these issues by providing investors with diversification across manager styles and professional oversight of fund operations that can provide the necessary degree of due diligence. In addition, many such funds hold shares in hedge funds otherwise closed to new investment allowing smaller investors access to the most sought-after managers. However, the diversification, oversight and access comes at the cost of a multiplication of the fees paid by the investor. One would expect that the information advantage of funds of funds would more than compensate investors for these fees. Unfortunately, individual hedge funds dominate fund of funds on an after-fee return or Sharpe ratio basis. In this paper we argue that the disappointing after-fee performance of some fund of funds might be explained by the nature of this fee arrangement, and that fund of funds providers may actually benefit from considering other possible fee arrangements. These alternative arrangements will improve reported performance and may make funds of funds more attractive to a growing institutional clientele.

1 Introduction

Despite the growing interest in hedge funds, it is difficult for many individual and institutional investors to participate in this area of the market. Minimum wealth levels and sophisticated investor requirements constrain many small investors. Legal limits on the number of US investors allowed in hedge funds effectively place a lower bound on the size of investment most hedge fund managers will accept. In fact, many otherwise attractive hedge funds are closed to new investment. For those open to new investment, the minimum unit size is usually quite substantial. Thus, even for smaller institutions and endowments it can be expensive and in many cases impractical to invest in hedge funds with a prudent degree of diversification. Unlike registered investment companies, hedge funds are not required—indeed by most legal interpretations not allowed to publically disclose performance and holdings information that might be construed

[a]NYU Stern School of Business, New York, NY, USA.

[b]Yale School of Management, International Center for Finance, New Haven, CT 06520-8200.

[c]University of Massachusetts at Amherst—Department of Finance and Operations Management, Amherst, MA 01003, USA.

*Corresponding author. NYU Stern School of Business, 44 West 4th Street, New York, NY 10012-1126, USA. Tel.: 212-998-0306; e-mail: sbrown@stern.nyu.edu

as solicitation materials. This has the unfortunate effect of making it more difficult for potential hedge fund investors to evaluate managers on a comparative basis. In addition, little public information exists about fund operations and their holdings and investment strategies are typically undisclosed for strategic reasons.

Funds of funds (sometimes in this context referred to as "funds-of-hedge funds") (FOF) are financial intermediaries established to address several of these issues. They are hedge funds themselves which hold shares in other investment companies and charge a fee for doing so. According to Tremont TASS (Europe) Limited (hereafter TASS), a London-based information and research company dedicated to the alternative investment industry, FOFs comprise a significant proportion of the hedge fund business. As of December 2003, the TASS hedge fund database contains 4301 hedge funds, including 2589 survived funds and 1712 dissolved funds. The total assets under management are about $330 billion. According to TASS, 23%, or 605 of the surviving funds are classified as FOFs. The fraction of funds classified as FOFs has risen considerably over time. At the beginning of 2000, only 15% of the funds were classified by TASS as FOFs.

The typical FOF invests in a range of hedge funds. They allow investors to participate in hedge fund investments that are otherwise closed, and allow for diversification across hedge funds. They also provide professional management services and access to information that would be difficult or expensive to obtain on a fund by fund basis by the investor. For this reason, some authors argue that the appropriate index of hedge fund return is indeed the return on well-managed FOFs.[1]

However, the major disadvantage of this arrangement is the cost to the investor. In addition to the fees charged by the FOF, they effectively pass on to the investor all fees charged by the constituent funds, since, in most cases, they report their raw returns after all of the underlying manager fees are paid. A common concern among practitioners is that this double fee arrangement might induce FOF managers to invest in unduly risky hedge funds to ensure that the returns gross of fees are sufficiently large to absorb the FOF fees charged. While it is true that the FOF structure allows for diversification and hence reduction of risk at the fund level, there is an often overlooked cost to this diversification. The more diversified the fund is, the greater the likelihood that the investor will incur an incentive fee on one or more of the constituent managers, regardless of overall FOF performance. In fact, there is a significant probability that the incentive fee will be so large that it absorbs all of the annual fund return.

The fact that FOFs incur incentive fees is not of itself a reason to avoid FOF investments. After all, an informed investor who invests in the underlying hedge funds would incur the same fees. However, such an investor would be able to hedge the incentive fee component at least to the extent that they could understand the underlying hedge fund positions. The problem arises as a result of the fact that investors choose to invest in FOFs precisely because they lack this necessary information. They are willing to pay management fees to FOFs to acquire information that is expensive or otherwise unavailable to them on an individual basis. On the other hand, FOFs are not obliged under current regulations to provide investors with current information on positions they take in constituent funds, let alone the positions taken by the underlying hedge funds. For this reason, FOF investors cannot hedge the incentive fees that are passed on by the FOF. The expected value of this unhedged fee then becomes a deadweight cost that impairs the performance of FOF investments. We document that this fee can be quite substantial, and is one reason for the relatively poor performance experience of most FOFs.

The extent to which agents can hedge incentive fee contracts is of course a central issue in the emerging literature on management incentives in the investment management industry. Most researchers assume (e.g., Carpenter, 2000) that managers cannot hedge their incentive contracts. Ability to hedge the contract converts the incentive feature into just another form of manager compensation unrelated to performance. In many cases this constraint is descriptively accurate. Money managers are frequently constrained from trading on their own account where such trading can represent a clear conflict of interest. While it may be difficult, if not impossible, to hedge incentive fee payments owing to hedge fund managers, at least FOF managers are not faced with this institutional constraint, and may in fact be better situated to hedge the fee component than is the average hedge fund investor.

What emerges from this theoretical literature is the implication that if incentive fees are effective, they will be more effective at the hedge fund or individual manager level than at the FOF level. Our empirical results provide support for this conjecture. Consistent with the results presented in Elton *et al.* (2003) for mutual funds, we find evidence that incentive fees are associated with higher risk-adjusted performance for hedge funds. Some funds charge no incentive fees, while other funds charge fees that are 20% or more of the return above benchmark. Hedge fund Sharpe ratios bear a significant and positive relationship with the rate at which incentive fees are charged. The same result does not follow for FOFs. Here the rate at which incentive fees are charged is unrelated to performance.

The reason FOF providers do not hedge underlying fund fees is that it is difficult and expensive to do so. Even with their informational advantage most FOF providers would find it impossible to completely hedge incentive fees due to the range and complexity of the underlying fund investments. However, it is possible under certain circumstances to hedge these fees at least in part, either as is often done, by charging an incentive fee on the basis of aggregate FOF performance, or by constructing partial hedges using correlated derivative positions.[2] By doing so they would eliminate at least in part a deadweight cost which we show can be quite substantial. Where it is possible to do so, FOF managers can gain a clear advantage by eliminating the deadweight cost associated with the fee on fee structure and thereby report higher returns.

A central objective for many FOF providers is to attract institutional clients who have more of a long term focus than do retail investors. Fee on fee arrangements are common in brokerage arrangements serving high net worth individuals. However, they are not common in institutional fund management contexts because of a concern about the possibility of conflict that arises through such secondary fee arrangements. By shedding this so-called "wrap account" fee structure, the FOF provider may open the market to a new and significant institutional clientele.

In the remainder of this paper we describe the data used in the study and then in Section 3 document some of the differences between FOFs and the hedge funds in which they invest, not only in their observed characteristics, but also in the extent to which fee structures are related to performance. In Section 4 we provide some examples that give an illustrative order of magnitude on incentive fees and the deadweight cost they impose. In Section 5 we document an emerging fee structure arrangement that may yield superior after-fee returns for investors, and yet be approximately revenue neutral for FOF managers. Section 6 concludes.

2 Data

We use the dataset provided by TASS which contains data on after-fee returns for the period February 1989–December 2003. Anecdotal evidence suggests that fees on average have fallen since that date due to the entry of CALPERs into the hedge fund market, but this is not indicated in the TASS database, which suggests that the fees voluntarily reported to TASS subsequent to that date may not be accurate. The dataset also includes the TASS "graveyard"—funds that existed in the period 1994 to the present but which have since dropped from the active fund sample. The last 3 months of data were excluded because of concerns about late reporting by a subset of hedge funds covered in the report. TASS also provides data on the considerable variety of fee structures used by hedge funds, including management and incentive fees. Among other things, it documents performance benchmarks used in calculating fees, redemption charges, and other expenses payable by the investor. An accompanying file of notes records the many exceptions to standard fee structures. For example, in a number of cases, the incentive fee charged per dollar return in excess of the performance benchmark increases as a function of the positive performance realized by the fund in excess of benchmark. In most cases, this performance benchmark is zero, but in many cases the fund has to earn a fixed return typically 10%, and sometimes even as high as 30 or even 50% before incentive fees are charged. In other examples, the fund has to earn a return in excess of the Treasury Bill rate, LIBOR or some other performance index benchmark. Highwatermark provisions typically require fund managers to make up losses relative to their benchmark from previous years before earning an incentive fee in the current period. This provision makes the valuation of the hedge fund management contract an interesting challenge (c.f. Goetzmann *et al.*, 2003).

To examine the relationship between fee structures and after-fee return, we use the total after-fee return provided by TASS for all hedge funds it surveys. However, to study the magnitude of incentive fees and to examine their impact on return we need some measure of before-fee returns. While the TASS database, in common with other hedge fund data providers, gives only returns after fees have been paid, it is possible using the fee schedules provided by TASS to calculate an approximation of the before-fee return.[3] The resulting before-fee numbers are an approximation for several reasons. In the first place, there is some variation in when fees are computed and charged. In the overwhelming majority of cases, the fees are calculated on an annual basis, although there are a few instances where the fees are computed and payable on a quarterly basis, and one instance where fees are charged on the basis of a 5-year return period. We assume for simplicity that all fees are computed and payable on an annual cycle. For this reason, in the results that use before-fee returns, we are forced to exclude funds for which we have less than one full calendar year of data. In addition, a minority of funds charge management fees that vary with the size of account. We also ignore this qualification in our before-fee results. Since we assume that highwatermark provisions are met as of the first year of survivorship free data (1994), we impart an upward bias in 1995 calculated incentives.[4] Finally, there were 12 cases where the algorithm used to compute before-fee returns failed, and for this reason those funds were excluded from the before-fee analysis.[5]

3 Characteristics and Performance of Fund of Funds[6]

Table 1 provides the basic statistics for FOFs and hedge funds. As expected, FOFs provide significant diversification potential. The notion that FOFs are unduly risky is not supported in the data. Not only do FOFs reduce by more than a third the standard deviation of monthly hedge fund returns, but they also significantly reduce the value at risk of hedge fund investment.[7] This value at risk result is particularly significant, as it is based on an examination of returns after all fees are paid. A fiduciary who is

Table 1 Descriptive statistics of fund of funds and hedge funds.

	Fund of funds (FOF)			Hedge funds (HF)			
Variable	No.	Mean	Std dev.	No.	Mean	Std dev.	t_{FOF-HF}
Mean return[a]	797	0.6051	0.5555	3239	0.9734	1.4092	−11.65**
Std. dev. of return[a]	797	2.6019	2.3265	3239	4.2996	0.0218	−20.60**
Skewness[a]	797	−0.1623	1.2545	3239	0.0508	1.3027	−4.26**
Kurtosis[a]	797	3.4866	6.0510	3239	3.4136	6.7108	0.30
Lower 5% fractile[a]	797	−3.4748	4.1965	3239	−6.5418	6.5504	16.31**
1st autocorrelation[a]	797	0.1627	0.1911	3239	0.0978	0.2027	8.48**
2nd autocorrelation[a]	797	0.0180	0.1899	3239	0.0283	0.1797	−1.39
3rd autocorrelation[a]	797	0.0150	0.1420	3239	0.0117	0.1576	0.57
Assets	827	$118.94	$590.86	3378	$127.58	$549.18	−0.38
Personal investment[b]	862	0.31	0.46	3439	0.42	0.49	−6.19**
Management fee	862	1.51	0.75	3439	1.40	0.79	3.81**
Incentive fee	862	9.06	7.64	3439	18.46	5.91	−33.69**
Leverage[b]	862	0.55	0.50	3439	0.71	0.45	−8.57**
Age	797	66.39	47.06	3239	62.43	43.52	2.160
Notice period	862	33.58	28.6	3439	26.05	25.28	7.07**
Minimum investment	856	$0.37	$0.85	3335	$0.78	$5.06	−4.44**

[a]Estimated for funds with a minimum of 1 year of continuous data.
[b]Dummy variables: 1 if yes and 0 if no.
**Significant at 1% level.
*Significant at 5% level.

Data are from Tremont TASS (Europe) Limited (TASS). There are 4301 hedge funds, including 2589 survived funds and 1712 dissolved funds as of December 2003. There are 862 funds of funds and 3439 hedge funds. A total of 605 out of 862 funds of funds are live funds while 257 (or 29.8%) are dissolved. In contrast, 1984 out of 3439 hedge funds are live funds while 1455 (or 42.3%) are dissolved. Assets and minimum investments are in millions of dollars.

primarily concerned about the downside risk associated with hedge fund investment should seriously consider a FOF vehicle.

However, as noted before, diversification is not the only reason why investors invest in FOFs. These instruments provide the investor with professional management and due diligence services, as well as access to otherwise closed funds. One would expect that investors would be prepared to pay for these services, but that the additional return would compensate them for any fees charged. Unfortunately, that is not the case. The average monthly after-fee return for FOFs is 0.61%, only a little less than two-thirds of the 0.97% return for hedge funds over the same period of time, a difference that is both economically and statistically significant. The result was the same when broken down by styles of management, with the differences in average after-fee returns greatest for Emerging Markets, Global Macro, and Long–Short Equity Hedge styles. In each of these cases, the differences are all statistically significant with t-values in excess of 3.0.[8]

This discrepancy has been noted in the finance literature. Fung and Hsieh (2000), for example, find that at least part of the reported under-performance of FOFs may be attributed to survivorship which effectively biases upwards the reported performance of individual hedge funds. According to Liang (2003), the annual survivorship bias for hedge funds is 2.32% per year while the bias is 1.18% for FOFs. The 1.14% difference in survivorship bias is not big enough for explaining the magnitude of performance difference between hedge funds and FOFs. FOFs which actually hold the shares of hedge funds when they become available, and experience the monetary losses when they are incurred, perhaps better represent the actual investment performance of the hedge fund investor. Fung and Hsieh persuasively argue that FOFs are perhaps a better index of aggregate hedge fund performance. We are of course sympathetic to the survivorship story—particularly since the use of annual returns still includes some conditioning on survival. For this reason, it is essential to include returns on all defunct or non-reporting funds contained in the TASS graveyard file. The survival issues are important, but it is also useful to focus on the role of FOF fees as an additional explanation for the poor relative performance of FOFs.[9]

Table 1 documents some additional differences between hedge funds and FOFs. On average, FOFs are similar in size to the hedge funds in which they invest. However, an important difference is that fewer fund managers have a stake in their own funds. While 31% of FOF managers have a personal investment in their own funds, the corresponding percentage is 42% for hedge fund managers. The difference is significant at the 1% level. This result suggests that perhaps the underlying hedge funds are more incentive aligned than FOFs. Probably the most interesting result in Table 1 is the difference in management and incentive fees between the two fund groups. The median management fee for FOFs is 1.5%, compared to 1% for hedge funds, reflecting the nature of the two-tier fee structure of FOFs. Both FOFs and hedge funds typically charge an incentive fee expressed as a percentage of fund returns over a specified benchmark. In addition both FOFs and hedge funds are typically required to make up for past losses before incentive fees may be charged (the "highwatermark provision"). However, the median incentive fee charged by FOFs is only 10%, compared to 20%

Table 2 Performance and risk: fund of funds versus hedge funds.

	Fund of funds[a]			Hedge Funds[a]				
Year	Mean return	Median return	Sharpe ratio	Mean return	Median return	Sharpe ratio	t-value (return)	t-value (Sharpe)
1994	−0.3233	−0.4530	−0.2961	0.1072	0.1642	−0.0141	−4.54**	−6.51**
1995	0.8238	0.8613	0.2399	1.3895	1.2888	0.3835	−5.43**	−3.75**
1996	1.0470	1.0800	0.4074	1.4447	1.3631	0.4480	−5.45**	−1.13
1997	1.0036	1.1218	0.3590	1.4596	1.3407	0.3845	−5.54**	−0.84
1998	0.0530	0.1694	−0.0478	0.4210	0.6672	0.0988	−3.38**	−6.26**
1999	1.6584	1.4776	0.5696	2.0594	1.4181	0.4013	−3.76**	5.80**
2000	0.5910	0.6875	0.2228	0.7589	0.8900	0.2050	−2.09*	0.62
2001	0.3187	0.4236	0.1045	0.5002	0.5568	0.1678	−3.39**	−2.59**
2002	0.1480	0.1682	0.0898	0.2100	0.2475	0.1428	−1.26	−1.63
2003	0.7914	0.7658	0.8206	1.3736	1.0117	0.5795	−11.43**	6.99**

[a]Numbers are calculated using funds with a minimum of 6-month return history within each year.
**Significant at 1% level.
*Significant at 5% level.

The table reports the annual average return for the funds in the TASS database including defunct funds after 1993. The mean returns are reported in the second and the fourth column. The median returns are reported in the third and sixth column. The average Sharpe ratio for funds is based on calculations for the corresponding year of data, and is recorded in the fourth and seventh column. Column 8 reports a t-test of the difference in the mean return for hedge funds versus funds of funds. Column 9 reports the results of a t-test for differences in the mean Sharpe ratio for hedge funds versus funds of funds.

for hedge funds. The differences in fees reflect the different incentives of FOF managers and hedge fund managers.[10]

Since FOFs provide significant diversification potential, an investor might expect that the reward to volatility ratio is higher for FOFs than it is for the average hedge fund. In Table 2, we report the average Sharpe ratio on an annual basis for FOFs and hedge funds during the 9-year period from 1994 to 2003, the period for which we have survivorship-free data. FOFs offer consistently lower Sharpe ratios, as well as lower average returns in many of the years documented. The same result follows when we break the funds down by the amount under management. There is little difference in Sharpe ratios across FOF size categories, while the Sharpe ratio for hedge funds increases with the size of the fund, from 0.3657 for funds in the range of $100–150 million, to 0.4722 for funds with in excess of $500 million under management. The implication is that direct investment in individual hedge funds, on average yields a higher reward to variability ratio—and that a levered position in FOFs that matched the expected return of the hedge fund sample is in fact *riskier* at least in terms of standard deviation. The data suggest either that FOF managers have not done a particularly good job at selecting superior hedge funds, or that the fees they charge more than capture the benefits they deliver.[11]

A cross-sectional analysis of the FOF universe is perhaps more instructive, since it allows us to compare managers that are subject to similar survival conditioning and similar evaluation by the investment community. In Table 3, we examine the extent to which FOF fees are related to performance. The FOF fee structure can be broken

Table 3 Regression results of Sharpe ratio on management and incentive fees.

	Fund of funds			Hedge Funds		
Variable	Estimate	Std error	t-value	Estimate	Std error	t-value
Intercept	−0.8203	0.1041	−7.88**	−1.0203	0.0589	−17.32**
Management	−0.0736	0.0156	−4.73**	−0.0145	0.0082	−1.76
Incentive	0.0026	0.0015	1.73	0.0045	0.0012	3.91**
Fund age	−0.0009	0.0003	−3.02**	−0.0006	0.0002	−3.31**
Log(assets)	0.0701	0.0057	12.23**	0.0713	0.0032	22.26**
N	688			N	2948	
R^2	22.90%			R^2	15.58%	
Adj R^2	22.45%			Adj R^2	15.47%	

**Significant at 1% level.

Data are from Tremont TASS (Europe) Limited (TASS). The dependent variable in the regression is Sharpe ratio of each fund; the independent variables are management fee, incentive fee, fund age, and logarithm of fund assets. Sharpe ratios are estimated using funds with a minimum 12-month return history.

down into the incentive fee that gives the rate at which incentive fees are charged, and the management fees which represent the fixed percentage of assets under management used to pay for management expenses and other fees. As noted before, there is a rich variety of ways in which the incentive fee benchmark is specified, but this variation is not reflected in Table 3.

A linear regression of after-fee performance on the rate at which incentive fees are charged finds no connection between the two. Cross-sectionally, it appears on the other hand that FOF managers that charge higher management fees achieve a lower risk adjusted return. Interestingly, no such relationship exists for hedge funds taken as a whole. It appears that the management fee for the typical FOF company is a deadweight load that has the effect of simply reducing after-fee return. On the other hand, the rate at which incentive fees are charged does have a significant positive relationship with risk adjusted returns for individual hedge funds. The conclusion is clear. While the fee structure appears to provide an appropriate incentive for hedge fund managers, it does not appear to motivate FOF managers to achieve superior returns. It is important to note that the table shows the relationship between the rate of fees charged and current performance in the cross-section of funds. It does not test the proposition that high current fees are associated with higher future performance. This is a very interesting issue for future research.

4 An Example

The FOF charges incentive fees based on the after-fee return to the individual hedge fund. This implies that the ultimate investor may end up paying incentive fees regardless of how well or poorly the FOF actually performs. To see how this might happen, consider a very simple numerical example given in Table 4. In this example we assume for simplicity that all funds charge a standard 20% incentive fee over a zero benchmark with no fixed management fee. With just three funds, the first and second funds may

Table 4 Example of positive incentive fees due on negative fund of fund returns.

Variable	Hedge fund 1	Hedge fund 2	Hedge fund 3	Fund of funds
Start of year ($M)	$1.00	$1.00	$1.00	$3.00
Annual return (before fee)	20%	40%	−75%	−5%
End of year ($M)	$1.20	$1.40	$0.25	$2.85
Incentive fee ($M)	$0.04	$0.08	$0.00	$0.12
Incentive fee ratio				4%
Annual return (after fee)	16%	32%	−75%	−9%

In this hypothetical example, a fund of funds is established with $1 million invested in each of three hedge funds that earn (before fees) 20, 40 and −75%. Each of these funds charge an incentive fee of 20% above a zero benchmark. For simplicity, none of the funds charge a management fee.

perform well, earning 20 and 40%, respectively. However, if the third fund performs sufficiently poorly, the overall fund may end up losing money. In this example, the before-fee return is −5%. However, there are incentive fees owing to the first two funds, amounting in total to 4% of the assets at the start of the year. This 4% represents an additional fee that is subtracted from returns in calculating the after-fee returns. In this example, the after-fee return correspond to a loss of 9%. While the investor escapes the FOF incentive fee because of a negative portfolio return, he or she must pay the incentive fees to the underlying managers. While an accounting of the incentive fees of the underlying managers is generally not explicitly provided to the FOF investor, the fees are nevertheless genuine monetary expenses that the intermediary institution pays and passes through to the client.

The example given in Table 4 is obviously an extreme example meant to illustrate the point. Under realistic circumstances, can it ever happen that an investor is liable for incentive fees when the fund as a whole loses money? Unfortunately, the answer is yes. To examine in some greater detail the relationship between fees and returns, we consider an example where FOF managers provide diversification services. However, consistent with the results in Table 1, the FOF managers do not add to returns through active selection and weighting of component hedge funds. We calculate the historical returns on FOFs from 1995 to the end of 2003 constructed by choosing the constituent funds at random from the set of hedge funds in business at the beginning of the period. As funds leave the sample, they are replaced by other funds in business at the time. We perform this exercise first for FOFs comprising only one fund, and then we consider what happens when we add more funds to the FOF. Stating returns on the underlying managers on a before-fee basis allows us to decompose the return to the FOF investor into the portion attributable to the underlying portfolio, the portion attributable to underlying manager fees, and the portion attributable to the FOF fees.

In Figure 1 we take the first case, where the hypothetical funds consist of only one fund. The data corresponds to all 830 hedge funds which according to TASS were operating at the start of 1995 and for which we were able to compute before-fee returns, excluding all FOFs. We then compute the realized annual returns to 830 hypothetical FOFs each investing in one and only one of these funds.[12] In this example, the incentive fees charged by the funds and the highwatermark benchmark before which fees are paid

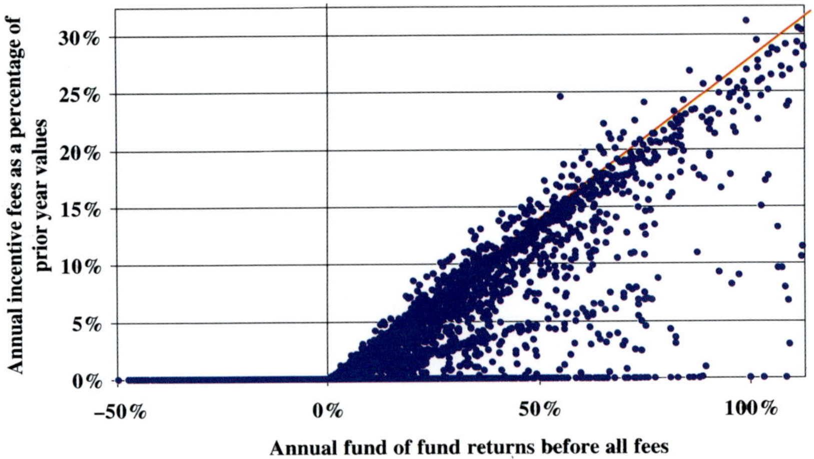

Figure 1 Incentive fees and performance: fund of funds with one fund, 1995–2003.

correspond to the actual fees and benchmarks listed by TASS for each of the funds. The hypothetical FOFs charge a 10% incentive fee over and above a zero benchmark. The solid line gives the relationship between returns and incentive fees suggested by an incentive fee schedule where the FOFs charge an incentive fee on top of the 20% of return fee charged by the individual fund.[13] Funds may actually charge less than this, either because they have more modest incentive fee schedules, or because of the requirement that they earn back past losses before they are awarded this incentive fee (the highwatermark provision). Most funds employ a zero benchmark before they are entitled to an incentive fee, while some have a fixed benchmark or a benchmark based on an index return (T Bill rate, LIBOR, or other benchmark).

We see that there is a great variation in realized before-fee return across years and across funds. It is important to note that extreme returns may be on a very small base. The largest return recorded in the database was 441%. This return, as high as it was, did not generate an incentive fee, as in this particular case the fund lost 95.6% of its value in the prior year. The quadrupling of value was insufficient to erase the prior year losses. As noted above, the losses could even be greater, as we exclude from our database funds immediately prior to failure. One of the major attractions of FOFs is that they provide the investor with the opportunity to diversify and hence alleviate this volatility.

In Figure 2 we consider the same period of data, for a set of 830 hypothetical funds equally invested as of the beginning of 1995 in five hedge funds chosen entirely randomly from the set of available funds.[14] Diversification decreases the incidence of extreme returns, both negative and positive. At the same time however, diversification appears to be costly. The more diversified the FOF, the greater is the chance that at least one of the funds generates an incentive fee to an underlying manager. Since the FOF provides after-fee returns to the investor, the investor may in effect be paying an incentive fee regardless of the performance of the overall fund. In fact, we find that the investor may actually end up paying incentive fees to the underlying managers

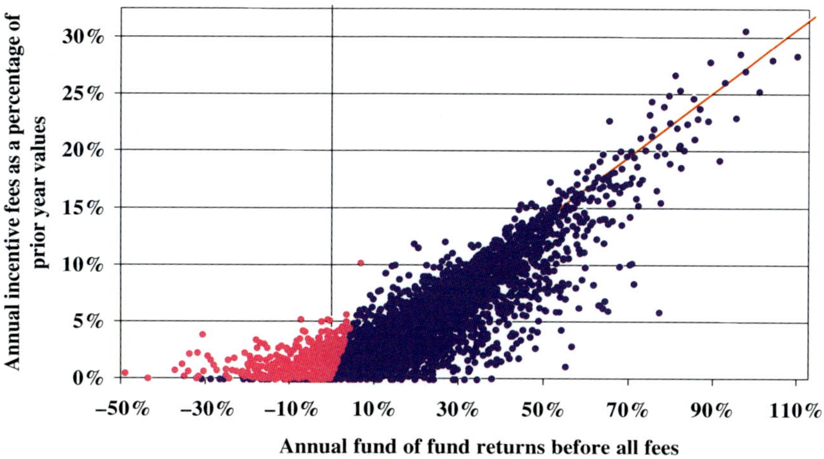

Figure 2 Incentive fees and performance: funds of funds with five funds, 1995–2003.

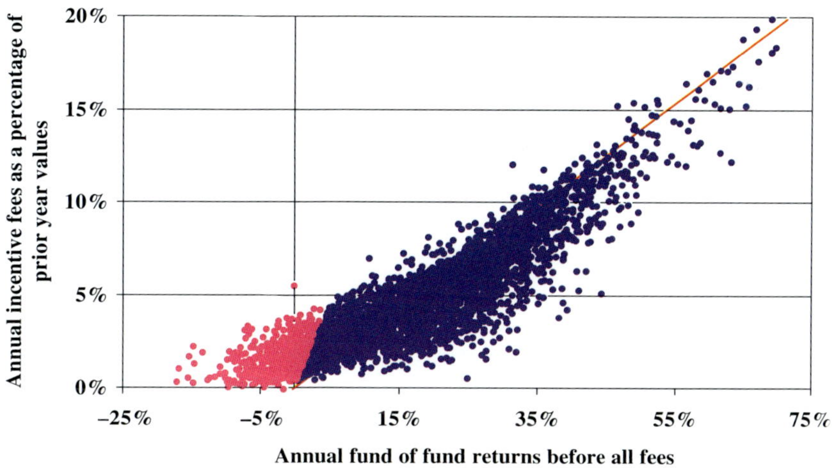

Figure 3 Incentive fees and performance: funds of funds with 20 funds, 1995–2003.

that exceed the annual return on the fund. In the figure we highlight the 18.22% of fund/year returns for which this is the case. Comparing Figures 1 and 2 we find that diversifying into as few as five funds can substantially increase the probability of paying fees on negative returns. When the fund earns less than 20% before fees, the additional fees can amount to between 2 and 3% of assets at the start of the year. It is important to note that these fees do not accrue to the FOF provider when the fund as a whole loses money. Rather, these are incentive fees paid to individual funds and are passed on to investors in the form of after-fee returns through the FOF vehicle. When we consider a case of ten funds chosen at random, the FOF investor almost always has to pay an incentive fee to an underlying manager. In fact out of 7470 fund years, there was only ten cases, or 0.1339% of the funds in which no incentive fees were charged, despite fund returns falling as low as −29% per annum on a before-fee basis. Funds that lose money on a before-fee basis lose on average an additional 1.1% on an after-fee basis accounting for incentive fees paid, and this additional burden can rise to as much as 5.7%. When we go to 20 funds per FOF (Figure 3), the incentive fees paid resemble what would be charged under a fee structure that charged an additional 2.5% management fee plus an incentive fee on returns in excess of a 15% benchmark criterion.

It is very important to note that the fact that investors end up paying incentive fees when the FOF loses money is of course not a criticism of the FOF diversification strategy. Individual investors investing in the same funds would suffer the same fees, and diversification does not increase the fee burden. To take a very simple example, suppose a FOF were to be fully invested in a hedge fund with a 2:1 leveraged position in a S&P 500 contract. Again, for simplicity assume that all assets are lognormally distributed with zero drift and a zero risk-free rate. The investor would pay an incentive fee half of the time. The expected value of this fee is increasing in volatility and would equal 4.2% if annual volatility is 40 percent.[15] On the other hand, if the fund invested half of the funds in a hedge fund comprising a leveraged S&P 500 position, and half of the funds in a fund that maintained an equivalent short position, then the investor would pay half of the incentive fee all of the time. The expected value of both the incentive fee and of total returns is identical in both cases.

The difference of course is that the individual informed investor can potentially hedge the incentive fees charged by the hedge fund, whereas they may choose to invest in the FOF precisely when the necessary information for hedging purposes is unavailable or expensive to acquire. In the simplified fact situation given above, the Black–Scholes

Table 5 Deadweight cost estimates associated with not hedging fund incentive fees.

Year	N	Average incentive fee as percentage of a start of year value (%)	Average cost of hedging incentive fee (%)	Average deadweight cost (%)	t-Value
1995	802	5.02	1.61	3.42	5.70
1996	932	5.02	1.38	3.64	7.61
1997	1126	4.91	1.29	3.62	6.11
1998	1278	3.22	1.21	2.01	4.76
1999	1405	7.37	1.00	6.37	6.19
2000	1546	3.76	0.96	2.81	5.54
2001	1618	2.58	0.89	1.69	3.68
2002	1722	1.95	0.70	1.25	4.30
2003	1565	3.04	0.50	2.54	3.28

For every hedge fund included in the March 2000 TASS database including all defunct funds but excluding designated funds of funds we infer before-fee returns on the basis of reported after-fee returns, fee structures, and benchmarks reported to TASS for the fund. For each fund we first calculate the magnitude of incentive fees implied by the incentive fee provisions and stated benchmarks, allowing for the highwatermark provision that adjusts benchmarks to require the manager to recoup past losses before an incentive fee is charged. We then compute the Black–Scholes value of the incentive fee contract, based on the contract provisions, current Treasury Bill rate and measure of historical volatility based on the time series of before-fee returns for that fund. The cross-sectional average difference between the *ex post* realized incentive fee and the *ex ante* cost of hedging that fee we term the average deadweight cost associated with not hedging fund incentive fees. We provide t-values for this quantity.

value of the incentive fee call option is 3.2%. The difference (in this example, 1%) is always positive and an increasing function of volatility, and amounts to a significant deadweight cost associated with not hedging the underlying hedge fund incentive fees. In a more realistic setting, the magnitude of this deadweight cost will depend in a complicated way on the capital market assumptions, the incentive fee, benchmark and highwatermark provisions. Taking the historical fund volatilities and incentive fee arrangements from the TASS database, it is possible to estimate the magnitude of the deadweight cost for each of the years 1995–2003 (Table 5).

5 Alternative Fee Structures

The results reported in Tables 2 and 3 suggest that far from encouraging FOF managers to seek out higher risk adjusted returns, the current incentive fee on fee arrangements represent a deadweight cost passed on to investors, payable whether or not the fund as a whole makes a positive return, consistent with the example given in Section 4. The challenge is to discover whether there are any alternative fee arrangements which might serve the purpose of reducing this deadweight cost and thereby improving reported performance.

As we note above, the fee on fee arrangement is a feature of retail wrap accounts common in the wealth management business. However, there is no general uniformity in fee arrangements, and this is an area that is highly negotiable in practice. It is understandable therefore that large institutions entering this market are putting pressure on fees charged. One area of negotiation may be in the fee structure itself. Large institutions are not responsible for the annual bonus payments made to star managers within managed accounts, but rather negotiate a fee for managing the total account. In the same way, they might begin to expect FOF providers to absorb incentive fees of individual hedge funds in return for a fixed fee/incentive fee package paid to the FOF provider. It ought to be possible to negotiate a fee package at the FOF level that would end up at least approximately revenue neutral to the FOF provider. Investors in the FOF would only pay incentive fees on positive performance. Finally, this policy would concentrate attention on adding value at the FOF level where the FOF manager can in fact earn a substantial incentive fee.

Indeed, it is the practice elsewhere in the funds management business for the fund management company to absorb fees and expenses in return for a fee charged at the fund level. Mutual funds, for instance, frequently compensate money managers employed by them using annual bonuses and other forms of performance related compensation. These incentive fees are then considered part of the management expenses that are passed on to investors in the form of a management fee computed on the basis of a flat percentage of the assets under management.[16] Very rarely do mutual funds charge incentive based fees, and SEC guidelines require that any such fees be symmetric in nature.[17] The very prevalence of this type of arrangement suggests the conjecture that it may in fact resolve a number of the agency issues that arise in the context of fund management.

The net cost to the fund of funds providers may not be that great. Take the simple case where a fund of funds provider charges a 20% incentive fee on returns in excess of the annual Treasury Bill rate, in return for which the fund absorbs any and all similar incentive fees charged by the constituent funds. If all of the constituent funds have a similar volatility, then the economic cost to the fund is easy to calculate and will depend only on the volatility of the underlying funds and the extent to which fund diversification reduces aggregate fund volatility.

To see this, note that essentially the fund is short a portfolio of $k \times p$ call contracts where k is the number of funds in the fund of funds, and p is the incentive fee for each (in this case, 20%), where the exercise price for each call is equal to the future value of the beginning of year fund value at the riskless rate of interest. It is long p calls on a portfolio consisting of k funds. It is possible to determine the appropriately hedged cost of providing this service to fund clients.[18] If for simplicity we neglect the highwatermark provision typical in such incentive contracts,[19] rearranging the Black–Scholes formula, one can easily show that not only is the net cost positive, but it depends only on the volatility of the original funds and the extent to which diversification reduces that volatility.[20] Furthermore, this value is small in absolute value. In Figure 4 we plot the net cost as a function of the volatility of the underlying funds and the extent to which diversification reduces the risk of the overall fund. For the data considered in Section 2, the median fund had a volatility of 17.1%. A five-fund portfolio reduces the median

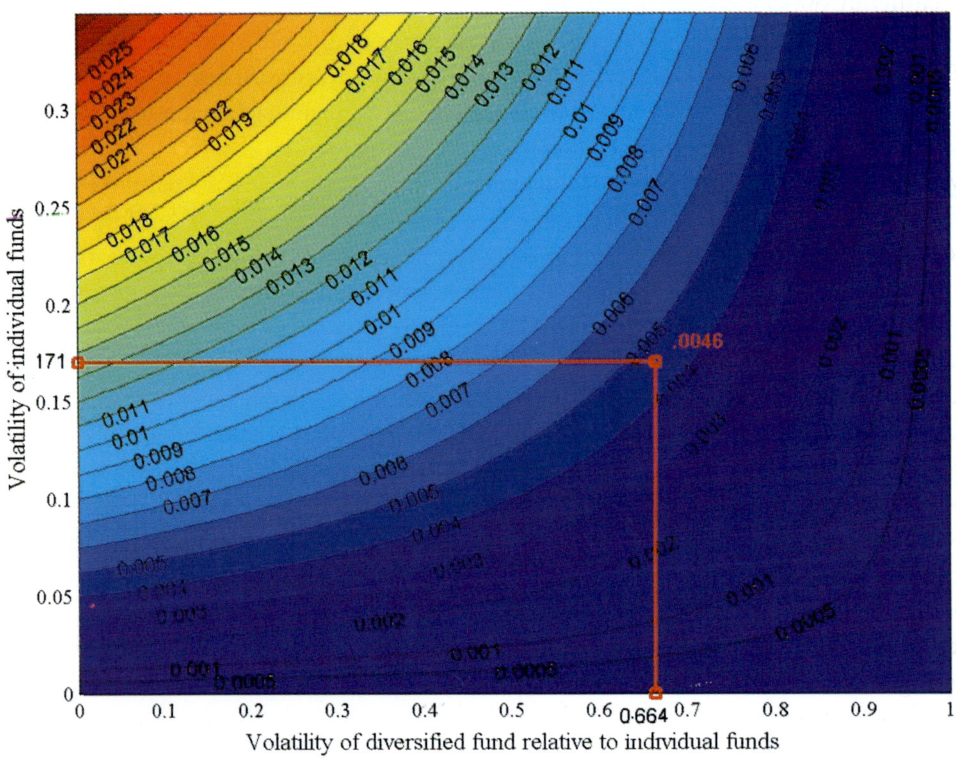

Figure 4 Cost of absorbing individual fund incentive fees.

Table 6 Effect of alternative fee arrangements on average Sharpe ratios.

Year	Actual results	Fee on fee arrangement			Alternative fee arrangement			Difference		
		5 funds	10 funds	20 funds	5 funds	10 funds	20 funds	5 funds	10 funds	20 funds
1995	0.2399	0.3793	0.4431	0.5406	0.4576	0.5413	0.6576	0.0782	0.0982	0.1170
1996	0.4074	0.3129	0.3722	0.4004	0.3964	0.4658	0.5025	0.0834	0.0936	0.1021
1997	0.3590	0.2698	0.2945	0.3044	0.3601	0.3887	0.4040	0.0903	0.0942	0.0996
1998	−0.0478	−0.0809	−0.0927	−0.1064	−0.0137	−0.0137	−0.0156	0.0672	0.0790	0.0908
1999	0.5696	0.3553	0.4164	0.4603	0.4930	0.5736	0.6252	0.1377	0.1572	0.1649
2000	0.2228	−0.0239	−0.0189	−0.0329	0.0812	0.0924	0.0855	0.1051	0.1113	0.1184
2001	0.1045	−0.0326	−0.0441	−0.0739	0.1371	0.1058	0.1006	0.1698	0.1499	0.1745
2002	0.0898	−0.0788	−0.1081	−0.1473	−0.6728	0.0517	0.0200	−0.5940	0.1598	0.1673
2003	0.8206	0.6844	0.7726	0.8784	0.8124	0.9777	1.1001	0.1280	0.2052	0.2217

This table reports the average Sharpe ratios computed for 830 hypothetical funds of funds created from an equal investment in 5, 10, and 20 hedge funds chosen at random as of December 1994. Failing funds were replaced in the portfolio by a random choice of funds active at that time. In the fee on fee case each case the hypothetical fund charges 1% management fee and a 10% incentive fee. The incentive is charged on the basis of after fee returns from the underlying hedge fund over and above a zero benchmark. In the alternative fee arrangement case, the underlying incentive fees charged by the hedge funds are paid for by the fund of funds manager in return for a 28% incentive fee (10% on top of 20% incentive above a zero benchmark) plus a 1.48% management fee. The Sharpe ratios are computed for each hypothetical fund on the basis of calculated returns after all management and incentive fees are paid. The reported differences are all significant at the 1% level. The actual results column gives the average Sharpe ratios for actual funds of funds, as reported in Table 2.

volatility by 66.4%. As a result, the cost is calculated as 0.46% of the initial fund value. This is certainly much smaller than the two percent of fund value deadweight cost that the existing fee arrangement penalizes fund of funds investors.[21] The figure also illustrates the tradeoff between increased cost and volatility reduction resulting from fund of funds diversification. A fund that invests in many small high-risk hedge funds would anticipate the largest benefit from diversification in terms of risk reduction. However, when each of these small funds charges a substantial incentive fee, the net cost can be large (top left corner of the figure).

The net cost to the investor of this alternative incentive fee arrangement may be quite small. In Table 6 we report the average Sharpe ratios for random portfolios of 5, 10, and 20 hedge fund portfolios, along with the reported Sharpe ratios for all funds of funds over the same period of time. It is important to note that by random selection of hedge fund portfolios we are making the unrealistic or worst case assumption that the FOF manager is not adding value by selection of hedge funds. By the same token, the portfolio is not being manipulated to artificially increase the Sharpe ratios reported. Nevertheless, it is interesting to note that these random portfolios experienced Sharpe ratios an order of magnitude similar to those of managed funds of funds over the same period of time. We report the differences in average Sharpe ratios as an appropriately scaled measure of the cost to the investor of switching from the standard fee on fee arrangement to an alternative where for an additional 0.46% fixed management fee, the fund of fund manager replaces the individual incentive fee with an incentive fee computed on the basis of total fund return over a zero highwatermark. In each case, the Sharpe ratio for the investor improves under the alternative fee arrangement, while at the same time the fund of fund manager is made revenue-neutral in expectation. In other words, the additional uncertainty he or she faces is compensated. Consistent with the analysis above, the benefit to the investor of this new fee arrangement increases in each case as the fund of funds becomes more diversified.

The puzzle then is why more FOF providers do not absorb incentive fees in exchange for a simple fee structure with a slightly higher management fee and an incentive fee component that covers the underlying hedge fund fees. Such an arrangement would lead to a major improvement in reported performance at small cost to the FOF provider, while at the same time increasing the institutional market for these funds. For the fact is, few do.[22] While much of the financial risk to the FOF can be eliminated by having the FOF charge an incentive fee on its own account, not all of it is. It is impractical to consider hedging this risk, although this might be possible in certain specialized instances where the risk might be absorbed by hedging derivative positions highly correlated with each hedge fund strategy. Small FOF providers simply cannot afford this magnitude of financial risk or otherwise obtain insurance against it.

It is worth bearing in mind that when properly explained to the clientele, funds that agree to absorb incentive fees would be able to charge higher fees on their own account. This might then be particularly attractive strategy for an emerging class of FOF managers who invest in a diversified set of funds within the same hedge fund family. In this instance, any disparity in fees would then just be a book entry offset. It would also be an attractive strategy for the very limited number of FOF providers who understand the positions taken by the underlying hedge funds sufficiently well that they can actually implement the necessary incentive fee hedges.[23]

6 Conclusion

Despite the popularity of hedge funds as an alternative asset class, the high degree of fund specific risk and the lack of transparency give most reasonable fiduciaries pause. In addition, many of the most attractive hedge funds are closed to new investment. FOFs resolve these issues by providing investors with an appropriate degree of diversification and professional management that can provide the necessary degree of due diligence. In addition, many such funds hold shares in hedge funds otherwise closed to new investment. The chief disadvantage of FOFs is the high fees that are typically charged, with an incentive fee component that may under certain circumstances exceed the realized return on the fund. In addition to the fees charged by the FOF, the FOF typically passes on to the investor all fees charged by the constituent funds in the form of after-fee returns.

As we note, one of the principal advantages of the FOF arrangement is that it allows for diversification. But the more diversified the fund is, the greater the likelihood that the investor will incur an incentive fee regardless of overall fund performance. In fact there is a significant probability that the incentive fee will be so large that it absorbs all of the annual fund return. The fact that investors end up paying incentive fees when the FOF loses money is of course not a criticism of the FOF diversification strategy. Individual investors investing in the same funds would suffer the same fees, and diversification does not increase the fee burden as an informed investor would face the same fees if they diversified on their own account. The problem arises because investors lack information necessary to hedge incentive fees charged by the underlying hedge funds and passed on to the investor through the FOF in the form of after-fee returns. This inability to hedge underlying incentive fees represents a deadweight cost that may tend to explain the relatively poor historical performance of FOFs relative to the hedge funds in which they invest. This cost arises because the ultimate investor, not the FOF manager, bears the cost of incentive fees incurred whether or not the overall fund makes money. In addition, the data does not indicate that the current incentive fee on fee arrangement leads to superior returns.

An alternative arrangement that would limit this deadweight cost and that is, in fact, common in other areas of the investment management business would have the FOF absorb the individual incentive fees generated by individual managers in exchange for a fixed fee/incentive fee charged at the FOF level. It is worth bearing in mind that when properly explained to the clientele, funds that agree to absorb incentive fees would be able to charge higher fees on their own account. As a result, a fixed fee/incentive fee arrangement could be devised which would be on average revenue neutral for the FOF provider. However, some financial risk remains, and we believe that this is the major reason why this alternative arrangement is not yet in common use.

Yet there are significant opportunities for FOF providers who can in fact absorb underlying hedge fund fees in return for a management fee/incentive fee charged at the level of the FOF. Such FOF providers would include funds that specialize in particular hedge fund subcategories, FOF managers who invest in hedge funds under the same corporate umbrella, and the very small minority of FOFs that understand the underlying positions sufficiently well to hedge them at least in part through derivative contracts in correlated securities.

Acknowledgments

We should like to acknowledge the extremely helpful and constructive comments of John Bilson, Edwin Elton, Ravi Dattatreya, Erol Emed, Martin Gruber, Bruce Grundy, Richard Green, Adriaan Klop, Richard McAloney, Frank Milne, Tom Schneeweis, Peter Swan and Laurens Swinkels, without of course implicating them in any errors of omission or commission that remain. We would also like to thank participants at the 2002 SIRCA Funds Management conference, Sydney and 2003 EFA Meetings in Glasgow, and presentations at Boston College, Melbourne University, New York Fed, Queens University and Wharton financial Institutions Center for helpful comments.

Notes

[1] Fung and Hsieh (2000).

[2] Fung and Hsieh (1997b, 2001) and Agarwall and Naik (2004) show that many hedge fund positions are highly correlated with long and short positions in benchmark derivative securities.

3 There is no uniformity in fee schedules across funds. A wide variety of benchmarks and highwatermark provisions are commonly in use, and in some cases, incentive fees are in fact a nonlinear function of return. In a small minority of cases these fees are dependent on the size of the investment with a discount offered for large fund holders. The fee schedules used to construct before-fee returns were based on the incentive fees and management fees reported in the December 2003 version of the TASS database with a zero benchmark. Results were checked by constructing the exact fee schedules determined from a close reading of the Notes section of the TASS database for a large subsample of the funds in our study. These fee schedules reflected the exact benchmark and high watermark provisions of each and every hedge fund contract. While the benchmark variation and nonlinearity of fee schedules is accounted for, it is not possible to adjust for variations by size of investment. The results reported in the paper were not sensitive to the use of precise fee schedules.

4 Brown *et al.* (2001) show that not meeting the highwatermark provision two years in a row is a good predictor of fund failure and hence departure from our database in later years of our sample.

5 The algorithm used to compute before-fee returns is as follows. For each year, the annual incentive fee was computed on the basis of an estimate of prior year before-fee returns. The estimate of before-fee returns is updated by adding back to the after-fee returns for each month, one twelfth of the annual fee expressed as a fraction of the prior month value accumulated at the estimated before-fee return. Convergence is achieved when successive estimates of the before-fee return differ in absolute value by less than 10^{-11} within 35 iterations. This algorithm failed in only 12 cases. These cases corresponded to short-lived funds with extraordinary volatility of returns.

6 Liang (2003) provides a detailed descriptive analysis of the difference between hedge funds and FOFs.

7 As indicated in Table 1, the lower 5% fractile of the empirical distribution of monthly fund returns is three percentage points higher for FOFs. This difference is significant at the 1% level. The range of FOF returns is also more limited, with the best fund earning an average of 3.12% on a monthly basis (over 10 months), while the worst performing fund in the sample earned −0.06% (over 84 months), a range that no doubt can be attributed in part to seasoning factors.

8 There are a disproportionately large number of very small hedge funds and funds of funds in the TASS database. Larger funds (in excess of $100 million in assets) experienced slightly higher average returns. The risk was also lower, with lower standard deviations and mean lower 5% fractile of −3.91% for hedge funds and −1.91% for FOFs. However, excluding the smaller funds does not affect in any way the comparison between hedge funds and FOFs given in Table 1. Both returns and risk measures are lower for FOFs than for hedge funds over the same period of time.

9 Survival issues would suggest that hedge funds that survive have persistent returns (Brown *et al.*, 1992). Brown *et al.* (1999) show that while hedge fund returns are not generally persistent, there is some negative persistence in FOF returns. This persistence is better explained by a negative drag on after fee performance due to fees than by a survival argument.

10 Twenty-nine percent of the larger FOFs in our sample (in excess of $100 million) do not charge any incentive fee, although the median fee is the same (15%) and one fund charges as much as 25% of the return above benchmark. The story is similar with management fees, although only one fund charges no management fees, 86% charge in the region of 1–2% management fee.

[11] Differences in Sharpe ratios do not necessarily indicate differences in skill where returns are left-skewed due to inclusion of derivative securities or option-like trading strategies (Goetzmann *et al.*, 2002). However, in this case FOF returns are actually more left skewed (average skewness −0.162) than are individual fund returns which are not on average skewed (average skewness 0.051) and the difference is significant at the 1% level. For this reason, it is difficult to attribute the higher Sharpe ratio of individual funds to increased negative skewness in the distribution of returns. This argument does not affect the cross-sectional results reported later in the paper. Lo (2002) advises care in the interpretation of hedge fund Sharpe ratios where positive autocorrelation in monthly returns can cause an upward bias in the estimated ratios. While the average first and second autocorrelation coefficients are significant (albeit smaller in magnitude than for the sample that Lo (2002) reports), they are significantly higher for the FOF sample. Hence we cannot attribute a lower FOF average Sharpe ratio to an autocorrelation artifact.

[12] To deal with the fact that not all 830 funds survived the entire period we assume that the FOF manager was astute enough to withdraw funds the month prior to the fund leaving the database, and reinvest the proceeds in another hedge fund in operation at that time. This will of course typically overstate the realized returns, as funds fail without prior warning, and in many cases there are restrictions that prevent such rapid withdrawals.

[13] These incentive fees and the benchmark correspond to the median numbers recorded in the TASS database.

[14] It is important to note that this illustration does not represent the actual trading results of any actual FOF, but is meant to be illustrative of the nature of the fee/return relationship implied by reported fee arrangements. FOF providers would not normally choose funds at random, and furthermore a survey of FOF providers show that the actual number of hedge funds held by FOF is close to 13 (Liang, 2003).

[15] For an initial fund value $S = 1$, the expected fee is given as $0.2\,(E(S|S > 1) - 1)\Pr(S > 1)$. If the annual return on the fund is lognormal with zero drift and volatility 0.2, the conditional expectation $E(S|S > 1)$ is 1.42 (Johnson and Kotz, 1970, p. 129), and the expected fee is 4.2% of initial fund value.

[16] Carpenter (2000) describes the consequences of these manager incentive payments on their risk-taking behaviors.

[17] Incentive fees are relatively new to the mutual fund industry, and are discussed in Elton *et al.* (2003).

[18] Presumably the fund of funds provider is in a better position to hedge the individual manager incentive fee contracts than is the ultimate investor, given that he or she has timely and accurate information on position sizes.

[19] Goetzmann *et al.* (2003) describe the adjustments that must be made to account for the highwatermark provision.

[20] The formula is $2p(N[\sigma_0/2] - N[\sigma_1/2])$ for time to maturity τ 1 year, $S = 1$ and $K = S\,e^{r\tau}$, where σ_0 is the volatility of the k underlying funds, and σ_1 is the volatility of the portfolio of those funds. This formula does not depend on the risk-free rate or number of funds.

[21] Using a portfolio of calls in place of the desired call on the portfolio is akin to certain inefficient dynamic trading strategies which also result in net positive deadweight costs to investors (Dybvig, 1986).

[22] There are very few funds in the TASS survey which offer to absorb incentive fees of the funds under its management in the event that the fund as a whole lost money. There are reports

that several large institutional investors are beginning to negotiate such arrangements with fund of funds providers both in the United States and in Europe.

23 There is an interesting parallel here to mutual fund companies investing in publically issued stock of corporations that compensate their managers in the form of bonus incentive arrangements. While incentive bonus payments rarely reach as high as 20% of net revenue, the argument in this section suggests that mutual funds might be able to improve reported performance by using traded derivatives to hedge these incentive payments.

References

Agarwal, V. and Naik, N. (2004). "Risks and Portfolio Decisions Involving Hedge Funds." *Review of Financial Studies* **17**, 63–98.

Brown, S., Goetzmann, W., Ibbotson, R., and Ross, S. (1992). "Survivorship Bias in Performance Studies." *Review of Financial Studies* **5**, 553–580.

Brown, S., Goetzmann, W., and Ibbotson, R. (1999). "Offshore Hedge Funds: Survival and Performance." *Journal of Business* **72**, 91–117.

Brown, S., Goetzmann, W., and Park, J. (2001). "Careers and Survival: Competition and Risk in the Hedge Fund and CTA Industry." *Journal of Finance* **61**, 1869–1886.

Carpenter, J. (2000). "Does Option Compensation Increase Managerial Risk Appetite." *Journal of Finance* **55**, 2311–2331.

Elton, E., Gruber, M., and Blake, C. (2003). "Incentive Fees and Mutual Funds." *Journal of Finance* **58**, 779–804.

Fung, W. and Hsieh, D. (1997a). "Survivorship Bias and Investment Style in the Returns of CTAs: The Information Content of Performance Track Records." *Journal of Portfolio Management* **24**, 30–41.

Fung, W. and Hsieh, D. (1997b). "Empirical Characteristics of Dynamic Trading Strategies: The Case of Hedge Funds." *Review of Financial Studies* **10**, 275–302.

Fung, W. and Hsieh, D. (2000). "Performance Characteristics of Hedge Funds and Commodity Funds: Natural vs. Spurious Biases." *Journal of Financial and Quantitative Analysis* **35**, 291–307.

Fung, W. and Hsieh, D. (2001). "The Risk in Hedge Fund Strategies: Theory and Evidence from Trend Followers." *Review of Financial Studies* **14**, 313–341.

Goetzmann, W., Ingersoll, J., and Ross, S. (2003). "High Water Marks and Hedge Fund Management Contracts." *Journal of Finance* **58**, 1685–1718.

Goetzmann, W., Ingersoll, J., Spiegel, M., and Welch, I. (2002). "Sharpening Sharpe Ratios." Yale ICF Working Paper No. 02-08, http://ssrn.com/abstract_id=302815.

Henriksson, R. D. and Merton, R. C. (1981). "On Market Timing and Investment Performance. II. Statistical Procedures for Evaluating Forecasting Skills." *Journal of Business* **54**(4), 513–533.

Johnson, N. L. and Kotz, S. (1970). "*Continuous Univariate Distributions—1.*" Boston: Houghton Mifflin Company.

Liang, B. (2003). "On the Performance of Alternative Investments: CTAs, Hedge Funds, and Funds-of-Funds." http://ssrn.com/abstract = 378140.

Lo, A. (2002). "The Statistics of Sharpe Ratios." *Financial Analysts Journal* **July/August**, 36–52.

Park, J. and Staum, J. (1999). "Fund of Fund Diversification: How Much is Enough?" *Journal of Alternative Investments* **Winter**, 29–42.

Sharpe, W. (1981). "Decentralized Investment Management." *Journal of Finance* **36**, 217–234.

Spurgin, R. B. (2001). "How to Game Your Sharpe Ratio." *The Journal of Alternative Investments* **4**(3), 38–46.

Keywords: Hedge funds; funds-of-funds; incentive fees

Journal of Investment Management
Vol. 2, No. 4 (2004), pp. 57–75

EXTRACTING PORTABLE ALPHAS FROM EQUITY LONG/SHORT HEDGE FUNDS

William Fung[a,*] *and David A. Hsieh*[b]

This paper shows empirically that Equity Long/Short (Equity L/S) hedge funds have significant alpha to both conventional as well as alternative (hedge fund-like) risk factors utilizing hedge fund data from three major data bases. Following the terminology introduced in Fung and Hsieh (2003) Journal of Fixed Income ***58****, 16–27, we call these Equity alternative alphas (or Equity AAs for short). Equity AAs are extracted from Equity L/S hedge fund returns by first identifying the systematic risk factors inherent in their strategies. Hedging out these systematic risk factors, the resultant AA return series are empirically shown to be independent of systematic risks during normal as well as stressful conditions in asset markets. This provides collaborative evidence that AA returns are portable across conventional asset-class indexes. By modeling the AA return series as GARCH(1,1)–AR(1) processes, it is shown that the unconditional return distributions are normal with time-varying variance free of serial correlations, skewness, and kurtosis. Alpha-enhanced equity alternative are constructed admitting higher mean return, better annual returns, and Sharpe ratios to the S&P 500 index over the sample period 1996–2002.*

1 Introduction

Alternative Investment Strategies (AIS for short), in their purest form, are those investment strategies whose return are not dependent on the behavior of primary asset classes (e.g., stocks and bonds). In other words, AIS are designed to deliver the proverbial "pure alpha." As such, AIS are often also referred to as absolute return strategies—absolute return in the sense that performance is not at the mercy of primary asset classes' performance.

Empirical experience, however, had often proved otherwise. At the worst of times, when primary asset classes are in distress, AIS often experience poor performance. This has attracted skeptics to question whether AIS "alphas" are no more than a redundant bull-market phenomenon. As such, what value it adds to a portfolio of primary asset classes remains unknown.

The range of AIS is wide—from hedge funds to venture capital investments. In this paper, we focus on the more liquid portion of AIS—equity-oriented hedge fund strategies. The reasons for our choice will become apparent as our analysis unfolds. Suffice to say that if a convincing case cannot be made for equity-oriented hedge funds

[a]Centre for Hedge Fund Research and Education, London Business School, London, UK.

[b]Fuqua School of Business, Duke University, Durham, NC, USA.

*Corresponding author.

to be included in an institutional portfolio of primary asset classes, then it is doubtful if hedge funds will ever make a meaningful performance difference to large institutional portfolios.

The first known hedge fund was founded by A.W. Jones in 1949. Unlike the typical equity mutual fund, Jones' fund took long and short positions in equities. This style of investing is now called Equity Long/Short (Equity L/S), to distinguish it from newer hedge fund styles, such as Global/Macro and Convertible Arbitrage that came along well after Jones' time. The key attributes to this style of trading are—the ability to use short sales, and the ability to use leverage. It is, to date, the most basic form of alternative strategy to the commonly accepted long-only equity investing.

Even though Equity L/S is one of the oldest hedge fund styles, interest in it has remained strong over the years. As of March 2003, the TASS database has 3068 hedge funds (excluding funds-of-hedge funds). Roughly 40% are classified as having Equity L/S as the primary investment style. In fact, the next largest style (Managed Futures) has only 15% of the total number of funds. Here, one encounters a major reason for our focus on this particular style of hedge fund strategies. Failure to identify alphas from equity hedge funds will eliminate some 40% of the hedge fund universe from the quest for alternative returns to conventional asset classes.

In this paper we demonstrate that Equity L/S hedge funds can be engineered to offer significant alphas to portfolios of primary asset classes. Following the work of Fung and Hsieh (2002b, 2003a, 2004), alternative alphas (zero beta with respect to conventional asset-class indexes as well as alternative systematic risk factors; refer to these as AAs for short) are extracted from the returns of diversified portfolios of Equity L/S hedge funds. It is shown that these AAs are not sensitive to conventional asset-class indexes and alternative risk factors under normal, as well as extreme market conditions. In other words, AAs are *portable* as well as *more than "just a bull-market phenomenon."*

However, incorporating AA returns into a conventional asset allocation framework calls for a more detailed analysis of their distributional properties. Since the initial findings of Fung and Hsieh (1997)[1] where hedge fund returns were reported to have fatter tails than those of standard asset classes such as stocks and bonds, different explanations on this phenomenon have been put forward. The evidence thus far points to the observed departure from return normality being a consequence of the nonlinear, option-like nature of hedge fund strategies—see, for example, Fung and Hsieh (2001) and Agarwal and Naik (2004). However another, less documented, plausible cause of the observed fat-tailed return distribution is that the moments of the return distribution are time-varying. The systematic effect of nonlinear, option-like strategies on the return distribution should be greatly mitigated once the systematic risk factors have been isolated. This in turn implies that the resultant distribution of the AA return series should exhibit much less leptokurtosis.

It is shown in this paper that the fat-tailed behavior of Equity L/S hedge funds returns come primarily from their exposure to the spread between small cap and large cap stocks. Once this exposure is removed from the return series through hedging, kurtosis is reduced dramatically. By modeling the resultant AA return series as a GARCH(1,1)–AR(1) process, we show that each return series is normally distributed with time-varying variance.[2] This conclusion has important implications for portfolio construction and asset allocation strategies. It tells us that the standard mean–variance model applies to alternative Equity L/S alphas despite the reported non-normal return distributions of the underlying hedge fund returns.

The paper is organized as follows. Section 2 describes the data set used and the empirical methodology. AA return series are extracted from Equity L/S hedge funds in Section 3. Section 4 analyzes the distribution properties of these AA return series, while Section 5 puts forth a method for incorporating AAs into a portfolio of conventional assets with minimal disruption to the portfolio's existing risk profile. Concluding remarks are given in Section 6.

2 Establishing the Risk Structure of Equity L/S Hedge Funds: Data and Methodology

2.1 Data

It is only appropriate to begin our analysis by acknowledging that hedge fund investing is not risk free. More specifically, not only are Equity L/S hedge funds not risk-free, they actually exhibit systematic exposure to market risk. In general, Equity L/S hedge funds carry a long bias. The key question is what other systematic risk factors do these strategies carry and is there a significant alpha after adjusting for systematic risks?

We begin by introducing terminology. In Fung and Hsieh (2003a, 2004), we introduced the concept of alternative alphas and alternative betas. Defining conventional asset-class indexes as the primary risk factors, alternative risk factors are those that lie outside the set of conventional asset-class indexes such as stocks and bonds. Typically, they are long/short combinations and sector specializations of conventional asset-class indexes such as value to growth spread and small cap stocks. What we need to know is how many risk factors, conventional, and alternative, are systematically present in Equity L/S hedge fund returns.

In a related study, Fung and Hsieh (2003b) analyzed individual equity-oriented hedge funds from the three major sources of hedge fund data—Hedge Fund Research (HFR), TASS, and Morgan Stanley Capital International (MSCI). It was shown that equity-oriented hedge funds have two major exposures—the equity market as a whole (as proxied by the S&P 500 index), and the spread between small cap and large cap stocks (as proxied by the difference between the Wilshire Small Cap 1750 index and the Wilshire Large Cap 750 index). This paper focuses on the property of diversified portfolios of Equity L/S hedge funds constructed from the same data sources—the HFR Equity Hedge index, a comparable, equally weighted Long/Short Equity index constructed from the funds in the TASS database,[3] and the MSCI Long Bias (North American) index.

2.2 Identification of common risk factors

To identify the common risk in Equity L/S hedge funds, we regress the three indexes on the Fama and French (1992) 3-factor model augmented with the Jegadeesh and

Table 1(a) Regression of HFR Equity Hedge index on 4-factor model (1994–2002).

	2-Factor	3-Factor	4-Factor	Nonlinear
Intercept	**0.0102**	**0.0103**	**0.0091**	**0.0076**
	0.0011	*0.0012*	*0.0011*	*0.0022*
Mkt-RF	**0.4383**	**0.4385**	**0.4721**	**0.4426**
	0.0270	*0.0300*	*0.0273*	*0.0307*
SMB	**0.2646**	**0.2648**	**0.2496**	**0.2545**
	0.0412	*0.0399*	*0.0373*	*0.0350*
HML		0.0006	0.0232	
		0.0458	*0.0389*	
MOM			**0.0851**	
			0.0236	
|Mkt-Rf|				0.0191
				0.0519
|SMB|				0.0602
				0.0488
R^2	0.8109	0.8109	0.8374	0.8156
Adjusted R^2	0.8073	0.8055	0.8312	0.8084

Standard errors in italics. Coefficients in bold are statistically significant at the 1% level.
2-factor model: Rm-Rf and SMB from Fama and French (1992).
3-factor model: Rm-Rf, SMB, and HML from Fama and French (1992).
4-factor model: Rm-Rf, SMB, and HML from Fama and French (1992), and MOM from Carhart (1997).

Titman (1993) momentum factor, as implemented in Cahart (1997). The results are shown in Tables 1(a)–(c).

Table 1(a) contains the regression results of the HFR Equity Hedge index on the various risk factors. In all regressions, the two most important risk factors are the excess return of the market (Mkt-Rf) and the spread between small cap and large cap stocks (SMB). The spread between high book-to-market and low book-to-market stocks (HML) is not statistically significant in any regression. In addition, the momentum factor (MOM), while statistically significant in the 4-factor regression, does not add substantial explanatory power beyond the 2-factor regression in terms of adjusted R^2. Similar results on the TASS and MSCI indexes are reported in Tables 1(b) and 1(c), respectively.

To complete the analysis, we check for evidence of market timing ability using the Henriksson and Merton (1981) method of adding absolute values of the regressors (|Mkt-Rf| and |SMB|) to the regressions. Statistical significance of these nonlinear variables would be consistent with the presence of significant market timing strategy in Equity L/S hedge funds. As shown in the last columns of Tables 1(a)–(c), neither nonlinear factor is statistically significant for all three indexes. In light of these findings, we elected to focus our analysis on the 2-factor model (based on factors Mkt-Rf and SMB).[4]

Table 1(b) Regression of CTI Long/Short Equity index on 4-factor model (1994–2002).

	2-Factor	3-Factor	4-Factor	Nonlinear
Intercept	**0.0112**	**0.0113**	**0.0102**	**0.0073**
	0.0011	*0.0012*	*0.0011*	*0.0023*
Mkt-RF	**0.4987**	**0.4857**	**0.5162**	**0.5068**
	0.0244	*0.0306*	*0.0298*	*0.0247*
SMB	**0.2939**	**0.2820**	**0.2690**	**0.2851**
	0.0261	*0.0311*	*0.0293*	*0.0269*
HML		−0.0285	−0.0086	
		0.0404	*0.0382*	
MOM			**0.0772**	
			0.0198	
|Mkt-Rf|				0.0451
				0.0442
|SMB|				0.0643
				0.0382
R^2	0.8570	0.8576	0.8759	0.8627
Adjusted R^2	0.8542	0.8535	0.8711	0.8573

Standard errors in italics. Coefficients in bold are statistically significant at the 1% level.

Table 1(c) Regression of MSCI Long Bias fund averages on 4-factor model (1994–2002).

	2-Factor	3-Factor	4-Factor	Nonlinear
Intercept	**0.0110**	**0.0105**	**0.0097**	**0.0078**
	0.0012	*0.0012*	*0.0011*	*0.0025*
Mkt-RF	**0.5803**	**0.6193**	**0.6431**	**0.5848**
	0.0279	*0.0311*	*0.0289*	*0.0294*
SMB	**0.3023**	**0.3386**	**0.3278**	**0.2875**
	0.0511	*0.0463*	*0.0424*	*0.0404*
HML		0.0876	**0.1036**	
		0.0416	*0.0353*	
MOM			**0.0603**	
			0.0248	
|Mkt-Rf|				0.0142
				0.0490
|SMB|				0.0843
				0.0620
R^2	0.8670	0.8720	0.8808	0.8725
Adjusted R^2	0.8644	0.8683	0.8761	0.8676

Standard errors in italics. Coefficients in bold are statistically significant at the 1% level.

3 Creating an Alternative Alpha Series for Equity L/S Hedge Funds

Having identified the risk structure of Equity L/S hedge funds, two of the Fama–French factors—one primary asset-class risk factor, and one alternative spread risk factor, we

Table 2 Annual alphas of the equity hedge fund portfolios (1996–2002).

Year	S&P	HFR-α	TASS-α	MSCI-α
1996	22.96%	13.43%	14.82%	0.71%
1997	33.36%	13.34%	9.39%	6.89%
1998	28.58%	15.48%	13.51%	9.40%
1999	21.04%	30.46%	33.27%	27.29%
2000	−9.11%	8.79%	8.52%	14.03%
2001	−11.88%	0.79%	2.76%	6.34%
2002	−22.10%	3.76%	6.28%	4.66%
Average	**10.22%**	**11.48%**	**12.65%**	**9.35%**
SD	16.24%	5.41%	9.97%	5.09%
Average/SD	0.629	2.122	1.269	1.837

Averages in bold are statistically significant at the 1% level.

S&P: Standard and Poors 500 index.
HFR-α: alpha of HFR Equity Hedge index.
TASS-α: alpha of the equally weighted average of TASS Long/Short Equity Funds.
MSCI-α: alpha of MSCI Long Bias (North American) index.

can now proceed to neutralize these systematic risk factors to obtain an AA return series. For the purpose of this exercise, we consider the three Equity L/S indexes as *equity hedge fund portfolios*, or EHFPs for short.

The alphas of these portfolios are extracted as follows. For each month, the regression coefficients (betas) of the previous 24 monthly returns on the two risk factors—the S&P 500 index, and the Small–Large spread (measured as the Wilshire Small Cap 1750 index minus the Wilshire Large Cap 750 index[5]) are used as hedge ratios. The monthly returns from a short position in the S&P 500 index, and the Small–Large spread, in proportion to the regression coefficients are subtracted from the returns of the EHFP. The resulting return is the AA of the portfolio spanning the period January 1996–December 2002. These return series are respectively denoted as HFR-α, TASS-α, and MSCI-α. Refer to these returns series as the AA return series for short.

Table 2 tabulates the annualized AA returns, from 1996 to 2002. On average, these AAs are roughly of the same magnitude as the S&P's average annual return of 10.22%. However, their standard deviations are much lower and their information ratios are uniformly higher than that of the S&P 500 for the same period. In addition, while the S&P had negative returns in 2000, 2001, and 2002, the annualized AA returns are uniformly positive.

To ensure that the alphas have no linear or nonlinear dependence on the returns of standard benchmarks—an important property of *portability*—we use the method developed in Fung and Hsieh (1997). The monthly returns of eight standard conventional asset-class indexes—US equities, non-US equities, emerging market equities, US bonds, non-US bonds, gold, trade-weighted dollar index, and the 1-month Eurodollar deposit rate—are individually sorted from worst to best into quintiles. The average return for each quintile of the asset-class indexes and the average of the corresponding months for the respective AA return series are graphed in Figures 1–8.

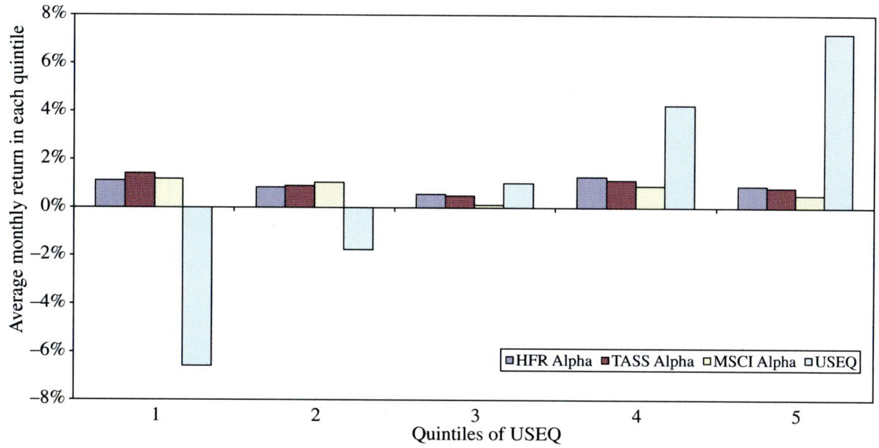

Figure 1 Alphas in different quintiles of USEQ.

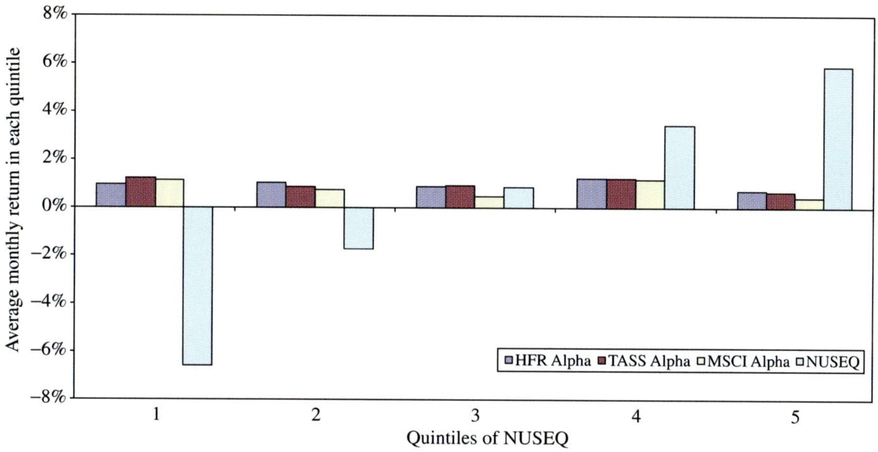

Figure 2 Alphas in different quintiles of NUSEQ.

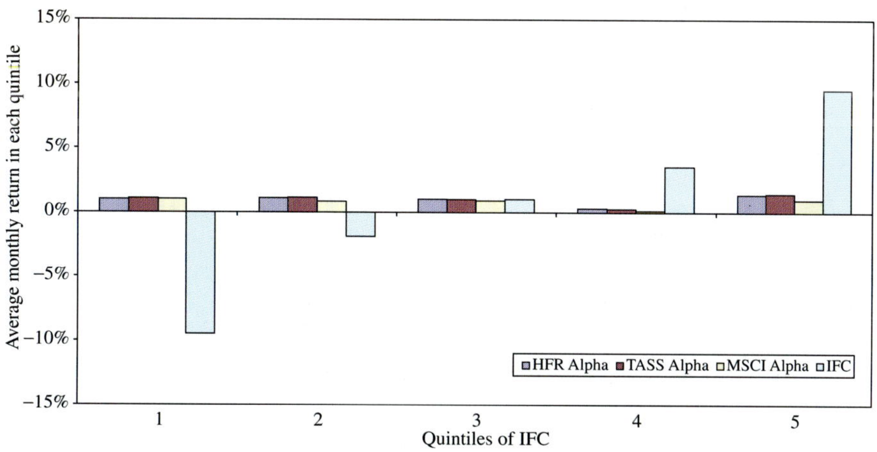

Figure 3 Alphas in different quintiles of IFC.

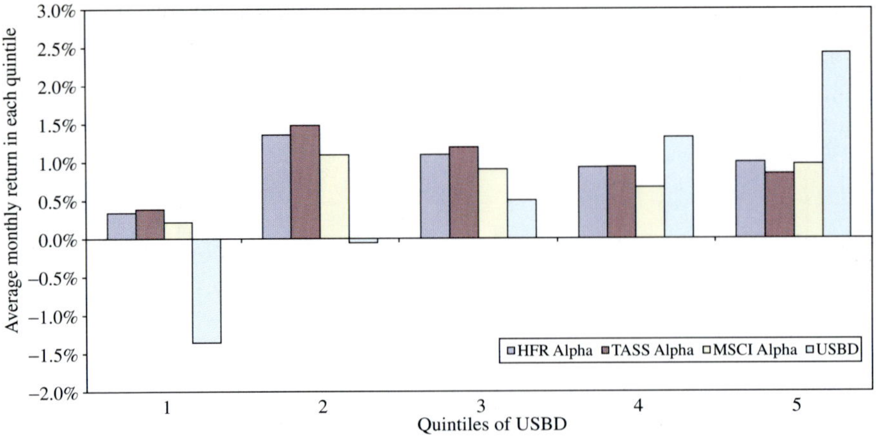

Figure 4 Alphas in different quintiles of USBD.

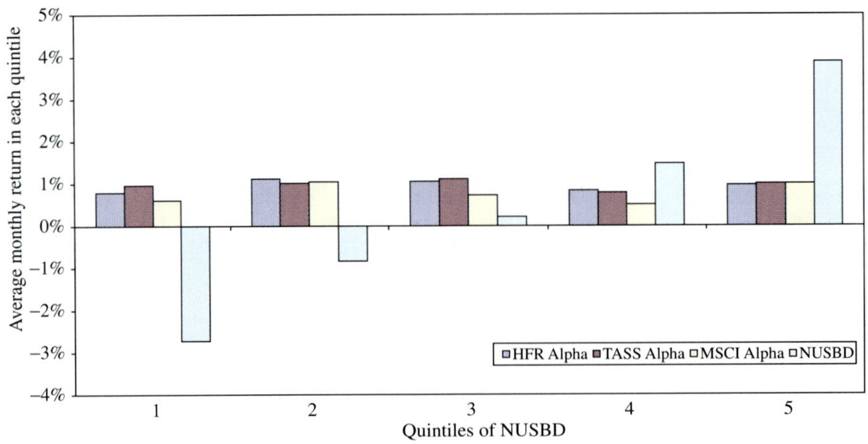

Figure 5 Alphas in different quintiles of NUSBD.

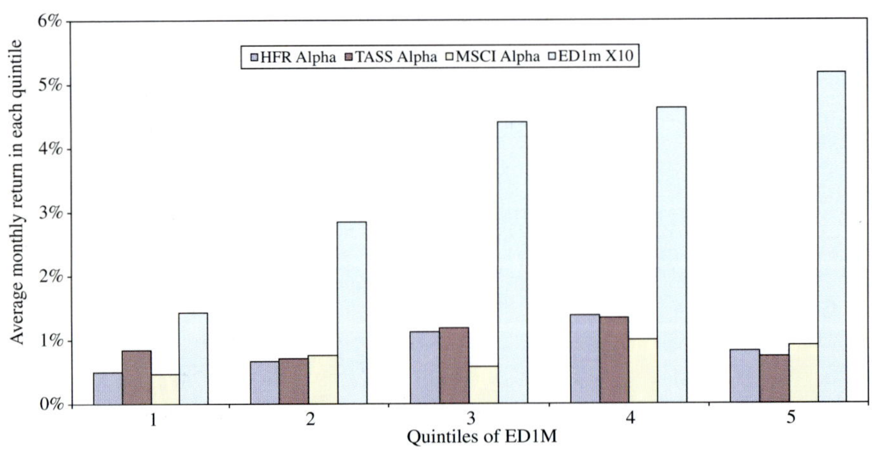

Figure 6 Alphas in different quintiles of ED1M.

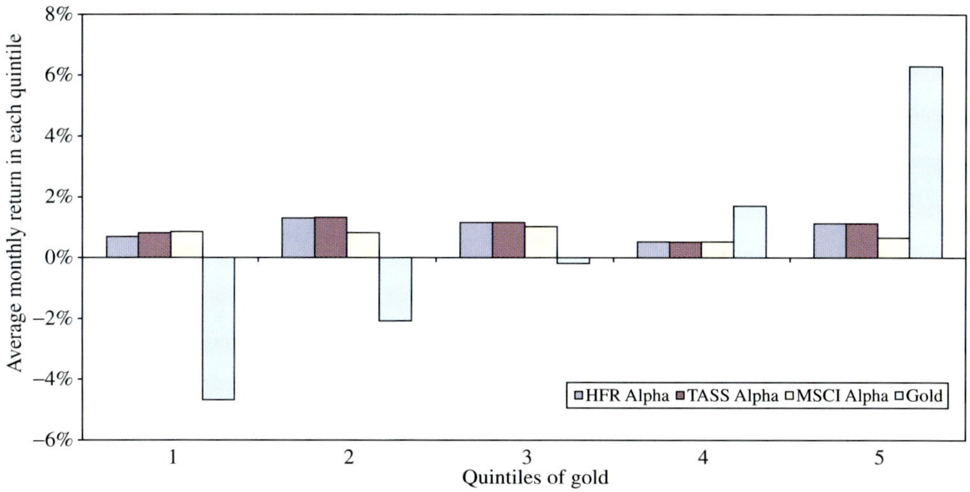

Figure 7 Alphas in different quintiles of gold.

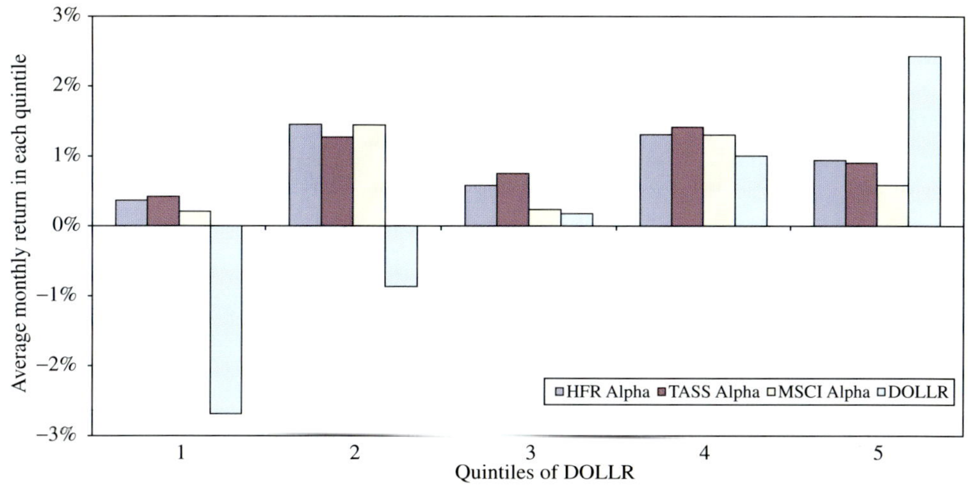

Figure 8 Alphas in different quintiles of DOLLR.

The general flat patterns of the AAs indicate that they have little relation to the eight conventional asset-class indexes. To complete the analysis, we perform the same check on the dependence of these alphas on the seven hedge fund risk factors (Asset-Based Style factors or ABS factors for short) reported in Fung and Hsieh (2004). These ABS factors include two equity-oriented risk factors (S&P 500, Small Cap minus Large Cap or SC-LC), two bond-oriented risk factors (the change in the 10-year constant Treasury yield, the change in the credit spread as measured by the difference between the Moody's Baa bond yield and the 10-year constant Treasury yield), and three trend-following risk factors (trend following on bonds, trend following on currencies, and trend following on commodities). Figures 9–15 show that there is no strong dependence on these seven hedge fund risk factors similar to the pattern observed using conventional asset-class indexes.

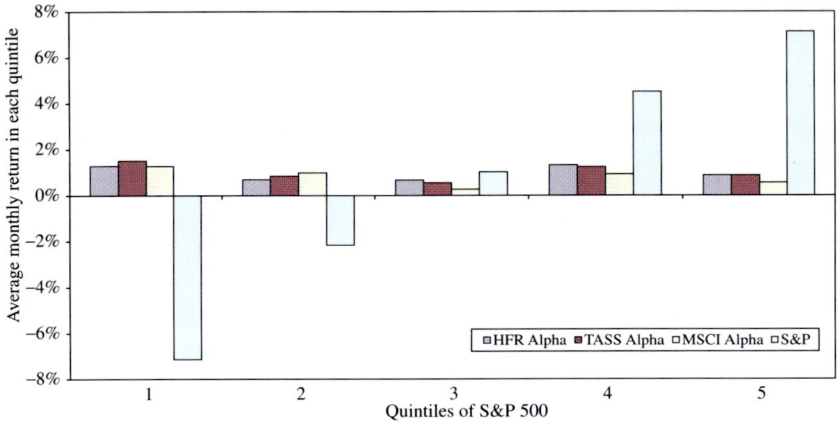

Figure 9 Alphas in different quintiles of S&P 500.

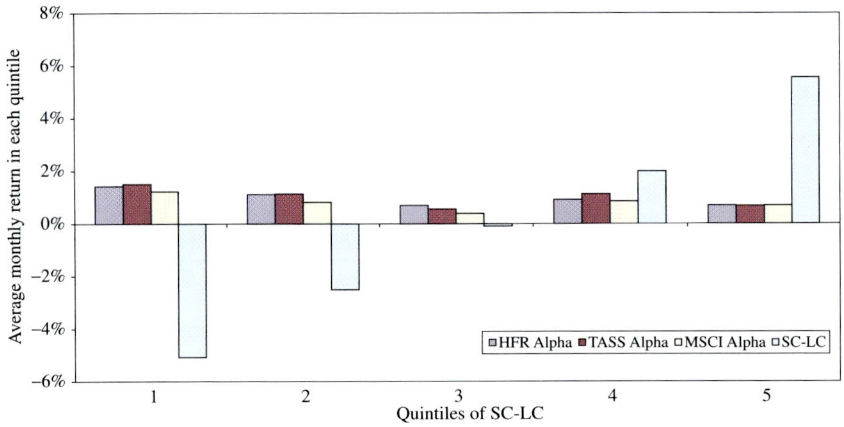

Figure 10 Alphas in different quintiles of SC-LC.

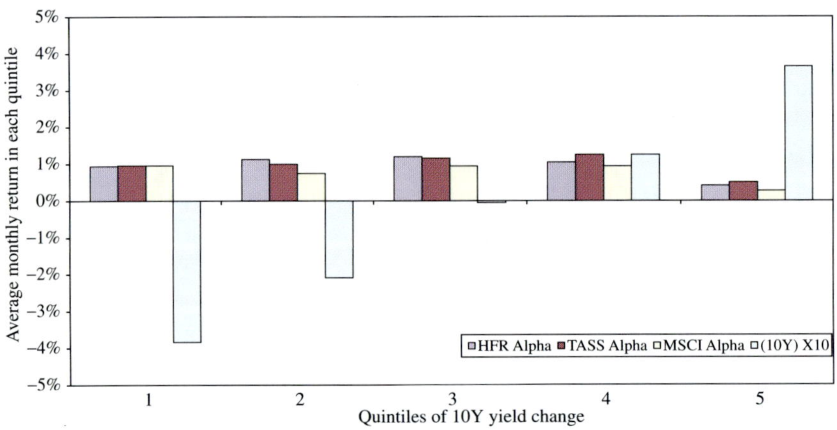

Figure 11 Alphas in different quintiles of 10Y yield change.

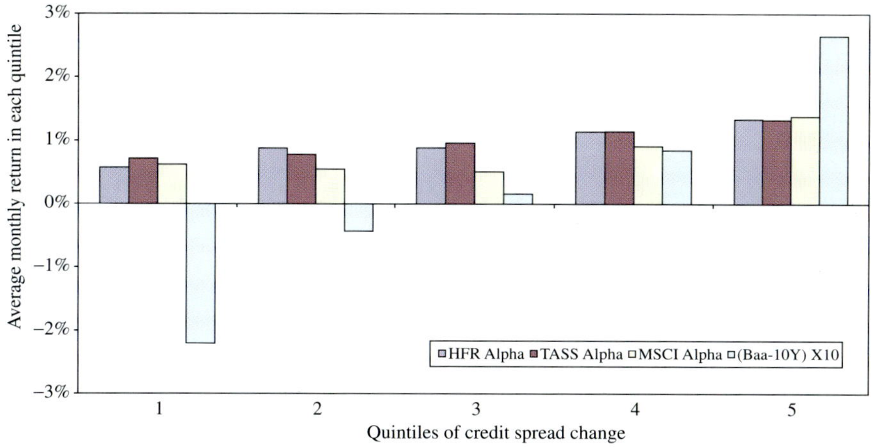

Figure 12 Alphas in different quintiles of credit spread change.

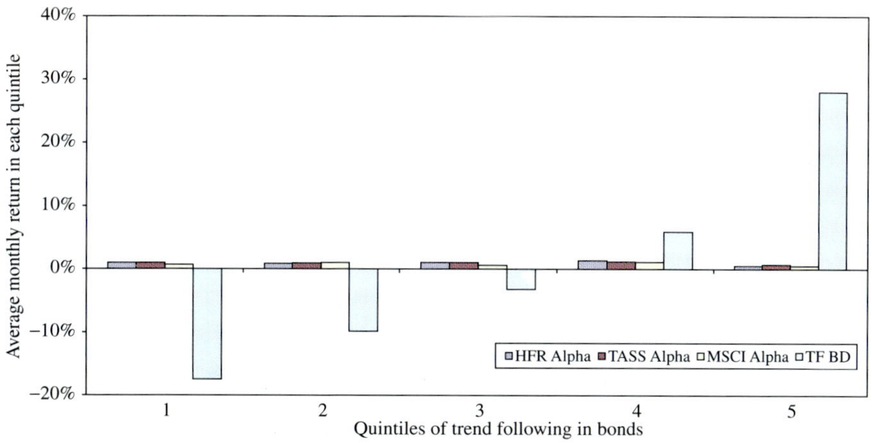

Figure 13 Alphas in different quintiles of trend following in bonds.

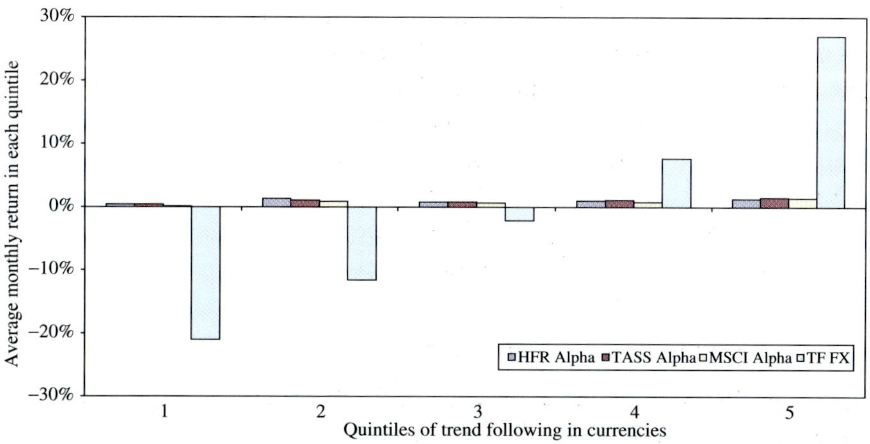

Figure 14 Alphas in different quintiles of trend following in currencies.

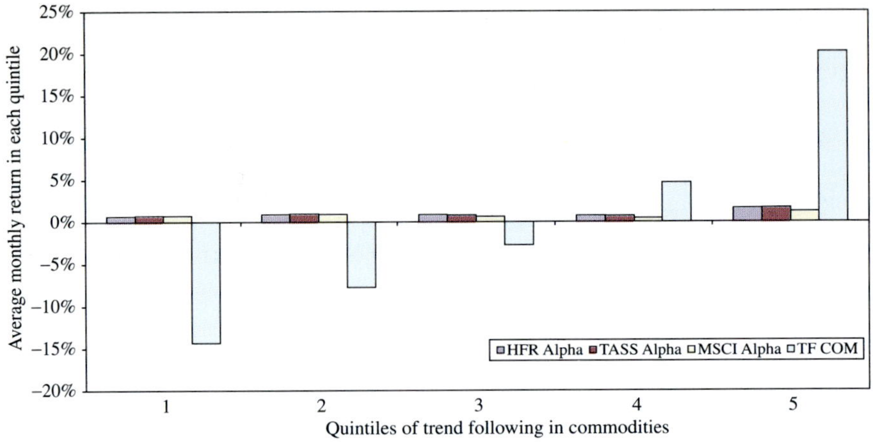

Figure 15 Alphas in different quintiles of trend following in commodities.

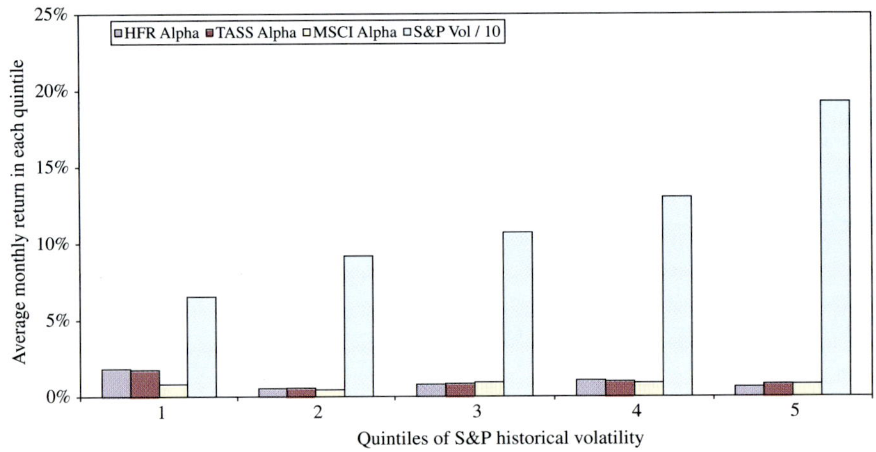

Figure 16 Alphas in different quintiles of S&P historical volatility.

We further check for the dependence of alphas on market volatility. Figure 16 depicts the average alphas for each quintile of the 21-day historical volatility of the S&P 500 index. Figure 17 is the corresponding figure for the 21-day historical volatility of the SC-LC factor. There is no strong evidence that alphas are related to market volatility.

Figures 18–20 show how the exposures change over time. Figure 18 has the 24-month rolling betas against the S&P 500 and SC-LC risk factors for the HFR Equity Hedge Index. Figures 19 and 20 are the corresponding figures for the CTI Equity L/S Index and the MSCI Long Bias Index.

4 Distributional Properties of Portable AAs

The results in Section 3 tell us something about the conditional distribution of AAs (conditional on most known risk factors, conventional, and alternative). This section completes the analysis by analyzing the unconditional distribution of AAs.

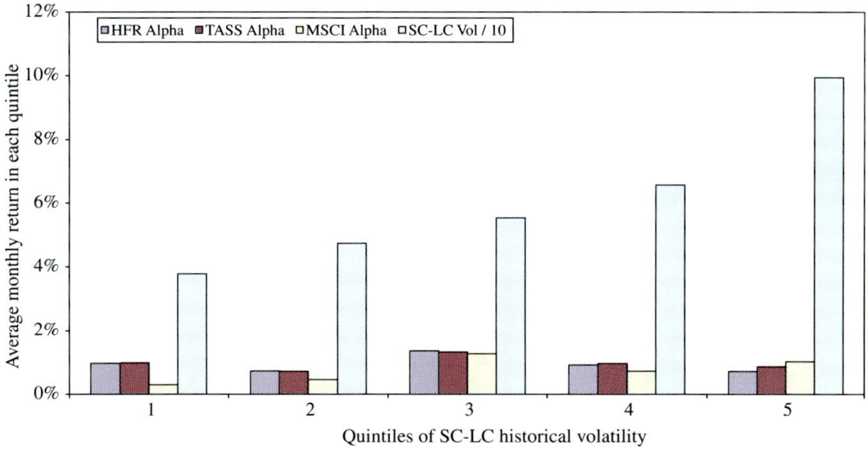

Figure 17 Alphas in different quintiles of SC-LC historical volatility.

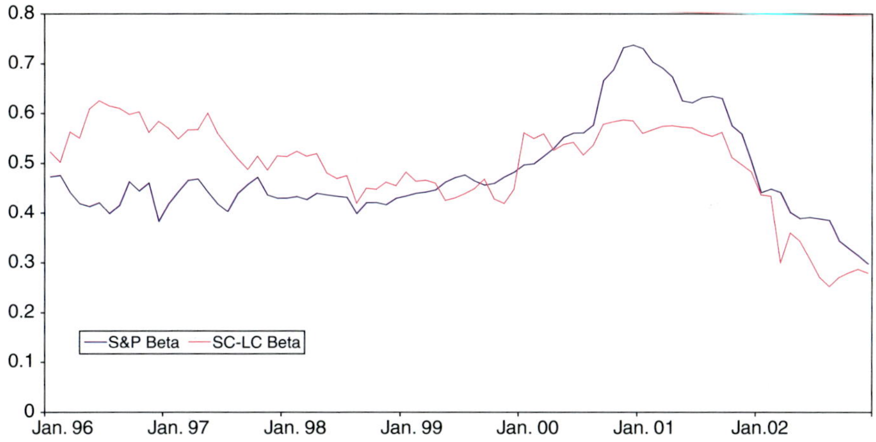

Figure 18 24-Month rolling betas: HFR Equity Hedge.

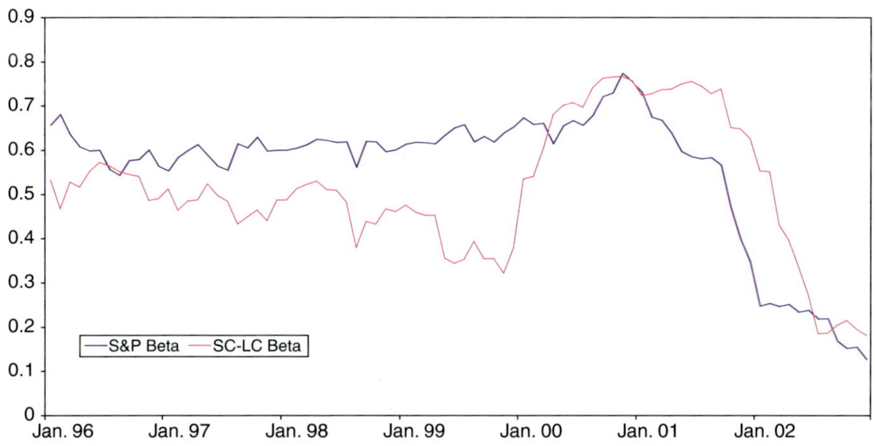

Figure 19 24-Month rolling betas: CTI Equity Long–Short.

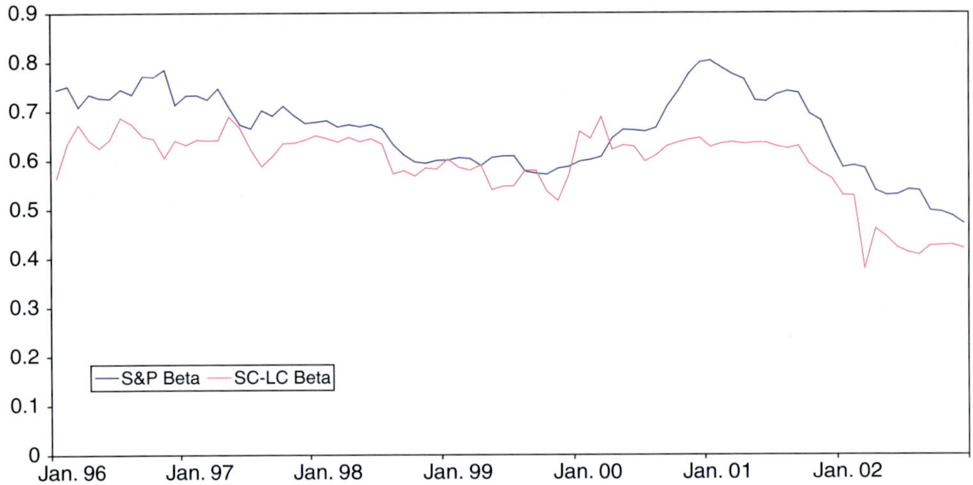

Figure 20 24-Month rolling betas: MSCI Long Bias.

It was noted in Fung and Hsieh (1997) that hedge fund returns tend to have excess kurtosis, or fat-tailed distributions—an observation that has since been confirmed by other researchers such as Amin and Kat (2003). Although there is no single conclusive theory as to why this occurs, one sufficient condition seems most likely. Suppose that the strategies used by most hedge fund managers are nonlinear, option-liked in character. This will certainly lead to observed returns from hedge funds to depart from normality. Thus far, theoretical models of hedge fund strategies proposed in Fung and Hsieh (2001), Mitchel and Pulvino (2001), and Agarwal and Naik (2004) have all point to option-like characteristics. While these are sufficient conditions for certain hedge fund strategies to exhibit non-normal return distributions, they are not necessary conditions for all hedge funds return to exhibit systematic departure from normality. Certainly, up to the time of writing, no theoretical option-like model of Equity L/S strategies has been put forward. Our empirical results have not confirmed option-like market timing characteristics from Equity L/S hedge funds—at least not at the level of a diversified portfolio of such strategies. Yet, Table 3 shows that the three EHFPs all have excess kurtosis (that are statistically different from zero).

Table 3 Excess kurtosis of hedge fund portfolios (Jan. 1994–Dec. 2002).

Excess kurtosis	S&P	SC-LC	HFR	TASS	MSCI
Raw returns	0.169	**4.046**	**1.451**	**2.905**	**1.043**
Alphas			**1.011**	0.888	**1.184**

Coefficients in bold are statistically significant at the 1% level.

S&P: Standard and Poors 500 index.
HFR: HFR Equity Hedge index.
TASS: Equally-weighted average of TASS Long/Short Equity funds.
MSCI: MSCI Long Bias (North American) index.

As the primary interest of this paper is on the series of AA returns extracted from the EHFPs, it is important to know whether leptokurtic return behavior survives the alpha extraction process. Table 3 shows that a substantial part of the observed excess kurtosis in the EHFPs' returns is due to exposures to the systematic risk factors. Although the S&P has virtually no excess kurtosis the alternative risk factor, the SC-LC factor, exhibits a high degree of excess kurtosis. However when we reach the level of the AA series, where exposures to the two systematic risk factors have been removed, the resulting returns exhibit substantially less excess kurtosis.

Next we examine the other source of observed leptokurtic return behavior—the possibility of time-varying moments of the return distribution. A frequent cause of kurtosis in financial time series is time-varying volatility, as shown in the pioneering work of Engle (1982) and Bollerslev (1986). To investigate this, we fit GARCH(1,1)–AR(1) models to the alphas of the three portfolios using the following specification:

$$u_t = c + \rho u_{t-1} + (h_t)^{1/2} e_t, \quad e_t \sim N(0, h_t)$$
$$h_t = s + a(e_{t-1})^2 + b h_{t-1}$$

In the first equation, the *u*s are the AA return series from the three EHFPs. In this specification, there is a constant term, c. A first-order autoregressive term, u_{t-1}, to capture any serial correlation that may potentially arise from infrequent trading of the securities in the underlying hedge fund portfolios. The error term, e_t, is assumed to be normally distributed with zero mean and variance h_t following the standard GARCH(1,1) process specified by the second equation.

Table 4 reports the maximum likelihood estimates using the same procedure as in Hsieh (1988). Several results are worthy of note. First, the serial correlation of the AA series is small—the coefficients are between 0.15 and 0.24—and are not statistically different from zero. Fung and Hsieh (2002b) asserted that the reported lagged dependency between hedge fund returns and the S&P 500 index returns in Asness *et al.* (2001) could be due the choice of benchmark rather than purported measurement error. Based on the GARCH(1,1)–AR(1) model of the AA returns series with explicitly identified systematic risk factors, the results in Table 4 provide direct evidence that the AA return series are indeed serial correlation-free as asserted in Fung and Hsieh (2002b).

Second, although four of the six GARCH(1,1) coefficients are not statistically different from zero, the joint test on the lack of GARCH(1,1) indicates that it is present in the TASS AA return series, and are also likely in the HFR and MSCI AA return series.

Third, the kurtosis of the standardized residuals is no longer statistically different from zero. Fourth, the insignificant kurtosis in the standardized residuals together with the lack of skewness is consistent with the proposition that the AA return series are normally distributed, with time-varying variances.

These results on the distributional property of the AA return series lead to the comforting conclusion that standard mean–variance analysis can be applied to AAs extracted from EHFPs. However, an explicit model of the time-varying variance process needs to be constructed.[6]

Table 4 GARCH(1,1)-AR(1) model of alphas.

	HFR-α	TASS-α	MSCI-α
c	**0.007998**	**0.006398**	0.004866
	0.002335	*0.001255*	*0.002233*
ρ	0.155580	**0.236075**	0.232230
	0.128093	*0.084019*	*0.127301*
s	0.000095	**0.000005**	0.000040
	0.000087	*0.000002*	*0.000044*
a	0.153903	0.028006	0.111228
	0.123220	*0.034218*	*0.109217*
b	0.442002	**0.949146**	**0.694664**
	0.392391	*0.041245*	*0.276933*
χ^2 test $a = 0$ and $b = 0$	3.36	18.65	4.42
p-value	0.1861	0.0000	0.1096
Standardized residuals			
Excess kurtosis	0.617	0.888	0.627
Skewness	0.262	0.228	0.180

Coefficients in bold are statistically significant at the 1% level. Standard errors are in italics.

HFR-α: HFR Equity Hedge index alphas.
TASS-α: Equally weighted average of TASS Long/Short Equity funds alphas.
MSCI-α: MSCI Long Bias (North American) index alphas.
GARCH(1,1)–AR(1) model of alphas:

$u_t = c + \rho u_{t-1} + (h_t)^{1/2} e_t;\ h_t = s + a(e_{t-1})^2 + bh_{t-1}.$

5 The Role of Portable Alternative Alphas in a Conventional Asset-Class Portfolio

One way to add value utilizing portable alphas is to create an alpha-enhanced alternative to conventional equity investments. This section reports the results of one such approach.[7]

In extracting the AA return series from the EHFPs, two overlay transactions were taken—a short position on the S&P 500 index to mitigate the persistent directional exposure to the equity market in general, and a short position on the spread between small cap and large cap stocks. However, if one proxies the Small Cap exposure by the Russell 2000 index[8] and the large cap exposure the S&P 500 index, then the net hedging transactions amount to a net short positions on the S&P 500 index as well as the Russell 2000 index. This has generally been the case since the beta of the EHFP returns to the S&P 500 index tended to be larger than the beta to the Small Cap/Large Cap spread factor.

To create an alpha-enhanced conventional passive equity investment (say the S&P 500 index) synthetically, all one needs to do is to replace the existing cash investment

Table 5 Return of the portable alpha portfolios (1996–2002).

Year	S&P	HFR-F	TASS-F	MSCI-F
1996	22.96%	36.92%	39.1%	24.25%
1997	33.36%	46.75%	42.5%	40.79%
1998	28.58%	45.42%	45.0%	40.73%
1999	21.04%	54.08%	58.6%	52.33%
2000	−9.11%	−2.56%	−2.2%	2.84%
2001	−11.88%	−12.50%	−10.8%	−7.43%
2002	−22.10%	−20.56%	−18.4%	−19.86%
Average	10.22%	17.79%	18.60%	16.78%
SD	16.24%	18.89%	18.36%	18.42%
Corr. w/ S&P	1.000	0.949	0.951	0.948
Excess kurtosis	0.169	−0.055	−0.346	0.324
Skewness	**−0.601**	−0.254	−0.156	−0.114
Sharpe ratio	0.355	0.401	0.770	0.911

Excess kurtosis and skewness coefficients in bold are statistically significant at the 1% level. S&P: Standard and Poors 500 index.

HFR-F: HFR Equity Hedge index plus futures.
TASS-F: Equally weighted average of TASS Long/Short Equity funds plus futures.
MSCI-F: MSCI Long Bias (North American) index plus futures.
Sharpe ratio: (Average return − Risk Free Return)/standard deviation, where the risk-free return is the average return of the 3-month Treasury bill from 1996 until 2002.

in the S&P 500 index by its futures contract equivalent, and invest the capital released into Equity L/S hedge funds on a hedged basis—hedged against the two systematic risk factors so as to extract the AA returns described in the previous sections. Refer to these as the *alternative alpha portfolio*(s) (AA portfolio(s) for short, one for each of the three hedge fund indexes, HFR, TASS, and MSCI).

Table 5 shows the annual returns of the three AA portfolios. Each has an average return that is higher than the S&P 500 index. The annual return in each year from 1996 until 2002 is superior to that of the S&P for all three portable alpha portfolios. By design, all three AA portfolios have returns that are highly correlated to the S&P 500 index with similar return standard deviations. However, all three AA portfolios have better Sharpe ratios than the S&P 500 index.

Lastly, we note that the returns of the AA portfolios do not have excess kurtosis and no significant skewness. In contrast, over this sample period, the distribution of the S&P 500 index's monthly return has a statistically significant skewness to the left. Interestingly, one could argue that these AA portfolios are more amenable to conventional mean–variance asset allocation models than the S&P 500 index.

The results in Section 3 showed that AAs are uncorrelated (during both normal and stressful markets) to most conventional asset-class indexes; the same replication procedure used here can be applied to other conventional asset-class indexes to create alpha-enhanced alternatives. Alpha-enhanced alternatives that offer better risk-adjusted returns without the baggage of nonlinear return distributions that are often reported on hedge fund investments.

6 Concluding Remarks

Unlike long-only equity mutual funds, equity hedge funds are a mixture of alpha and beta bets. However, hedge fund risks are known to differ from conventional asset-class risks. Consequently, to extract the alpha returns from Equity L/S hedge funds necessitated the identification of both conventional as well as alternative risk factors. Although we are able to show that diversified portfolios of Equity L/S hedge funds can be adequately modeled using a simple 2-factor model, it must be noted that less diversified indexes such as CSFB/Tremont's Long/Short Equity index's returns can exhibit less well-conditioned return characteristics, as the 2-factor model can only capture 66.5% of return variation in terms of adjusted R^2. The precise process through which diversification simplifies the return generation process is still unknown with hedge fund returns.[9] Research to-date points to nonlinear factors at work driving the performance of hedge fund strategies.

Against this background, we analyzed the distributional properties of the AA return series extracted from EHFPs using the 2-factor model. Conditional on the outcomes of eight conventional asset classes, the AA return series display no abnormal behavior. These results are interpreted to support the state-independent nature as well as portability of AAs. What remains to be done is to see how these AA return series can be incorporated into conventional asset allocation models. Since, conventional asset allocation models tend to rely on a mean–variance framework, we proceeded to analyze the unconditional return distribution of the AA return series.

Modeling the AA return series as a GARCH(1,1)–AR(1) process we are able to show that these return series are normally distributed with time-varying variance. This allows us to create alpha-enhanced equity alternatives (AA portfolios; one for each of the three databases) to the S&P 500 index's returns using Sharpe ratios as performance criteria. Over the sample period 1996–2002, these AA portfolios are highly correlated to the S&P 500 index but outperformed the S&P 500 index each year for all seven years. The AA portfolios have higher mean returns and better Sharpe ratios compared to the S&P 500 index. To what extent similar alpha-enhanced portfolios can be constructed relative to other asset-class indexes remains a subject for future research; thus far, the framework and empirical results established here provide a promising start.

Notes

1 Also reported in later studies by other researchers such as Amin and Kat (2003).

2 Free of skewness and serial correlation.

3 This is an equally weighted index of TASS hedge funds that are designated as Long/Short equity hedge funds includes both live and dead funds within the TASS database. The choice of such a construction is to maintain comparability with the other two indexes both in terms of the number of funds in the index as well as the index construction method. It is these

considerations that precluded the use of the CSFB/Tremont Long/Short equity index, which is both smaller in scope and is value-weighted by construction.

4 It shall become obvious why this choice is more than just a preference for simplicity. In extracting alphas from hedge fund returns, certain amount of hedging is required. The more factors a model admits, the more cumbersome will be the attendant hedging process, and at some point, the simulated alphas can become unrealistic propositions.

5 The choice of the Wilshire indexes rather than the academic series from Fama and French is an attempt to move closer to a more readily commercially available data source.

6 The theory and empirical construct for such a model is well beyond the scope of this paper, nonetheless, it remains an important area for future research.

7 An approach that combines the hedged EHFPs, the S&P 500 index futures and the Russell 2000 index to generate alpha-enhanced equity alternatives.

8 The Russell 2000 index is by far a more practicable candidate for short sale transactions than the Wilshire indexes as both futures contracts and ETFs exist mimicking the Russell 2000 index. We note also that the returns of the Russell 2000 index are highly correlated to the Wilshire Small Cap 1750 index that we used in constructing the AA returns series.

9 Or to what extent the index construction method of the CSFB/Tremont index impeded the process of diversification is also unclear.

References

Agarwal, V. and Naik, N. (2004). "Risks and Portfolio Decisions Involving Hedge Funds." *Review of Financial Studies* **17**(1) (Spring), 63–98.

Amin, G. and Kat, H. (2003). "Hedge Fund Performance 1990–2000: Do the Money Machines Really Add Value?" *Journal of Financial and Quantitative Analysis.*

Bollerslev, T. (1986). "Generalized Autoregressive Conditional Heteroskedasticity." *Journal of Econometrics* **31**, 307–327.

Carhart, M. (1997). "On Persistence in Mutual Fund Performance." *Journal of Finance* **52**, 57–82.

Engle, R. (1982). "Autoregressive Conditional Heteroscedasticity with Estimates of Variance of UK Inflations." *Econometrica* **50**, 987–1007.

Fama, E. and French, K. (1992). "The Cross-Section of Expected Stock Returns." *Journal of Finance* **47**, 427–465.

Fung, W. K. H. and Hsieh, D. A. (1997). "Empirical Characteristics of Dynamic Trading Strategies: The Case of Hedge Funds." *Review of Financial Studies* **10**, 275–302.

Fung, W. K. H. and Hsieh, D. A. (2001). "The Risk in Hedge Fund Strategies: Theory and Evidence from Trend Followers." *Review of Financial Studies* **14**, 313–341.

Fung, W. K. H. and Hsieh, D. A. (2002a). "The Risk in Fixed-Income Hedge Fund Styles." *Journal of Fixed Income* **58**, 16–27.

Fung, W. K. H. and Hsieh, D. A. (2002b). "Asset-Based Hedge-Fund Styles Factors for Hedge Funds." *Financial Analysts Journal* **12**, 6–27.

Fung, W. K. H. and Hsieh, D. A. (2003a). "The Risk in Hedge Fund Strategies: Alternative Alphas and Alternative Betas." In: Lars Jeager (ed.), *The New Generation of Risk Management for Hedge Funds and Private Equity Investments*. Euromoney Books, 2003, Chapter 5.

Fung, W. K. H. and Hsieh, D. A. (2003b). "Estimating the Risk Premium in Equity Long/Short Hedge Funds." Working Paper, London Business School and Duke University.

Fung, W. K. H. and Hsieh, D. A. (2004). "Constructing Hedge Fund Benchmarks: A Risk Based Approach." *Financial Analyst Journal,* forthcoming.

Henriksson, R. D. and Merton, R. C. (1981). "On Market Timing and Investment Performance II: Statistical Procedures for Evaluating Forecasting Skills." *Journal of Business* **41**, 867–887.

Hsieh, D. A. (1988). "Statistical Properties of Daily Foreign Exchange Rates: 1974–1983." *Journal of International Economics* **24**, 129–145.

Jagedeesh, N. and Titman, S. (1993). "Returns to Buying Winners and Selling Losers: Implications for Stock Market Efficiency." *Journal of Finance* **48**, 93–130.

Merton, R. C. (1981). "On Market Timing and Investment Performance I. An Equilibrium Theory of Value for Market Forecasts." *Journal of Business* **54**, 363–407.

Sharpe, W. (1992). "Asset Allocation: Management Style and Performance Measurement." *Journal of Portfolio Management* **18**, 7–19.

Journal of Investment Management
Vol. 2, No. 4 (2004), pp. 106–129

AIRAP—ALTERNATIVE RAPMs FOR ALTERNATIVE INVESTMENTS

*Milind Sharma**

This paper highlights the inadequacies of traditional RAPMs (risk-adjusted performance measures) and proposes AIRAP (alternative investments risk-adjusted performance), based on Expected Utility theory, as a RAPM better suited to alternative investments. AIRAP is the implied certain return that a risk-averse investor would trade off for holding risky assets. AIRAP captures the full distribution, penalizes for volatility and leverage, is customizable by risk aversion, works with negative mean returns, eschews moment estimation or convergence requirements, and can dovetail with stressed scenarios or regime-switching models. A modified Sharpe ratio is proposed. The results are contrasted with Sharpe, Treynor, and Jensen rankings to show significant divergence. Evidence of non-normality and the tradeoff between mean–variance merits vis-à-vis *higher moment risks is noted. The dependence of optimal leverage on risk aversion and track record is noted. The results have implications for manager selection and fund of hedge funds portfolio construction.*

1 Introduction

The heterogeneity of hedge fund strategies, their idiosyncratic bets, the complexity inherent in their dynamic trading and the extra degrees of freedom they possess (given the absence of leverage or shorting constraints), makes the task of judging managerial skill and performance particularly daunting. An increasingly popular alternative is to invest indirectly through fund of hedge funds (FoHFs hereafter). Liew (2002) suggests that, FoHFs with "good discernment," can outperform their passively indexed counterparts. However, "good discernment" presupposes the existence of "good RAPMs."[1]

A flurry of recent papers such as Goetzmann *et al.* (2002), Spurgin (2001), and Bernardo and Ledoit (2000) have highlighted the inadequacies of traditional RAPMs such as the Sharpe ratio (hereafter SR). Alternatives and modifications to SR have been proposed, such as, Madan and McPhail (2000), Shadwick and Keating (2002a),[2] or Kazemi *et al.* (2003) while Leland (1999) proposes modifying the CAPM beta. In that vein, this paper introduces the proposed RAPM, AIRAP (alternative investments risk-adjusted performance), as the certainty equivalent. We follow the CRRA (constant

Deutsche Bank, 60 Wall St, 3rd Floor, Integrated Credit Trading, NY, NY 10005.
E-mail: milind_sharma@db.com

*Director and Senior Proprietary Trader at Deutsche Bank. The author expresses his gratitude to Peter Carr, Kent Osband and an anonymous referee for valuable correspondence. Opinions, errors and omissions are solely those of the author and do not represent those of any employers, past or present.

relative risk aversion) framework of Osband (2002) but take the distribution-free route along the lines of CARA (constant absolute risk aversion) solutions by Davis (2001). This is the first paper to investigate the utility of certainty equivalence as a RAPM for hedge funds and to contrast the significantly different rankings obtained *vis-à-vis* SR and Jensen's alpha (JA). Sharma (2003) applies the AIRAP framework to re-visit empirical tests as well as to contrast hedge fund (HF) strategies at the index and fund levels.

This paper is organized as follows: Section 2 surveys traditional RAPMs. Section 3 reviews the expected utility framework and justifies our choice of the CRRA. A closed form, distribution-free solution for AIRAP is derived under CRRA. Secion 4 analyzes the dataset used and presents rank correlations and reversals of competing RAPMs both at the strategy and hedge fund levels. Evidence of non-normality and the trade-off between mean-variance profile *vis-à-vis* higher moments is also examined. Section 5 investigates the impact of leverage on RAPMs while Section 6 proposes a composite ranking system for HFs based on AIRAP. Section 7 discusses caveats and concludes with thoughts on further research.

2 Survey of RAPMs

While there exists no consensus on how to measure risk or risk-adjusted performance for HFs, the menagerie of RAPMs in circulation that could be applied includes SR, JA, Modigliani-Squared (M^2), M^2-alpha, M^3, SHARAD,[3] Treynor, information ratio (IR), Sortino, Calmar, Sterling, Gain/Loss, etc. Related performance statistics include Max Drawdown, number of months to recovery, peak–trough, VAMI (value added monthly index), up/down market returns, upside/downside capture, etc. Finally, the associated risk metrics are beta, active risk, total risk, variance, semi-variance (upside/downside and capture), MAD (mean absolute deviation), VaR, VarDelta, Marginal VaR, CVaR (Conditional VaR or expected shortfall), CDaR (conditional drawdown at risk), etc.

Absolute RAPMs consider portfolio returns in excess of the risk-free rate (viz., SR and Treynor) or zero (Calmar and Sterling). Relative RAPMs on the other hand, consider portfolio returns in excess of benchmark (IR), Beta-adjusted benchmark (JA) or some threshold of minimum acceptable return[4] (Sortino). SR and IR use the standard deviation of differential returns in the denominator to risk adjust, Treynor uses Beta, Sortino uses downside deviation (DD), Calmar uses max drawdown over 3 years and Sterling uses the average of max drawdowns over each of the past 3 years. Benchmark risk-equivalent RAPMs such as M^2, M^2-alpha, M^3, and SHARAD lever/de-lever portfolio performance in order to risk-equalize with the benchmark volatility, while borrowing at the risk-free rate. Since M^2 is an affine transform of SR it always produces the same rankings. Further, M^2-alpha is a close cousin of Treynor and produces identical rankings. Hence, we do not dwell on either M^2 measures separately. M^3 was proposed by Muralidhar (2000) to augment M^2 by explicitly adjusting for benchmark correlation while SHARAD goes yet further by adjusting for disparate performance history (length of manager track records). Both M^3 and SHARAD differ from SR and are particularly germane to institutional benchmark relative performance measurement and risk-budgeting considerations. Despite the progressive institutionalization of hedge funds, correlation adjustment and tracking-error budgeting do not presently appear central to a class of investments still largely perceived as an absolute return class.

The applicability and appropriateness of these RAPMs to HFs is a function of the efficacy of their associated risk measure in capturing HF risk. To the extent that *none* of standard deviation, Beta, downside deviation or Max Drawdown is a sufficient risk statistic *under non-normality, none* of the corresponding RAPMs should suffice for hedge funds. That said, each of these has its attractions worth highlighting. Calmar and Sterling are well suited for presenting the "worst case" picture since they take into account Maximum Drawdown, that is, the worst losing streak. Sortino, on the other hand, only adjusts by DD. The benefit is that DD does not penalize for upside variability but only for under-performance *vis-à-vis* some threshold of MAR. For predictably asymmetric returns, Sortino can be a better *ex post* RAPM than SR since DD will in that case pick up on the realized skew and produce better portfolio rankings. Indeed, generalizing to the notion of lower partial moments (LPMs hereafter) can yield a host of new risk and corresponding risk-adjusted measures. The zeroeth LPM is just Shortfall risk or the frequency of under-performance *vis-à-vis* some MAR. The first LPM is just the mean under-performance, while the second LPM turns out to be Downside Variance.

2.1 The risk of RAPM shortfall

Recent literature highlights the vulnerability of traditional RAPMs given the vagaries of leverage, non-normality, and derivatives usage—issues which typify hedge fund returns. In the domain of risk measures, even the most popular candidates such as VaR fall short in that they cannot handle liquidity, credit or tail risk that are often characteristic of hedge funds. Further, VaR is not a "coherent risk measure"[5] under non-normality, a deficiency that has led to the growing preference for Expected Shortfall (as a quantifier of tail risk), coupled with coherent scenario testing.

Amongst absolute RAPMs, we first consider Treynor. Treynor can be *magnified without bound*, via beta in the denominator. As a market neutral HF approaches beta-neutrality (as it should in order to uphold truth in advertising), Treynor approaches infinity. This is an issue for non-directional strategies in general, hence, Treynor is unsatisfactory for ranking/comparison of HFs.

Sortino performs a valuable function in adjusting by DD but can look deceptively high/favorable (upon trend reversal) if the *ex post* estimation is based on a period of upwardly trending returns, since downside deviation underestimates the two-sided risk if the estimation period is not long enough to include loss periods. In this case, SR would perform better since standard deviation is not as vulnerable to a skewed sample when the underlying population is symmetrical.

Jensen's alpha is *not leverage invariant*. Instead, it scales in direct proportion with leverage thereby providing the perverse incentive to increase leverage without bound. In fact HF strategies, particularly relative-value strategies such as fixed-income or statistical arbitrage, are known to employ significant leverage in order to scale up their alpha. Assuming only IID returns for the market proxy, Leland (1999) shows that alpha can be systematically misguided because the CAPM beta ignores higher moments. Even if the single index CAPM world sufficed, Roll (1978) shows the arbitrariness of alpha rankings. If the benchmark used is mean–variance efficient, the securities market line is unable to discern out-performance. If not, then there exists some other non-efficient index which can reverse the ranking obtained.

Perhaps the most commonly used and widely respected RAPM in industry circulation is the SR. Sharpe has held the industry and academics in good stead since it was coined by its namesake and Nobel laureate in 1966. It has many desirable properties such as proportionality to the t-statistic (for returns in excess of zero) and the centrality of SR squared to optimal portfolio allocation.

However, SR is leverage invariant and it is not as intuitive as M^2, M^3, and SHARAD which measure performance in basis point terms. It does not incorporate correlations nor can it handle iceberg risks lurking in the higher moments. Further, even the SR ratio can be "gamed" by manipulating the returns profile. Spurgin (2001) has a recipe, which entails truncating the right tail. Similarly, Goetzmann *et al.* (2002) derive the optimal static strategy via short OTM puts and calls which maximizes the SR ratio. This corresponds to a distribution with a truncated right tail (i.e., smooth monthly returns) but fat left tail (the periodic crashes). They remark, "the 'peso problem' may be ubiquitous in any investment management industry that rewards high Sharpe ratio managers." Bernardo and Ledoit (2000) specifically demonstrate the limitations of the SR under non-normality. They show that outside the realm of normality, attractive investments (such as arbitrage opportunities) can have arbitrarily low SR ratios while poor investments may have high SR ratios. Although, given normality, SR suffices in completely characterizing investment desirability, "outside normality, it is impossible to make general statements that are preference-free other than no-arbitrage."[6]

A number of cases manager hubris based on short but impressive track records (possibly attributable to short option profiles) have been documented. Jorion (2000)[7] points this out for LTCM's risk signature. Similarly, the well respected, Neiderhoffer, became victim to short OTM puts as a result of a sudden 7% market drop on October 27, 1997. Lo (2001) observes, "Shorting deep out-of-the-money puts is a well known artifice employed by unscrupulous hedge-fund managers to build an impressive track record quickly." More recently, Naik and Agarwal (2003)[8] find the majority of HF strategies being characterized by short option profiles. They extend the previous findings of Mitchell and Pulvino (2001)[9] for Merger Arbitrage. While there are isolated cases that put manager integrity into question, the broader issue remains one of investor suitability and whether that necessitates regulating access to hedge fund investments.

To assess suitability we must ask—Are hedge fund investors unwittingly underwriting disaster insurance unbeknownst to them? The operative principle in insurance is that risk transfer should result in the concentration of risk with the less risk-averse party. Arguably, the existing requirement of investor accreditation (which limits the audience to the less risk-averse) should assuage suitability concerns, although the emergence of vehicles that lower those requirements may not. The issue is germane to HFs not only because of their extensive use of derivatives and the option like characteristics of their incentive fees/survival likelihoods, but also because they are often marketed on the basis of RAPMs such as the SR. To the extent that financial intermediaries (such as registered brokers) are sufficiently trained to assess suitability and investors sufficiently aware of risks (when viewed as "stand-alone" investments) then the focus can shift to the potential portfolio level benefits of adding HFs based on marginal risk-return characteristics.

Bookstaber and Clarke (1981) show that options can skew portfolio returns distribution, rendering the mean–variance framework inadequate. Fama (1976) provides evidence of leptokurtosis for individual stocks.[10] While market participants may be anecdotally or peripherally aware that the crash of 1987 was an ab-"normal" 27 sigma event, they may perceive the relevance of higher moments as merely an esoteric concern. Table 1 shows negative skew and excess positive kurtosis for the S&P 500 over each of the trailing 10, 20, 30 and 40-year periods[11] (Feb. 1962–Jan. 2002). Goodness of fit tests for the past 40 years confirms our suspicion. Table 10 shows rejections of normality by Bera-Jarque at the 99% level and by Lilliefors at the 95% level. Figure 1

Table 1 Negative skew and excess positive kurtosis for the S&P 500.

S&P 500 mo returns	Excess Kurt	Skew	Vol.	Av. monthly return
40 years [2/62–1/02]	1.91	(0.32)	4.33	0.97
30 years [2/72–1/02]	2.20	(0.36)	4.49	1.06
20 years [2/82–1/02]	2.96	(0.67)	4.43	1.29
10 years [2/92–1/02]	1.10	(0.66)	4.04	1.10

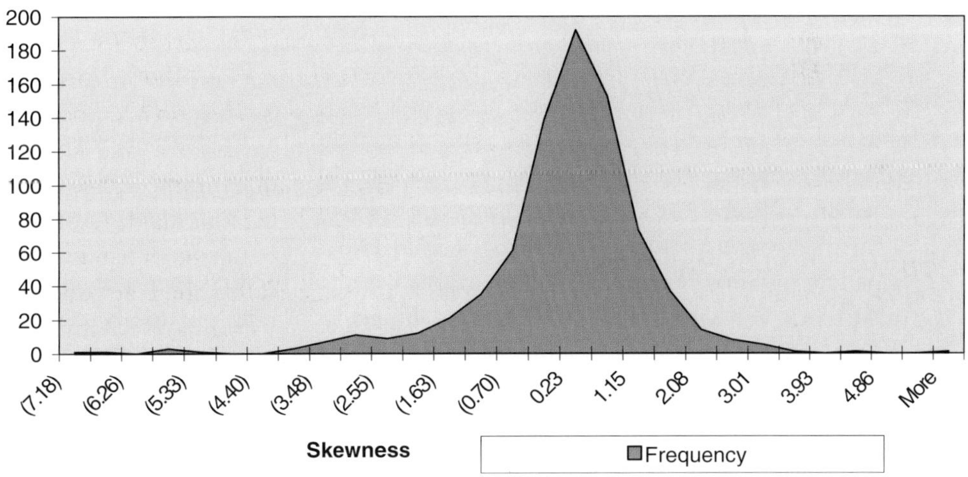

Figure 1 Distribution of skewness.

The distribution of HF skewness shows mild negative skew of −1.24 apparently due to the counterbalancing effect of including CTAs. Still the left tail is longer given min of −7.18 versus max of 5.78 while mean, median, and mode are all negative.

Source for 787 HFs used is Hedge Fund Research, Inc., © HFR, Inc., www.hedgefundresearch.com

Table 2 Sharpe ratios (negative mean returns).

EACM 5 years (1997–2001)	Bond * Hedge	FI hedge fund
Ann vol	6.02%	12.04%
Ann % Excess TR	−4.50%	−4.50%
Ann Sharpe	(0.75)	(0.37)

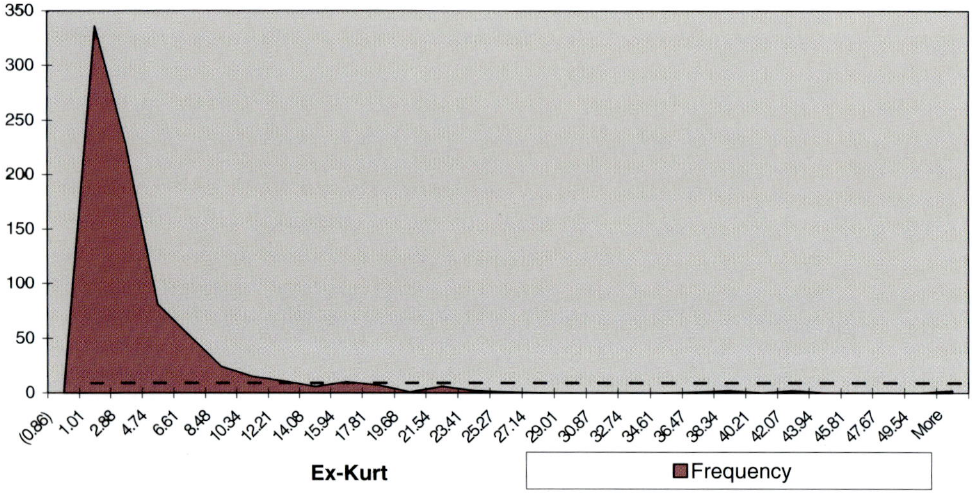

Figure 2 Distribution of excess kurtosis.

The distribution of excess kurtosis for hedge funds during the 5 years (Jan. 97–Dec. 01) is clearly right skewed (+4.54) with a long right tail (max of 51.4 but min of −0.086). Average Ex-Kurt of 3.0 is significantly non-Gaussian with 87.4% of all funds in positive territory.

Source for 787 HFs used is Hedge Fund Research, Inc., © HFR, Inc., www.hedgefundresearch.com

and Table 3 show for the HF case that the mean, median, and mode of skewness are all negative as is the skew of skewness. Worse yet, Figure 2 and Table 3 show that the mean, median and mode of kurtosis (in excess of normality) are significantly positive with positive skew and kurtosis of kurtosis.

Sharpe (1994) himself remarks, "comparisons based on the first two moments of a distribution do *not take into account possible differences* among portfolios in other moments or in distributions of outcomes across states of nature that may be associated with *different levels of investor utility*."[12] Clearly then, what is needed is a measure that incorporates investor preferences via risk aversion and that which adjusts for iceberg risks lurking in the higher moments.

Finally, SR is plagued by another deficiency, which limits its utility during bear markets. Table 2 uses the EACM Bond Hedge index (1997–2001) to show that a fund with the same excess return (−4.5%) but twice the risk (12%) has an SR twice as good instead of its being twice as worse. This happens because −0.37 is larger than −0.74 even though smaller in absolute magnitude.

Table 3 RAPM stats—HFR universe (787 funds, 1997–2001).

Spearman correlations	ExTR	Vol	Skew mo	Excess Kurt mo	Treynor	Jensen	Beta	Sharpe	AIRAP	MSR
ExTR	1.00	0.06	0.26	0.02	0.41	0.90	0.08	0.73	0.76	0.49
Vol	0.06	1.00	0.22	(0.13)	(0.32)	0.11	0.55	(0.50)	(0.47)	(0.73)
Skew mo	0.26	0.22	1.00	(0.18)	0.11	0.32	(0.03)	0.07	0.14	(0.02)
Excess Kurt mo	0.02	(0.13)	(0.18)	1.00	0.10	0.04	(0.05)	0.12	0.08	0.14
Treynor	0.41	(0.32)	0.11	0.10	1.00	0.34	0.04	0.60	0.50	0.57
Jensen	0.90	0.11	0.32	0.04	0.34	1.00	(0.16)	0.66	0.66	0.43
Beta	0.08	0.55	(0.03)	(0.05)	0.04	(0.16)	1.00	(0.23)	(0.24)	(0.37)
Sharpe	0.73	(0.50)	0.07	0.12	0.60	0.66	(0.23)	1.00	0.86	0.92
AIRAP	**0.76**	**(0.47)**	**0.14**	0.08	**0.50**	**0.66**	**(0.24)**	**0.86**	1.00	**0.80**
MSR	0.49	(0.73)	(0.02)	0.14	0.57	0.43	(0.37)	0.92	0.80	1.00
Significance										
ExTR	—	0.11	0.00	0.57	—	—	0.03	—	—	—
Vol	0.11	—	0.00	0.00	—	0.00	—	—	—	—
Skew mo	0.00	0.00	—	0.00	0.00	—	0.44	0.05	0.00	0.53
Excess Kurt mo	0.57	0.00	0.00	—	0.01	0.29	0.17	0.00	0.02	0.00
Treynor	—	—	0.00	0.01	—	—	0.23	—	—	—
Jensen	—	0.00	—	0.29	—	—	0.00	—	—	—
Beta	0.03	—	0.44	0.17	0.23	0.00	—	0.00	0.00	—
Sharpe	—	—	0.05	0.00	—	—	0.00	—	—	—
AIRAP	—	—	0.00	0.02	—	—	0.00	—	—	—
MSR	—	—	0.53	0.00	—	—	—	—	—	—

Table 3 (*Continued*)

Stats/RAPMs	Mean ExTR	Median ExTR	Vol	Skew	Excess Kurt	SR	Treynor	Jensen	Beta (S&P)	ExTR	AIRAP	Risk Prem	MSR
Pearson Correl (AIRAP)	**0.22**	0.12	**(0.74)**	**0.06**	**(0.09)**	**0.46**	**(0.01)**	**0.37**	**(0.38)**	0.62	1.00	(0.82)	0.06
Mean	0.69%	0.58%	16.55%	(0.14)	3.02	0.75	0.05	6.22%	0.29	6.53%	−0.02%	6.55%	13.65
Standard Error	0.02%	0.03%	0.46%	0.04	0.19	0.03	0.16	0.28%	0.02	0.28%	0.49%	0.39%	3.05
Median	0.59%	0.53%	13.83%	(0.01)	1.28	0.57	0.19	5.64%	0.20	6.01%	2.99%	2.97%	2.13
Mode	0.78%	0.75%	46.06%	(0.37)	4.00	0.09	(0.03)	14.36%	(1.45)	−7.19%	−46.41%	39.22%	(0.18)
Standard Deviation	0.66%	0.73%	12.87%	1.23	5.39	0.82	4.43	7.93%	0.46	7.92%	13.78%	10.82%	85.69
Sample Variance	0.00%	0.01%	1.66%	1.50	29.08	0.67	19.60	0.63%	0.21	0.63%	1.90%	1.17%	7,341.92
Kurtosis	4.87	3.77	4.98	5.89	28.46	14.57	103.59	5.71	2.26	2.19	10.70	22.44	235.44
Skewness	1.20	(0.03)	1.78	(1.24)	4.54	2.68	(6.82)	0.84	0.32	0.23	(2.73)	4.12	14.70
Minimum	−1.54%	(0.03)	0.00	(7.18)	(0.86)	(1.72)	(60.66)	−24.36%	(1.75)	(0.25)	(0.93)	0.00	(74.00)
Maximum	5.25%	0.04	1.00	5.78	51.41	7.54	38.93	66.53%	2.12	0.45	0.26	0.89	1,600.14

AIRAP is positively correlated with ExTR, skew, Treynor, Jensen, SR and negatively with Vol and Beta as per intuition.
All AIRAP correlations are highly significant.

Table 4 EACM sub-indexes.

EACM sub-indexes	Relative value				Event driven			Equity hedge fds			Global AA		Shorts	Index
Summary Stats—5 years [1997–2001]	Long/short equity	Convertible hedge	Bond hedge	Multi-strategy	Risk arbitrage	Bankruptcy/ distressed	Multi-strategy	Domestic long bias	Domestic opportunistic	Global/ international	Discretionary	Systematic	Short sellers	SP500
Mean ExTR mo	0.00%	0.32%	−0.37%	0.73%	0.35%	0.29%	0.73%	0.66%	1.06%	0.58%	0.19%	0.19%	0.25%	0.59%
Median ExTR mo	0.09%	0.50%	0.15%	0.97%	0.49%	0.51%	0.86%	0.35%	0.85%	0.66%	0.03%	−0.16%	−0.46%	0.71%
Vol ExTR Ann	2.98%	5.99%	6.02%	8.44%	4.87%	6.22%	6.18%	21.93%	12.91%	13.05%	10.19%	12.06%	22.78%	17.91%
Skew ExTR mo	(0.56)	**(2.11)**	**(2.12)**	**(4.61)**	**(2.49)**	**(1.87)**	**(2.31)**	(0.06)	1.03	0.22	**(2.60)**	0.62	0.72	(0.54)
Excess Kurt ExTR mo	1.65	**6.28**	**5.76**	**24.70**	**9.06**	**8.32**	**11.49**	0.23	2.14	0.89	**14.90**	1.15	0.47	(0.16)
Ann Sharpe	0.02	0.65	(0.73)	1.04	0.86	0.56	1.41	0.36	0.99	0.54	0.22	0.19	0.13	0.39
Ann Treynor	(0.10)	0.60	(1.24)	2.20	0.31	0.22	0.57	0.10	0.62	0.16	0.07	(0.44)	(0.03)	0.07
Ann Jensen's Alpha	0.09%	3.40%	−4.67%	8.51%	3.24%	2.34%	7.64%	2.04%	11.28%	3.92%	−0.01%	2.65%	10.55%	0.00%
CAPM Beta	(0.01)	0.06	0.04	0.04	0.13	0.16	0.15	0.83	0.20	0.44	0.32	(0.05)	(1.08)	1.00
Corr to S&P500	(0.03)	0.19	0.10	0.08	0.49	0.46	0.45	0.68	0.28	0.60	0.56	(0.08)	(0.84)	1.00
Lilliefors GoF test (2-sided, 95%)	0	1	1	1	1	1	1	0	0	0	1	0	0	
Bera-Jarque GoF test (2-sided, 95%)	1	1	1	1	1	1	1	0	1	0	1	1	0	
P value Lilliefors (2-sided, 95%)	0.10	NaN	NaN	NaN	NaN	0.04	NaN	NaN	NaN	NaN	NaN	0.11	NaN	
P value Bera-Jarque (2-sided, 95%)	0.05	—	—	—	—	—	—	0.97	0.00	0.37	—	0.04	0.07	
Ann ExTR	0.01%	3.75%	−4.50%	8.75%	4.14%	3.32%	8.89%	5.66%	12.60%	6.37%	1.72%	1.59%	0.46%	5.61%
Ann AIRAP [CRR = 4]	−0.13%	3.16%	−5.06%	7.32%	3.75%	2.69%	8.23%	−1.71%	10.08%	3.77%	−0.14%	−0.49%	−6.42%	**0.45%**
Ann Risk Prem [CRR = 4]	0.13%	0.59%	0.55%	**1.43%**	0.39%	0.63%	0.66%	**7.37%**	2.52%	2.59%	1.86%	2.08%	**6.88%**	5.16%
Modified SR	0.05	6.38	(8.12)	6.12	10.66	5.27	13.46	0.77	5.01	2.45	0.93	0.76	0.07	1.09

AIRAP vs SR [#Reversals, Total#, %Rev]	11	13	85%
MSR vs SR [#Reversals, Total#, %Rev]	7	13	54%

For GoF tests 1 corresponds to REJECTION of Normality.
Bera-Jarque: The Null assumes normality with unspecified mean and variance in addition to standardized skew and kurtosis being asymptotically normal and independent.
Lilliefors: Modifies Kolmogorov–Smirnov. Test statistic used is max|Empirical CDF − Gaussian CDF|. *P*-values outside [0.01, 0.20] are reported as NaN.
All stats are annualized and based on Excess TR.

Table 4 (*Continued*)

	ExTR	Vol	Skew mo	Excess Kurt mo	Treynor	Jensen	Beta	Sharpe	AIRAP	MSR
Spearman correlations										
ExTR	1.00	0.23	(0.05)	0.24	0.85	0.65	0.60	0.90	0.84	0.74
Vol	0.23	1.00	0.57	(0.53)	(0.06)	0.37	0.27	(0.07)	(0.20)	(0.25)
Skew mo	(0.05)	0.57	1.00	(0.85)	(0.25)	0.31	(0.07)	(0.30)	(0.19)	(0.43)
Excess Kurt mo	0.24	(0.53)	(0.85)	1.00	0.49	(0.01)	0.05	0.54	0.48	0.60
Treynor	0.85	(0.06)	(0.25)	0.49	1.00	0.66	0.37	0.94	0.84	0.86
Jensen	0.65	0.37	0.31	(0.01)	0.66	1.00	(0.06)	0.63	0.57	0.47
Beta	0.60	0.27	(0.07)	0.05	0.37	(0.06)	1.00	0.39	0.37	0.35
Sharpe	0.90	(0.07)	(0.30)	0.54	0.94	0.63	0.39	1.00	0.87	0.93
AIRAP	0.84	(0.20)	(0.19)	0.48	0.84	0.57	0.37	0.87	1.00	0.77
MSR	0.74	(0.25)	(0.43)	0.60	0.86	0.47	0.35	0.93	0.77	1.00
Two-sided correlation p-values										
ExTR	—	0.45	0.87	0.43	0.00	0.02	0.03	0.00	0.00	0.00
Vol	0.45	—	0.04	0.06	0.84	0.21	0.36	0.82	0.51	0.42
Skew mo	0.87	0.04	—	0.00	0.40	0.31	0.82	0.32	0.54	0.14
Excess Kurt mo	0.43	0.06	0.00	—	0.09	0.97	0.87	0.06	0.09	0.03
Treynor	0.00	0.84	0.40	0.09	—	0.01	0.22	0.00	0.00	0.00
Jensen	0.02	0.21	0.31	0.97	0.01	—	0.84	0.02	0.04	0.10
Beta	0.03	0.36	0.82	0.87	0.22	0.84	—	0.19	0.22	0.24
Sharpe	0.00	0.82	0.32	0.06	0.00	0.02	0.19	—	0.00	0.00
AIRAP	0.00	0.51	0.54	0.09	0.00	0.04	0.22	0.00	—	0.00
MSR	0.00	0.42	0.14	0.03	0.00	0.10	0.24	0.00	0.00	—
Ascending rands by RAPM										
L/S Eq	2	1	8	5	3	3	3	2	6	2
Converts	7	3	6	8	11	8	6	9	8	11
Bond Hedge	1	4	5	7	1	1	4	1	2	1
RV Multi-Strategy	11	7	1	13	13	11	5	12	11	10
Risk Arb	8	2	3	10	9	7	7	10	9	12
Bankruptcy/ D	6	6	7	9	8	5	9	8	7	9
ED Multi-Strategy	12	5	4	11	10	10	8	13	12	13
Dom Long	9	12	9	1	6	4	13	6	3	5
Dom Opp	13	10	13	6	12	13	10	11	13	8
Global International	10	11	10	3	7	9	12	7	10	7
GAA Discretionary	5	8	2	12	5	2	11	5	5	6
GAA Systematic	4	9	11	4	2	6	2	4	4	4
Shorts Sellers	3	13	12	2	4	12	1	3	1	3

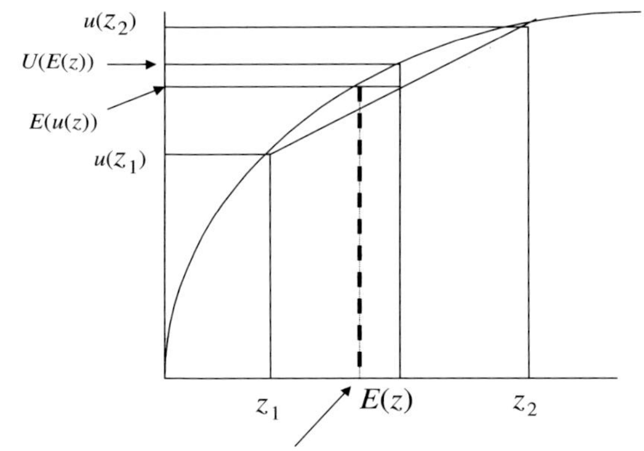

Figure 3 AIRAP (certainty equivalent for CRRA = 4) under risk aversion.

3 Expected Utility Theory and AIRAP

Expected Utility theory is central to the foundations of modern economics and dates back to the axiomatization of Von Neumann and Morgenstern (1944). Under Transitivity, Completeness, Independence, and the Archimedean axioms, investor preferences have an Expected Utility representation (which is unique up to affine transforms). The Expected Utility property allows for the expression of the Von Neumann–Morgenstern utility U of a lottery (with payoffs z_1 and z_2 and probabilities p and $(1-p)$) as $[p \cdot u(z_1) + (1-p) \cdot u(z_2)]$. Here u: $x \rightarrow R$ is the real-valued Bernoulli utility, which is a function of payoffs (as opposed to lotteries for U). Allowing a lottery to be represented by the real-valued random variable w enables us to use the fact of U representing preferences over lotteries to be equivalently stated in terms of preferences over cumulative distributions F:

For lotteries w and w':

$$F_w \geq F_{w'} \equiv U(F_w) \geq U(F_{w'}), \quad \text{where } U(F_w) = \int_R u(x)\, \mathrm{d}F_w(x)$$

For RAPMs to be useful they should incorporate risk aversion since the investor expects to be paid a risk-premium for owning risky assets. In this case, risk aversion is embodied by the concavity of u (risk-proclivity by convexity and risk-neutrality by linearity).

Given the concavity of u and Jensen's inequality we obtain[13]:

$$u(E(z)) = u(pz_1 + (1-p)z_2) > pu(z_1)(1-p)u(z_2) = E(u)$$

Risk aversion is captured by $u(E) > E(u)$, since the utility of the mean but certain payoff $E(z)$ exceeds the utility of the uncertain lottery (with payoffs z_1 and z_2). The *certainty equivalent* lottery can thus be defined as that lottery which pays CE(z) and has the same utility as the uncertain lottery (Figure 3), that is, $u(\text{CE}(z)) = E(u)$. Risk-aversion qua concavity entails that the payoff $\text{CE}(z) < E(z)$. Hence, the Risk-Premium is defined as,

$$\text{RP}(z) = [E(z) - \text{CE}(z)], \quad \text{where } \text{RP}(z) \geq 0$$

Table 5 Percentage rejections of normality versus % rank reversals.

HFR Intra-Style (97–01)	# Rejections	% Rejections	# Funds Tot	# Reversals	% Reversals
Shorts	4	36	11	9	82
Eq non-hedged	22	37	60	53	88
Converts arb	20	51	39	34	87
Merger arb	19	66	29	29	100
Event driven	35	80	44	41	93
Full HFR universe	418	53	788	787	100

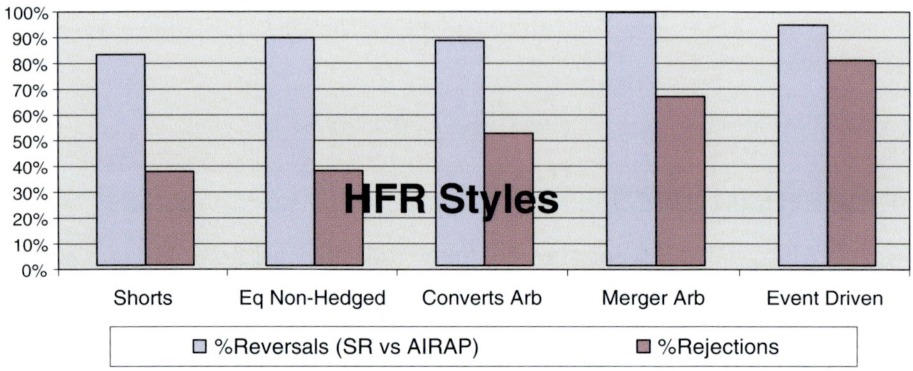

Rejections of Normality are based on Bera–Jarque GoF test (2-sided, 95%).
Reversals are rank reversals between Sharpe and AIRAP.

In the RAPM world, CE(z) is the *implied equivalent return* that the risk-averse investor desires with *certainty* in exchange for the *uncertain return* from holding *risky assets*. Consequently, RP(z) ≥ 0 (under risk-aversion) is the price paid for trading off the risky asset with CE(z). Hence, certainty equivalence provides an intuitive risk adjustment for our definition of AIRAP. By stripping out varying risk premia earned, it facilitates a fair comparison of HF performance. Further, strict monotonicity and continuity[14] of the chosen utility function ensure invertibility, resulting in CE(z) rankings that are identical to maximizing $E(u)$, since by definition, CE(z) $= u^{-1}(E(u))$.

We now proceed with choosing the appropriate form of utility. The standard mean–variance framework is justified either on the basis of tractability of quadratic utility (for arbitrary distributions) or multivariate normality (for arbitrary preferences). However, neither assumption is satisfactory. Quadratic utility displays satiation[15] and IARA (Increasing Absolute Risk Aversion), since it views risky assets as inferior goods. Nor does it not show skewness preference while normality is a poor assumption for HFs (Table 5). In fact, HF data does not even usually satisfy the premises of the central limit theorem (see Getmansky *et al.*, 2003).

A CRRA formulation has the benefit of being impartial to wealth level (which is to be expected of asset managers from a fiduciary perspective), excluding negative wealth (consistent with hedge fund losses under limited liability being bounded below by the principal invested) and *scale invariance*. For instance, a high net worth family in the top 39.1% tax bracket[16] will be relatively indifferent to a \$10,000 loss (<3.4% of income) *vis-à-vis* a family at the poverty line[17] for whom the same loss amounts to 55.3% of income. See Osband (2002) for an exposition of utility functions and the relative merits of CARA versus CRRA.

The best-known measure of risk aversion is Arrow–Pratt, which quantifies the normalized magnitude of concavity of u times wealth via its second derivative. Assuming concavity, monotonically increasing and twice differentiable utility, CRRA is tantamount to requiring that the Arrow–Pratt RRA coefficient is a constant c:

$$-\frac{u''(w)}{u'(w)}w = c$$

We assume the NAV (net asset value) process represents HF total returns (since dividends are rare),

$$\%\mathrm{TR}_t = \frac{(\mathrm{NAV}_t - \mathrm{NAV}_{t-1})}{\mathrm{NAV}_{t-1}}$$

CRRA utility corresponds to the family of power utility functions defined for terminal wealth, W_{T} as,

$$U(W_{\mathrm{T}}) \equiv \frac{W_{\mathrm{T}}^{(1-c)} - 1}{(1-c)}, \quad c \neq 1, \ c \geq 0 \quad \text{and}$$

$$U(W_{\mathrm{T}}) \equiv \ln(W_{\mathrm{T}}), \ \text{ when } c = 1$$

Given that terminal wealth is just the initial wealth compounded at %TR,

$$W_{\mathrm{T}} = W_0 * (1 + \mathrm{TR})$$

and CRRA rankings are scale invariant, then $U(W_{\mathrm{T}})$ rankings are the same as $U(1 + \mathrm{TR})$.

$$U(1+\mathrm{TR}) \equiv \frac{(1+\mathrm{TR})^{(1-c)} - 1}{(1-c)}, \quad c \neq 1, \ c \geq 0 \quad \text{and}$$

$$U(1+\mathrm{TR}) \equiv \ln(1+\mathrm{TR}) \quad \text{when } c = 1$$

For a finite discrete distribution[18] (true for any histogram of empirical returns), we can now solve directly for CRRA CE from EU $= U$, albeit not explicitly parsed in terms of higher moments. Let p_i represent the probability of the ith return of N observed $\mathrm{TR}_{i,i=1,\ldots,N,}$, such that:

$$\mathrm{EU} \equiv \sum_i \left[\frac{(1+\mathrm{TR})^{(1-c)} - 1}{(1-c)}\right] \cdot p_i = U$$

$$\Leftrightarrow \left[\sum_i p_i \cdot (1+\mathrm{TR})^{(1-c)} - \sum_i p_i\right] = (1+\mathrm{CE})^{(1-c)} - 1$$

$$\Leftrightarrow \left[\sum_i p_i \cdot (1+\mathrm{TR}_i)^{(1-c)}\right] = (1+\mathrm{CE})^{(1-c)}$$

$$\Leftrightarrow \mathrm{AIRAP} = \mathrm{CE} = \left[\sum_i p_i \cdot (1+\mathrm{TR}_i)^{(1-c)}\right]^{\frac{1}{(1-c)}} - 1,$$

when $c \neq 1$ and $c \geq 0$

To avoid restrictive or questionable distributional assumptions, one can now proceed with any one of many available non-parametric estimation techniques. We emphasize the generality of this result, since the choice of non-parametric method is a matter of taste, and the resulting AIRAP estimate need not be tied to it. Still it is worth highlighting a particularly simple solution that results from fitting a histogram where p_k = [frequency of % Returns in the kth bin/N], $k = 1, \ldots, M$. Since arbitrariness in the choice of bin size results in arbitrariness of M and precision of the AIRAP estimate, we set the bin width[19] as:

$$\varepsilon := \frac{1}{2} * \mathrm{Min}\{|\mathrm{TR}_i - \mathrm{TR}_j|\}, \quad \forall\, i \neq j$$

Starting with the leftmost observation, the ε-bins are centered on each TR_i such that all distinct TR_i fall in exactly one bin. Thus, for all non-empty bins, $p_i = 1/N$. Substituting with $1/N$[20] for p_i in AIRAP yields a convenient closed form simplification. When $c = 1$, one proceeds in a similar manner to solve for AIRAP under log utility:

$$\mathrm{EU} \equiv \sum_i \ln(1 + \mathrm{TR}_i) \cdot p_i = U \equiv \ln(1 + \mathrm{CE})$$

$$\Leftrightarrow \ln\left\{\prod_i (1 + \mathrm{TR}_i)^{p_i}\right\} = \ln(1 + \mathrm{CE})$$

$$\Leftrightarrow \mathrm{AIRAP} = \mathrm{CE} = \left[\prod_i (i + \mathrm{TR}_i)^{p_i}\right] - 1, \quad c = 1$$

Again setting $p_i = 1/N$ provides a closed form solution that has a straightforward spreadsheet implementation. In general, any non-parametric estimate as outlined above has the dual benefit of being distribution free and of capturing all observed moments. Note that an analogous derivation is obtainable under exponential utility (CARA), which would be a special case of the closed form solution in Davis (2001) for histograms.[21] Hence, AIRAP could be formulated for CARA with ease. For comparison, we note that Madan and McPhail (2000) as well as Davis (2001) use exponential utility while Osband (2002) and Leland (1999)[22] use power utility.

3.1 Recommended Arrow–Pratt coefficient

For power utility, $c > 0$ represents risk-aversion. When $c = 0, U(\mathrm{TR})$ is linear in %TR and AIRAP is simply the arithmetic mean or in the annualized case it is the geometrically compounded monthly arithmetic mean excess return. For $c = 1$, logarithmic utility results in AIRAP as the geometric mean of monthly excess returns.[23] Since $0 < c < 1$ implausibly allows rational investors to entertain bets potentially resulting in insolvency, we restrict our attention to $c \geq 1$. In the latter case, the pain of insolvency is unbounded, precluding bets that could risk total ruin.

The plausible range for c is from 1 to 10. Osband (2002) suggests using c from 2 to 4. Ait-Sahalia *et al.* (2001) propose a resolution to the equity premium puzzle by examining data on the consumption of luxury goods[24] by the very rich who also constitute the majority of equity ownership. Their point estimate of $c = 3.2$ (s.e. 2.2) for ultra-high net-worth individuals[25] seems most pertinent to HF investors. To be quite conservative we assume $c = 4$, in which case the CRRA agent is willing to risk no more than one-fifth of his or her wealth for even odds of doubling.

The dependence of this approach on parameter c may be viewed as undesirable from a practical standpoint, given the ongoing academic debate over the true value of c and its implications for the equity risk premium puzzle. However, for RAPM purposes this is not an impediment. As long as we can target a plausible but fixed c, the ranking of all funds under AIRAP will be comparable and consistent. There is a *possible significant benefit* to the *flexibility* of being able to tweak risk-aversion. Technology can enable financial advisors/investment managers to query data on investor risk preferences and map them to an individualized c, thereby generating *customized AIRAP rankings*.

4 Data and Analysis

We use 5 years of monthly data (Jan. 1997–Dec. 2001),[26] for the EACM (Evaluation Associates Capital Markets) indexes for our index level analysis, since these indexes are recognized for their style pure categorization. The EACM100 is an equally weighted, annually re-balanced composite of 100 funds rigorously screened to represent five strategies (13 style sub-indexes). It has adequate data history (extending to 1996) and does not allow closed funds. At the individual fund level (where EACM does not disclose constituents), we resort to the HFR[27] universe given its wide usage and recognition for lower survivorship bias. Of the 2445 entries in HFR as of June 2003, only 887 HFs existed for the entire 5-year period. 100 time series corresponding to HFR indexes were excluded. The final 787 HFs include on and offshore funds, FoHFs, managed futures, as well as sector HFs.

Our dataset is long enough to be meaningfully subject to analysis, without being too long to be afflicted by more survivorship bias. Further, the choice of this period was motivated by the desire to include the Asian crisis (1997), the Russian crisis and LTCM debacle (1998), the bubble era (through 1999) and the subsequent Nasdaq collapse. We do not explicitly adjust for survivorship, instant history, selection and other well-known biases, since the objective is to study *relative* rankings. Table 6 shows the aggregate statistics for the first four moments and various RAPMs with regard to the HFR universe. This in conjunction with Figure 2 shows the distribution of ExKurt to be right skewed (+4.54) with a long right tail given a max of 51.4. Average ExKurt of 3 is significantly non-Gaussian with over 87% of funds showing positive ExKurt. The mean skewness is −0.14, while the skewness of skew is also negative (−1.24). This could have been worse at the composite level if not for the counterbalancing effect (Table 4) of Managed Futures and Macro funds in the sample.

We display rank correlations and reversals between SR, JA and power utility (AIRAP) for the full HFR universe of 787 funds, as a function of c (between 0.1 and 30), in Table 7. RAPM ranks and correlations for the 13 EACM style sub-indexes appear in Table 4. The SR rank correlations (Table 7) are similar to Fung and Hsieh

Table 6 RAPM summary—HFR universe (787 funds, 1997–2001).

	Average	Median	Min	Max
ExTR	6.53%	6.01%	−25.10%	44.76%
Vol	16.55%	13.83%	0.12%	100.07%
Skew mo	(0.14)	(0.01)	(7.18)	5.78
Excess Kurt mo	3.02	1.28	(0.86)	51.41
Treynor	0.05	0.19	(60.66)	38.93
Alpha	6.2%	5.6%	−24.4%	66.5%
Beta	0.29	0.20	(1.75)	2.12
Sharpe	0.75	0.57	(1.72)	7.54
AIRAP	−0.02%	2.99%	−93.25%	25.63%
MSR	13.65	2.13	(74.00)	1,600.14

The Table 6 shows the aggregate statistics for the first four moments and various RAPMs based on 787 individual hedge funds in the HFR universe for the 5-year period.

Table 7 AIRAP, Sharpe and Jensen Alpha as a function of risk-aversion.

CRR	# Reversals SR*	# Reversals JA*	% Reversals SR	% Reversals JA	AIRAP vs SR	AIRAP vs Alpha	F&H'99
0.1	781	779	99	99	0.59	0.89	0.49
0.2	780	775	99	98	0.61	0.89	0.50
0.3	784	777	99	99	0.63	0.90	0.52
0.4	783	776	99	98	0.64	0.90	0.53
0.5	786	776	100	98	0.66	0.91	0.55
1	783	772	99	98	0.73	0.90	0.52
1.5	784	783	99	99	0.78	0.86	0.68
2	787	785	100	100	0.82	0.82	0.73
2.5	785	784	100	99	0.84	0.78	0.77
3	785	784	100	99	0.86	0.74	0.81
3.5	786	783	100	99	0.86	0.70	0.84
4	787	786	100	100	0.86	0.66	0.85
4.5	786	786	100	100	0.87	0.63	0.87
5	783	787	99	100	0.87	0.60	0.89
10	785	784	100	99	0.80	0.34	0.89
15	788	786	100	100	0.74	0.23	0.87
20	788	786	100	100	0.70	0.17	0.85
25	784	787	99	100	0.68	0.14	0.83
30	786	787	100	100	0.66	0.11	0.81

AIRAP versus Sharpe and Jensen represent Spearman rank correlations. Correlation with Jensen tapers off rapidly.

F&H'99: Rank correlations of [power utility, SR] from Fung and Hsieh (1999).
% Reversals SR show nearly 100% rank reversals between Sharpe and AIRAP.
% Reversals JA show nearly 100% rank reversals between Jensen and AIRAP.

Data: 787 funds in HFR for the period 1997–2001.
Source: Hedge Fund Research, Inc., © HFR, Inc., www.hedgefundresearch.com

(1997) except that their study used 233 funds, defined SR in terms of total not excess returns and did not look across style categories and databases. More importantly, their objective was to check for the near sufficiency of mean-variance in portfolio construction as opposed to the suitability of RAPMs for HFs.

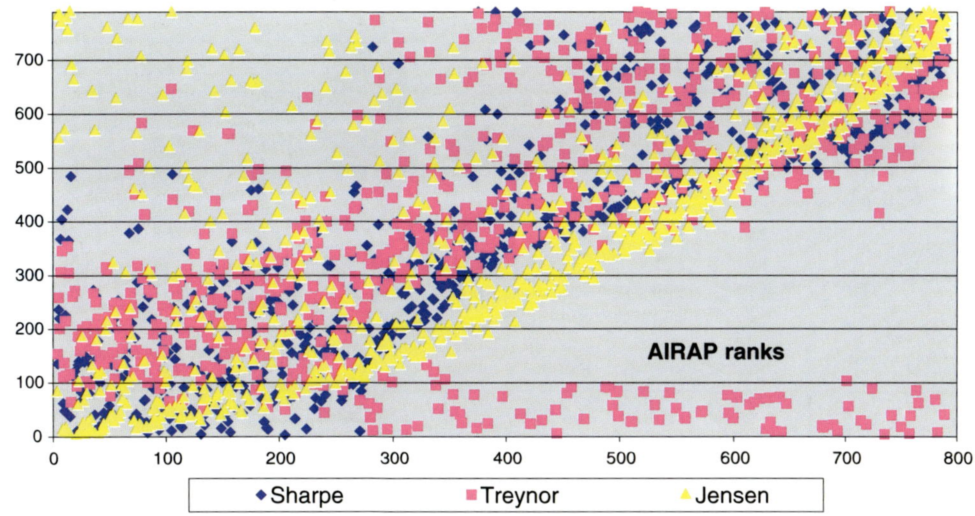

Figure 4 Comparative RAPM rankings (HFR universe).

All RAPM ranks are in ascending order with higher ranks being more desirable.
AIRAP (CRRA = 4) rankings are shown on the x-axis.
The abundance of off-diagonal data shows the extent of divergence between the 3 RAPMS *vis-à-vis* AIRAP.
The cluster of pyramids in the top left represents high JA funds demoted by AIRAP.
The cluster of squares at the bottom right represents high AIRAP funds demoted by Treynor.
Source for 787 HFs used is Hedge Fund Research, Inc., ©HFR, Inc., www.hedgefundresearch.com

The performance of SR in ranking hedge funds is significantly misleading with respect to the investor's true utility rankings as per both ranks reversals and correlations (Table 7). Pearson correlations (Table 3) are even weaker at 0.46, 0.37 and −0.01 for SR, JA, and Treynor, respectively. Our correlations (Table 7) are similar to Fung and Hsieh (1997) for CRRA in the range [3, 5] but theirs drop off much faster for lower values of CRRA while ours decline faster for higher levels of risk aversion. Further correlations of AIRAP with Alpha decrease dramatically with increasing risk-aversion. This may be explicable since AIRAP imposes a steeper risk penalty, as an increasing (but non-linear) function of risk-aversion while Alpha is invariant with regard to risk-aversion.

Scatter plots of RAPM rankings (Figure 4) with the abundance of off-diagonal funds visually confirm the noted lack of correlation and that the picture is essentially the same for CRRA in the 2–4 range. Treynor with the lowest AIRAP correlation of 0.49, erroneously penalizes funds with slight negative beta exposures or negative means, resulting in the cluster to the south-east corner. Alpha on the other hand (+0.66 correlation), creates a cluster to the north-west comprised of funds that are in most cases either negative beta or where the CAPM beta fails to capture risk. Short sellers are grossly misrepresented due to their negative betas, resulting in JA being artificially boosted and Treynor being inappropriately depressed. Table 8 of representative funds shows that #512 has the worst AIRAP rank (1) even though SR ranks it as 133 (of 787), because not only are returns low (10) and 56% Vol extreme (786 rank) but iceberg risks are high (ExKurt is 682 while Skew rank is 58). On the other hand, #235 has

Table 8 Representative fund RAPM comparisons.

Fund ID	AIRAP	Sharpe	Treynor	Jensen	Beta	ExTR	Vol	Skew	ExKurt
229	**13**	482	62	**788**	25	787	**787**	719	590
230	11	362	302	753	786	679	**781**	398	507
231	10	420	351	777	783	747	**780**	373	550
235	202	1	48	65	176	69	8	423	74
272	2	234	256	**781**	655	223	**788**	**788**	**786**
512	1	133	151	81	771	**10**	**776**	58	**682**
636	**788**	699	599	**776**	635	784	545	667	361
762	373	**788**	784	221	143	201	2	485	174

Fund ID	AIRAP	Sharpe	Treynor	Jensen	Beta	ExTR	Vol	Skew mo	ExKurt
229	−48.57%	0.76	(1.27)	66.53%	(0.50)	37.92%	83.16%	1.13	3.23
230	−51.15%	0.53	0.19	20.27%	1.75	14.09%	61.08%	0.01	2.27
231	−51.64%	0.62	0.23	25.93%	1.64	20.12%	60.23%	(0.05)	2.68
235	−2.76%	−1.72	(1.40)	−2.88%	0.02	−2.72%	1.60%	0.07	(0.10)
272	−86.14%	0.34	0.49	29.23%	0.69	3.03%	100.07%	5.78	41.15
512	−93.25%	0.15	0.06	−2.09%	1.45	−13.39%	56.17%	(1.82)	6.00
636	25.63%	1.54	0.48	25.40%	0.62	31.96%	19.32%	0.80	1.13
762	2.41%	7.54	9.38	2.37%	0.00	2.41%	0.32%	0.22	0.34

the worst SR (1) due to negative mean and low Vol (8). AIRAP correctly handles the negative mean and boosts the rank by 201 notches since the higher moments are tame and Vol exceptionally low. Fund #229 has the highest Alpha (787 rank due to negative beta), middle of the pack SR (482) but AIRAP is 775 notches lower because of the penalty for extreme 83.2% Vol. For EACM sub-indexes, AIRAP penalizes on average 2% more than JA does. It is systematically lower than Alpha for all but Event Driven sub-indexcs. In the case of Multi-Strategy Relative Value, the penalty is 1.2% more largely due to the −4.6 skew and ExKurt of nearly 25.

To show that AIRAP conveys new information not already captured by traditional RAPMs, we show Spearman rank and Pearson correlations[28] in Table 3. For the HFR universe, AIRAP is positively correlated with ExTR, Skew, Treynor, Jensen, and SR but negatively correlated with Volatility and Beta as one would expect. To the extent that a large dispersion in mean–variance profiles has been documented across strategies and these effects often dominate higher order effects, one should expect drastic rank reversals for the full HFR universe that aggregates across strategies. We find that *% rank reversals are in excess of 99% across the board*, that is, at the broad universe level, there is *almost no agreement between AIRAP and Sharpe or Alpha rankings*. This observation needs to be tempered by the realization that for a given rank order $\langle 1, 2, \ldots, 787 \rangle$ the trivial permutation $\langle 2, 3, \ldots, 787, 1 \rangle$ results in 100% reversals despite near-perfect correlation. The key is that the magnitude of some of these reversals (in addition to their prevalence) can be substantial as per Figure 4, anecdotal evidence above and the rank correlations previously noted.

Rank discrepancies at the intra-strategy level are likely to be fewer if HFR strategies are sufficiently style-pure to reduce heterogeneity. While the 90% average reversal rate from intra-strategy rankings in Table 5 is somewhat lower, it is well known that the self-proclaimed style of managers in databases such as HFR need not be a reliable indicator of the factors they load on. The magnitude of intra-strategy rank discrepancies and how that relates to the aggregate level across databases is further documented in Sharma (2003).

Strategies with higher iceberg risks like HFR Merger Arbitrage and Event Driven seem to have higher reversal rates (Table 5) than more liquid strategies like Shorts (82%). Short Sellers do display a much lower incidence of non-Gaussian profile (36%) as compared to Event Driven (80%). Indeed, our results for EACM sub-indexes (Table 4) show Event Driven as well as Relative Value and Event Driven multi-strategy being demoted a notch under AIRAP. Liquid equity strategies with controlled volatility such as Domestic Opportunistic, Global and Long/Short do move up 2–4 notches. It would therefore appear that style categories exhibiting greater departures from normality (i.e., higher moment risks) also exhibit greater rank discrepancies between SR and AIRAP. However, the picture is muddied by the complex interaction of volatility with higher moments (since manifestation of higher kurtosis can percolate into volatility/skewness and vice versa) and the fact that the higher magnitude volatility penalty often dominates. For example, high volatility (despite innocuous higher moments) results in AIRAP severely penalizing Long Biased (RP = 7.37%) and Short EACM sub-indexes (RP = 6.9%). This interaction is often easier to disentangle at the individual fund level than at the aggregate category level.

The related claim—*high Sharpe ratios in hedge funds may represent a trade off for higher moment risk*—is investigated in Sharma (2003). Here we simply note the positive (and statistically significant) rank correlation of SR with excess kurtosis for both EACM and HFR data (Tables 3 and 4). To the extent that some HF strategies pay for a better mean–variance profile by assuming iceberg risks, it seems less plausible that they are better exploiting inefficiencies or expanding the investment opportunity set. At least part of their *mean–variance attraction may stem from the pre-meditated but potentially suicidal (short volatility) act of scooping up pennies before the onslaught of the steamroller.*

Scott and Horvath (1980) show that *risk-averse investors prefer positive odd central moments (such as skewness) and dislike even central moments (such as kurtosis).* Unlike traditional RAPMs (which are largely oblivious to the impact of higher moments), AIRAP critically *penalizes for negative skew and positive kurtosis.*

5 Impact of Leverage

Traditionally, the leverage invariance of SR has been considered desirable. This makes sense for traditional investments since leverage is neither central to the investment strategy nor usually permissible under existing regulation (e.g., with mutual funds). If used at all, leverage is usually employed by means external to the core investment vehicle, perhaps at the allocation level or through structured products.

Leverage to the hedge fund manager is a critical extra degree of freedom, especially for relative value/arbitrage strategies. The *decision, whether to use leverage and to what extent is integral to the hedge fund investment process.* The impact of leverage on the

Table 9 Change in RAPMs versus change in leverage.

Leverage factor	2	5	10	15	Response
Leverage increase	2.00	2.50	2.00	1.50	
ExTR arith	2.00	2.50	2.00	1.50	Linear
Vol	2.00	2.50	2.00	1.50	Linear
Skew	1.00	1.00	1.00	1.00	Invariant
Excess Kurtosis	1.00	1.00	1.00	1.00	Invariant
Sharpe	1.00	1.00	1.00	1.00	Invariant
Treynor	1.00	1.00	1.00	1.00	Invariant
Alpha	2.00	2.50	2.00	1.50	Linear
Beta	2.00	2.50	2.00	1.50	Linear
AIRAP	1.76	1.35	−1.83	4.78	Non-Linear
ExTR geom	1.98	2.40	1.76	1.14	Non-Linear
RiskPrem (Arith)	4.15	6.98	4.88	2.43	Non-Linear

realized distribution should not be ignored.[29] For ranking and comparison purposes, either we must use un-levered returns or account for leverage directly. Given the lack of transparency with HFs, computing un-levered returns may be impractical. Besides, investor utility is a function of the realized total return achieved not some hypothetical un-levered return which may have been achieved had the manager not made the wise or unwise decision to use a given degree of leverage. Hence, appropriately accounting for leverage requires accommodating preferences, that is, a good hedge fund RAPM *should encapsulate aversion to excessive leverage under risk-aversion.*

To understand how AIRAP incorporates leverage, we consider only financing leverage, that is, the impact of levered exposure to the same risky fund enabled through borrowing. This suffices since AIRAP already adjusts for the market risk of the underlying fund based on returns data. Table 9 shows the impact of leverage on EACM 100. We assume that n-times leverage corresponds to the excess return scaled up by n, since the differential return is a self-financed portfolio. Hence, the mean monthly excess return of 0.40% doubles to 0.80% for 2× and rises to 6% for 15× leverage. Volatility, Beta, and Alpha rise also linearly by exactly the leverage factor n. Since Alpha rises in proportion to leverage, it is inappropriate for HFs as it indiscriminately rewards higher leverage without bound. The proportional rise in Beta does not sufficiently penalize for the rise in volatility under risk aversion, even though skew and excess kurtosis are unchanged. Sharpe and Treynor on the other hand are leverage invariant.[30] They are oblivious to the impact of leverage since the first and second moments[31] rise in tandem and cancel out.

$$\text{Sharpe}_{P,\text{Levered}} = \frac{\mu_{P,\text{Levered}}}{\sigma_{P,\text{Levered}}} = \frac{n * \mu_P}{n * \sigma_P} = \text{Sharpe}_P$$

$$\text{Treynor}_{P,\text{Levered}} = \frac{\mu_{P,\text{Levered}}}{\beta_{P,\text{Levered}}} = \frac{n * \mu_P}{n * \beta_P} = \text{Treynor}_P$$

$$\alpha_{P,\text{Levered}} = R_{P,\text{Levered}} - \beta * R_B = n * (R_P - \beta * R_B) = n * \alpha_P$$

$$\beta_{P,\text{Levered}} = \rho * \frac{\sigma_{P,\text{Levered}}}{\sigma_B} = \rho * \left(\frac{n * \sigma_P}{\sigma_B}\right) = n * \beta_P, \quad \because \sigma_{P,\text{Levered}} = n * \sigma_P$$

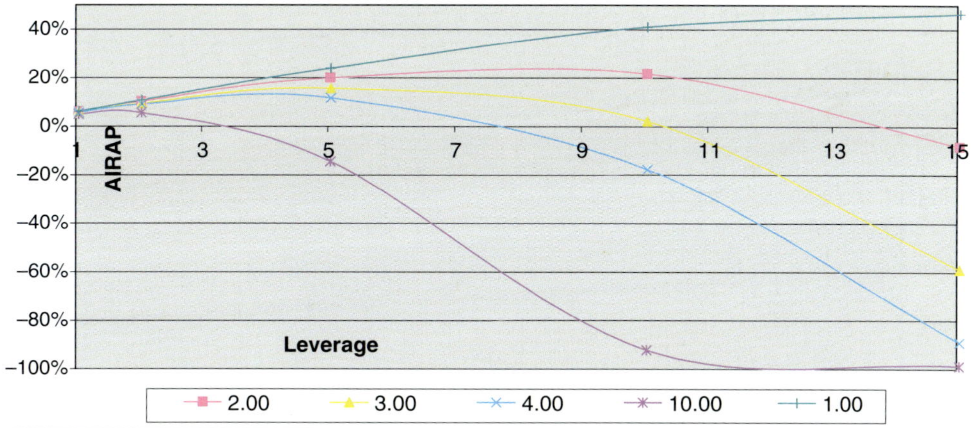

CRRA/ Leverage	1	2	5	10	15
1.00	4.77%	9.44%	22.63%	39.85%	45.23%
2.00	4.62%	8.84%	18.48%	20.32%	−9.44%
3.00	4.48%	8.24%	14.39%	0.86%	−60.10%
4.00	4.33%	7.64%	10.30%	−18.89%	−90.27%
10.00	3.47%	4.07%	−15.83%	−93.48%	−100.00%

Figure 5 AIRAP across CRRA and Leverage for EACM100®.

AIRAP penalizes for increased leverage as a function of risk-aversion. The impact of leverage on the returns distribution is captured via credit for the higher mean and penalty for the higher volatility as a function of the CRR parameter. For example, in going from 5× to 10×, RP jumps by 46.4%, from 12.3 to 58.7% (CRR = 4), turning AIRAP negative (−18.9% despite +39.8% Excess TR) in Table 9. The alpha of 37.3% and static 0.90 SR would have misled us in this instance. Assuming lower risk-aversion, for example, CRR = 2, AIRAP only turns negative in going from 10× to 15× (Figure 5). Hence, AIRAP provides risk-adjustment for leverage customized to the investor's risk-aversion. An AIRAP based Sharpe ratio, defined as a function of CRR would also respond to leverage (since the denominator incorporates risk-aversion) though not identically:

$$\text{MSR-AIRAP} = \frac{\text{Excess TR}}{\text{RP}(4)}$$

The difference is attributable to penalizing for Risk-Premium multiplicatively (in MSR-AIRAP) *vis-à-vis* additively (in AIRAP).

Finally, the dependence of AIRAP on leverage[32] (Table 9), tells both the HF manager and the institutional investor what degree of leverage is optimal for a given track record. Standard optimization techniques (qua first and second order conditions in terms of the partial derivative of AIRAP on leverage) can provide the *optimal leverage*, which *maximizes* AIRAP. Figure 5 shows the AIRAP profile across varying leverage for a range of CRRA. For the growth-optimal case, the Kelly criterion[33] provides the answer (Figures 6 and 7).

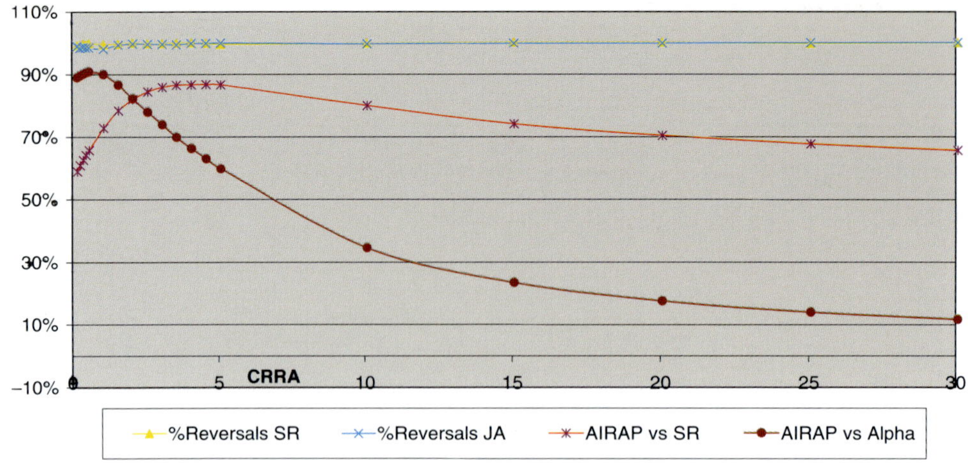

Figure 6 Percentage reversals and rank correlations by risk aversion.
AIRAP versus Sharpe and Jensen represent Spearman rank correlations.
Correlation with Jensen tapers off rapidly.
% Reversals SR show nearly 100% rank reversals between Sharpe and AIRAP.
% Reversals JA show nearly 100% rank reversals between Jensen and AIRAP.
Data: 788 funds in HFR for the period 1997–2001.
Source: Hedge Fund Research, Inc., ©HFR, Inc., www.hedgefundresearch.com

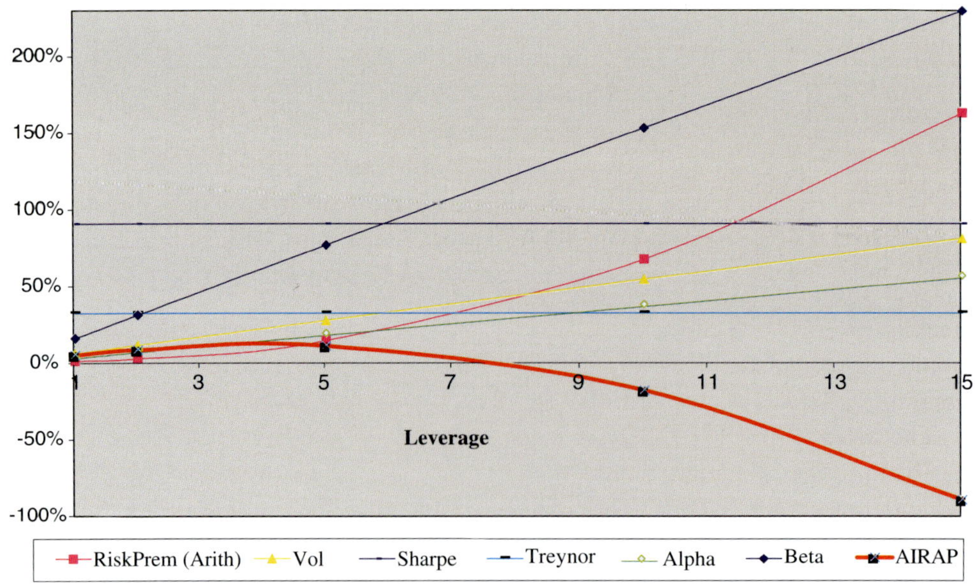

Figure 7 RAPMs versus Leverage (CRR = 4)—EACM 100.

6 Hedge Fund Peer Percentile Rankings

Realized HF peer rankings within category[34] can be directly calculated based on realized AIRAP. However, for a prospective measure that may better handle iceberg risks without

Table 10 Goodness of-fit-test results.

	40 Years—Two Sided goodness of fit			
GoF tests	Asympt P_{val}	Test stat	95% Critical value	99% critical value
Lilliefors	0.0486*	0.0408	0.0404	0.0503
Bera-Jarque	—*,**	77.2904	5.9915	9.2103

* and ** correspond to 95 and 99% levels of significance, respectively.

the complications of a regime switching implementation, we propose (for future implementation) a composite percentile ranking framework based on a weighted average of the funds style category percentile and stressed scenario percentile. The weights should be fixed from intra-style category testing (e.g., $w_1 = 0.7$ and $w_2 = 0.3$) such that:

$$\begin{aligned}&\text{Composite AIRAP \%tile}\\&\quad = \{\mathrm{w}_1 * \text{AIRAP Style \%tile} + \mathrm{w}_2 * \text{AIRAPStress \%tile}\}, \quad \text{and}\\&\quad \text{AIRAP Style \%tile}\\&\quad = 5_{\mathrm{y}} \text{ AIRAP \%tile ranking within style category}\end{aligned}$$

Given that most HFs have a far shorter history than their traditional counterparts, this may appear to be impractical counsel. However, a number of simulation and optimization techniques have emerged for back-filling history, which can remedy the paucity of available data. Attractive candidates include fitting optimal factor or style exposures to fund profiles based on available history. This will allow one to *extend the style signature back in time* via factor or style exposures that have adequate history. A plethora of multi-factor models have been proposed for HFs, for example, Schneeweis and Spurgin (1998)[35] or Fung and Hsieh (1997).[36] Further, one can use style analysis—originally proposed by Sharpe (1992) for mutual funds—and applied to HFs[37] by Agarwal and Naik (1999) or Fung and Hsieh (1998).[38] Indexes better known for their style pure classification schema (such as Standard & Poors, EACM, or Zurich) should be used to extend backwards the earliest known weighted average *style signature* (assuming no style drift) to facilitate calculation of AIRAP Style %tile.

The inclusion of AIRAP Stress %tile is warranted due to dormant dangers that may be lurking in the higher moments but not manifest in the 5-year trailing period. Industry consensus is required for establishing representative, preset crash test scenarios encompassing credit, interest rate, volatility and equity events. Obvious candidates for equity include 1987 and 2000, 1994 for fixed income, while 1997 and 1998 may suffice for credit and default scenarios. Incorporating historical crises is critical to capturing higher moment risks, hence potential rank reversals: For example, the volatility spike resulting from the Russian default dealt swift justice to short volatility players, whose previously pristine track records abruptly realized the dormant dangers of their "true" risk profile. In fact, using just the 3-year period (Dec. 99–Nov. 02), which omits these credit and volatility spikes, shows rather different results with Non-Directional strategies displaying dramatically lower kurtosis (even less than directional strategies during this period) and more favorable skew.

7 Caveats and Conclusion

AIRAP presents a radical departure from preference free RAPMs in circulation. At the same time, it benefits from the familiar and established lineage of Expected Utility theory. Salient features of AIRAP, which enhance its suitability as a RAPM for hedge funds include:

- Appropriate treatment of leverage for hedge funds.
- Distribution free framework eschews unrealistic assumption of Normality.
- Incorporation of investor preferences via Power utility, which given CRRA is more realistic than Quadratic utility underlying mean–variance. Risk adjustment is neither ad hoc, nor does it misrepresent upside risk. Downside variance is penalized more.
- AIRAP better handles non-normality since it directly utilizes the full empirical distribution. Unlike higher order approximations (e.g., MSR based on a Cornish–Fisher modified VaR expansion), there is no sacrifice in accuracy due to the truncation of higher order terms.
- Scale invariance of CRRA inherent to AIRAP.
- Consistent rankings even when mean excess returns are negative.[39]
- Intuitively expressed in familiar units of performance.
- AIRAP maximization is equivalent to maximizing EU. Hence, it can be utilized for portfolio optimization as in the case of FoHFs.
- AIRAP can better handle non-directional/market-neutral strategies.
- AIRAP can be expressed as a modified SR[40] to preserve the reward-risk format.
- No complications regarding the estimation of higher moments, co-moments or convergence of Taylor series.
- AIRAP can dovetail with regime switching models or be combined with scenario stresses, for handling iceberg risks. While regime-switching models provide a systematization of the ad hoc scenario analysis prevalent in practice, they do require regime identification and technical complexities that may present barriers to practicability.
- Possible to use closed form solution with easy spreadsheet implementation.

Traditional portfolio construction of FoHFs based on SR maximization can result in a bias towards illiquidity and short volatility. Measures such as AIRAP that mitigate the vulnerabilities of SR can help circumnavigate the dangers lurking in higher moments. As FoHF portfolio construction usually entails a two-step top-down procedure where the optimal style weights are determined before individual manager weights, refining the first optimization (by transcending the mean–variance framework) should help in avoiding the pitfalls of improperly weighting styles. Getting the style allocation decision right also means that the FoHF manager can focus more on the "selection" challenge of picking the right managers and performing the necessary due diligence to avoid operational risk or fraud. We have demonstrated the criticality of AIRAP to the "selection" challenge via better rankings. AIRAP as presented in this paper maximizes ease of practical use at the stand-alone fund level. We leave the application of EU theory towards FoHF portfolio construction using marginal considerations and correlations with other investments as fodder for future research.

Effects such as putatively managed or stale pricing[41] may also be masking the true statistical properties. Lo (2002) and Getmansky *et al.* (2003) have documented the extent of serial correlation observed in HF returns and its upward bias on RAPMs like SR. Hence, it would be interesting to apply AIRAP to unsmoothed returns since it would adjust for illiquidity/stale pricing in addition to higher moment risks. To the extent that survivorship would likely bias means and skews upwards while depressing the true volatilities and kurtoses, it appears that even if one were to adjust for survivorship, the divergence between AIRAP and SR or JA reported here would only be exacerbated. Although SR would also drop given the mean–variance impact it may not be impacted as much as AIRAP upon incorporation of higher moments.

Meantime, a healthy debate on the "near adequacy" of SR and the mean–variance framework continues. Barring *ex ante* prescience, it appears that one should err on the side of caution by also considering RAPMs such as AIRAP which stand a better chance of survival in stressed scenarios.

Notes

1 Risk-Adjusted Performance Measures.

2 Shadwick, W. and Keating, C. (2002). "A Universal Performance Measure." *Journal of Performance Measurement* **6**(3), 59–84.

3 The SHARAD (Skill, History and Risk-Adjusted) RAPM has been proposed by Muralidhar (2001/2002) as an extension of M^3 (see Muralidhar, 2000), since it explicitly adjusts for disparate performance history. Muralidhar, A. (2001). "Skill, History and Risk-Adjusted Performance." *Journal of Performance Measurement*, **Winter** (2001). Muralidhar, A. (2000). "Risk-Adjusted Performance—The Correlation Correction." *Financial Analysts Journal* **56**(5), 63–71.

4 MAR hereafter.

5 Artzner *et al.* (1999). "Coherent Measures of Risk." *Mathematical Finance* **9**(3), 203–208.

6 Bernardo and Ledoit (1996), p. 7.

7 Jorion, P. (2000). "Risk Management Lessons from LTCM." *European Financial Management.*

8 Naik, N. Y. and Agarwal, V. (2003). "Risk and Portfolio Decisions Involving Hedge Funds." *Review of Financial Studies*, forthcoming.

9 Mitchell, M. and Pulvino, T. (2001). "Characteristics of Risk and Return in Arbitrage." *The Journal of Finance* **56**(6), 2135–2175.

10 On the other hand, Koski and Pontiff (1996) find that the use of derivatives in mutual funds does not significantly alter either risk or return profile. However, derivatives do significantly alter kurtosis for mutual funds, but the bias is not systematic (presumably because they are also being used for hedging and to reduce returns variability which would decrease kurtosis). The situation with hedge funds appears to be quite different. Koski, J. L. and Pontiff, J. (1996). "How are Derivatives Used? Evidence from the Mutual Fund Industry." Working paper series, Wharton Financial Institutions Center.

11 The effect would be more pronounced with daily instead of monthly data.

12 The italicization is mine.

13 EU measures are complete, transitive, and convex like the underlying preferences.

14 This follows from the inverse function theorem. Continuity and existence of the inverse makes the original function a homeomorphism.

15 The assumption is that rational investors prefer more to less and view risky assets as normal goods. See Huang, C. and Litzenberger, R. (1988). *Foundations for Financial Economics*, Prentice-Hall, NJ.

16 Top marginal tax rate of 39.1% for Head of Household kicks in at $297,350 threshold (2001 IRS tax schedule).

17 For a four-person family, the poverty line is defined as $18,100 in 2002 (cf. *Federal Register*, Vol. 67, No. 31, February 14, 2002, pp. 6931–6933).

18 This derivation ignores subtleties such as rebalancing, transaction costs, etc.

19 This could be called the degenerate histogram method. The end result resembles the L_p norm, for $p = (1 - c)$, except that $p \neq 0$ and $p \leq 1$.

20 This works even if one occasionally encounters k returns that are identical since the frequency in the overlapping bins simply add up to k/N, the probability assigned to that TR_i at the mid-point.

21 Davis (2001) also has CE solutions for exponential utility (but none for power utility) under a host of other distributions.

22 Leland (1999) only assumes IID returns for the market proxy but given "perfect" markets in his framework, it turns out that the representative investor must have power utility.

23 Given our use of the geometric mean (annualized) in measuring average performance, RP $= 0$ corresponds to $c = 1$. If instead, we were to use the geometrically compounded (annualized) monthly arithmetic mean, then $c = 0$ would correspond to RP $= 0$. However, for long horizons the latter diverges significantly from the average annualized performance a fund investor would obtain.

24 Their contention is that NIPA and household survey data used in prior literature (on basic goods consumption) overstates risk aversion by an order of magnitude.

25 This estimate of RRA is implied from "Luxury Retail Sales (US Retailers)." For perspective, they also find that the c implied by "Charitable Contributions of Rich" is 4.7 (s.e. 3.3).

26 It is best to use data post 1994 since most databases exhibit severe survivorship biases prior to 1994.

27 Hedge Fund Research, Inc., © HFR, Inc., www.hedgefundresearch.com

28 Rank correlations are to be preferred in assessing the co-dependence since the data suggests non-linear dependence rendering Pearson correlation less appropriate.

29 We take the liberty of not maintaining a clear distinction between instrument leverage within a hedge fund and levered exposure to a hedge fund (such as within a FoHF) since we are only working with returns and not positions.

30 We also assume that the numerators in SR and Treynor are annualized arithmetically to ensure that leverage invariance still holds.

31 As before we assume excess returns.

32 While it is better to chart this with the base case being un-levered performance, it is clear that the unit of leverage for the independent variable here (EACM100) is simply a multiple of the leverage already inherent to the EACM100 index.

33 Kelly, J. L. (1956). "A New Interpretation of Information Rate." *Bell Systems Technical Journal* **35**, 917–926.

[34] Morningstar appears to have recently adopted a similar framework (although their research is not fully in the public domain). Arguably that may not be necessary for mutual fund rankings, but it does provide further validation of the practicality of such an approach. There are also press reports indicating that they are using the Stutzer index.

[35] Schneeweis, T. and Spurgin, R. (1998). "Multifactor Analysis of Hedge Fund, Managed Futures, and Mutual Fund Return and Risk Characterisitcs." *Journal of Alternative Investments* **1**, 1–24.

[36] Fung, W. and Hsieh, D. (1997). "Empirical Characteristics of Dynamic Trading Strategies: The Case of Hedge Funds." *The Review of Financial Studies* **10**, 275–302.

[37] Weisman and Abernathy (2001) propose a non-parametric alternative via Generic Model Decomposition. However, their approach requires subjective judgement in the choice of variables for each fund on a case by case basis. See Weisman, A. and Abernathy, J. D. (2001). "The Dangers of Historical Hedge Fund Data." In: Leslie Rahl (ed.), *Risk Budgeting—A New Approach to Investing*. Risk Books.

[38] Fung, W. and Hsieh, D. (1998). "Performance Attribution and Style Analysis: From Mutual Funds to Hedge Funds." Working Paper.

[39] Given two portfolios with the same negative mean excess return, SR will erroneously rank the one with higher risk (hence less negative ratio) as the better porftfolio.

[40] However, MSR-AIRAP inherits some of the disadvantages of SR.

[41] See Asness, C., Krail, R. and Liew, J. (2001). "Do Hedge Funds Hedge?" *Journal of Portfolio Management* **28**(1), 6–19.

References

Agarwal, V. and Naik, N. Y. (1999). "On Taking the 'Alternative' Route: Risk, Rewards, Style and Performance Persistence of Hedge Funds." LBS Working Paper.

Ait-Sahalia, Y., Parker, J., and Yogo, M. (2001). "Luxury Goods and the Equity Premium." NBER Working Paper Series.

Bernardo, A. E. and Ledoit, O. (2000). "Gain, Loss and Asset Pricing." *Journal of Political Economy* **108**(1), 144–172.

Bookstaber, R. and Clarke, R. (1981). "Options can Alter Portfolio Return Distributions." *Journal of Portfolio Management* 7, 63–70.

Bookstaber, R. (2000). "Understanding and Monitoring the Liquidity Crisis Cycle." *Financial Analysts Journal* **Sept./Oct.**, 17–22.

Davis, R. E. (2001). "Decision Policy Optimization Via Certainty Equivalent Functions for Exponential Utility." *Advances in Mathematical Programming and Financial Analysis* **6**, 89–113.

Fung, W. and Hsieh, D. (1999). "Is Mean–Variance Analysis Applicable to Hedge Funds?" *Economic Letters* **62**, 53–58.

Getmansky, M., Lo, A. W., and Makarov, I. (2003). "An Econometric Model of Serial Correlation and Illiquidity in Hedge Fund Returns." NBER Working Paper 9571.

Goetzmann, W. N., Ingersoll, J. E., Spiegel, M., and Welch, I. (2002). "Sharpening Sharpe Ratios." Yale School of Management Working Paper.

Kazemi, H., Mahdavi, M., and Schneeweis, T. (2003). "Generalized Sharpe Ratio: A Defense Against Sharpened Sharpe Ratios." CISDM Working Paper.

Krause, A. and Litzenberger, R. (1976). "Skewness Preference and the Valuation of Assets." *Journal of Finance* **31**, 1085–1100.

Leland, H. (1999). "Beyond Mean–Variance: Performance Measurement in a Non-Symmetrical World." *Financial Analysts Journal* **Jan.–Feb.**, 27–36.

Levy, H. and Markowitz, H. M. (1979). "Approximating Expected Utility by a Function of Mean and Variance." *The American Economic Review* **69**(3), 308–317.

Madan, D. and McPhail, G. S. (2000). "Investing in Skews." Working Paper, University of Maryland.

Markowitz, H. M. (1959). *Portfolio Selection: Efficient Diversification of Investments.* New Haven, CT: Yale University Press.

Muralidhar, A. (2000). "Risk-Adjusted Performance—The Correlation Correction." *Financial Analysts Journal* **56**(5), 63–71.

Osband, K. (2002). *Iceberg Risk.* New York: Texere.

Roll, R. (1978). "Ambiguity when performance is Measured by the Securities Market Line." *The Journal of Finance* **33**(4), 1051–1069.

Scott, R. and Horvath, P. (1980). "On the Direction of Preference for Moments of Higher Order than the Variance." *The Journal of Finance* **35**(4), 915–919.

Sharma, M. (2003). "A.I.R.A.P.—Alternative views on Alternative Investments." Forthcoming.

Sharpe, W. (1992). "Asset Allocation: Management Style and Performance Measurement." *Journal of Portfolio Management* **winter** 7–19.

Sharpe, W. (1994). "The Sharpe Ratio." *The Journal of Portfolio Management* **20**(1), 49–59.

Spurgin, R. B. (2001). "How to Game Your Sharpe Ratio." *The Journal of Alternative Investments* **4**(3), 38–46.

Keywords: Hedge funds; risk adjusted performance; certainty equivalent; AIRAP